Biodiversity, Genetic Resources and Intellectual Property

Debates about access and benefits sharing (ABS) have moved on in recent years. An initial focus on the legal obligations established by international agreements like the United Nations' *Convention on Biological Diversity* and the form of obligations for collecting physical biological materials have now moved to a far more complex series of disputes and challenges about the ways ABS should be implemented and enforced: repatriation of resources, technology transfer, traditional knowledge and cultural expressions, open access to information and knowledge, naming conventions, farmers' rights, new schemes for accessing pandemic viruses and sharing DNA sequences, and so on. Unfortunately, most of this debate is now crystallised into apparently intractable discussions such as implementing the certificates of origin, recognising traditional knowledge and traditional cultural expression as a form of intellectual property, and sovereignty for Indigenous peoples. Not everything in this new marketplace of ABS has been created *de novo*. Like most new entrants, ABS has disrupted existing legal and governance arrangements. This collection of chapters examines what is new, what has been changed, and what might be changed in response to the growing acceptance and prevalence of ABS of genetic resources.

Biodiversity, Genetic Resources and Intellectual Property: Developments in Access and Benefit Sharing of Genetic Resources addresses current issues arising from recent developments in the enduring and topical debates about managing genetic resources through the ABS regime. The book explores key historical, doctrinal, and theoretical issues in the field, at the same time developing new ideas and perspectives around ABS. It shows the latest state of knowledge and will be of interest to researchers, academics, policymakers, and students in the fields of intellectual property, governance, biodiversity and conservation, sustainable development, and agriculture.

Charles Lawson is a Professor at the Australian Centre for Intellectual Property in Agriculture, Griffith Law School, Griffith University, Australia.

Kamalesh Adhikari is AIBE Research Fellow in Food Security and Member of the ARC Laureate Project 'Harnessing Intellectual Property to Build Food Security', TC Beirne School of Law, The University of Queensland, Australia.

Routledge Research in Intellectual Property

Available:

Well-Known Trade Marks
A Comparative Study of Japan and the EU
Hiroko Onishi

Contemporary Issues in Pharmaceutical Patent Law
Setting the Framework and Exploring Policy Options
Bryan Mercurio and Daria Kim

Protecting Intellectual Property in the Arabian Peninsula
The GCC states, Jordan and Yemen
David Price and Alhanoof AlDebasi

Biodiversity, Genetic Resources and Intellectual Property
Developments in Access and Benefit Sharing
Charles Lawson and Kamalesh Adhikari

Forthcoming:

Intellectual Property, Finance and Corporate Governance
Janice Denoncourt

Intellectual Property and Conflict of Laws
Moral Rights and Alternatives to the Copyright Qualifications
Hanan Almawla

Pharmaceutical Patent Protection and World Trade Law
The Unresolved Problem of Access to Medicines
Jae Sundaram

Intellectual Property Branding in the Developing World
A New Approach for Non-Technological Innovation and Success Stories
Tshimanga Kongolo

Biodiversity, Genetic Resources and Intellectual Property

Developments in Access and Benefit Sharing

Edited by
Charles Lawson and Kamalesh Adhikari

Routledge
Taylor & Francis Group

LONDON AND NEW YORK

First published 2018 by Routledge

2 Park Square, Milton Park, Abingdon, Oxfordshire OX14 4RN

52 Vanderbilt Avenue, New York, NY 10017

Routledge is an imprint of the Taylor & Francis Group, an informa business

First issued in paperback 2020

Library of Congress Cataloging in Publication Data
A catalog record for this book has been requested

ISBN: 978-1-138-29862-0 (hbk)
ISBN: 978-0-367-59217-2 (pbk)

Typeset in Galliard
by Taylor & Francis Books

CL – For CP and Victoria
KA – For Nikunja and Rishita

Contents

List of illustrations

Figures

Tables

Notes on contributors

Kamalesh Adhikari is AIBE Research Fellow in Food Security and Member of the ARC Laureate Project 'Harnessing Intellectual Property to Build Food Security' in the TC Beirne School of Law at The University of Queensland, Australia. Kamalesh's current research focuses on the role of networks, informality and community seed banks in shaping seed regulation across developing and least-developed countries. Kamalesh is also undertaking a critical account of the concept of farmers' rights in intellectual property law.

Edwin Bikundo is a Senior Lecturer in the Griffith Law School, Griffith University, Australia. Edwin's current teaching and research interests lie in International and Comparative Law as well as Legal Theory. Recent and ongoing aspects of this span the different legal regimes governing land and sea and their literary origins, the law on the use of force as seen through a musical lens and the German myth of Faust in international law.

Fran Humphries is a Research Fellow with the Law Futures Centre and a member of the Australian Centre for Intellectual Property in Agriculture at Griffith University, Australia. Her research focuses on laws governing aquatic genetic resources and aquaculture as well as laws relating to ecological governance in Northern Australia.

John Hunter is an Aboriginal postdoctoral researcher at Macquarie University, Australia from the Gamilaraay and Wiradjuri people of New South Wales. He works in areas related to Aboriginal community development, community capacity building, environmental management and enriching communities through culture, arts and history. His research strongly supports programmes which develop intergenerational healing and wellbeing through the maintenance and revival of traditional Aboriginal knowledge.

Charles Lawson is a Professor in the Australian Centre for Intellectual Property in Agriculture at the Griffith Law School, Griffith University, Australia. Charles' current research interests focus on the information systems linking biology data around the globe, seeking efficient and effective ways of making this data available.

Paul Martin is the Director of the Australian Centre for Agriculture and Law in the School of Law at the University of New England, Australia. He also is on the Governing Board of the International Union for Conservation of Nature (IUCN) Academy of Environmental Law. Paul's current research includes a multi-country evaluation of the effectiveness of implementation of environmental conventions, and research into engagement and behavioural strategies affecting the implementation of laws.

Margaret Raven is a postdoctoral fellow at the Department of Geography and Planning, Macquarie University, Australia. She is a recipient of the Macquarie University Fellowship for Indigenous Researchers. Margaret's current research interests are food geographies, Indigenous food security, Indigenous knowledge and biodiversity, protocols and other regulatory regimes of controlling the flow of knowledge.

Matthew Rimmer is a Professor in Intellectual Property and Innovation Law at the Faculty of Law, at the Queensland University of Technology (QUT), Australia. Matthew leads the Leader of the QUT Intellectual Property and Innovation Law Research Program. Matthew's current research broadly addresses many areas including digital copyright, gene patents, biotechnology regulation, access to essential medicines, plain packaging of tobacco products, renewable energy, clean technologies, and climate change, traditional knowledge and Indigenous intellectual property, three dimensional printing, remix culture, and the maker movement, trade, and media and information technology law.

Daniel Robinson is an Associate Professor in the School of Humanities and Languages at the University of New South Wales, Australia. He is also a Research Fellow at the International Centre for Trade and Sustainable Development (ICTSD), Geneva, and a member of the Australian Centre for Intellectual Property in Agriculture. Daniel's current research interests are on Indigenous knowledge and biodiversity, community protocols, Indigenous laws, access and benefit-sharing regimes, 'biopiracy' and related issues, trade and environment.

Manuel Ruiz Muller is Director of the International Affairs and Biodiversity Program of the Peruvian Society for Environmental Law (SPDA). For the past two decades, Manuel has been doing research and publishing in the field of access to genetic resources, agrobiodiversity, food security, intellectual property and indigenous peoples. At present, Manuel is a Senior Advisor and Researcher with SPDA, and a private consultant for German Society for International Cooperation (GIZ), United Nations Conference on Trade and Development (UNCTAD), World Intellectual Property Organization (WIPO), and other organisations.

Jay Sanderson is an Associate Professor in the School of Law at the University of the Sunshine Coast, Australia. Jay is also an adjunct Research Fellow with the Law Futures Centre, Griffith University. Jay's current research focuses on trade and certification marks, particularly as they relate to agriculture, food and psychology.

Drossos Stamboulakis is a Lecturer in the School of Law at the University of the Sunshine Coast, Australia. Drossos' current research focuses on international commercial law, with an emphasis on contract law, cross-border legal regulation, and transnational commercial dispute resolution (including both private international law and international arbitration).

Leanne Wiseman is an Associate Professor in the Australian Centre for Intellectual Property in Agriculture at the Griffith Law School, Griffith University, Australia. Leanne's research interests currently focus on the legal issues arising from agricultural data, including the intersection of copyright and open access to the collection, aggregation and dissemination of on-farm data.

Abbreviations

ABS	Access and benefit sharing
ACAM	Australian Collection of Antarctic Microorganisms
ACCC	Australian Competition and Consumer Commission
ACIPA	Australian Centre for Intellectual Property in Agriculture
AIBE	Australian Institute of Business and Economics
AMLRC Act	*Antarctic Marine Living Resources Conservation Act 1981* (Cth)
ASEAN	Association of Southeast Asian Nations
ATCM	Antarctic Treaty Consultative Meeting
ATEP Act	*Antarctic Treaty (Environmental Protection) Act 1980* (Cth)
B2B	Business to business
BASIC countries	Four newly industrialised countries – Brazil, South Africa, India and China
BioCode	International Code of Biological Nomenclature
BOLD	Barcode of Life Data System
Bonn Guidelines	*Bonn Guidelines on Access to Genetic Resources and Fair and Equitable Sharing of the Benefits Arising out of their Utilization*
BRICS countries	Five emerging national economies – Brazil, Russia, India, China and South Africa
CAML	Census of Antarctic Marine Life
CBD	United Nations' *Convention on Biological Diversity*
CBD COP	Conference of the Parties to the *Convention on Biological Diversity*
CCAMLR	*Convention on the Conservation of Antarctic Marine Living Resources*
CCAMLR Commission	Commission for the Conservation of Antarctic Marine Living Resources

CGIAR	Consultative Group on International Agricultural Research
CITES	*Convention on International Trade in Endangered Species*
CMB	Catchment Management Board
COP	Conference of the Parties
Cth	Commonwealth
Cultivated Plant Code	International Code of Nomenclature for Cultivated Plants
CWAATSICH	Charleville and Western Areas Aboriginal and Torres Strait Islander Community Health Limited
DDBJ	DNA Data Bank of Japan
DITC	Division on International Trade in Goods and Services, and Commodities
DNA	Deoxyribonucleic acid
Doha Declaration	*Doha Ministerial Declaration on TRIPS*
DOIs	Digital Object Identifiers
DivSeek	Diversity Seek
EMBL	European Molecular Biology Laboratory
EPBC Act	*Environment Protection and Biodiversity Conservation Act 1999* (Cth)
EPBC Regulations	*Environment Protection and Biodiversity Conservation Regulations 2000* (Cth)
EU Regulation	*Regulation of the European Union on Compliance Measures for Users from the Nagoya Protocol on Access to Genetic Resources and the Fair and Equitable Sharing of Benefits Arising from their Utilization in the Union,* No 511/2014 of the European Parliament and of the Council of 16 April 2014
Eurisco	European Search Catalogue for Plant Genetic Resources
FAO	Food and Agriculture Organization of the United Nations
FPIC	Free, prior and informed consent
GEF	Global Environment Facility
GenBank	NIH genetic sequence database
GeneSys	Global Gateway to Genetic Resources
GRIN-Global	Germplasm Resource Information Network
GUIDs	Globally Unique Identifiers
ICTSD	International Centre for Trade and Sustainable Development
IGAE	*Inter-Governmental Agreement on the Environment*

IGC	World Intellectual Property Organization's Intergovernmental Committee on Intellectual Property and Genetic Resources, Traditional Knowledge and Folklore
IK	Indigenous knowledge
INBIO	National Biodiversity Institute of Costa Rica
IP	Intellectual property
IPA	Indigenous Protected Areas
IRGC	International Risk Governance Council
ISBN	International Standard Book Number
ISHS	International Society for Horticultural Science
ISO	International Standards Organization
ISSN	International Standard Serial Number
IUCN	International Union for Conservation of Nature
IUPGRFA	*International Undertaking on Plant Genetic Resources for Food and Agriculture*
LSIDs	LifeScience Identifiers
Madrid Protocol	*Protocol on Environmental Protection to the Antarctic Treaty*
MAT	Mutually agreed terms
Micro B3 Agreement	*Micro B3 Model Agreement on Access to Marine Microorganisms and Benefit Sharing*
MTA	Material transfer agreements
Nagoya Protocol	United Nations' *Nagoya Protocol on Access to Genetic Resources and the Fair and Equitable Sharing of Benefits Arising from Their Utilization to the Convention on Biological Diversity*
NCA	*Nationally Consistent Approach for Access to and the Utilisation of Australia's Native Genetic and Biochemical Resources*
NGOs	Non-governmental organisations
NIH	National Institute of Health (USA)
NSW	New South Wales (Australia)
NZ	New Zealand
PCT	Patent Cooperation Treaty
PGRFA	Plant Genetic Resources for Food and Agriculture
PIC	Prior informed consent
PIP Framework	World Health Organization's *Pandemic Influenza Preparedness Framework for the Sharing of Influenza Viruses and Access to Vaccines and Other Benefits*
Plant Code	International Code of Nomenclature for algae, fungi and plants

Plant Treaty	Food and Agriculture Organization of the United Nations' *International Treaty on Plant Genetic Resources for Food and Agriculture*
POPs	*Stockholm Convention on Persistent Organic Pollutants*
QUT	Queensland University of Technology
R&D	Research and development
RCEP	*Regional Comprehensive Economic Partnership*
RNA	Ribonucleic acid
SCAR-MarBIN	Marine BioTRIPS
SDGs	United Nations' *Sustainable Development Goals*
SMTA	Standard Material Transfer Agreement
SMAMLRC Act	*Antarctic Marine Living Resources Conservation Act 1981* (Cth)
SPDA	Peruvian Society for Environmental Law
TK	Traditional knowledge
TPP	*Trans-Pacific Partnership*
TRIPS (Agreement)	World Trade Organization's *Agreement on Trade-Related Aspects of Intellectual Property Rights*
UEBT	Union of Ethical BioTrade
UK	United Kingdom
UN	United Nations
UNCLOS	United Nations' *Convention on the Law of the Sea*
UNCTAD	United Nations Conference on Trade and Development
UNDP	United Nations Development Programme
UNDRIP	United Nations' *Declaration for the Rights of Indigenous Peoples*
UPOV	*International Union for the Protection of New Varieties of Plants*
US (and USA)	United States of America
UTZ	An independently monitored "program and label for sustainable farming" of tea, coffee, cocoa and hazelnuts
WA	Western Australia
WHO	World Health Organization
WIPO	World Intellectual Property Organization
WISM-GPA	World Information Sharing Mechanism for the implementation of the Global Plan of Action
WTO	World Trade Organization

Acknowledgements

This collection started as a conversation about the 'other' issues that need to be addressed for an effective implementation of national and international regimes on access and benefit sharing (ABS). There is a vast literature about the governance of ABS for genetic resources and other biological materials. Most of it, however, focuses on many of the same issues. Our brief was to try to address some of those 'other' issues, and in this way, bring forward some new perspectives around the discourse on ABS. Discussions among our colleagues set in motion the idea of asking experts to write about what they thought were new and important issues rather than identifying an issue and then seeking an expert. The outcome has been a welcome journey leading to the completion of this collection. In bringing this all together we acknowledge the generous support of the Australian Centre for Intellectual Property in Agriculture (ACIPA) at Griffith University and the Australian Research Council Australian Laureate Fellowship (FL150100104) funded by the Australian Government and led by Professor Brad Sherman (Laureate Fellow) at The University of Queensland. We also acknowledge our colleagues, and in particular Carol Ballard, for their insight, support and assistance that they extended to accomplish this project.

1 Biodiversity, genetic resources and intellectual property

Charles Lawson and Kamalesh Adhikari

The ongoing debates about access to and commercial use of biodiversity and genetic resources, and the application of intellectual property over gene-based products and technologies, have attracted a huge body of academic commentary and critique. While these debates have continued with some progress at international and national levels, there remains a number of issues that are yet to be addressed. The new dimension to the ongoing debates about biodiversity, genetic resources and intellectual property is the growing use of new biological technologies and knowledge systems such as genetics, genomics, synthetic biology and bioinformatics. These technologies and knowledge systems have made genetic resources more valuable because of their potential to address the pressing global challenges of agricultural growth, food security, public health, climate change and environmental sustainability, including meeting the *Sustainable Development Goals* (SDGs) of the United Nations. To deliver on potential solutions to these global challenges the demand for the use of the materials of biodiversity and genetic resources is rising, but the perennial questions of who can provide or obtain access to these resources, who gains the benefits from such access, and how to ensure that genetic resources are accessed and used in a fair and equitable way still remain.

Perhaps the turning point for the current debates about access to and use of biodiversity and genetic resources can be traced to the adoption of the United Nations' *Convention on Biological Diversity* (CBD) in 1992[1] that formally recognised the sovereignty of Nation States to control their biodiversity and genetic resources. While there had been important developments preceding this international agreement[2] – for example under the *Antarctic Treaty* in 1950s,[3] the *Outer Space Treaty* in the 1960s, the *Convention on the Law of the Sea* in the 1970s/1980[4] and the *International Undertaking on Plant Genetic Resources for Food and Agriculture* in the 1980s[5] – it was the CBD that delivered

---

1 (1992) 1760 UNTS 79 (CBD).
2 See Charles Lawson, *Regulating Genetic Resources: Access and Benefit-sharing in International Law* (Edward Elgar, 2012).
3 (1959) 19 ILM 860.
4 (1982) 1833 UNTS 3.
5 FAO Conference, *Report of the Conference of FAO, Twenty-second Session* (1983) C 1983/REP, [285] (Resolution 8/83).

a multilateral obligation and a mechanism that Nation States do have sovereignty over their biodiversity and genetic resources. In doing so, the CBD also stated that access would be according to the Nation States' laws, and that access be subject to the prior informed consent (PIC) and to mutually agreed terms (MAT) including an agreement about the benefits to be shared between the providers and users of genetic resources.[6] More recently this basic mechanism has been further clarified through the *Nagoya Protocol on Access to Genetic Resources and the Fair and Equitable Sharing of Benefits Arising from their Utilization to the Convention on Biological Diversity* (Nagoya Protocol).[7] There are also similar and compatible schemes for the governance of access to some agricultural plants under the *International Treaty on Plant Genetic Resources for Food and Agriculture* (Plant Treaty)[8] and to human pandemic influenza virus under the *Pandemic Influenza Preparedness Framework for the Sharing of Influenza Viruses and Access to Vaccines and Other Benefits* (PIP Framework).[9] Similar and compatible schemes are also being developed under the *Law of the Sea Convention*,[10] and for various classes of organisms like microorganisms, livestock and forestry, although these are in the very early stages of negotiation.[11]

The basic mechanisms of accessing biodiversity and genetic resources on the one hand, and sharing the benefits accrued from the access and use of these resources on the other hand, can be conveniently and simplistically separated into: (1) the access elements; and (2) the benefit sharing elements. According to this characterisation of the process, the legalities of access and benefit sharing (ABS) are essentially about the terms and conditions of access (such as PIC) and the terms and conditions of benefit sharing (such as MAT). And never far from this is the role of intellectual property and how this either promotes or undermines any ABS. This might be conceptualised as a model where the conservators of biodiversity and genetic resources come together with the owners of technology and intellectual property to deliver a commercialisable product for benefits (monetary and non-monetary) that are then shared *both* promoting conservation *and* rewarding the technology and intellectual property owners

---

6   CBD, Arts 1, 3 and 15.

7   Conference of the Parties to the Convention on Biological Diversity, *Report of the Tenth Meeting of the Conference of the Parties to the Convention on Biological Diversity* (2010) UNEP/CBD/COP/10/27, [103] and Annex (Decision X/1, Annex 1 (Nagoya Protocol), pp 89–109).

8   [2006] ATS 10 (Plant Treaty).

9   World Health Organization, *Pandemic Influenza Preparedness: Sharing of Influenza Viruses and Access to Vaccines and Other Benefits* (2011) A64/8, Attachment 2 (PIP Framework). This was adopted by the Member States of the World Health Organization: World Health Organization, *Pandemic Influenza Preparedness: Sharing of Influenza Viruses and Access to Vaccines and Other Benefits*, Sixty-fourth World Health Assembly (2011) WHA64.5, [1].

10 See United Nations General Assembly, *Letter Dated 13 February 2015 from the Co-Chairs of the Ad Hoc Open-ended Informal Working Group to the President of the General Assembly* (2015) A/69/780.

11 See Lawson, above n 2, pp 241–246.

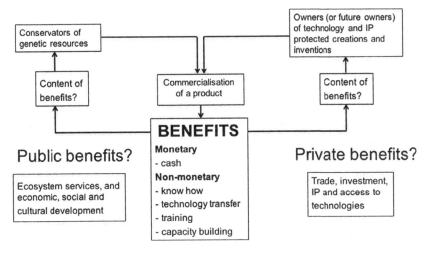

Figure 1.1 Basic model of ABS highlighting the public and private benefits
Notes: According to this basic model the conservers of biological and genetic resources come together with the owners of technology (and intellectual property (IP)) to create a commercialisable product that generates benefits, both monetary and non-monetary, and public and private. With these benefits the conservers are incentivised to conserve and the owners of technology and IP are incentivised (and rewarded) for their creations and inventions.

(Figure 1.1). Conceived in this simplistic way there is a virtuous cycle that not only promotes the conservation of valuable biodiversity and genetic resources, but also advances the development of such biodiversity and genetic resources into economically useful production.

Under the CBD (and the Nagoya Protocol) the ABS legalities are sorted out between the party holding the biodiversity and genetic resource and the party wanting to access that biodiversity and genetic resource. This is achieved through a bilateral contract where the contract establishes PIC and MAT, including benefit sharing conditions for providers as well as users of genetic resources. Under the Plant Treaty and the PIP Framework, these legalities have been reduced to a standard form contract that covers both PIC and MAT (including benefit sharing). Although these legalities appear to follow a simple conceptual model, the details are and remain contentious especially now that broader concerns are being engaged. Recalling that the CBD was negotiated in the shadow of negotiations to establish the World Trade Organization and its trade (and intellectual property) agreements, the CBD has a broader remit than just conserving biodiversity and aims to address broader global concerns about sustainable development and other social goals. These broader concerns also include the conception of Traditional Knowledge in the CBD (and the Nagoya Protocol).[12] Similar to the conception of Traditional Knowledge in

12 See CBD, Arts 8(j) and 10(c); Nagoya Protocol, Art 7.

the CBD and the Nagoya Protocol are the embodiments of Farmers' Rights to plant genetic resources and Traditional Knowledge in the Plant Treaty[13] and of genetic sequence data in the PIP Framework.[14] Importantly, however, these basic legalities remain contested. The incorporation of Traditional Knowledge, Farmers' Rights and genetic sequence data in international agreements consequently raises a challenging new dimension for the governance of intellectual property. This also means that the simplistic model for ABS set out in Figure 1.1 does not account for the current contestation around the governance of ABS for biodiversity and genetic resources. The legal and policy issues reach much more broadly and now reflect a plethora of different agendas, including economic development, sustainable development, Indigenous Peoples' sovereignty, and so on.

To address some of these contestations about ABS around the CBD, the Nagoya Protocol, the Plant Treaty and the PIP Framework, we convened a workshop ('Developments in Access and Benefit Sharing of Genetic Resources Workshop') hosted by the Australian Centre for Intellectual Property in Agriculture at Griffith University and Professor Brad Sherman's (ARC Laureate Fellow) ARC Laureate Project 'Harnessing Intellectual Property to Build Food Security' at The University of Queensland. Rather than identifying an issue and then seeking an expert, we approached experts to write about what they thought were important issues. Each participant was just asked to prepare and discuss a paper falling within the workshop theme of how different aspects of the law have addressed the concerns associated with the access and use of biodiversity and genetic resources (very broadly conceived). The intention was to allow a large discretion for scholars around the workshop theme, perhaps addressing perspectives that are often lost or under-represented in the literature. This collection is the result of the workshop and reflects the diversity of perspectives and the task that remains to find a common ground. Interestingly, the various perspectives that we present in this book demonstrate that even the basic ABS legalities remain deeply contested and that the issues addressed do not fall neatly into discreet themes. Rather, the various perspectives about the governance of biodiversity, genetic resources and intellectual property reflect the complex of legalities for a robust ABS regime. This accounts for our arranging the perspectives according to the alphabetic order of authors rather than trying to impose some kind of thematic order. This also accords with our workshop conclusions that the discourse in this area of law has advanced significantly, and that the current debates are taking place at a very high level of sophistication. The various contributions demonstrate what has been operationalised and what remains aspirational, and also that the contested issues are complex and require a careful consideration not simply by scholars but also by policymakers, development

---

13 See Plant Treaty, Art 9.
14 See PIP Framework, Art 5.2.4.

practitioners, community groups and private entities. Each contribution provides a challenge and articulates an optimistic solution.

In Kamalesh Adhikari's chapter, 'Reconceptualising Access: Moving Beyond the Limits of International Biodiversity Laws', he addresses the fundamental conception of access, that is, what it means when we access biodiversity and genetic resources. Kamalesh argues that access is more than just the physical performative act of providing and obtaining genetic resources for some kind of benefit sharing between resource providers and resource users. He reconceptualises access in a broader context of the governance of genetic resources, de-linking access and benefit sharing and addressing the question: are users of genetic resources obligated to share the benefits from accessing genetic resources? Kamalesh argues that access is a mechanism of benefit sharing in the context of the CBD, the Nagoya Protocol and the Plant Treaty. Kamalesh also argues that there is a need to revisit the traditional conceptualisation of access over 'tangible resources' in the light of the new technologies and knowledge systems that lead to the access and use of 'intangible resources' such as digital genetic sequence data. Following an examination of national and regional laws on ABS, Kamalesh concludes that the international community needs to address the inconsistent approaches that countries have adopted while defining 'access' in their domestic laws. The reconceptualisation of access, Kamalesh argues, is needed if the goal is to make bilateral and multilateral mechanisms of access more robust and effective.

Edwin Bikundo's chapter 'Aligning Means and Ends to Benefit Indigenous Peoples under the Convention on Biological Diversity and the Nagoya Protocol' addresses the legal complex around the place of Indigenous Peoples in international law. Edwin focuses on critiquing the use and non-use of the term 'people' in the CBD's ABS mechanism. The problem Edwin explores is that in the CBD it is axiomatic that the Contracting Parties to the CBD are not only Nation States but can also only *be* Nation States as the sole legal form with full legal personality in international law. The consequence, Edwin argues, by engaging with the work of German jurist Carl Schmitt and Italian philosopher Giorgio Agamben, is that the way the system is set up is such that access is the *means* by which the *State* is to meet the *ends* of sharing benefits with Indigenous *peoples*. The problem Edwin identifies is that 'the people' as such, and consequently Indigenous Peoples, cannot maintain their specificity in the absence of the Nation State form, and that the presence of the Nation State's political form promotes homogeneity and therefore erases Indigenous identity. This is a bleak prognosis for those Indigenous Peoples seeking to assert their sovereignty through claims to Traditional Knowledge under the CBD. This is, however, a call to the elites representing Indigenous Peoples to carefully reconsider their roles and how they go about engaging in these forums on behalf of those they represent.

Fran Humphries's 'Banking on a Patent Solution for Sharing Antarctica's *ex situ* Genetic Resources' reviews the ABS regulation of Antarctica's *ex situ* genetic resources and the scant legal basis requiring the benefits be used to achieve the *Antarctic Treaty*'s objectives of cooperation and freedom of scientific investigation. The *Antarctic Treaty* provides an intriguing alternative scheme for the jurisdictions beyond the CBD. Fran argues that the proposed instrument under the *Convention on the Law of the Sea* might address some of the jurisdictional complexity, but in the meantime the evolving system of patent law defences may prove to be an unexpected ally for achieving the *Antarctic Treaty*'s objectives. More broadly, Fran's contribution highlights the importance of engaging with the existing laws, in this case patents, to exploit their existing potential to address the concerns associated with the ABS of Antartica's *ex situ* genetic resources.

Charles Lawson's chapter 'Nomenclature as a Standardised Metadata System for Ordering and Accessing Information about Plants' addresses the critical issue of biological information about genetic resources as an important benefit to be shared under the CBD, the Nagoya Protocol, the Plant Treaty and the PIP Framework. Charles argues that names have the potential to act as a standardised metadata system for ordering and accessing all the biological information about plants that are increasingly being collected, stored, searched, retrieved and integrated through computers. He asserts that naming according to the existing code (rules about naming) provides a superior metadata structure because they enable information linking across diverse information collections and they retain the benefit of being rule-based, memorable, understandable and communicable compared to disembodied signs like Globally Unique Identifiers (GUIDs), LifeScience Identifiers (LSIDs) and Digital Object Identifiers (DOIs). While he accepts that the GUIDs, LSIDs and DOIs do have a role, he argues this is in addition to plant names to distinguish the various biological entities despite some of the inherent problems with the naming codes.

Paul Martin's 'Free Prior Informed Consent – Mere Politics or Meaningful Change?' addresses the contours of free PIC (FPIC) as a critical component of ABS. Paul considers that while many things are unknown about how FPIC will translate into jurisprudence and governance processes and what impacts this will have for the goals of conservation of biodiversity and ABS, the eventual costs, benefits and outcomes will be determined by legal and administrative details, by the specific issues that are the focus of application and contestation, and by context. Given the uncertainty of these variables, Paul argues, risk management is justified so that there are positive outcomes from adopting FPIC through law and public policy.

Matthew Rimmer's 'The *Trans-Pacific Partnership* and Sustainable Development: Access to Genetic Resources, Informed Consent, and Benefit Sharing' considers the impact of the regional trade agreement – the *Trans-Pacific Partnership* (TPP) – on the SDGs. While apparently distant from ABS debates, Matthew demonstrates how several chapters of the TPP impinge upon the SDGs, potentially undermining the United Nations' efforts to promote sustainable development and equality throughout the Pacific region, and that the exclusion of many developing countries, least-developed countries and small island states from the preferential trade deals flows through to the debate over access to genetic resources, informed consent and benefit sharing. Matthew's chapter demonstrates the interrelationship of ABS with the broader global policy debates about the SDGs and trade, and the need to factor these debates into considerations about ABS.

The chapter by Daniel Robinson, Margaret Raven and John Hunter, 'The Limits of ABS Laws: Why Gumbi Gumbi and other Bush Foods and Medicines need Specific Indigenous Knowledge Protections' presents case studies where Indigenous knowledge associated with endemic species in Australia has been utilised for research and/or commercialisation, and where patents have been issued for those uses disclosed by Indigenous knowledge. This sets voice to the concerns about the cultural and spiritual integrity of Indigenous knowledge and how that knowledge is being unfairly appropriated for commercial gains using patents and other intellectual property. Daniel, Margaret and John conclude that regulating ABS and modifying intellectual property laws may play a role, but a more progressive move would be towards greater recognitions of Indigenous customary laws and community protocols.

Manuel Ruiz Muller's chapter, 'Reshaping the International Access to Genetic Resources and Benefit Sharing Process? Overcoming Resistance to Change and Correction' sets out an overview of why designing operational ABS frameworks may have been so difficult and, in particular, the reasons why policy makers and practitioners seem so reluctant to consider a more efficient regulatory and institutional alternative. Manuel argues that a solution to realise the objective of ABS under the CBD and the Nagoya Protocol lies in the conceptual framework of 'bounded openness'. The concept of 'bounded openness' starts from the proposition that 'the utilization of genetic resources [is] the utilization of natural information, which invites the application of the economics of information and the justification of rents'.[15] Manuel laments the resistance to any re-definition of genetic resources as natural information and to a change in direction away from bilateralism of MAT, PIC and ABS contracts. He attributes the resistance to technocracy, path dependency, principal-agent problems, studied ignorance and the subtle dominance of lawyers limiting the scope for other possibilities. Manuel calls for creativity, innovation and sound policy and legal approaches to realise the fairness and equity dimensions in ABS.

And in the final chapter, Jay Sanderson, Leanne Wiseman and Drossos Stamboulakis's 'Certified ABS: The Union for Ethical BioTrade and the Use of Trade and Certification Marks to Encourage and Facilitate Behaviour Change' addresses a broader view of ABS and considers how trade and certification marks can be used to encourage and facilitate a fair and equitable sharing of benefits that arise from the use of biodiversity, genetic resources, and any associated Traditional Knowledge. Jay, Leanne and Drossos argue that trade

15 Joseph Vogel, 'Foreword: "On the Silver Jubilee of 'Intellectual Property and Information Markets: Preliminaries to a New Conservation Policy'"' in Manuel Ruiz Muller, *Genetic Resources as Natural Information: Policy Implications for the Convention on Biological Diversity* (EarthScan, 2015) p xviii.

and certification marks represent a complementary, flexible and responsive option to also encourage and facilitate ABS. Their hope is that ABS marks can facilitate a market-driven low-intervention nudging of consumers and producers towards ABS practices such as equitable pricing, PIC and MAT.

The conclusions from the workshop's contributors were that ABS is currently not working and that new approaches are needed to rethink, reconceptualise and (re)consider drastic alternatives. While the contributors' considered that there were significant hurdles to pass, they were also optimistic that these hurdles could be passed. They agreed that good outcomes were possible with a mastery of interdisciplinary solutions and that an effective governance of ABS required resolution at the level of individuals and communities rather than a single global standard. Again, however, the complexity of the ABS forums as a crucible for broader debates distantly related to ABS posed difficulties in finding new solutions. We hope the contributions add to the solutions and thank the contributors for their engagement in bringing the workshop to a satisfying conclusion.

2 Reconceptualising access

Moving beyond the limits of international biodiversity laws

Kamalesh Adhikari

2.1 Introduction

The international circulation of genetic resources is not a new phenomenon. The movement of these resources, whether in the form of plants, animals, seeds or germplasm, has been taking place for centuries and has had an important impact on global agriculture and food security. Over time, national food supplies and production systems have benefited from the flow of these resources between countries. Indeed, in 2014 it was estimated that foreign crops contributed 68.7 per cent of the food supplied and 69.3 per cent of the food produced in countries around the world.[1] The international flow of genetic resources has also had an important impact on sectors such as pharmaceuticals and biotechnology, in particular by making it possible for technological innovations based on the genetic materials of plants, animals and microorganisms that have been accessed from forests, water resources, farmers' fields and gene banks.[2]

Despite these benefits, the international movement of genetic resources has also generated a number of questions and concerns. These include: should genetic resources be made subject to ownership, access and use through intellectual and other property rights, or should they be treated as a common heritage of the global community?; what are the rights and responsibilities of States in relation to the access and flow of genetic resources between and within nations?; and, how should the interests of Indigenous Peoples,

---

1 Colin Khoury, Harold Achicanoy, Anne Bjorkman, Carlos Navarro-Racines, Luigi Guarino, Ximena Flores-Palacios, Johannes Engels, John Wiersema, Hannes Dempewolf, Julian Ramírez-Villegas, Nora Castañeda-Álvarez, Cary Fowler, Andy Jarvis, Loren Rieseberg and Paul Struik, *Estimation of Countries' Interdependence in Plant Genetic Resources Provisioning National Food Supplies and Production Systems*, Research Study 8 (Secretariat of the International Treaty on Plant Genetic Resources for Food and Agriculture, 2014) available at <http://www.planttreaty.org/sites/default/files/files/ITPGRFA_Interdependence_text_2015_9_18_0_Main%20text.pdf> (accessed 16 May 2017).
2 For some estimates of the benefits derived from the use of genetic resources in pharmaceutical, biotechnology and other sectors, see Patrick ten Brink (ed.), *The Economics of Ecosystems and Biodiversity in National and International Policy Making* (Earthscan, 2011).

including local and farming communities, be protected when their genetic resources and traditional knowledge are accessed by others, for example, for commercial use by pharmaceutical, cosmetic and food industries?

In attempting to address these concerns, the international regulatory landscapes for the governance of genetic resources have changed significantly over the past few decades. Until the 1950s, there was no international law dealing with the access and commercial use of genetic resources. This situation changed when a series of international regulatory instruments were negotiated, debated and concluded in the decades thereafter. Some of these instruments – such as the 1961 *International Union for the Protection of New Varieties of Plants* (UPOV) and the 1995 *Agreement on Trade-Related Aspects of Intellectual Property Rights* (TRIPS) of the World Trade Organization – govern the rules of intellectual property for genetic resources.[3] Some other instruments – which are the focus of this chapter, such as the 1992 *Convention on Biological Diversity* (CBD) and the 2001 *International Treaty on Plant Genetic Resources for Food and Agriculture* (Plant Treaty) – aim to facilitate the access and use of genetic resources by requiring the resource users to share the benefits accrued from the utilisation of genetic resources with the resource providers.

A lot has been written about the objectives, nature and scope of the legal measures that the CBD and the Plant Treaty have established.[4] In recent years, there has also been a proliferation in the number of studies that have assessed the effectiveness and impact of the legal regimes that countries have introduced in accordance with these international agreements.[5] These studies provide important insights into a range of key concepts and issues about bioprospecting, biopiracy, Indigenous knowledge, free and prior informed consent, access permits, material transfer agreements, and monetary and non-monetary benefit sharing. Despite this, however, one area that has yet to receive any real sustained attention is the concept of 'access'. This is probably because there is a tendency to consolidate access and benefit sharing (ABS)

---

3 For a comprehensive account of the *International Union for the Protection of New Varieties of Plants* (UPOV) and the *Agreement on Trade-Related Aspects of Intellectual Property Rights* (TRIPS) and how their intellectual property systems protect plant varieties and genetic resources, see Lionel Bently and Brad Sherman, *Intellectual Property Law* (4th edition, Oxford University Press, 2014).

4 See, for examples, Michael Halewood, Isabel López Noriega and Sélim Louafi, (eds.), *Crop Genetic Resources as a Global Commons: Challenges in International Law and Governance* (Routledge, 2013); Manuel Ruiz and Ronnie Vernooy (eds.), *The Custodians of Biodiversity: Sharing Access to and Benefits of Genetic Resources* (Routledge, 2012); Geoff Tansey and Tasmin Rajotte (eds.), *The Future Control of Food: A Guide to International Negotiations and Rules on Intellectual Property, Biodiversity and Food Security* (Earthscan, 2008).

5 See, for example, Jorge Cabrera Medaglia, Frederic Perron-Welch and Freedom-Kai Phillips, *Overview of National and Regional Measures on Access to Genetic Resources and Benefit-sharing: Challenges and Opportunities in Implementing the Nagoya Protocol* (Centre for International Sustainable Development Law, 2014). Also see Carmen Richerzhagen, *Protecting Biological Diversity: The Effectiveness of Access and Benefit-sharing Regimes* (Routledge, 2013).

into a unified concept and not to focus on the role that 'access' on its own plays in a broader context of the governance of genetic resources.[6]

To the extent that scholars have considered the meaning of access, it is usually assumed that access is merely the physical performative act of providing and obtaining genetic resources for some kind of benefit sharing between resource providers and resource users. In this chapter, I move beyond this way of thinking about access, seeking instead to explore the meaning of access in a broader historical and emerging context of the governance of genetic resources. In doing so, I investigate three questions: (1) how did access emerge as a concern?; (2) how has access been perceived by relevant international agreements?; and, (3) how should we reconceptualise access in a broader context of the governance of genetic resources?

2.2 How did access emerge as a concern?

While access to genetic resources is generally considered to have first emerged as a global issue in the 1980s, questions about access had arisen previously.[7] One early situation where access was made visible as a concern was in relation to UPOV. Initially designed to address the commercial interests of European plant breeders and seed companies, UPOV was the first international agreement to grant intellectual property over new plant varieties.

After its entry into force in 1968, UPOV ensured that breeders who bred or discovered new plant varieties could control the production, reproduction and sale of the seeds of new plant varieties through the exercise of a set of exclusive rights.[8] As there were concerns that farmers' access to the seeds of protected plant varieties would be restricted due to breeders' rights, UPOV recognised a

---

6 See an analysis of the concept of ABS in Carmen Richerzhagen, 'Effective Governance of Access and Benefit-sharing Under the Convention on Biological Diversity' (2011) 20 *Biodiversity and Conservation* 2243. ABS as a concept has also been discussed in several policy documents and scholarly research: see, for example, Thomas Greiber, Sonia Peña Moreno, Mattias Ahrén, Jimena Nieto Carrasco, Evanson Kamau, Jorge Cabrera Medaglia, Maria Julia Oliva, Frederic Perron-Welch and Natasha Ali China Williams, *An Explanatory Guide to the Nagoya Protocol on Access and Benefit-sharing* (International Union for Conservation of Nature and Natural Resources, 2012).

7 A number of studies discuss or refer to the history of the international negotiations on access to genetic resources in the context of some specific developments that first occurred in the 1980s at the United Nations and the United Nations Food and Agriculture Organization (FAO): see, for example, Kerry ten Kate and Sarah Laird, *The Commercial Use of Biodiversity: Access to Genetic Resources and Benefit-sharing* (Earthscan, 1999).

8 UPOV has been criticised by a number of scholars for various reasons including the implications of breeders' rights for small-scale farmers, especially in developing countries. For a summary of criticisms against UPOV and a response to such criticisms by the Vice Secretary-General of UPOV, see Jay Sanderson, 'Why UPOV is Relevant, Transparent and Looking to the Future: A Conversation with Peter Button' (2013) 8 *Journal of Intellectual Property Law and Practice* 615.

so-called 'farmers' privilege'.[9] The provisions on the farmers' privilege allowed farmers to save and re-sow the seed harvested from protected varieties for their own use. Over time, UPOV strengthened breeders' rights leading to further concerns for farmers.[10] There were concerns that new rights would restrict the ability of farmers to access the seeds of protected plant varieties and that the private seed industry would be the sole beneficiary of the monopolisation of genetic resources. Concerns were also raised that UPOV did not require plant breeders to share the benefits with germplasm providers (farmers), even though breeders regularly obtained access to germplasm for breeding and commercialisation of new varieties from gene banks, farmers' fields and natural habitats.

Access to genetic resources was also raised as a concern in the United Nations in the 1960s. To protect access to natural resources, the United Nations passed the *General Assembly Resolution 1803 (XVII)* in 1962 addressing the sovereignty of natural resources. Although it did not explicitly mention biological or genetic resources, this resolution was the first international instrument to recognise the sovereign right of peoples and nations over natural resources. The resolution stated that 'the right of peoples and nations to permanent sovereignty over their natural wealth and resources must be exercised in the interest of their national development and of the well-being of the people of the State concerned'.[11] It is important to note that as a result of Article 1 of the *International Covenant on Civil and Political Rights*[12] and the *International Covenant on Economic, Social and Cultural Rights*,[13] by 1966 the concept of permanent State sovereignty over a State's own natural resources had already become a general principle of international law.[14]

9   UPOV had also recognised 'breeders' exemption' allowing for the access and use of the protected plant varieties for the purpose of breeding. For an analysis of breeders' exemption and how access and benefit sharing laws impact further breeding, see Charles Lawson, 'The Breeder's Exemption Under UPOV 1991, the Convention on Biological Diversity and its Nagoya Protocol' (2015) 10 *Journal of Intellectual Property Law and Practice* 526.

10   UPOV was revised in 1972, 1978 and 1991 to strengthen breeders' rights which some scholars argue has restricted the ability of farmers to save, exchange and sell the seed harvest from protected plant varieties: see, for example, Robert Tripp, Niels Louwaars and Derek Eaton, 'Plant Variety Protection in Developing Countries: A Report from the Field' (2007) 32 *Food Policy* 354.

11   United Nations General Assembly, *Permanent Sovereignty over Natural Resources*, GA Res 1803 (XVII), UN GAOR, 17th sess, 1194th plen mtg, UN Doc A/RES/1803, Art 1.

12   United Nations General Assembly, *International Covenant on Civil and Political Rights*, GA Res 2200 (XXI), 21st sess, 1496th plen mtg, UN Doc A/RES/21/2200, Art 1.

13   United Nations General Assembly, *International Covenant on Economic, Social and Cultural Rights*, GA Res 2200 (XXI), 21st sess, 1496th plen mtg, UN Doc A/RES/21/2200, Art 1.

14   For further discussion on the recognition of permanent sovereignty of peoples and nations over natural resources, see Erica-Irene Daes, *Indigenous Peoples'*

These developments, coupled with the advent of modern biotechnology and genetic engineering, had a significant impact on international negotiations that were taking place in the 1980s and 1990s. As developed countries were making use of the open flows and collections of germplasm from different locations and obtaining intellectual property over plant varieties, developing countries argued for an international legal regime to regulate the inequitable use of germplasm at the 1981 conference of the United Nations Food and Agriculture Organization (FAO). Developing countries expressed the view that an international legal regime was necessary to address the disparity of gene bank facilities between the developing and the developed world and to regulate developed countries' excessive control and use of the germplasm stored in gene banks.[15] There was a concern that only 15 per cent of all international collections of germplasm was designated for preservation and use in developing countries, while the rest of the accessions were stored in developed countries and in the Consultative Group on International Agricultural Research (CGIAR) Centers.[16] There were also concerns in relation to who owned and controlled the use of germplasm that international gene banks (such as the CGIAR Centers) had collected from countries around the world.[17]

After long and protracted negotiations, the *International Undertaking on Plant Genetic Resources for Food and Agriculture* (IUPGRFA) was adopted at the 1983 conference of the FAO. Although the IUPGRFA was non-binding, it was the first international agreement to govern the conservation and use of genetic resources that are important for food and agriculture. The IUPGRFA was conceptualised to operate on the principle that plant genetic resources were the heritage of humankind and that they should be available to all people without restriction.[18] Based on this principle, governments and institutions with plant genetic resources under their control were directed to 'allow access to samples of such resources, and to permit their export, where the resources have been requested for the purposes of scientific research, plant breeding or genetic resource conservation'.[19] They were also required to provide samples of plant

---

Permanent Sovereignty over Natural Resources: Final Report of the Special Rapporteur (2004) E/CN.4/Sub.2/2004/30. For a detailed analysis of the history and the evolution of the concept of sovereignty within different entities of the United Nations, see Charles Lawson, *Regulating Genetic Resources: Access and Benefit Sharing in International Law* (Edward Elgar Publishing, 2012).

15 For further details of the concerns of developing countries, see Regine Andersen, 'Governing Agrobiodiversity: International Regimes, Plant Genetics and Developing Countries', Dissertation (University of Oslo, 2007).

16 Andersen, ibid, cites Cary Fowler, *Unnatural Selection: Technology, Politics and Plant Evolution* (Gordon and Breach, 1994).

17 Commission on Plant Genetic Resources, *The Global System for the Conservation and Utilization of Plant Genetic Resources* (1991) CPGR/91/5.

18 Food and Agriculture Organization of the United Nations, *Report of the Conference of FAO*, Twenty-second Session, C 1983 (1983) [285] (Resolution 8/83, Art 1).

19 Ibid, [285] (Resolution 8/83, Art 5).

genetic resources free of charge, either through mutual exchange or on mutually agreed terms.[20]

Rather than ending international tensions, the IUPGRFA's concept of unrestricted access to plant genetic resources served to generate further debate among FAO members. On the one hand, developed countries felt that the IUPGRFA failed to address the concerns of plant breeders and the seed industry. In particular, developed countries held the view that making plant genetic resources available for third parties without restriction would undermine the rights of plant breeders and the seed industry.[21] Developed countries were also concerned that the IUPGRFA had defined plant genetic resources in such a way that the concept of unrestricted access would also extend to cover 'newly developed plant varieties' and 'special genetic stocks (including elite and current breeders' lines and mutants)'.[22] The notion that privately owned plant varieties and special genetic stocks should be made available without restrictions led the American Seed Trade Association, and other seed industry groups of the developed world, to declare that the IUPGRFA 'strikes at the heart of free enterprise and intellectual property'.[23] The coverage of new plant varieties and special genetic stocks for unrestricted access also resulted in the registration of reservations to the IUPGRFA by a group of developed countries including Canada, France, Germany, Japan, New Zealand, Switzerland, the United Kingdom and the United States of America. These countries further argued for the recognition of intellectual property within the framework of the IUPGRFA.[24]

In contrast to the positions taken by developed countries at the FAO, developing countries argued that the contribution that their governments and farmers had made to the conservation and continued availability of plant germplasm were neither recognised nor rewarded. In particular, among developing countries:

> there was a growing feeling of the inequality of a system that rewarded the contributions of some innovators to the development of plant genetic

20 Ibid.

21 Jack Kloppenburg and Daniel Lee Kleinman, 'The Plant Germplasm Controversy' (1987) 37 *Bioscience* 190. For an argument that the principle of unrestricted access to all plant germplasm was not acceptable for countries with highly developed seed industries, also see Roger Sedjo, 'Property Rights, Genetic Resources, and Bio-technological Change' (1992) 35 *Journal of Law and Economics* 199.

22 Other than newly developed varieties and special genetic stocks (including elite and current breeders' lines and mutants), the IUPGRFA had defined plant genetic resources to also cover cultivated varieties (cultivars), obsolete cultivars, primitive cultivars (landraces), and wild and weed species: see IUPGRFA, Art 2.1.

23 As quoted in Shawn Sullivan, 'Plant Genetic Resources and the Law Past, Present, and Future' (2004) 135 *Plant Physiology* 10.

24 Kerry ten Kate and Carolina Lasén Díaz, 'The Undertaking Revisited: A Commentary on the Revision of the International Undertaking on Plant Genetic Resources for Food and Agriculture' (1997) 6 *Review of European, Comparative & International Environmental Law* 284.

resources through plant variety protection and patents, but failed to recognize the important contribution over time of farmers' innovations in selecting and breeding, as well as conserving, plant genetic resources.[25]

In an attempt to address the concerns of both developed and developing countries, two additional resolutions were annexed to the IUPGRFA in 1989. The first resolution stated that 'plant genetic resources are a *common* heritage of mankind to be preserved, and to be *freely available for use*, for the benefit of present and future generations' (emphasis added).[26] The resolution also recognised that plant breeders' rights that have been protected under UPOV *are not incompatible* with the IUPGRFA. However, as the IUPGRFA's acceptance of UPOV allowed plant breeders and the seed industry to exclude their plant varieties and genetic materials from the common heritage, developing countries argued for the recognition of farmers' rights to counterbalance plant breeders' rights.[27] This eventually led to a second resolution, which stated that farmers (as well as countries in all regions) should be able to 'participate fully in the benefits derived, at present and in the future, from the improved use of plant genetic resources, through plant breeding and other scientific methods'.[28]

The consensus reached as a result of these two resolutions did not, however, resolve the tensions that had arisen between developing and developed countries. Additional concerns were raised about how to interpret the concept of common heritage in relation to the access and use of plant genetic resources, as well as how to implement farmers' rights over plant genetic resources. As a way forward, it was recognised in 1991 that farmers' rights would be implemented through the creation of an international fund and that the concept of common heritage should be subject to the sovereign rights of States over their own plant genetic resources.[29]

This recognition of States' sovereign rights over plant genetic resources played a decisive role in the design of the framework of the CBD in 1992. The CBD was the first international instrument to establish rules of a binding

---

25 Gerald Moore and Witold Tymowski, *Explanatory Guide to the International Treaty on Plant Genetic Resources for Food and Agriculture* (International Union for Conservation of Nature and Natural Resources, 2005).

26 See Food and Agriculture Organization of the United Nations, *Report of the Conference of FAO*, Twenty-fifth Session, C 1989 (1989) [108] (Resolution 4/89) *(emphasis added)*.

27 For some early debates about farmers' rights, see Keystone Center, *Final Consensus Report: Global Initiative for the Security and Sustainable Use of Plant Genetic Resources*, Third Plenary Session, 31 May–4 June 1991, Oslo, Norway (Keystone Center, 1991) available at <https://idl-bnc.idrc.ca/dspace/bitstream/10625/12710/1/IDL-12710.pdf> (accessed 16 May 2017).

28 Food and Agriculture Organization of the United Nations, *Report of the Conference of FAO*, Twenty-fifth Session, C 1989 (1989) [108] (Resolution 5/89).

29 Food and Agriculture Organization of the United Nations, *Report of the Conference of FAO*, Twenty-sixth Session, C 1991 (1991) [104] (Resolution 3/91).

nature for the conservation, access, use and the sharing of the benefits that arise from the use of genetic resources. Drawing on the *Charter of the United Nations*[30] and the principles of international law, the CBD reaffirmed that 'States have sovereign rights over their own biological resources'.[31] The CBD also stated that national governments had 'the authority to determine access to genetic resources'.[32] It was anticipated that this would not be used by any Contracting Party to restrict other Contracting Parties' access to genetic resources if the access was for 'environmentally sound uses'.[33] Rather, Contracting Parties were required to facilitate access to genetic resources in the form of mutually agreed terms that ensured commercial and other uses of genetic resources, and benefit sharing between resource providers and resource users.[34] It was also anticipated that Contracting Parties would make legal arrangements to provide prior informed consent for access to genetic resources from their territories,[35] and to 'respect, preserve and maintain knowledge, innovations and practices of indigenous and local communities'.[36]

While the CBD provided a strong legal basis for establishing State-based access regimes, the framework established by the CBD to govern the genetic resources of plants, animals and microorganisms was beset by a number of limitations. In particular, the CBD did not cover the genetic materials collected prior to its entry into force and the germplasm stored in international gene banks, such as the CGIAR Centers' collections. The CBD also did not address farmers' rights that were being discussed as a counterbalance to intellectual property at the FAO. It was recognised that solutions to these limitations should be sought within the IUPGRFA.[37]

Finally, after a number of years of further negotiations, FAO member countries agreed to address the limitations of the CBD, as well as other issues in relation to the governance of plant genetic resources through a separate legal regime. In 2001, FAO member countries replaced the IUPGRFA with the Plant Treaty, a legally-binding international agreement that governs access to the plant genetic resources that are important for food and agriculture. The Plant Treaty, in harmony with the CBD, aimed to promote the conservation and sustainable use of plant genetic resources and to ensure the fair and equitable sharing of the benefits arising from their use. In an attempt to address the

---

30 United Nations. *Charter of the United Nations.* 24 October 1945, 1 UNTS XVI, available at <http://www.un.org/en/charter-united-nations/> (accessed 11 June 2017).

31 In the CBD, states' sovereign rights have been recognised over 'biological resources' (Preamble) and 'natural resources' (Art 15.1).

32 CBD, Art 15.1.

33 The CBD does not clarify the term 'environmentally sound uses' (Art 15.2).

34 CBD, Art 15.4.

35 CBD, Art 15.5.

36 CBD, Art 8(j).

37 For further discussion on these issues, see Secretariat of the Convention on Biological Diversity. *Handbook of the Convention on Biological Diversity Including its Cartagena Protocol on Biosafety* (3rd edition, CBD Secretariat, 2005) pp 406–408.

concerns of developing countries, the Plant Treaty also recognised farmers' rights to plant genetic resources including traditional knowledge. Although the Plant Treaty and the CBD were designed to operate in tandem, the way they govern access to genetic resources is different.

2.3 How is access perceived?

In the past few decades, the term 'access' has emerged as a problematic concept among scholars in fields as diverse as public health (access to medicines and health services),[38] natural resource management (access to land and forests),[39] science and innovation (access to technologies and knowledge),[40] and food security (access to food and farm inputs).[41] While a lot has been written on the topic, there is no agreed-upon understanding of access among scholars. For example, while some scholars such as Schlager and Ostrom define access as 'the right' to enter a defined physical area and benefit from resources,[42] others such as Ribot and Peluso define access as 'the ability' to benefit from resources, proposing a theory of access that builds on the notion of power.[43]

In this chapter, I do not intend to use a definition of access that focuses on tangible resources such as land and forests. Neither do I seek to frame a new definition of access that neatly explains the dynamics of access associated with two important components of genetic resources – that is, tangible components (such as cells, tissues, plant parts, and sexual and vegetative seeds) and intangible components (such as information contained in genetic resources and their derivatives, including traditional knowledge or any new knowledge, for example, genetic sequence information).[44] Rather, in this section I explore how the term 'access' has been specifically used and perceived by the legal

---

38 See, for example, Maryam Bigdeli, Bart Jacobs, Goran Tomson, Richard Laing, Abdul Ghaffar, Bruno Dujardin, and Wim Van Damme, 'Access to Medicines from a Health System Perspective' (2013) 28 *Health Policy Plan* 692.

39 See, for example, Edella Schlager and Elinor Ostrom, 'Property-rights Regimes and Natural Resources: A Conceptual Analysis' (1992) 68 *Land Economics* 249.

40 See, for example, Fiona Murray and Scott Stern, 'Do Formal Intellectual Property Rights Hinder the Free Flow of Scientific Knowledge?: An Empirical Test of the Anti-commons Hypothesis' (2007) 63 *Journal of Economic Behaviour and Organization* 648.

41 See, for example, Kerstin Mechlem, 'Food Security and the Right to Food in the Discourse of the United Nations' (2004) 10 *European Law Journal* 631.

42 Schlager and Ostrom, above n 39, p 250.

43 Jesse Ribot and Nancy Lee Peluso, 'A Theory of Access' (2003) 68 *Rural Sociology* 153. See also Jesse Ribot, 'Theorizing Access: Forest Profits Along Senegal's Charcoal Commodity Chain' (1998) 29 *Development and Change* 307.

44 For a comprehensive discussion on tangible and intangible features of plant genetic resources and why a theoretical framework that deals with tangible natural resources does not explain the case of plant genetic resources, see Michael Halewood, 'What Kind of Goods are Plant Genetic Resources for Food and Agriculture? Towards the Identification and Development of a New Global Commons' (2013) 7 *International Journal of the Commons* 278.

regimes that govern genetic resources. I also consider whether it is necessary to reconceptualise access in a broader context of the governance of genetic resources.

The CBD and the Plant Treaty use access as a key term to shape the governance of genetic resources. Although States are able to exercise their sovereign rights to determine access to genetic resources in their respective jurisdictions, each Contracting Party is obligated to exercise such rights in a way that facilitates access and makes genetic resources available for commercial and other uses in other territories. Accordingly, Article 15 of the CBD and Article 10 of the Plant Treaty establish a number of rules and principles for facilitating access to genetic resources between or among member countries.

Although access is at the core of both the CBD and the Plant Treaty, neither provides a definition of 'access'. The 2010 *Nagoya Protocol on Access to Genetic Resources and the Fair and Equitable Sharing of Benefits Arising from their Utilization* (Nagoya Protocol),[45] which is a supplementary agreement to the CBD, does not define 'access' either. What access means depends on the contexts in which it has been used in the international agreements.

The CBD uses the term 'access' in two specific ways.[46] The first is where access means the physical performative act of providing and obtaining genetic resources. The notion that access is a physical performative act that leads both to the use of genetic resources and to the sharing of the benefits accruing from such use is reflected in the obligations of each Contracting Party. According to the CBD, Contracting Parties are required to 'create conditions to facilitate access to genetic resources' for other Contracting Parties and to share 'the benefits arising from the commercial and other utilization of genetic resources' with Parties providing the resources.[47]

The second way 'access' is used in the CBD is to refer to access as a mechanism of sharing the benefits that accrue from the use of genetic resources. The notion that access could be seen as a mechanism of benefit sharing is reflected in the CBD's third objective: 'the fair and equitable sharing of the benefits arising out of the utilization of genetic resources, including *by appropriate access to genetic resources*' (emphasis added).[48] However, as I discuss further in the next section, Contracting Parties are required to ensure that while sharing benefits derived from access to genetic resources, they take into

---

45 Conference of the Parties to the Convention on Biological Diversity, *Report of the Sixth Meeting of the Conference of the Parties to the Convention on Biological Diversity* (2010) UNEP/CBD/COP/10/27, [103] and Annex (Decision X/1, Annex, pp 89–109) (Nagoya Protocol on Access to Genetic Resources and the Fair and Equitable Sharing of Benefits Arising from their Utilization to the Convention on Biological Diversity) (Nagoya Protocol).

46 Access has also been used in relation to *access to technology* in both the CBD, Arts 1 and 16, and the Plant Treaty, Art 13.2(b). In this chapter, I do not focus on that issue.

47 CBD, Art 15.7.

48 CBD, Art 1 (emphasis added).

consideration all rights over those resources, including any applicable intellectual or other property rights.[49]

The Plant Treaty uses the term 'access' in the same two specific ways as the CBD. The first is where access means the physical performative act of providing and obtaining plant genetic resources. This is reflected in the obligations of each Contracting Party. The Plant Treaty requires its Contracting Parties to establish a Multilateral System for facilitating 'access to plant genetic resources for food and agriculture' and sharing 'the benefits arising from the utilization of these resources'.[50] The establishment of a Multilateral System is intended to facilitate physical access to a predetermined set of 64 genetic resources listed in Annex 1 of the Plant Treaty. In order to facilitate physical access to plant genetic materials, Contracting Parties are obligated to include Annex 1 plant genetic resources in the Multilateral System and others such as the CGIAR Centers are invited to make their genetic resources available for access through the Multilateral System.[51] Providers and users of the Multilateral System are then obligated to adhere to a non-negotiable standard material transfer agreement for the access and sharing of plant materials.[52] Any access to plant materials under the Plant Treaty should be 'solely for the purpose of utilization and conservation for research, breeding and training for food and agriculture' and no user is allowed to claim intellectual property or other property rights over materials that are 'in the form received from the Multilateral System'.[53]

The second way 'access' is used in the Plant Treaty is as a mechanism made in relation to benefit sharing. Article 13.2 of the Plant Treaty requires users of plant materials to return the improved plant genetic material when such material has been developed from germplasm that has been accessed from the Multilateral System.[54] The objective of this provision is to ensure that users of the Multilateral System are able to access improved germplasm, albeit only for the purposes of further research, breeding and training.[55] If users of the Multilateral System decide not to include improved plant materials in the Multilateral System, they must pay a predetermined percentage of the monetary benefits derived from the commercialisation of those plant materials to the multilateral

49 Ibid.
50 Plant Treaty, Art 10.
51 Plant Treaty, Arts 11.2 and 11.5.
52 Plant Treaty, Art 12.4.
53 Plant Treaty, Arts 12.3(a) and 12.3(d).
54 According to the Plant Treaty, Art 13.2(d)(ii) 'the standard Material Transfer Agreement ... shall include a requirement that a recipient who commercializes a product that is a plant genetic resource for food and agriculture and that incorporates material accessed from the Multilateral System, shall pay ... an equitable share of the benefits arising from the commercialization of that product, except whenever such a product is available without restriction to others for further research and breeding'.
55 Plant Treaty, Art 12.3(a) provides that access to plant materials under the Multilateral System shall only be 'for the purpose of utilization and conservation for research, breeding and training for food and agriculture'.

fund of the Plant Treaty.[56] However, as is the case with the CBD, it is a requirement that benefit sharing by access to improved varieties and genetic materials be facilitated, while taking into account applicable property rights and access laws of the Contracting Party.[57]

Another provision that recognises access as a mechanism of benefit sharing is Article 9.3 of the Plant Treaty. The Article recognises the farmers' right to 'save, exchange, reuse and sell farm-saved seed' as an attempt to create a legal space for farmers to access the seeds of plant varieties for customary seed saving, sharing, use and sale.[58] In particular, the recognition of the farmers' right to seed aims to address the concerns associated with the curtailment of the farmers' privilege by UPOV in the 1991 amendments and by other intellectual property laws.[59] However, the limitation within the Plant Treaty is that the implementation of farmers' rights, including the right to seed, is at the discretion of the Contracting Party – 'Contracting Part[ies] should, as appropriate, and subject to [their] national legislation, take measures to protect and promote Farmers' Rights'.[60]

The two ways in which access has been used in the CBD and the Plant Treaty – namely as a physical performative act and as a mechanism of benefit sharing – suggest that access is a central idea behind the governance of genetic resources. However, there has not been any significant progress towards the implementation of the access regimes of these international agreements. To date, only 60 of the 196 member countries have implemented domestic laws to regulate access to genetic resources as required by the CBD.[61] This shows a

---

56 Plant Treaty, Art 13.2(d)(ii) and Article 6.7 of the Standard Material Transfer Agreement of the Plant Treaty.

57 Plant Treaty, Art 13.2(b)(i).

58 While the Plant Treaty, Art 9 recognises a set of farmers' rights, Art 9.3 states that 'Nothing in this Article shall be interpreted to limit any rights that farmers have to save, use, exchange and sell farm-saved seed/propagating material, subject to national law and as appropriate'. For a detailed account of farmers' rights issues, see Michael Halewood (ed.), *Farmers' Crop Varieties and Farmers' Rights: Challenges in Taxonomy and Law* (Routledge, 2016); Stephen Brush, 'Farmers' Rights and Protection of Traditional Agricultural Knowledge' (2007) 35 *World Development* 1499.

59 For arguments that farmers' rights to plant genetic resources are important for the protection of customary seed saving and sharing practices and that the idea of farmers' rights addresses the restrictions imposed by UPOV, see Suman Sahai, 'CoFaB: A Developing Country Alternative to UPOV', in Ratnakar Adhikari and Kamalesh Adhikari (eds.), *Farmers' Rights to Livelihood in the Hindu-Kush Himalayas* (South Asia Watch on Trade, Economics and Environment, 2003) pp 26–32.

60 Plant Treaty, Art 9.2 states 'The Contracting Parties agree that the responsibility for realizing Farmers' Rights, as they relate to plant genetic resources for food and agriculture, rests with national governments. In accordance with their needs and priorities, each Contracting Party should, as appropriate, and subject to its national legislation, take measures to protect and promote Farmers' Rights'.

61 See, for example, Jerome Reichman, Tom Dedeurwaerdere and Paul Uhlir, *Governing Digitally Integrated Genetic Resources, Data, and Literature: Global*

lack of willingness among a majority of Contracting Parties to implement the CBD. This lack of motivation may be based on the fact that there are very few concrete examples of resource provider countries that have been able to derive significant benefits from access agreements with resource user countries. In the words of Tvedt and Schei, access and benefit sharing laws have 'not succeeded as an innovative benefit-sharing mechanism from business back to providing countries for genetic resources'.[62] The failure of the CBD to deliver on its promises has been summarised by Kamau, Fedder and Winter:

> Seventeen years have elapsed since the CBD entered into force ... Although much has transpired and tremendous work done in relation to biodiversity protection, barely are there any effectively and efficiently functioning measures/regimes for access and benefit sharing.[63]

There has also been limited progress in relation to the implementation of the Multilateral System of the Plant Treaty. It is important to recall that the subject matter that can be accessed under the Plant Treaty depends entirely on the plant genetic resources that have been included in the Multilateral System.[64] In accordance with the provisions of the Treaty, CGIAR Centers were the first to include plant genetic resources in the Multilateral System. Member countries are also obliged to include the plant genetic resources that are under their control and management and in the public domain in the Multilateral System.[65] However, so far only 39 of the 142 Contracting Parties have informed the Plant Treaty Secretariat about the inclusion of their plant genetic materials for facilitated access through the Multilateral System. While Contracting Parties are required to encourage private individuals and institutions in their jurisdictions to include their materials in the Multilateral System,[66] there has not been any significant progress on this front. To date, only a few institutions in India, Costa Rica, Kenya, France and Peru have informed the Plant

Intellectual Property Strategies for a Redesigned Microbial Research Commons (Cambridge University Press, 2016) p 94.

62 Morten Tvedt and Peter Schei, 'The Term Genetic Resources: Flexible and Dynamic while Providing Legal Certainty' in Sebastian Oberthür and Kristin Rosendal (eds.), *Global Governance of Genetic Resources: Access and Benefit Sharing After the Nagoya Protocol* (Routledge, 2014) pp 29–30.

63 Evanson Kamau, Bevis Fedder and Gerd Winter, 'The Nagoya Protocol on Access to Genetic Resources and Benefit Sharing: What is New and What are the Implications for Provider and User Countries and the Scientific Community?' (2010) 6 *Law, Environment and Development Journal* 246, 248.

64 Plant Treaty, Art 11.

65 For a comprehensive discussion on the obligations of the CGIAR Centers and member countries of the Plant Treaty, see Carlos Correa, 'Plant Genetic Resources Under the Management and Control of the Contracting Parties and in the Public Domain', in Michael Halewood, Isabel López Noriega and Sélim Louafi (eds.), *Crop Genetic Resources as a Global Commons: Challenges in International Law and Governance* (Routledge, 2013) p 177.

66 Plant Treaty, Art 11.3.

Treaty Secretariat that their materials are included in the Multilateral System.[67]

The limitations in relation to the implementation of the bilateral and multilateral access regimes of the CBD and the Plant Treaty point towards an important question: why have these international regimes not been able to deliver on their promises? The response to this question lies in the answer to another question: how can access be more broadly conceptualised? It is to this question that I now turn.

2.4 How to reconceptualise access?

There is a tendency among scholars, policymakers and development practitioners to think about access and benefit sharing as a unified concept. Such a composite understanding of access and benefit sharing gives an impression that access is directly linked to benefit sharing. But a key question here is: are users of genetic resources obligated to share the benefits for *accessing* genetic resources?

The CBD and the Plant Treaty suggest that it is not access that obliges resource users to engage in benefit sharing. Rather, benefit sharing is triggered by the utilisation of genetic resources.[68] The CBD requires its Contracting Parties to develop mutually agreed terms of sharing 'the benefits arising from the commercial or other utilization of genetic resources'.[69] Likewise, the Plant Treaty's focus is on mobilising a multilateral fund to share the benefits accrued from 'the utilization of plant genetic resources'.[70] Neither of these international agreements explain what the utilisation of genetic resources means. To address this issue, the Nagoya Protocol to the CBD defines the utilisation of genetic resources as: 'to conduct research and development on the genetic and/or biochemical composition of genetic resources, including through the application of biotechnology'.[71]

What this elaboration by the Nagoya Protocol reinforces is the notion that access and utilisation are two separate concepts. While the utilisation of genetic resources in this context means research and development that may lead to potential benefits and the sharing thereof, access merely means a physical performative act that may lead to the utilisation of genetic resources. However, this is a narrow way of thinking about access. Such a conceptualisation

---

67 These data are based on the information available at the Plant Treaty's website <http://www.fao.org/plant-treaty/areas-of-work/the-multilateral-system/collec tions/en> (accessed 16 May 2017).

68 For further discussion on this issue, see Berne Declaration and Natural Justice, *Access or Utilisation – What Triggers User Obligations? A Comment on the Draft Proposal of the European Commission on the Implementation of the Nagoya Protocol on Access and Benefit Sharing* (2013) available at <http://naturaljustice.org/wp -content/uploads/2015/09/Nagoya-Protocol-Submission.pdf> (accessed 16 May 2017).

69 CBD, Art 15.7.

70 Plant Treaty, Art 10.2.

71 Nagoya Protocol, Art 2.

underestimates the pivotal role that access plays (or can play) in legal regimes that govern to genetic resources. There is a need to reconsider how we think about the concept of access in the broader context of the governance of genetic resources for a number of reasons. Of these, three stand out.

The first is the need to recognise access as a mechanism of benefit sharing. However, what is worrying is that there is no explicit provision or recognition of any measure in the CBD that helps to meet an important objective of the CBD, that is the sharing of benefits by providing *appropriate access* to genetic resources. It is also surprising that much scholarly research and policy negotiations do not tend to think about access as a mechanism of benefit sharing. This is probably because there are legal complexities that constrain the realisation of the objective of recognising access as a mechanism of benefit sharing. One such complexity appears from the obligation of each Contracting Party, as reflected in the CBD's goal, to ensure that intellectual and other property rights are taken into account while sharing the benefits by providing *appropriate access* to genetic resources.[72]

One may argue that a reason why some scholars and development practitioners have promoted the idea of open access to crop germplasm is for the same purpose, namely to address the restrictions created by intellectual property and to share the benefits by providing unrestricted access to genetic resources. One example of an attempt to address the restrictions created by intellectual property over access to genetic resources is the Open Source Seed Initiative.[73] Although this initiative faced a number of problems in its use of legal licences to exchange germplasm, it has facilitated open access to a common pool of crop germplasm in which plant breeders, farmers, gardeners and seed companies have offered their seeds as 'open source-pledged seeds'.[74] The goal here is to ensure that no user of open source-pledged seeds is allowed to restrict other users' ability to access and use these seeds or derivatives thereof by any legal means, including patents and plant breeders' rights.[75] However, it should be noted that the Open Source Seed Initiative, and other similar open access schemes, operate outside of the framework of the international agreements.

As is the case with the CBD, the Plant Treaty also faces a number of challenges in its goal to recognise access as a mechanism of benefit sharing. To date, no country, person or entity has included a new genetic material that has

---

72 CBD, Art 1 (emphasis added).
73 For different examples of open source initiatives, see Janet Hope, *Biobazaar: The Open Source Revolution and Biotechnology* (Harvard University Press, 2009).
74 Claire Luby, Jack Kloppenburg, Thomas Michaels and Irwin Goldman, 'Enhancing Freedom to Operate for Plant Breeders and Farmers Through Open Source Plant Breeding' (2015) 55 *Crop Science* 2481. For a detailed account of the challenges of the Open Source Seed Initiative, also see Jack Kloppenburg, 'Re-purposing the Master's Tools: The Open Source Seed Initiative and the Struggle for Seed Sovereignty' (2014) 41 *Journal of Peasant Studies* 1225.
75 For details see Claire Luby and Irwin Goldman, 'Freeing Crop Genetics Through the Open Source Seed Initiative' (2016) 14 *PLoS Biology* e1002441.

been derived from the material accessed from the Multilateral System in the Plant Treaty's system of access and benefit sharing. The implementation of farmers' rights – mainly in relation to ensuring farmers' access to plant genetic resources – has also been a major challenge. At the national level, countries that have introduced laws and regulations to protect farmers' rights to plant genetic resources have not been able to generate any evidence of benefits for farmers, including in relation to farmers' access to protected plant varieties for the purpose of customary seed saving and sharing.[76]

At the international level, developed and developing countries have not been able to reach consensus on issues related to the implementation of farmers' rights. Developed countries express the view that protecting farmers' rights falls under the national purview and should not conflict with the rights and obligations under other relevant international laws such as UPOV and TRIPS. In contrast to the views of developed countries, developing countries believe that implementing farmers' rights requires international support and that such support should include identifying measures to address the restrictions that intellectual property and other seed laws create for the realisation of farmers' rights.[77]

In an attempt to address the concerns of both developed and developing countries, in its 2015 *Resolution on the Implementation of Article 9, Farmers' Rights*, the Governing Body of the Plant Treaty invited all member countries 'to consider reviewing and, if necessary, adjusting (their) national measures affecting the realization of Farmers' Rights'.[78] In the resolution, the Governing Body also urged the Secretary of the Plant Treaty to engage further with the UPOV Secretariat and the World Intellectual Property Organisation to 'finalize the process for identification of possible areas of interrelations' between their intellectual property instruments and the Plant Treaty.[79]

---

76 Some studies show that while developing countries have adopted diverse approaches to implement farmers' rights, any real benefits for farmers are yet to be ensured. See, for example, the case of Brazil and India in Karine Peschard, 'Seed Wars and Farmers' Rights: Comparative Perspectives from Brazil and India' (2017) 44 *Journal of Peasant Studies* 144.

77 For specific positions taken by developing and developed countries during recent negotiations on farmers' rights, see IISD Reporting Service, 'Summary of the Sixth Session of the Governing Body of the International Treaty on Plant Genetic Resources for Food and Agriculture: 5–9 October 2015' (2015) 9(656) *Earth Negotiations Bulletin* 12 October 2015 available at <http://enb.iisd.org/download/pdf/enb09656e.pdf> (accessed 16 May 2017). See also Kamalesh Adhikari, *Farmers' Rights: Global Contexts, Negotiations and Strategies*, Policy Brief No 19 (South Asia Watch on Trade, Economics and Environment, 2009) available at <http://www.sawtee.org/publications/Policy-Brief-17.pdf> (accessed 16 May 2017).

78 Governing Body of the International Treaty on Plant Genetic Resources for Food and Agriculture, *Sixth Session of the Governing Body of the International Treaty on Plant Genetic Resources for Food and Agriculture* (2015) IT/GB-6/15/Report, [34] and Appendix A.5 (Resolution 5/2015 'Implementation of Article 9, Farmers' Rights').

79 Ibid, Appendix A.5, [12]. For an analysis of the interlinkages between TRIPS, UPOV, CBD and the Plant Treaty, see also Jonathan Curci, *The Protection of*

The second reason why it is necessary to think about access more broadly relates to the objects regulated by the CBD and the Plant Treaty, specifically traditional knowledge and genetic resources.[80] In this context, an important question is: what kinds of things are included within the scope of traditional knowledge and genetic resources? The CBD and the Plant Treaty do not define traditional knowledge. However, as these agreements require their Contracting Parties to regulate the access and use of traditional knowledge that are *related to* or *associated with* genetic resources, the definition of genetic resources is key to the governance of the access regimes.[81]

The CBD defines genetic resources as 'genetic material of actual or potential value' and genetic material as 'any material of plant, animal, microbial or other origin containing functional units of heredity'.[82] Similarly, the Plant Treaty defines plant genetic resources as 'plant genetic material of actual and potential value' and plant genetic material as 'any material of plant origin, including reproductive and vegetative propagating material, containing functional units of heredity'.[83] Despite these definitions, there is little clarity about the subject matter actually covered by access to genetic resources or plant genetic resources. The definition of genetic resources in the international agreements does not cover all possible derivatives that can be extracted from these resources. For example, enzymes derived from genetic materials or biochemicals for commercial use by pharmaceutical, food and cosmetic industries may remain outside of the scope of the definition of genetic resources adopted by the international agreements.[84] This is because enzymes may not contain 'functional units of

Biodiversity and Traditional Knowledge in International Law of Intellectual Property (Cambridge University Press, 2010) pp 50–85.

80 It is important to also note that the Nagoya Protocol, Art 7, as an elaboration of the provisions on traditional knowledge of the CBD, specifically deals with access to traditional knowledge associated with genetic resources providing 'each Party shall take measures, as appropriate, with the aim of ensuring that traditional knowledge associated with genetic resources that is held by indigenous and local communities is accessed with the prior and informed consent or approval and involvement of these indigenous and local communities, and that mutually agreed terms have been established'. In the case of the Plant Treaty, issues in relation to the access, use and protection of traditional knowledge are covered by Art 9 on farmers' rights.

81 There is no agreed-upon definition of traditional knowledge. For some critical insights on the concept of traditional knowledge, see Miranda Forsyth, 'How Can Traditional Knowledge Best be Regulated? Comparing a Proprietary Rights Approach with a Regulatory Toolbox Approach' (2013) 25 *The Contemporary Pacific* 1. For a comprehensive discussion about Indigenous Peoples and traditional knowledge, see Peter Drahos, *Intellectual Property, Indigenous People and their Knowledge* (Cambridge University Press, 2014).

82 CBD, Art 2.

83 Plant Treaty, Art 2.

84 Morten Tvedt and Peter Schei, 'The Term "Genetic Resources": Flexible and Dynamic while Providing Legal Certainty' in Sebastian Oberthür and Kristin Rosendal (eds.), *Global Governance of Genetic Resources: Access and Benefit Sharing After the Nagoya Protocol* (Routledge, 2014) pp 23–24.

heredity', which is a requirement to qualify as genetic material under the CBD and the Plant Treaty.[85]

In the backdrop of the ambiguity created by the way genetic resources are defined in the CBD and the Plant Treaty, two elaborations made by the Nagoya Protocol are relevant here. First, the Nagoya Protocol clarifies that the utilisation of genetic resources means research and development involving the *genetic and/or biochemical composition* of genetic resources. Second, by providing a definition of 'derivatives', the Nagoya Protocol also includes biochemical compounds *that do not* contain functional units of heredity within the scope of genetic resources.[86]

Given these changes, has the question of what constitutes the subject matter of access been fully addressed? Probably not. This is because the CBD, the Nagoya Protocol and the Plant Treaty only cover the regulation of physical access to tangible samples of genetic resources or materials. Although these agreements explicitly deal with access to and/or protection of traditional knowledge, they do not cover access in relation to intangible genetic information. Yet this is where the real value of genetic resources lies.[87]

In the emerging context of rapidly advancing knowledge systems and technologies such as genomics, synthetic biology and bioinformatics, there is evidence that access to intangible genetic information (for example, digital genetic sequence information) is more important than access to physical genetic materials.[88] In this context, a number of pertinent questions arise: how will the CBD and the Plant Treaty govern the application of new technologies that copy genetic materials synthetically? Will the use of digital genetic sequence information derived from genetic resources of one country, then transferred electronically to another country for commercial use, be subject to regulation under these international agreements?[89]

---

85 Although in simple terms, genes, which are made up of DNA, are considered the basic and functional units of heredity, there does not exist clarity about the scientific meaning and legal scope of the functional unit of heredity. For a comprehensive discussion on the definitional limits of genetic resources, derivatives and functional units of heredity: see Tvedt and Schei, ibid, pp 18–30; Bevis Fedder, *Marine Genetic Resources, Access and Benefit Sharing: Legal and Biological Perspectives* (Routledge, 2013) pp 35–37.

86 Nagoya Protocol, Art 2 defines derivative as 'a naturally occurring biochemical compound resulting from the genetic expression or metabolism of biological or genetic resources, even if it does not contain functional units of heredity'.

87 On the significance of genetic information, see Joseph Vogel, Nora Álvarez-Berríos, Norberto Quiñones-Vilches and Jeiger Medina-Muñiz, 'The Economics of Information, Studiously Ignored in the Nagoya Protocol on Access to Genetic Resources and Benefit Sharing' (2011) 7 *Law, Environment and Development Journal* 52.

88 Margo Bagley, *Digital DNA: The Nagoya Protocol, Intellectual Property Treaties, and Synthetic Biology*, Virginia Public Law and Legal Theory Research Paper No 11 (2015) available at <http://dx.doi.org/10.2139/ssrn.2725986> (accessed 16 May 2017).

89 See Charles Lawson and Michelle Rourke, 'Open Access DNA, RNA and Amino Acid Sequences: The Consequences and Solutions for the International Regulation of Access and Benefit Sharing' (2016) 24 *Journal of Law and Medicine* 96.

Within the negotiations surrounding the CBD, questions emanating from the growing use of synthetic biology and the informational components of genetic resources have started to attract significant attention.[90] For example, in order to address concerns associated with digital genetic sequence information, an *Ad Hoc* Technical Expert Group was formed in December 2016 at the Conference of the Parties to the CBD. The Expert Group is mandated to discuss the definition and scope of the terminology 'genetic sequence information on genetic resources' and to report back about the potential implications of digital genetic sequence information for the regulation of access to and use of genetic resources.[91]

The question of intangible subject matter is also a concern for the Plant Treaty. Negotiations under the Plant Treaty have started to discuss the implications that the informational components of plant genetic resources have for the scope and operation of the Plant Treaty. A number of concerns in relation to the 'dematerialization of genetic resources' were raised at the Sixth Session of the Governing Body of the Plant Treaty held in October 2015.[92] Some countries believed that there was a need to develop legal measures to regulate access to intangible genetic information and, in so doing, ensure that the 'dematerialization of genetic resources does not lead to the dematerialization of benefit-sharing'.[93]

The third reason why it is important to reconsider how we think about access is because it will help us to address the inconsistent approaches that countries have adopted while defining 'access' in their domestic laws. For example, the *Andean Decision No. 391 Establishing the Common Regime on Access to Genetic Resources* defines access as 'obtaining and use of genetic resources conserved *in situ* and *ex situ*, of their by-products and, if applicable, of their intangible components, for purposes of research, biological prospecting, conservation, industrial application and commercial use, among other things'.[94] An important feature of the Andean Decision is that access does not merely mean the physical performative act of *obtaining* genetic resources or

---

90 For some negotiating issues of the CBD, see Bruce Manheim, 'Regulation of Synthetic Biology under the Nagoya Protocol' (2016) 34 *Nature Biotechnology* 1104.

91 Decision Adopted by the Conference of the Parties to the Convention on Biological Diversity, CBD/COP/DEC/XIII/16, available at <https://www.cbd.int/doc/decisions/cop-13/cop-13-dec-24-en.pdf> (accessed 18 May 2017).

92 For further discussion on the dematerialisation of genetic resources and associated concerns, see Carolina Roa, Ruaraidh Sackville Hamilton, Peter Wenzl and Wayne Powell, 'Plant Genetic Resources: Needs, Rights, and Opportunities' (2016) 21 *Trends in Plant Science* 633.

93 IISD Reporting Service, 'ITPGRFA GB 6 Highlights' (2015) 9(654) *Earth Negotiations Bulletin* 8 October 2015 available at <http://enb.iisd.org/vol09/enb09654e.html> (accessed 18 May 2017).

94 Andean Decision No. 391 *Establishing the Common Regime on Access to Genetic Resources*, Title I available at <http://www.wipo.int/wipolex/en/text.jsp?file_id=223610> (accessed 18 May 2017).

their by-products and intangible components. Instead, access also extends to include the *use* of genetic resources including their by-products and intangible components. Another important feature of the way access is defined in the Andean Decision is its coverage of a broad range of intangible components, that is 'all know-how, innovation or individual or collective practice, with a real or potential value, that is associated with the genetic resource, its by-products or the biological resource that contains them, whether or not protected by intellectual property rights'.[95]

African countries have also defined access in their relevant regional and national laws. In the *African Model Legislation for the Protection of the Rights of Local Communities, Farmers and Breeders, and for the Regulation of Access to Biological Resources*, access is defined as 'the acquisition of biological resources, their derivatives, community knowledge, innovations, technologies, or practices'.[96] This definition is different from the definition articulated by the Andean Decision in a number of ways. First, the definition adopted by the African Model covers access to biological resources and not simply genetic resources. Second, unlike the definition of access in the Andean Decision, the African Model does not expand the meaning and scope of access by covering a wide range of commercial and non-commercial motives such as research, biological prospecting, conservation, industrial application and commercial use. Third, the African Model defines access to mean the *acquisition* but not the *utilisation* of the accessed resources or knowledge. However, it is important to note that despite being a member of the African Community, Ethiopia has created its own definition of access. In its *Access to Genetic Resources and Community Knowledge, and Community Rights Proclamation*, Ethiopia defines access to mean the *collection, acquisition, transfer* or *use* of genetic resources and/or community knowledge.[97]

The focus on the utilisation of genetic resources in the definition of access adopted by Ethiopia and the Andean Decision is also apparent in other national laws. For example, Bhutan's *Interim Access and Benefit Sharing Policy* defines 'access to genetic resources' as 'the utilization of genetic resources from Bhutan irrespective of whether they are accessed *in situ* or *ex situ* for the purpose of conducting any research and/or development on the genetic and/or biochemical composition of genetic resources including through the application of biotechnology'.[98] What is unique and interesting here is that Bhutan's *Access*

95 Ibid.
96 *African Model Legislation on Access and Benefit Sharing*, Part II available at <http://www.wipo.int/edocs/lexdocs/laws/en/oau/oau001en.pdf> (accessed 18 May 2017).
97 *Access to Genetic Resources and Community Knowledge, and Community Rights Proclamation 482/2006* (Ethiopia), Art 2 available at <http://www.wipo.int/edocs/lexdocs/laws/en/et/et006en.pdf> (accessed 18 May 2017).
98 Bhutan's *Access and Benefit Sharing Policy* available at <http://www.gnhc.gov.bt/wp-content/uploads/2011/05/ABS_Policy_of_Bhutan_-Latest_31st_Oct_2012clean_1.pdf> (accessed 18 May 2017).

and Benefit Sharing Policy also defines 'access to traditional knowledge' as 'the utilization of traditional knowledge associated with genetic resources for the purpose of conducting any research and development'.[99]

Another regional law that defines access is the *Regulation of the European Union on Compliance Measures for Users from the Nagoya Protocol on Access to Genetic Resources and the Fair and Equitable Sharing of Benefits Arising from their Utilization in the Union* (EU Regulation). According to the EU Regulation, access means 'the acquisition of genetic resources and of traditional knowledge associated with genetic resources in a party to the Nagoya Protocol'.[100] One of the features of the EU Regulation is that it defines access to mean the *acquisition* and not the *utilisation* of genetic resources and traditional knowledge. This definition is similar to the way access is defined in the African Model. What is different about the EU Regulation compared to the African Model and other laws is that the European Union has defined access in the terms of the Nagoya Protocol.[101] What this means is that the EU Regulation is limited to the acquisition of subject matter the Nagoya Protocol specifically deals with, namely genetic resources and traditional knowledge.

Another important feature of the definition of access that distinguishes the EU Regulation from other regional and national laws is its intention to regulate only the acquisitions that have been made *in a country that is a member of the Nagoya Protocol*. This raises a number of questions and concerns. Will the access and use of genetic resources and traditional knowledge in a country that is not party to the Nagoya Protocol but a party to the CBD remain outside the scope of the EU Regulation? How would the European Union regulate the access and use of genetic resources and traditional knowledge in its member countries if such access or use had occurred after the CBD came into force in 1993 and before the Nagoya Protocol came into force in 2014?

Given that the Nagoya Protocol does not address the issue of temporal scope and the applicability of access laws before the protocol came into force, it is up to the Contracting Parties to address the matter in their own national or regional laws.[102] This means that in the backdrop of the issues generated by

---

99 Ibid.
100 *Regulation (EU) No 511/2014 of the European Parliament and of the Council of 16 April 2014 on Compliance Measures for Users from the Nagoya Protocol on Access to Genetic Resources and the Fair and Equitable Sharing of Benefits Arising from their Utilization in the Union,* Art 3 available at <http://eur-lex.europa.eu/legal-content/EN/TXT/PDF/?uri=CELEX:32014R0511&from=EN> (accessed 18 May 2017) (EU Regulation).
101 Nagoya Protocol, Art 3 states that 'This Protocol shall apply to genetic resources within the scope of Art 15 of the [CBD] and to the benefits arising from the utilization of such resources. This Protocol shall also apply to traditional knowledge associated with genetic resources within the scope of the [CBD] and to the benefits arising from the utilization of such knowledge'.
102 For further analysis of temporal scope and possible implications from the EU Regulation, see Berne Declaration and Natural Justice, *Access or Utilisation – What Triggers User Obligations? A Comment on the Draft Proposal of the European*

the Nagoya Protocol and the development of new access laws by countries such as the European Union member states, it is more likely for new access laws to suffer from further inconsistencies. This is mainly because developed and developing countries – which often hold conflicting positions on the issue of temporal scope and the applicability of access rules – may explore the meaning and scope of access in new national laws in ways that contradict each other. For example, while developed countries may assume that international laws (in this case the Nagoya Protocol) cannot be applied retroactively, developing countries may argue that the relevance of the CBD should not be ignored surrounding the issue of the applicability and scope of the access regimes. More specifically, the positions taken by developing countries suggest that all instances of access and/or utilisation of genetic resources and traditional knowledge – including acts that occurred after the CBD came into force in 1993 – should be subject to benefit sharing and other obligations in relation to access and use.[103]

2.5 Conclusions

The history of the negotiations of the CBD and the Plant Treaty suggests that access was a central idea behind the emergence and design of the framework for global governance of genetic resources. Historically, the recognition of intellectual property and the farmers' privilege in UPOV, the establishment of permanent sovereignty of States over natural resources by the membership of the United Nations, and the endeavour to implement the principle of common heritage by the FAO's IUPGRFA, all have played a pivotal role in advancing the notion of access in legal regimes related to genetic resources.[104]

Although access is at the core of the governance of genetic resources, the CBD, the Nagoya Protocol and the Plant Treaty do not define access. It is surprising that the concept of access has not received any real sustained

---

Commission on the Implementation of the Nagoya Protocol on Access and Benefit Sharing (2013) available at <http://naturaljustice.org/wp-content/uploads/2015/09/Nagoya-Protocol-Submission.pdf> (accessed 18 May 2017). See also see Mathias Buck and Clare Hamilton, 'The Nagoya Protocol on Access to Genetic Resources and the Fair and Equitable Sharing of Benefits Arising from Their Utilization to the Convention on Biological Diversity' (2011) 20 *Review of European Community and International Environmental Law* 47.

103 For further information on the positions of developed and developing countries pertaining to the temporal scope of the Nagoya Protocol, see IISD Reporting Service, 'ITPGRFA GB 6 Highlights' (2010) 9(544) *Earth Negotiations Bulletin* 1 November 2010 available at <http://enb.iisd.org/download/pdf/enb09544e.pdf> (accessed 18 May 2017).

104 Some other important international developments, which are beyond the scope of this chapter but hold an important role in relation to debates about access to genetic resources, include the intellectual property provisions of TRIPS and the development agenda that deals with access to genetic resources and traditional knowledge within the WIPO.

attention in policy negotiations and scholarly research. Attention is often placed on access and benefit sharing as a unified concept and not on the role that access on its own plays in the broader context of the governance of tangible and intangible genetic resources. It is usually assumed that access is merely the physical performative act of providing and obtaining tangible genetic resources. However, access is not limited to physical performative acts or to the use of tangible genetic resources. There is a need to reconceptualise access if the goal is to make bilateral and multilateral mechanisms of access more robust and effective.

One way to reconceptualise access would be to recognise access as a mechanism of benefit sharing. Since this is already a goal of the CBD and the Plant Treaty, some innovative measures could be explored within these international agreements to address property rights restrictions and to ensure that access to genetic resources is conceptualised as a mechanism of benefit sharing. In order to do so, engagements of the CBD and the Plant Treaty with relevant international agreements on intellectual property should be increased to explore legal space in which to recognise access as a means of benefit sharing. For example, incentives could be created for innovators of new plant varieties or genetic materials to include their germplasm in the Plant Treaty's Multilateral System or to offer such products as a means of benefit sharing through a bilateral system of access and benefit sharing. In doing so, lessons could also be learned from the challenges that open source initiatives have faced in their attempts to create open access regimes for plant breeders and farmers.

Likewise, incentives to implement the farmers' right to save, reuse, exchange and sell seeds of protected plant varieties could be identified and included as part of access and benefit sharing schemes. The implementation of the farmers' right to seed is probably more important for farmers, especially small-scale farmers of developing countries, than the access of plant germplasm under the Multilateral System. This is because while access to seeds of protected plant varieties for saving, reusing and selling purposes could have a direct contribution to the livelihood of small-scale farmers, the Multilateral System offers no direct or immediate benefits to farmers. The use of plant materials under the Multilateral System is restricted to research, breeding and training for food and agriculture. Most small-scale farmers, for example in developing and least-developed countries, may not directly benefit from the Multilateral System, unless they are supported by concrete measures for farmer-driven research and breeding on germplasm obtained through the Plant Treaty's standard material transfer agreement.

A second way to reconceptualise access would be to address the concerns associated with the growing trend of accessing, transferring and using the intangible components of genetic resources. An option would be to address the issue of access to and use of intangible genetic information, including digital genetic sequence information, in national and regional access regimes. However, as there is a risk of inconsistency in how countries define or regulate intangible genetic information in their national and regional regimes, some consensus on this issue is needed at the level of the CBD, the Nagoya Protocol and the Plant Treaty. As a solution, the definition of genetic resources in the international agreements could be expanded to deal with intangible genetic information, including digital genetic sequence information. This would help to extend the scope of access regimes to include both tangible and intangible genetic resources, thereby creating further avenues for potential benefit sharing.

Finally, a third way to reconceptualise access would be to address the inconsistent approaches that countries have adopted to define access in their laws. The inconsistency is evident in the way some countries have defined access as *acquisition* and some others as *utilisation* or both. The definitions of access adopted by national and regional laws are also inconsistent in terms of subject matter covered (biological resources, genetic resources, biochemicals, intangible components, traditional knowledge, etc.).

While countries may have their own rationales for the way they articulate the meaning of access in their laws, a number of concerns arise from the inconsistent way access has been interpreted. Inconsistent definitions not only lead national and regional laws to contradict each other but also create further challenges for the implementation of the international regimes. If Contracting Parties of the CBD, the Nagoya Protocol and the Plant Treaty are serious about making bilateral and multilateral mechanisms of access more robust and effective, they need to reconsider what they mean by access.

3 Aligning means and ends to benefit indigenous peoples under the Convention on Biological Diversity and the Nagoya Protocol

Edwin Bikundo

The very first article of the United Nations' *Convention on Biological Diversity* (CBD)[1] proclaims 'the fair and equitable sharing of the benefits arising out of the utilization of genetic resources' as one of its three objectives.[2] The other two objectives of the CBD are to conserve biological diversity and to use that diversity sustainably. The means to achieve these three objectives include 'appropriate access to genetic resources', 'appropriate transfer of relevant technologies', and 'appropriate funding'.[3] Both access to genetic resources and transfer of technologies moreover must take into account 'all rights' in a bifurcated fashion over resources on one hand and technologies on the other. It is important to note that the CBD's references to Indigenous Peoples are in a specific context of respecting, preserving and maintaining the 'knowledge, innovations and practices' of Indigenous Peoples 'embodying traditional lifestyles'.[4] More specifically, the CBD only talks about the 'desirability of sharing equitably benefits arising from the use of traditional knowledge, innovations and practices' of Indigenous Peoples.[5] What is more, the very first article of the CBD's protocol, the *Nagoya Protocol on Access to Genetic Resources and the Fair and Equitable Sharing of Benefits Arising from their Utilization to the Convention on Biological Diversity*,[6] singles out 'the fair and equitable sharing' as its sole objective in terms otherwise identical to the CBD without specifically referencing Indigenous Peoples.[7]

Being a multilateral convention it is axiomatic that the parties to the CBD are not only States but can also only *be* States as the sole legal form with full legal personality in international law. This is reinforced by the principle

---

1 *Convention on Biological Diversity* [1993] ATS 32, 1760 UNTS 79 12 (CBD).
2 CBD, Art 1.
3 CBD, Art 1.
4 CBD, Art 8(j).
5 CBD, Preamble.
6 Conference of the Parties to the Convention on Biological Diversity, *Report of the Tenth Meeting of the Conference of the Parties to the Convention on Biological Diversity* (2010) UNEP/CBD/COP/10/27, [103] and Annex (Decision X/1, Annex 1 (Nagoya Protocol), pp 89–109).
7 Nagoya Protocol, Art 1.

enunciated in the CBD that 'States have, in accordance with the *Charter of the United Nations* and the principles of international law, the sovereign right to exploit their own resources pursuant to their own environmental policies'.[8] The place of Indigenous Peoples is not explicitly provided for among the objectives of the CBD. Can it be read implicitly without reference to the State? Can sovereignty play a positive role as a means to the end of sharing the benefits from the use of genetic resources with Indigenous Peoples? To cite one instance, Clinton Benjamin an undergraduate law student and Indigenous Australian speaks favourably of the notion that a treaty with Aboriginal and Torres Strait Islander people would enable the recognition of what he considers the un-ceded sovereignty of the various Aboriginal Nations.[9] There is a certain risk though, inherent in this legalistic approach, as recognised by Alexis Wright who says:

> the law courts and governments of Australia do not want you to turn up on your own behalf, they want to hear and argue the Aboriginal story from the professional point of view, and the government provides the money or professional support mechanism so that these arguments can take place in the language of the court ... The plot line has always been for one outcome, to erode Aboriginal belief in sovereignty, self-governance and land rights, even when it has gotten to the point where most Aboriginal people have been silenced, or feel too overwhelmed to fight any more. Look at the years where it was impossible to mention the words treaty, sovereignty or even land rights without creating a major backlash in the media.[10]

The law and especially international law thus appears to be completely ambivalent. On the one hand being the solution and on the other the problem to be surmounted. This chapter examines the place of Indigenous Peoples in international law by critiquing the use as well as non-use of the term 'people' in the relevant legal and theoretical contexts. The argument is that the way the system is set up is such that access is the *means* by which the *State* is to meet the *end* of sharing benefits with Indigenous *Peoples*. The chapter approaches this question by engaging with the work of German jurist Carl Schmitt and Italian philosopher Giorgio Agamben to identify the points at which their work sharpens the dilemma at hand.

---

8 CBD, Art 3.
9 Clinton Benjamin, 'An Indigenous Treaty Would Create a Virtuous Circle of Self-determination', *The Guardian*, 8 February 2017, available at <https://www.theguardian.com/commentisfree/2017/feb/08/an-indigenous-treaty-would-create-a-virtuous-circle-of-self-determination> (accessed 25 April 2017).
10 Alexis Wright, 'What Happens When You Tell Somebody Else's Story?', *Meanjin Quarterly* (Summer 2016), available at <https://meanjin.com.au/essays/what-happens-when-you-tell-somebody-elses-story> (accessed 25 April 2017).

The specific problem identified is that 'the people' as such, and consequently Indigenous Peoples, cannot maintain their specificity in the absence of the State form and yet that the presence of the State's political form promotes homogeneity and therefore erases Indigenous identity. Enter then, Schmitt, the German legal and political thinker whose work encompassed not just issues surrounding sovereignty in *The Concept of the Political* and *Constitutional Theory*, or international law in the *Nomos of the Earth*, but also representation in *The Crisis of Parliamentary Democracy*. Each of these in different but related ways provides insights into the relationship between the States and Indigenous Peoples. For Schmitt 'Democracy requires, therefore, first homogeneity and second – if the need arises – elimination or eradication of heterogeneity'.[11] Furthermore, since the nineteenth century it has existed above all in membership in a particular nation; in national homogeneity.[12] Examples of this homogeneity of the population include national, religious, cultural, social, class or other types of common characteristics.[13]

This is why for him 'every democracy rests on the presupposition of the indivisibly similar, entire, unified people'.[14] That the indivisibility of the State can especially (but not only) be seen in a democracy is explained by Schmitt in terms that:

> In a democracy, where those who command and those who obey are identical, the sovereign, that is, an assembly composed of all citizens, can change laws and change constitutions at will; in a monarchy or aristocracy, 'where there are some who command and some who are commanded,' a mutual contract is possible ... and thus also a limitation of [S]tate power.[15]

Furthermore, modern politics is entirely subsumed by the State: '[t]he concept of the [S]tate presupposes the concept of the political'.[16] Schmitt states that '[a]ccording to modern linguistic usage, the [S]tate is the political status of an organized people in an enclosed territorial unit. This is nothing more than a general paraphrase, not a definition of the [S]tate'.[17] Schmitt then points out that:

> In one way or another 'political' is generally juxtaposed to '[S]tate' or at least is brought into relation with it. The [S]tate thus appears as something political, the political as something pertaining to the [S]tate – obviously an unsatisfactory circle.[18]

---

11 Carl Schmitt, *The Crisis of Parliamentary Democracy* (MIT Press, 1985) pp 8–9.
12 Ibid, pp 8–9.
13 Carl Schmitt, *Constitutional Theory* (Duke University Press, 2008) pp 392–393.
14 Carl Schmitt, *Legality and Legitimacy* (Duke University Press, 2004) p 29.
15 Schmitt, above n 11, pp 14–15.
16 Carl Schmitt, *The Concept of the Political* (University of Chicago Press, 2007) p 19.
17 Ibid, pp 19–20.
18 Ibid, p 20.

That sets the stage for him to express his infamous thesis on political enmity as being somehow constitutive of the State:

> The specific political distinction to which political actions and motives can be reduced is that between friend and enemy. This provides a definition in the sense of a criterion and not as an exhaustive definition or one indicative of substantial content.[19]

Importantly:

> The friend and enemy concepts are to be understood in their concrete and existential sense, not as metaphors or symbols, not mixed and weakened by economic, moral, and other conceptions, least of all in a private-individualistic sense as a psychological expression of private emotions and tendencies. They are neither normative nor pure spiritual antitheses.[20]

Schmitt utilises the terms 'identity' and 'representation' to expand the points above and bind the people and the State ever tighter.[21] To start with 'identity':

> State is a certain status of the people, specifically the status of political unity. State form is this unity's particular type of formation. The people are a subject of every conceptual definition of the [S]tate.[22]

Schmitt identifies two ways of achieving political unity. Either self-identity (no State without a people) or 'that the political unity of the people as such can never be present in actual identity and, consequently must always be *represented* by men personally' (emphasis added).[23] These opposed ways do not exclude each other. Indeed '[i]n every [S]tate, one or the other is stronger, yet both are part of the political existence of a people'.[24]

When it comes to the concept of 'representation' there are four components to note, according to Schmitt. First, '[r]epresentation can only occur in the *public* sphere'.[25] Representation is not a normative event or even a process, or a procedure. It is, rather, something *existential*. 'To represent means to make an invisible being visible and present through a publicly present one. The dialectic of the concept is that the invisible is presupposed as absent and nevertheless is simultaneously made present'.[26] Second, the 'political unity as a whole is

19 Ibid, p 26.
20 Ibid, pp 27–28.
21 Schmitt, above n 13, pp 239–392.
22 Ibid, p 239
23 Ibid, p 245.
24 Ibid, p 240.
25 Ibid, p 242.
26 Ibid, p 243

represented'.[27] Third, the representative is *independent*, neither functionary nor agent nor commissioner, and fourth, this is not just true of democracies but that even an absolute prince is also the sole representative of the political unity of the people.

Having seen how Schmitt dealt with the people and the State we can then turn to territory or land. Schmitt's idea of *Nomos* means the ordering of territory, law, regulation or norms and the concrete form in which a political, economic and social order becomes apparent.[28] As he puts it, not every seizure of land is a *Nomos* but every *Nomos* includes a taking of land.[29]

In an important essay *What is a People?*, Agamben, an important contemporary interlocutor of Schmitt, starts by highlighting and demonstrating how 'people' in numerous examples also indicates 'the poor, the underprivileged, and the excluded'.[30] That is, the concept of 'people' has the effect of connoting both the active subject of the political as well as those that are excluded as anything other than abject, passive subjects. He goes on to claim though that this ambiguity is no accident but rather 'reflects an ambiguity inherent in the nature and function of the concept of *people* in Western politics'.[31] This would make 'people' an 'oscillation between two opposite poles', not a unitary subject. This also maps it into Agamben's most famous conceptual pair *zoë*, or 'naked life' represented in people, and *bios*, or political existence representing People. This enables Agamben to even redefine the Marxist class struggle as between *People* and *people* and thus a global civil war that can only end when there are no people to speak of. Agamben continues his analysis of the so-called global civil war in a subsequent work, *Stasis: Civil War as a Political Paradigm*.[32]

The theses advanced in *Stasis* are first that civil war is the threshold between politicisation and de-politicisation (at least in the West), and second that the constitutive element of the State is the absence of a people.[33] It does leave open, however, whether the contemporary 'global civil war' (which is to say the so-called war on terror) has altered the meaning of these theses 'in an essential manner'.[34] The work divides into two chapters. The first is the eponymous 'Stasis' (in this chapter 'Stasis' stands for the first chapter, '*Stasis*' refers to the book while '*stasis*' indicates the phenomenon under consideration – as civil strife with elements of violent and extensive intra social breakdown). Stasis is the shorter chapter of the two and principally engages with Aristotle.

27 Ibid, p 245
28 Carl Schmitt, *The Nomos of the Earth in the International Law of the Jus Publicum Europaeum* (Telos Press Ltd., 2003) pp 70–78.
29 Ibid, p 80.
30 Giorgio Agamben, *Means Without End: Notes on Politics* (University of Minnesota Press, 2000) p 29.
31 Ibid, p 31
32 Giorgio Agamben, *Stasis: Civil War as a Political Paradigm* (Homo Sacer II, 2) (Stanford University Press, 2015).
33 Ibid, p ix.
34 Ibid.

The second is titled 'Leviathan and Behemoth', which not completely unexpectedly has Thomas Hobbes as its chief interlocutor.

Agamben states that 'a theory of civil war is completely lacking today' where 'hand in hand with the advance of global civil war' academic analysis is geared 'toward the conditions under which an international intervention becomes possible'.[35] His lament is that this 'seems incompatible with the serious investigation of a phenomenon that is at least as old as Western democracy'.[36] His work, however, does not purport to fill this gap on its own. Rather, it restricts itself to examining *stasis* (treated as synonymous with civil war) in Ancient Greece and in Thomas Hobbes's work as representing 'two faces ... of a single political paradigm' being 'the necessity of civil war' simultaneously with 'the necessity of its exclusion', both of which mutually 'maintain a secret solidarity' that Agamben 'seek[s] to grasp'.[37]

The notion of *stasis* 'constitutes a zone of indifference between the unpolitical space of the family and the political space of the city'.[38] For Agamben, 'in Greek politics civil war functions as a threshold of politicisation and depoliticisation, through which the house is exceeded in the city and the city is depoliticised in the family'.[39] He cites for authority how Greek law under Solon, the Athenian lawmaker punished with the loss of civil rights, 'the citizen who had not fought for either one of the two sides in a civil war'.[40] Therefore, 'not taking part in civil war amounts to being expelled from the polis and confined to the oikos'.[41] Per Agamben, according to Aristotle:

> the invention of amnesty ... with respect to civil war is thus the comportment most appropriate to politics. From the juridical point of view, *stasis* thus seems to be defined by two prohibitions, which perfectly cohere with one another: on the one hand, not participating in it is politically culpable; on the other, forgetting it once it has finished is a political duty.[42]

Rather provocatively, this is 'just the opposite, that is to say, of what civil war seems to be for the moderns: namely, something that one must seek to render impossible at every cost, yet that must always be remembered through trials and legal prosecutions'.[43]

Agamben concludes the chapter with: 'precisely when the polis appears in the reassuring figure of an oikos – the "Common European Home", or the

35 Ibid, p 2.
36 Ibid.
37 Ibid, p 4.
38 Ibid, p 16.
39 Ibid (emphasis removed).
40 Ibid, p 17.
41 Ibid.
42 Ibid, pp 20–21.
43 Ibid, p 22.

world as the absolute space of global economic management – then *stasis*, which can no longer be situated in the threshold between the oikos and the polis, becomes the paradigm of every conflict and re-emerges as terror'.[44] In February 2017 at the time of the workshop that gave birth to this book, this parting shot harked back to 1995 with *Homo Sacer: Sovereign Power and Bare Life*, as well as looked forward to the concerns addressed in 2003 by *State of Exception* and in 2007 by *The Kingdom and Glory*.[45]

The second chapter, Leviathan and Behemoth is an illustrated and sustained engagement with the iconic image of the biblical creature leviathan reproduced in the frontispiece to Thomas Hobbes's *Leviathan*. There are two versions of this image. While one of these versions was intended for general publication, the other was presented to the sovereign directly.[46] Peter Goodrich in a recent book *Legal Emblems and the Art of Law* states that: '[t]he frontispiece converts the text into an image, the code into a collection, and functions to veil; screen; and in the language of the theory of the mysteries of government, the *arcana imperii*, it obscures and protects through simulation'.[47] For Goodrich just as it is for Agamben, 'the dual role of the sovereign is the essence of Hobbes's *Leviathan*'.[48] According to Agamben, analysing the emblem requires the resources of both political philosophy and iconology. For him, 'it is reasonable to suppose that the author had intended to summarise in an image the entire content of the work (or at least its esoteric meaning)'.[49] He consequently interprets the emblem as 'a door or threshold that would lead, even if in a veiled manner, into the problematic nucleus of the book'.[50] This, contrarily to Schmitt's book on the same subject, is moreover not necessarily an esoteric reading.[51] However, Agamben concurs with Schmitt's hypothesis that the behemoth–leviathan opposition corresponds 'to the fundamental geopolitical opposition between land and sea'.[52]

Although he perhaps deems it too obvious to mention, Agamben's starting point of the centrality of civil war to Hobbes' state of nature is strengthened by the historical fact that *Leviathan* was conceived in, and responded to, the

44 Ibid, p 24.
45 Giorgio Agamben, *Homo Sacer: Sovereign Power and Bare Life* (Stanford University Press, 1998); Giorgio Agamben, *State of Exception* (University of Chicago Press, 2005); Giorgio Agamben, *The Kingdom and the Glory: For a Theological Genealogy of Economy and Government* (Homo Sacer II, 2) (Stanford University Press 2011).
46 Agamben, above n 32, pp 31 and 36.
47 Peter Goodrich, *Legal Emblems and the Art of Law: Obiter Depicta as the Vision of Governance* (Cambridge University Press, 2014) p 111.
48 Ibid, p 116.
49 Agamben, above n 32, p 25.
50 Ibid, p 21. See also Carl Schmitt, *The Leviathan in the State Theory of Thomas Hobbes: Meaning and Failure of a Political Symbol* (University of Chicago Press, 2008).
51 Agamben, above n 32, p 27.
52 Ibid, p 35.

context of the English Civil War.[53] Consequently, it is a crucial subterranean link between the two chapters. For Agamben the mortal god leviathan 'does not dwell within the city, but outside it'.[54] Further the city is devoid of its inhabitants.[55] The iconic image thus discloses that 'political representation is only an optical representation (but no less effective on account of this)'.[56] Indeed, 'at the very instant that the people chooses the sovereign it dissolves into a confused multitude'.[57] Consequently, 'the state of nature is the city from the perspective of civil war'.[58] Previously, in dialogue with Walter Benjamin and Schmitt, Agamben has described this oscillation as between 'constituent power and constituted power'.[59] To put it more emphatically, 'the state of nature is a mythological projection into the past of the civil war; conversely, civil war is a projection of the state of nature into the city: it is what appears when one considers the city from the perspective of the state of nature'.[60]

Furthermore, 'political theology appears in Hobbes in a decidedly eschatological perspective'.[61] For Agamben, 'it is certain that the political philosophy of modernity will not be able to emerge out of its contradictions except by becoming aware of its theological roots'.[62] This last remark from Agamben should be taken seriously before beginning to even consider whether and if so how legal fictions such as sovereignty can serve as appropriate means to achieve the ends of those whom are excluded from, and by it.

This is because it is yet to be demonstrated that Indigenous *Peoples* can become part of the *People* without losing their Indigenous identity in the process. This chapter begun by demonstrating that the CBD's referencing Indigenous Peoples did not preclude and is indeed predicated upon sovereign States under whom indigeneity is either subsumed by way of inclusion or is heterogeneous and therefore can only be excluded. Thinking through the issues with Schmitt and Agamben we can see that in a democracy homogeneity is presupposed. This homogeneity is of sovereign States. As a necessity Indigenous *Peoples* are always excluded.

---

53 Thomas Hobbes, *Leviathan* (Richard Tuck (ed), Cambridge University Press, 2005) pp xi, lii, 127, 138, 311 and 484.
54 Agamben, above n 32, p 37.
55 Ibid, p 37.
56 Ibid, p 41.
57 Ibid, pp 44–45. See also Agamben, above n 30, pp 30–31.
58 Agamben, above n 32, p 53.
59 Ibid, pp 30, 33, 36, 54 and 56.
60 Ibid, p 53.
61 Ibid, pp 47 and 60.
62 Ibid, pp 54 and 69.

4 Banking on a patent solution for sharing Antarctica's *ex situ* genetic resources[*]

Fran Humphries

4.1 Introduction

Economic and conservation interests in Antarctica's *ex situ* biological and genetic resources[1] are converging to create a perfect regulatory storm. On the one hand, an increasing interest in Antarctica's genetic resources for commercial purposes[2] could be expected to thrive in the absence of comprehensive access and benefit sharing (ABS)[3] obligations under the Antarctic Treaty System. On the other hand, efforts towards the conservation of migratory aquatic genetic resources[4] are hampered by a lack of coordination between and among *ex situ* gene banks or repositories. A growing concern is that the genetic resources that the *ex situ* gene banks hold in physical and digital forms, including the ones that are originally from the Antarctic Treaty Area, may be impacted by a complex array of national ABS regimes. At the heart of the regulatory storm is the global territorial approach to ABS that does not sit comfortably with the

---

[*] I thank Dr Chris Butler for his comments on the draft paper.
[1] Biological resources include 'genetic resources, organisms or parts thereof, populations, or any other biotic component of ecosystems with actual or potential use or value for humanity', 'genetic resources' mean 'genetic material of actual or potential value' and 'genetic material' means 'any material of plant, animal, microbial or other origin containing functional units of heredity': *Convention on Biological Diversity* (1992) 1760 UNTS 79 (CBD), Art 2. The CBD is a multilateral treaty providing a framework for national strategies and laws for the conservation and sustainable use of biological diversity.
[2] Antarctic Treaty Consultative Meeting, *An Update on Biological Prospecting in Antarctica, Including the Development of the Antarctic Biological Prospecting Database* (2008) ATCM 31, WP 011, Agenda Item 17, p 3.
[3] ABS refers to how genetic resources may be accessed from *in situ* or *ex situ* sources and how the benefits that arise from their use may be shared between users and providers of the genetic resource.
[4] Commission on Genetic Resources for Food and Agriculture, *Status and Trends in Aquatic Genetic Resources: A Basis for International Policy*, Background Study Paper No 37 (FAO, 2007) p 3. See also Ad Hoc Intergovernmental Technical Working Group on Aquatic Genetic Resources for Food and Agriculture, *Draft State of the World's Aquatic Genetic Resources for Food and Agriculture* (Commission on Genetic Resources for Food and Agriculture, 2016) CGRFA/AqGR-1/16/Inf.2, Provisional Agenda Item 4.

unique governance arrangements concerning the Antarctic Treaty Area. Many Consultative Parties to the Antarctic Treaty Consultative Meeting (ATCM)[5] are taking a wait-and-see approach to the possible regulation of Antarctica's *ex situ* genetic resources under the proposed United Nations' *Convention on the Law of the Sea* (UNCLOS)[6] on the conservation and sustainable use of marine biological diversity in areas beyond national jurisdiction (New Instrument).[7] Meanwhile, recipients and providers, including gene banks, of Antarctica's *ex situ* genetic resources must determine on a case-by-case basis whether a resource is subject to national ABS obligations. This chapter shows that the answer can depend on the location and the purpose of the use of, and the temporal link between, the physical and the digital resource in question. This creates a level of confusion and complexity that has the potential to undermine the objectives and principles of the *Antarctic Treaty*.[8]

There has been surprisingly little debate about whether leaving ABS of Antarctic *ex situ* genetic resources to multiple ABS systems outside the Antarctic Treaty System undermines the *Antarctic Treaty*'s principles including international cooperation and freedom of scientific investigation[9] that 'accords with the interests of science and the progress of all [hu]mankind'.[10] This chapter considers the question by firstly outlining the extent to which the ABS of Antarctica's *in situ* and *ex situ* genetic resources is regulated under the Antarctic Treaty System. It then argues that the gap in the *ex situ* regulation under the *Antarctic Treaty* is part of a bigger problem that undermines the opportunity for benefits to flow back to Antarctica, namely, the lack of coordination between *ex situ* repositories on aquatic sample, data, information and knowledge exchange. This is followed by an examination of the extent to which ABS regimes outside of the Antarctic Treaty System apply to Antarctic *ex situ* genetic resources. The chapter considers the bilateral territorial approaches to ABS under the United Nations' *Convention on Biological Diversity* (CBD)[11] and the *Nagoya Protocol on Access to Genetic Resources and the Fair and Equitable Sharing of Benefits Arising from Their Utilization to the Convention on Biological Diversity* (Nagoya Protocol).[12] The chapter also considers

---

5 See n 21 below and accompanying text.

6 *United Nations Convention on the Law of the Sea* (1994) 1833 UNTS 3 (*UNCLOS*).

7 *Development of an International Legally-Binding Instrument under the United Nations Convention on the Law of the Sea on the Conservation and Sustainable Use of Marine Biological Diversity of Areas beyond National Jurisdiction*, GA Res 69/292, UN GAOR, 69th sess, 96th plen mtg, Agenda Item 74(a), Supp No 49, UN Doc A/RES/69/292 (6 July 2015, adopted 19 June 2015) (*New Instrument Resolution*).

8 *Antarctic Treaty* (1961) 402 UNTS 71 (*Antarctic Treaty*).

9 *Antarctic Treaty*, Art II.

10 *Antarctic Treaty*, Preamble.

11 CBD, above n 1.

12 Conference of the Parties to the Convention on Biological Diversity, *Report of the Tenth Meeting of the Conference of the Parties to the Convention on Biological Diversity* (2010) UNEP/CBD/COP/10/27, [103] and Annex (Decision X/1,

the multilateral cooperative commons approaches under the *International Treaty on Plant Genetic Resources for Food and Agriculture* (Plant Treaty)[13] and the proposed New Instrument under UNCLOS. The result is a complex matrix of regulation that poses at least two significant challenges for the ABS of Antarctica's *ex situ* resources. First, the challenge of equitably treating changes of intent for the purpose of a resource's use. Secondly, the challenge of overcoming jurisdictional problems arising from the CBD's geographical origin approach to ABS, including the territorial limitations of laws and the extent to which physical and digital derivatives of the genetic resources fall within ABS regimes.

Under the *Antarctic Treaty*, sovereignty claims concerning Antarctica's resources are on hold.[14] Despite the perception of an unregulated open access approach to Antarctica's genetic resources,[15] this chapter shows that some countries appear to be regulating the sharing of Antarctic *ex situ* genetic resources that are located within their national territory. This chapter argues that the legal authority for regulation is tenuous and complicated. It becomes more complex when dealing with the abstract information and knowledge (the digital resources) separate to the physical resource sample. In the light of the increasing interest in commercialising and patenting inventions related to Antarctic genetic resources,[16] an additional layer of national regulation concerns the protection of exclusive rights over genetic resource inventions under patent law. This protection may further restrict access to Antarctic genetic resources on which the inventions are based. A significant difference, however, between ABS and patent law regimes lies in their mechanisms for benefit sharing. This chapter argues that benefits under the bilateral ABS regimes generally flow to the provider country and not Antarctica. It concludes on the other hand that the framework of defences under the World Trade Organization's *Agreement on Trade-Related Aspects of Intellectual Property Rights* (TRIPS)[17] offers a multilateral approach to sharing knowledge and technology concerning Antarctica's *ex situ* resources in a way that is consistent with

---

Annex 1 (Nagoya Protocol), pp 89–109). The *Nagoya Protocol* has not yet entered into force for Australia. It is a supplementary agreement to the CBD providing a transparent legal framework for the effective implementation of the fair and equitable sharing of benefits arising out of the 'utilization of genetic resources': Art 1.

13 *International Treaty on Plant Genetic Resources for Food and Agriculture* (2001) 2400 UNTS 303 (*Plant Treaty*).

14 *Antarctic Treaty*, Art IV.

15 See discussion of the open access approach in Antarctica in Bernard Herber, 'Bioprospecting in Antarctica: The Search for a Policy Regime' (2006) 42(221) *Polar Record* 139, 145.

16 Antarctic Treaty Consultative Meeting, *Biological Prospecting in Antarctica – the Need for Improved Information* (2013) ATCM 36, Agenda Item 17, WP 48, p 4.

17 *Marrakesh Agreement Establishing the World Trade Organization* (1994) 1869 UNTS 3, Annex 1C (*Agreement on Trade-Related Aspects of Intellectual Property Rights*) (*TRIPS*).

fulfilling the objectives of cooperation and freedom of scientific investigation under the *Antarctic Treaty*.

4.2 The framework governing Antarctic genetic resources

The Antarctic Treaty System establishes a distinct international framework for governing activities in waters beyond national jurisdiction of the area south of 60 degrees South latitude. The Antarctic Treaty System includes the *Antarctic Treaty*, the *Protocol on Environmental Protection to the Antarctic Treaty* (Madrid Protocol)[18] and the *Convention on the Conservation of Antarctic Marine Living Resources* (CCAMLR).[19] All claims for sovereignty over Antarctic waters, land and resources are on hold.[20] The governance of Antarctic waters, land and resources is dependent on cooperation between representatives of Contracting Parties to the *Antarctic Treaty* through the ATCM.[21] The ATCM exchanges information and recommends measures to governments in furtherance of principles and objectives of the *Antarctic Treaty* including the facilitation of scientific research[22] and international scientific cooperation in Antarctica.[23]

The ATCM has affirmed that the Antarctic Treaty System is the appropriate framework for managing the collection and use of biological material in the Antarctic Treaty Area.[24] Sharing the benefits of Antarctica is an important aim under the Antarctic Treaty System,[25] however the system does not directly regulate the ABS of Antarctica's biological resources.[26] Instead there are several provisions that apply to accessing *in situ* genetic resources and to the sharing of non-monetary benefits that arise from their use. The provisions do not govern the ABS of *ex situ* Antarctic genetic resources[27] but may arguably be relevant to determining the extent to which national legislation applies to *ex situ* physical and digital resources outlined later in this chapter.[28]

---

18 *Protocol on Environmental Protection to the Antarctic Treaty* (1991) 30 ILM 1455 (*Madrid Protocol*).
19 *Convention on the Conservation of Antarctic Marine Living Resources* (1980) 1329 UNTS 47 (*CCAMLR*).
20 *Antarctic Treaty*, Art IV.
21 *Antarctic Treaty*, Art IX(1).
22 *Antarctic Treaty*, Art IX(1)(b).
23 *Antarctic Treaty*, Art IX(1)(c).
24 Antarctic Treaty Consultative Meeting, *Biological Prospecting in Antarctica* (2013) ATCM 36, Resolution 6; Antarctic Treaty Consultative Meeting, *Collection and Use of Antarctic Biological Material* (2009) ATCM 32.
25 Thomas Greiber *et al.*, *An Explanatory Guide to the Nagoya Protocol on Access and Benefit-sharing*, Environmental Policy and Law Paper No 83 (International Union for Conservation of Nature, 2012) p 38.
26 Antarctic Treaty Consultative Meeting, *A Gap Analysis of the Antarctic Treaty System Regarding the Management of Biological Prospecting* (2009) ATCM 32, WP 26, Agenda Item 17, p 3 (*A Gap Analysis*).
27 Ibid, p 15 (regarding access); ibid, p 18 (regarding benefit sharing).
28 See below n 144 and following text.

A. Access provisions

Access to *in situ* resources must accord with the principle of freedom of scientific investigation and cooperation.[29] Access must be carried out for peaceful purposes[30] 'in the interest of all [hu]mankind'[31] and the preservation of the Antarctic environment.[32] This means, for example, that access to biological resources for developing new biological weapons would not be allowed,[33] but arguably access to develop new aquaculture products would meet these requirements. Contracting Parties are obliged to give prior notification to other Contracting Parties about expedition activities in Antarctica including the collection of biological material, through the Electronic Information Exchange System.[34] While this is not an obligation to seek permission before extraction akin to the CBD's access obligations of prior informed consent and mutually agreed terms,[35] it provides other Contracting Parties with an opportunity to voice their concerns about the proposed access.

Other Antarctic Treaty System instruments have requirements to obtain permits for access under certain circumstances. Under the Madrid Protocol, for example, the 'taking of native mammals, birds and plants' is prohibited except with a permit.[36] Permits would only be issued to provide specimens for scientific study or information, or to provide specimens for museums, herbaria or other educational or cultural institutions or uses.[37] Micro-organisms,[38] and arguably invertebrates like molluscs and sponges, fall outside the definition of 'native mammals, birds and plants'.[39] This means that there are no requirements for prior authorisation or permit restrictions on taking these organisms (unless domestic legislation provides otherwise)[40] other than the general environmental impact assessment obligations on researchers taking the samples.[41]

Marine living resources under the CCAMLR are also outside the scope of the Madrid Protocol's permit system.[42] The CCAMLR applies to fin fish, molluscs, crustaceans and all other species of living organisms, including birds,

---

29 *Antarctic Treaty, Art* II.
30 *Antarctic Treaty*, Art I.
31 *Antarctic Treaty*, Preamble.
32 *Antarctic Treaty*, Art IX(1)(f); *Madrid Protocol*, Art 2.
33 *A Gap Analysis*, above n 26, p 15.
34 *Antarctic Treaty*, Art VII(5); Antarctic Treaty Consultative Meeting, *Electronic Information Exchange System* (2005) ATCM 28, Agenda Item 17, Decision 10.
35 See below n 121 and accompanying text.
36 *Madrid Protocol*, Annex II, Art 3(1).
37 *Madrid Protocol*, Annex II, Art 3(2).
38 *A Gap Analysis*, above n 26, p 15.
39 See Antarctic Treaty Consultative Meeting, *A Case of Biological Prospecting* (2011) ATCM 34, IP 62, Agenda Item 17, p 3.
40 *A Gap Analysis*, above n 26, p 15.
41 *Madrid Protocol*, Arts 3, 8 and Annex 1.
42 *A Gap Analysis*, above n 26, p 15. Under Article 4, the *Madrid Protocol* is subordinate to other instruments within the Antarctic Treaty System and harvesting of marine living resources must comply with measures under the *CCAMLR*.

found south of the Antarctic Convergence (a wider area than the Madrid Protocol).[43] The objective of the CCAMLR is the conservation of marine living resources.[44] It is unclear whether it only applies to the harvesting and use of these resources as a source of protein,[45] rather than utilisation of the resource for its genetic material value to which ABS regimes apply.[46] Members must issue an authorisation (eg permit) to their flagged vessels before they can take the relevant resources.[47] Recently the Commission declared the world's largest marine park in the Ross Sea which will come into effect in December 2017.[48] Access restrictions in this area include a 'no take' zone in 72 per cent of the marine park.[49]

B. Knowledge sharing provisions

As with the access provisions above, the benefit sharing of genetic resources accessed from the Antarctic Treaty Area must support the continuance of freedom of scientific investigation and cooperation.[50] In other words, benefit sharing would need to accord 'with the interests of science and the progress of all [hu]mankind',[51] the peaceful use of Antarctica[52] and the preservation of the Antarctic environment.[53] The *Antarctic Treaty*, which entered into force before TRIPS, does not mention the relationship between these objectives and private interests like intellectual property. While there is no explicit prohibition on claiming intellectual property over Antarctica's genetic resources, the agreement to put sovereign rights on hold to fulfil a collective purpose of cooperation and scientific investigation that benefits all humankind would suggest that the proprietary interests of users of the resources would not outweigh the public interest in having the resource available in accordance with the *Antarctic Treaty*'s objectives.

The Antarctic Treaty System does not regulate the sharing of monetary benefits but does have provisions for sharing non-monetary benefits of using Antarctica's genetic resources.[54] These benefits arguably focus on sharing information and knowledge rather than sharing the physical specimens on

---

43 *CCAMLR*, Art I.
44 *CCAMLR*, Art II(1) and Preamble.
45 *CCAMLR*, Preamble.
46 See the definition of 'genetic resources' in CBD, Art 2.
47 See, eg, permit obligations under Australia's *Antarctic Marine Living Resources Conservation Act 1981 (Cth)* s 9.
48 See Commission for the Conservation of Antarctic Marine Living Resources, *Report of the Thirty-Fifth Meeting of the Commission* (2016) CCAMLR-XXXV.
49 See <https://www.ccamlr.org/en/news/2016/ccamlr-create-worlds-largest-ma rine-protected-area> (accessed 20 August 2017).
50 *Antarctic Treaty*, Art II.
51 *Antarctic Treaty*, Preamble.
52 *Antarctic Treaty*, Art I.
53 *Antarctic Treaty*, Art IX(1)(f); *Madrid Protocol*, Art 2.
54 *A Gap Analysis*, above n 26, p 17.

which the technologies are based.[55] Contracting Parties to the *Antarctic Treaty* are obliged to promote international cooperation for scientific investigation in Antarctica.[56] This requires to the greatest extent practicable the exchange of plans for scientific programmes, personnel and the exchange and free availability of 'scientific observations and results'.[57] It is difficult to determine the scope of this obligation because 'scientific observations and results' are not defined.[58] The phrase is likely, however, to include observations and results related to biological prospecting of genetic resources.[59] In 2015, Consultative Parties to the ATCM agreed on a consolidated list of information exchange requirements for science activities including information on the 'taking and harmful interference with flora and fauna species, location, amount, sex, age and purpose'.[60] The condition to record purpose at the time of taking the resources is relevant for determining the types of benefits that can be shared from their subsequent uses.[61]

The Madrid Protocol and CCAMLR have additional obligations for knowledge sharing within the scope of their jurisdictions. Under the Madrid Protocol, Parties are required to exchange information through annual reports on Protocol activities.[62] Parties are specifically required to exchange records and statistics on the numbers of native mammals, birds and plants taken annually,[63] but this arguably does not apply to invertebrates, fish and microorganisms. The only requirement for invertebrates is to exchange information on their status[64] but even then it only relates to native invertebrates.[65] Parties must also 'cooperate in the planning and conduct of activities'.[66] To achieve this goal, Parties must endeavour to among other things undertake joint expeditions and sharing the use of facilities and information that may be helpful in conducting activities.[67] Direct participation in joint marine research is often regarded as a more

---

55 See examples of non-monetary benefit sharing in *A Gap Analysis*, ibid, p 17.
56 *Antarctic Treaty*, Art II.
57 *Antarctic Treaty*, Art III.
58 Morten Walløe Tvedt, 'Patent Law and Bioprospecting in Antarctica' (2011) 47 (1) *Polar Record* 46, 52.
59 See Antarctic Treaty Consultative Meeting, *Biological Prospecting* (2005) ATCM 28, Resolution 7.
60 Antarctic Treaty Consultative Meeting, *Exchange of Information* (2015) ATCM 38, Decision 6, Annex ('Information Exchange Requirements').
61 Fran Humphries, 'The Rising Tide of Access and Benefit Sharing in Aquaculture' in Nigel Bankes, David VanderZwaag, and Irene Dahl, *Aquaculture Law and Policy: International, Regional and National Perspectives* (Edward Elgar, 2016) (*ABS in Aquaculture*) p 93.
62 *Madrid Protocol*, Art 17.
63 *Madrid Protocol* annex II, Art 6(1)(a).
64 *Madrid Protocol* annex II, Art 6(1)(b).
65 *Madrid Protocol* annex II, Art 1(d). See also *A Case of Biological Prospecting*, above n 39, p 3.
66 *Madrid Protocol*, Art 6.
67 *Madrid Protocol*, Art 6.

effective approach to technology transfer than pure information sharing because it promotes sustainable capacity building.[68]

Under the CCAMLR, the Commission for the Conservation of Antarctic Marine Living Resources (CCAMLR Commission) must facilitate research of Antarctic marine living resources.[69] Members are obliged to submit statistical, biological and other information[70] which may include information on the taking of biological resources for use of their genetic resources. Non-parties to the *Antarctic Treaty* may become members of the CCAMLR. Interestingly they are bound by Articles I, IV, V and VI of the *Antarctic Treaty*[71] (peaceful purpose objectives and sovereignty arrangements) but not specifically the knowledge sharing provisions under Articles II and III of the *Antarctic Treaty*.

A recurring theme for the *Antarctic Treaty*'s access and knowledge sharing rules is its cooperative approach to sharing information, samples, facilities and technical knowhow. It is important to keep in mind that its obligations are only imposed on parties to the relevant international instrument. Significantly for the increasingly commercial applications of genetic resources that originated in Antarctica,[72] the Antarctic Treaty System does not provide guidance on ABS of Antarctic *ex situ* resources, the role of intellectual property,[73] and how to balance proprietary interests and the interests of humankind.

4.3 Gap in regulating *ex situ* resources – the tip of the iceberg

Some Contracting Parties to the *Antarctic Treaty* are reluctant to provide for additional or specific ABS regulation[74] despite the regulatory gap relating to the use and sharing of Antarctic *ex situ* genetic resources, including those that are subsequently patented. The following discussion highlights how this regulatory gap is only the tip of the iceberg for the fair and equitable sharing of Antarctic *ex situ* genetic resources. It is indicative of a bigger problem that is lurking beneath the surface – the lack of coordination between *ex situ* repositories on aquatic sample, data, information and knowledge exchange (outlined in this section) and

---

68 Ad Hoc Open-ended Informal Working Group, *Intersessional Workshops Aimed at Improving Understanding of the Issues and Clarifying Key Questions as an Input to the Work of the Working Group in Accordance with the Terms of Reference Annexed to General Assembly Resolution 67/78: Summary of Proceedings Prepared by the Co-chairs of the Working Group* (Advanced, Unedited Version, New York, 19–23 August 2013) [128] (*IWG Intersessional Workshops*).

69 *CCAMLR*, Art IX.

70 *CCAMLR*, Art XX.

71 *CCAMLR*, Arts III and IV.

72 See below n 75 and accompanying text.

73 Petra Drankier *et al.*, 'Marine Genetic Resources in Areas Beyond National Jurisdiction: Access and Benefit-sharing' (2012) 27(2) *The International Journal of Marine and Coastal Law* 375, 419.

74 Antarctic Treaty Consultative Meeting, *Report of the ATCM Intersessional Contact Group to Examine the Issue of Biological Prospecting in the Antarctic Treaty Area* (2010) ATCM 33, WP 13, Agenda Item 17, p 7 [21].

the confusion about the extent to which national ABS obligations would apply to Antarctic deposits (outlined in the next section). This section outlines some of the uses of Antarctic *ex situ* genetic resources with particular emphasis on aquaculture, which is likely to increasingly become a beneficiary of Antarctica's genetic resources, making this an important perspective to consider.

Much of the recent commercial and patent activity concerning Antarctic organisms relates to krill while the 'rest is based on a variety of Antarctic source organisms which include micro-organisms, invertebrates (such sponges, tunicates, corals, sea stars and worms), vertebrates (such as fish) and plants (such as algae and Antarctic hairgrass)'.[75] Many uses of genetic material and derivatives concern pharmaceutical and industrial uses.[76] Although the literature lacks thorough analyses of trends relating specifically to aquaculture, there are some examples of Antarctic genetic resources being used for aquaculture purposes.[77] A good example is the interest in antifreeze gene technologies. A major issue for aquaculture is unseasonal cold winters which can severely damage production and brood fish stocks.[78] Further, the inability of fish without antifreeze proteins severely restricts suitable sites for aquaculture operations.[79] Researchers have focused their attention on antifreeze proteins and glycoproteins that reduce freezing temperatures by preventing ice-crystal growth.[80] Sources of patented antifreeze proteins and glycoproteins include deep sea cold ocean teleost fish from the Southern Ocean,[81] including areas covered by the Antarctic Treaty System. Uses of antifreeze protein technologies in breeding include direct injection of purified antifreeze protein into a host species to improve freezing resistance for farming,[82] or its use in cryopreservation of breeding material,[83] or the antifreeze gene's complete integration into the

75 Antarctic Treaty Consultative Meeting, *The Antarctic Biological Prospecting Database* (2009) ATCM 32, WP 1, Agenda Item 17, p 3.
76 *Biological Prospecting in Antarctica*, above n 16, p 3.
77 Antarctic Treaty Consultative Meeting, *Biological Prospecting in Antarctica: Review, Update and Proposed Tool to Support a Way Forward* (2007) ATCM 30, IP 67, Agenda Item 17, p 8.
78 John Beardmore and Joanne Porter, 'Genetically Modified Organisms and Aquaculture' (FAO, 2003) Fisheries Circular No. 989, FIRI/C989(3), p 4.
79 Choy Hew *et al.*, 'Liver-specific and Seasonal Expression of Transgenic Atlantic Salmon Harboring the Winter Flounder Antifreeze Protein Gene' (1999) 8 *Transgenic Research* 405, 406.
80 Beardmore and Porter, above n 78, p 4.
81 Jong Kyu Lee *et al.*, 'Molecular and Comparative Analyses of Type IV Antifreeze Proteins (AFPIVs) from Two Antarctic Fishes, *Pleuragramma antarcticum* and *Notothenia coriiceps*' (2011) 159 *Comparative Biochemistry and Physiology Part B: Biochemistry and Molecular Biology* 197, 204.
82 Such as rainbow trout: Garth Fletcher, Ming Kao and Ron Fourney, 'Antifreeze Peptides Confer Freezing Resistance to Fish' (1986) 64 *Canadian Journal of Zoology* 1897, 1898.
83 Heather Young and Garth Fletcher, 'Antifreeze Protein Gene Expression in Winter Flounder Pre-hatch Embryos: Implications for Cryopreservation' (2008) 57 *Cryobiology* 84, 84.

genome of the host species, which might then be expressed in the host's off-spring.[84] The use of antifreeze genes to develop transgenic fish species such as salmon[85] and tilapia[86] has attracted much attention. While the use of *ex situ* Antarctic genetic resources may be on the rise, difficulties in pinpointing bio-prospecting and patenting trends for their specific use in aquaculture are com-pounded by the lack of ABS rules documenting intent at the time of extraction, changes of intent and the subsequent use of *ex situ* Antarctic resources. In other words, a genetic resource may be extracted from Antarctic waters for non-commercial research purposes and then later stored in an *ex situ* facility and subsequently used for commercial aquaculture purposes without any benefits flowing back to Antarctica.

Ex situ collections are diverse and can include culture collections, germplasm collections, cell banks, stock centres, herbaria, zoos, museum collections and botanic gardens.[87] Unlike the current extensive system for the exchange of terrestrial plant germplasm collections which began in the early twentieth century,[88] the history of aquatic gene banks only goes back to the past few decades.[89] Collections of aquatic genetic resources can include living brood-stock or cryopreserved collections. Broodstock collections take up space and are more expensive than cryopreserved banks to replenish and maintain.[90] Storage ranges from simple bacteria strains to more complex organisms. One of the few collections in the world dedicated to the collection of Antarctic bacteria strains is the Australian Collection of Antarctic Microorganisms (ACAM).[91] There are also growing private and university Antarctic collections including those in the United States, Germany and Belgium.[92] Cryopreserva-tion of sperm from several fish species is also commonly practised.[93] The same technology, however, for eggs and embryos of aquatic species is not yet

84 Hew *et al.*, above n 79, 411.
85 Jay Sanderson and Fran Humphries, 'Unnaturally Natural: Inventing and Eating Genetically Engineered AquaAdvantage® Salmon and the Paradox of Nature' in Charles Lawson and Berris Charnley (eds), *Intellectual Property and Genetically Modified Organisms: A Convergence in Laws* (Ashgate, 2015) pp 185 and 188.
86 Antje Caelers, 'Expression of Endogenous and Exogenous Growth Hormone (GH) Messenger (m) RNA in a GH-transgenic Tilapia (*Oreochromis niloticus*)' (2005) 14 *Transgenic research* 95, 96.
87 Susette Biber-Klemm *et al.*, 'Ex Situ Collections of Plants and How they Adjust to ABS Conditions' in Evanson Chege Kamau, Gerd Winter and Peter-Tobias Stoll (eds), *Research and Development on Genetic Resources: Public Domain Approaches in Implementing the Nagoya Protocol* (Routledge, 2015) pp 207 and 208.
88 Bonwoo Koo *et al.*, *Saving Seeds: The Economics of Conserving Crop Genetic Ex Situ in the Future Harvest Centres of CGIAR* (CABI Publishing, 2004) p 2.
89 David Greer and Brian Harvey, *Blue Genes: Sharing and Conserving the World's Aquatic Biodiversity* (Earthscan, 2004) pp 67–68.
90 Ibid, p 67.
91 See <http://gcmd.nasa.gov/records/AADC_ACAM.html> (accessed 20 August 2017).
92 *Biological Prospecting – A Way Forward*, above n 77, p 10.
93 Greer and Harvey, above n 89, p 67.

viable[94] which severely limits the effectiveness of cryopreservation for aquatic gene banking.[95] Other options for gene banking include androgenesis, cloning, stem cell collections and other future technologies.[96] While there are a number of large state-run collections (for example in Norway, India, Russia and Finland), the bulk of cryopreserved material is held in small private or university-based banks, whose numbers are nowhere near those of plant repositories.[97]

Unlike the plant networks, there is 'no coordination between aquatic gene banks'.[98] Nor are there generally accepted protocols or regulations governing the access and use of aquatic resources; rather private law contracts are usually agreed between the providers and users of the resource 'and very little importance is given to [ABS] considerations'.[99] Similar uncoordinated contractual mechanisms are used for the exchange of aquatic genetic resources from broodstock collections. For example genetic material for marine shrimp or tilapia are improved by private breeding companies and then the genetically improved stocks are 'multiplied' by other hatchery facilities in order to provide enough animals to sell to farmers for grow-out.[100] The multiplier facilities may enter into contractual agreements, usually termed material transfer agreements (MTAs), with the breeding companies that set restrictions on how the multiplier hatcheries may use the genetically improved stocks. The terms of the MTAs often 'prevent the multiplier stations ... from selling the stock for breeding purposes without compensation' to the provider breeder.[101] However, the numerous groups involved in the production process from breed improvement to sale of live fish, combined with the highly fertile nature of many aquatic species, mean that there is substantial scope for failure to adhere to MTAs and for the unauthorised exchange of aquatic genetic material.[102] This lack of coordination for the exchange of aquatic germplasm has implications for determining which resources may have originated from Antarctica. Even when the origins can be traced back to Antarctica, the gap in regulating *ex situ* resources becomes a significant issue because a substantial proportion of the use of Antarctic specimens takes place in national laboratories.[103]

---

94 Paz Herráez, Elsa Cabrita and Vanesa Robles, 'Fish Gamete and Embryo Cryopreservation: State of the Art', in Garth Fletcher and Matthew Rise (eds), *Aquaculture Biotechnology* (Wiley-Blackwell, 2011) pp 303, 309–10.

95 Rex Dunham, *Aquaculture and Fisheries Biotechnology: Genetic Approaches* (CABI, 2nd ed, 2011) p 253.

96 See ibid, pp 253–254.

97 Greer and Harvey, above n 89, pp 33 and 68.

98 Ibid, p 67.

99 Devin Bartley *et al.*, *The Use and Exchange of Aquatic Genetic Resources for Food and Agriculture*, Background Study Paper No 45 (Commission on Genetic Resources for Food and Agriculture, 2009) p 24.

100 John Benzie, 'Use and Exchange of Genetic Resources of Penaeid Shrimps for Food and Agriculture' (2009) 1 *Reviews in Aquaculture*, 232, 235.

101 Bartley *et al.*, above n 99, p 25.

102 Ibid.

103 *A Gap Analysis*, above n 26, p 18.

In the context of genomics, proteomics, phenomics and bioinformatives, *ex situ* collections may include the digitalised forms of Deoxyribonucleic acid (DNA), ribonucleic acid (RNA) and proteins.[104] These kinds of 'omic' technologies are becoming increasingly important for innovation in aquaculture[105] and aquatic related research.[106] There are several global initiatives for storing genetic data, including the information relating to Antarctic genetic resources. The Census of Antarctic Marine Life (CAML) collates DNA barcode data for Antarctic marine species including life from the Southern Ocean and the Sub-Antarctic Islands. DNA barcoding is a technique that uses a short gene sequence from a standardised region of the genome as a diagnostic 'biomarker' for species.[107] There are also separate initiatives for specific species such as the barcode library for Antarctic sponges.[108] Coordination between depositories is complicated by the different means of entering data. For example, many genetic databases contain DNA sequences such as DNA Data Bank of Japan (DDBJ), European Molecular Biology Laboratory (EMBL) databank, and National Institute of Health's GenBank. However, there are few Antarctic barcodes in Genbank.[109] These barcodes are held in specially designed databases such as the Barcode of Life Data System (BOLD), which is an online workbench and receptacle for sequence data generated from Barcode of Life projects, such as the CAML project above.[110] Without proper coordination between databases, however, it is difficult to determine the geographical origin of the data and information for the purposes of ABS.

There is no centralised information or knowledge repository for the results of high seas research,[111] including the Antarctic waters of the Southern Ocean. The ATCM has called for 'further development of linked databases and geographically referenced maps, which can serve to improve the informational basis for discussions at the ATCM'.[112] ATCM parties set up a database for

---

104 Peter Johan Schei and Morten Walløe Tvedt, Fridtjof Nansen Institute, *The Concept of 'Genetic Resources' in the Convention on Biological Diversity and How It Relates to a Functional International Regime on Access and Benefit-Sharing* (2010) UNEP/CBD/WG-ABS/9/INF/1 (*The Concept of 'Genetic Resources'*) p 25.

105 See, eg, Pedro Rodrigues *et al.*, 'Proteomics in Aquaculture: Applications and Trends' (2012) 75 *Journal of Proteomics* 4325; Marco Saroglia and Zhanjiang (John) Liu (eds), *Functional Genomics in Aquaculture* (Wiley-Blackwell, 2012).

106 See, eg, Paul Oldham, *Global Status and Trends in Intellectual Property Claims: Genomics, Proteomics and Biotechnology* (2005) UNEP/CBD/WG-ABS/3/INF/4.

107 Rachel Grant and Katrin Linse, 'Barcoding Antarctic Biodiversity: Current Status and the CAML Initiative – A Case Study of Marine Invertebrates' (2009) 32 *Polar Biology* 1629, 1630.

108 For the recent assembly of a barcode library for Antarctic sponges see Sergio Vargas *et al.*, 'Diversity in a Cold Hot-Spot: DNA-Barcoding Reveals Patterns of Evolution among Antarctic Demosponges (Class Demospongiae, Phylum Porifera)' (2015) 10 *PLOS One*: e0127573 DOI: 10.1371/journal.pone.0127573.

109 Grant and Linse, above n 107, 1631.

110 Ibid.

111 *IWG Intersessional Workshops*, above n 68, [121].

112 *Biological Prospecting in Antarctica*, above n 16, p 4.

bioprospecting in Antarctica that included patenting information, effectively linking data, information and knowledge relating to Antarctic genetic resources. The Antarctic Biological Prospecting Database 'provides a searchable interface allowing the user to obtain information about research and commercial products arising from biological samples that were sourced from the Antarctic region'.[113] However, at the time of writing this chapter, the database had been taken offline. Other broader initiatives incorporate Antarctic information such as the Global Biodiversity Information Facility,[114] which was set up to make primary global biodiversity information more widely available, and the Ocean Biogeographic Information System,[115] which publishes information on the distribution of marine species.[116] The Marine Biodiversity Information Network (SCAR-MarBIN) compiles and manages information on Antarctic marine biodiversity by coordinating database networking.[117]

In summary, the regulatory vacuum outlined in the previous section combined with the lack of coordination between *ex situ* repositories and the subsequent loss of control over resources that originated from Antarctic waters makes it difficult to pinpoint the extent to which physical and digital Antarctic genetic resources contribute to aquatic research and development generally and aquaculture in particular. Significantly, the lack of coordination impedes the collection and exchange of detailed information needed to trace the origin of a given genetic resource to determine its status for the purpose of ABS under national laws as outlined in the following section.

4.4 The tidal wave of applicable ABS-related instruments

Private benefit sharing agreements and patent protection concerning Antarctic genetic resources have already begun despite the regulatory gaps in the Antarctic Treaty System. ATCM Parties have reported that some companies using Antarctic resources offer benefit sharing on an *ad hoc* basis in return for access.[118] This may include a mix of monetary benefits like fees per sample and licensing agreements, as well as non-monetary benefits, for example through training, capacity-building, research exchanges and technology transfer.[119] Given that no country has control over Antarctic resources and that the Antarctic Treaty System has no ABS mechanism, it would be interesting to know to whom or to what the benefits in these private agreements flow. The ABS of Antarctic *ex situ* resources is being influenced by a growing matrix of ABS-related international instruments including the CBD, the Nagoya

---

113 *The Antarctic Biological Prospecting Database*, above n 75, p 3.
114 See <www.gbif.org> (accessed 20 August 2017).
115 See <www.iobis.org> (accessed 20 August 2017).
116 Grant and Linse, above n 107, 1630.
117 See <http://www.scarmarbin.be> (accessed 20 August 2017).
118 Sarah Laird, Rachel Wynberg and Sam Johnston, *Recent Trends in the Biological Prospecting* (2006) ATCM 29, IP 116, Agenda Item 18, p 23.
119 Ibid.

Protocol, the Plant Treaty and the New Instrument under UNCLOS. This section explores the extent to which other ABS regimes apply to Antarctic genetic resources.

A. CBD's territorial approach

The CBD and the Nagoya Protocol provide a framework for a bilateral territorial approach to ABS of genetic resources. The CBD's significant shift from treating genetic resources as a common heritage of humankind to recognising the sovereign rights of countries over their resources[120] has created spatial and temporal complexities for the legal status of Antarctic genetic resources. The following discussion highlights that spatially, the reach of the ABS rules depends on whether Antarctic genetic resources are located *in situ* or *ex situ* (geographical origin) which may depend on the timing and circumstances of their extraction. Other temporal complexities arise in cases where derivatives of the genetic resource such as the abstract digital resource and synthetic derivatives are being used independently from the physical *in situ* or *ex situ* resource, at different points in time and for different purposes of extraction and subsequent use.

Under the framework of the CBD and the Nagoya Protocol, Contracting Parties have sovereign rights to control access to *in situ* and *ex situ* genetic resources within their jurisdiction (subject to exceptions addressed below), as well as control over their nationals' activities in relation to genetic resources located outside their territories.[121] This is subject to obligations to facilitate access for, and transfer to, other Contracting Parties' relevant technologies that make use of (*in situ* or *ex situ*) genetic resources.[122] In return for access, users must share with the provider country, on mutually agreed terms, the benefits ultimately gained from the subsequent use of the genetic resources. The benefits include the resource provider's participation in scientific and biotechnology research based on the genetic resources supplied[123] as well as the fair and equitable sharing of the results of research, development, commercial and biotechnological use of the resources.[124] More specifically, the CBD's supplementary agreement, the Nagoya Protocol, sets out the rules, procedures and compliance mechanisms for ABS. This more detailed system is based on access conditions set out in domestic permits issued by a contracting party to the CBD[125] that are linked to contractual benefit sharing agreements between

---

120 Keith Aoki and Kennedy Luvai, 'Reclaiming Common Heritage Treatment in the International Plant Genetic Resources Regime Complex' (2007) 35 *Michigan State Law Review* 35, 49.
121 CBD, Arts 3, 4 and 15(1).
122 CBD, Art 16(1).
123 CBD, Art 19(1).
124 CBD, Arts 15(7) and 19(2).
125 *Nagoya Protocol*, Arts 6(3)(c), 14(2)(c) and 17(2).

users and providers,[126] all of which operate within a compliance framework of national laws in user and provider countries.[127]

The ABS framework applies to genetic resources that are (a) provided by the country of origin, or (b) parties that have 'acquired' genetic resources 'in accordance with the [CBD]'.[128] Antarctica does not fall within the definition of a 'country of origin'.[129] The question therefore becomes whether Antarctica's genetic resources located in a national *ex situ* facility have been 'acquired ... in accordance with the [CBD]' – a term that is not defined under the CBD. Glowka argues that genetic resources are not acquired in accordance with the CBD if they are taken illegally from a country of origin, for example, without prior informed consent (if required by the country of origin).[130] Other circumstances may include acquiring genetic resources that were deposited in an *ex situ* facility before the CBD entered into force,[131] or those in repositories within the jurisdiction of nations that are not party to the CBD. The meaning or the timing of the term 'acquired' is also not defined in the CBD and may need clarification in national legislation.[132] As the following discussion highlights, the clarification may depend on the circumstances of the original accession of the relevant genetic resource from the Antarctic Treaty Area.

While the CBD is based on the principle of territorial sovereignty, it also applies to processes and activities carried out by a Contracting Party's nationals within its control beyond the limits of the national jurisdiction.[133] Even though there is no territorial application of laws to *genetic resources* in the Antarctic Treaty Area, the *people* located in Antarctica including scientific personnel, staff and observers in Antarctica are subject to the jurisdiction of their country of nationality.[134] The Nagoya Protocol does not have similar extra-territorial application because its scope is limited to ABS under Article 15 of the CBD[135] and not the CBD's extended scope in Article 4.[136] This means that the CBD's obligations may apply to users of Antarctica's *in situ* resources but not the Nagoya Protocol's obligations.[137]

---

126 Referred to as 'mutually agreed terms' in the *Nagoya Protocol*, Arts 5, 6(3)(g), 7, 12(3)(b) and 19.

127 Elisa Morgera, Matthias Buck and Elsa Tsioumani, 'Introduction' in Elisa Morgera, Matthias Buck and Elsa Tsioumani (eds), *The 2010 Nagoya Protocol on Access and Benefit-Sharing in Perspective: Implications for International Law and Implementation Challenges* (Martinus Nijhoff Publishers, 2013) p 9.

128 CBD, Arts 2 and 15(3).

129 CBD, Art 2.

130 Lyle Glowka *et al.*, *A Guide to the Convention on Biological Diversity*, Environmental Policy and Law Paper No 30 (IUCN, 1994) p 79.

131 Ibid, p 77.

132 Ibid, p 79.

133 CBD, Art 4(b).

134 *Antarctic Treaty*, Art VIII(1).

135 *Nagoya Protocol*, Art 3.

136 Greiber *et al.*, above n 25, p 74.

137 Ibid.

i. Argument that the CBD does not apply

Some commentators argue that the Antarctic Treaty Area is not a sovereign state and therefore cannot be a Contracting Party to the CBD. What this means is that within the meaning of the ABS framework of the CBD, the Antarctic Treaty Area cannot enter into mutually agreed terms, require prior informed consent, and be afforded benefits for subsequent uses of the genetic resources.[138] Under the CBD:

> access to genetic resources shall be subject to prior informed consent of the Contracting Party providing such resources, unless otherwise determined by that Party.[139]

The ATCM is a forum rather than a decision making body authorised with sovereign rights and would not similarly be deemed a Contracting Party with sovereign powers. The CCAMLR Commission does have a legal personality[140] but there is uncertainty about whether its mandate is limited to the use of genetic resources for consumption rather than for their genetic material potential.[141] One interpretation of Article 15(5) of the CBD is that in the absence of a 'state' with sovereign rights over the resources, there is no provider to whom prior informed consent is owed. The consequence is that the genetic resources cannot be taken 'in accordance with' the CBD and so the ABS provisions are not triggered (in effect a free access scenario). Once a commons resource has been extracted by a Contracting Party to the CBD, the extractor may then become the party from whom consent is required and benefits are afforded under the ABS framework. This is because, although the requirement to provide prior informed consent does not clarify the phrase 'the Contracting Party providing such resources', it is likely to have a similar meaning to the 'country providing genetic resources' under Article 2 of the CBD. In other words:

> the country supplying genetic resources collected from *in situ* sources, including populations of both wild and domesticated species, or taken from *ex situ* sources, which may or may not have originated in that country.[142]

Under this *res nullius* scenario,[143] the CBD's ABS obligations would not apply. The Antarctic genetic resource would be treated the same way as a

---

138 See, eg, Regine Andersen *et al.*, *International Agreements and Processes Affecting an International Regime on Access and Benefit Sharing under the Convention on Biological Diversity: Implications for its Scope and Possibilities of a Sectoral Approach*, FNI Report 3/2010 (Fridtjof Nansen Institute, 2010) p 21.

139 CBD, Art 15(5).

140 *CCAMLR*, Art VIII.

141 See above n 46 and accompanying text.

142 CBD, Art 2.

143 Where the genetic resources are available to the first person with the capacity and technology to exploit them, who also receives the benefits from their use to the

country's territorial genetic resources. In this case, the benefits of using the genetic resources flow back to the country taking the resource, and not for the benefit of the Antarctic Treaty System's collective purpose.

ii. Argument that the CBD does apply

A second 'collective scenario' is based on the unique governing arrangements of the Antarctic Treaty System where the genetic resources are subject to neither national sovereignty nor free access. Under this scenario, although Consultative Parties to the ATCM cannot exercise sovereign powers over resources within the Antarctic Treaty Area, collectively they have contracted to put into effect their access and knowledge sharing obligations under the Antarctic Treaty System within their national laws on behalf of one another. So for a Contracting Party to the CBD that is also a Consultative Party to the Antarctic Treaty System, the *res nullius* scenario would not apply. In effect, there is a reciprocal arrangement where prior informed consent is given on behalf of other Contracting Parties and resources are capable of being acquired 'in accordance with' the CBD.

For example, Australia is a party to the *Antarctic Treaty*, Madrid Protocol and CCAMLR. The *Antarctic Treaty Act 1960* (Cth) gives effect to the *Antarctic Treaty* in Australia and applies to observers, scientific personnel and accompanying staff within the meaning of the *Antarctic Treaty* who are nationals of a Contracting Party to the *Antarctic Treaty*.[144] Australia's obligations under the Madrid Protocol, including permit approvals and environmental impact assessments, are implemented through the *Antarctic Treaty (Environmental Protection) Act 1980* (Cth) (ATEP Act). These laws (that effectively put into effect the *Antarctic Treaty*'s access provisions) apply to any activity proposed to be undertaken by Australian citizens, organisations, expeditions and tour operators in any waters south of 60 degrees South including all waters.[145] Australia's obligations under CCAMLR, including permit approvals, are implemented through the *Antarctic Marine Living Resources Conservation Act 1981* (Cth) (AMLRC Act) that applies to the CCAMLR 'Convention Area' (marine areas south of the Antarctic Convergence).[146] These Acts apply to Australian citizens and organisations so foreign nationals and organisations based outside Australia need to contact their respective country's Antarctic administrative organisations for approval, unless their activity is part of the Australian Antarctic programme.[147] The Australian

exclusion of others; Charles Lawson, *Regulating Genetic Resources: Access and Benefit Sharing in International Law* (Edward Elgar, 2012) p 242.

144 *Antarctic Treaty Act 1960* (Cth) s 3.
145 *Antarctic Treaty (Environmental Protection) Act 1980* (Cth) (*ATEP Act*).
146 *Antarctic Marine Living Resources Conservation Act 1981* (Cth) s 3 (*AMLRC Act*).
147 'Guide to Administering Environmental Approvals' (Australian Antarctic Division, Department of the Environment, June 2014) p 5, available at <http://www.anta

government has advised that 'in accordance with the principles of the *Antarctic Treaty*, Parties are responsible for their own nationals and other Antarctic programmes will recognise approvals granted by Australia'.[148] Under this reciprocal 'collective scenario', the extracting party has an obligation for prior informed consent of the permitting country on behalf of the other parties to the Antarctic Treaty System. This means the genetic resources can be 'taken in accordance with' the CBD and therefore Antarctica's *in situ* and subsequent *ex situ* genetic resources may fall within the CBD's framework. The Nagoya Protocol's framework will not apply to Antarctic *in situ* resources but may apply to its *ex situ* resources depending on how a country implements its obligations.

While this reasoning may offer legal authority to regulate Antarctica's *ex situ* genetic resources under the CBD, the territorial application of laws means that benefits still flow to the provider country, unless otherwise negotiated under mutually agreed terms. To use the Australian example, the *Environment Protection and Biodiversity Conservation Act 1999* (Cth) (EPBC Act) puts into effect Australia's ABS obligations under the CBD. The EPBC Act only applies to the physical genetic resources in Commonwealth Areas,[149] which includes the Australian Antarctic Territory, generally the area south of 60 degrees South and between 45 degrees East and 160 degrees East.[150] This area largely represents Australia's claim that has been put on hold by the *Antarctic Treaty*. It does not apply to physical genetic resources or Australian nationals dealing with genetic resources in the broader Antarctic Treaty Area or CCAMLR waters outside Commonwealth Areas. Biological resources in land and waters administered by the Australian Antarctic Division are exempt from the ABS obligations under the EPBC Act.[151] This means that a permit is required to access Antarctic genetic resources but administratively, access is governed in accordance with the ATEP Act or the AMLRC Act. While these acts do not have specific benefit sharing laws, it is likely that government decision-makers will follow the process under the EPBC Act. If a party wishes to access an Antarctic genetic resource for non-commercial purposes, they must have written permission from the provider to use the resource in return for giving the provider the results of any research on the biological resource and a taxonomic duplicate of the sample.[152] If a party wishes to access a genetic resource for

rctica.gov.au/__data/assets/pdf_file/0008/142667/CD-14-21-Guide-to-Adm inistering-Environmental-Approvals-Handbook-2016-2018.pdf> (accessed 20 August 2017).
148 Ibid. See *ATEP Act* s 7(1).
149 *Environment Protection and Biodiversity Conservation Act 1999 (Cth) (EPBC Act)* s 525; *Environment Protection and Biodiversity Conservation Regulations 2000 (Cth) (EPBC Regulation)* reg 8A.02.
150 *Australian Antarctic Territory Acceptance Act 1933* (Cth) s 2.
151 Commonwealth of Australia, *Gazette: Government Notices*, No 6, 14 February 2007 'Declaration of Exempt Biological Resources under Part 8A *Environment Protection and Biodiversity Conservation Regulation 2000*' 537.
152 *EPBC Regulation*, reg 8A.13.

actual or potential commercial purposes, a benefit sharing agreement must be negotiated with the Commonwealth government's relevant delegate.[153] Among other things, the benefit sharing agreement must set out the purpose of access[154] and details of benefits to the access provider who in this case is the Australian government.[155] The only concession to the Antarctic Treaty Area is to include the details of any proposals of the user to benefit biodiscovery conservation 'in the area' if access is granted.[156] Arguably, this requirement is at the contractual discretion of the user, rather than a legislative obligation for benefits to flow to the Antarctic Treaty Area.

In summary, whether or not the CBD applies to Antarctica's *in situ* and *ex situ* genetic resources, the territorial application of laws means that there are no positive requirements for benefits to flow to the Antarctic Treaty Area in support of its knowledge sharing provisions, unless agreed between the parties that negotiate a contract over a specific genetic resource.

iii. The CBD's spatial and temporal complexities

The Australian example highlights the spatial and temporal complexities caused by the territorial approach to ABS laws that apply to collecting *in situ* Antarctic genetic resources and the subsequent taking of the same resources from *ex situ* facilities. This is because in keeping with the Antarctic Treaty System, the ATEP Act and the AMLRC Act apply to *in situ* Antarctic resources and not *ex situ* genetic resources of Antarctica.[157] Australian ABS obligations apply to genetic resources within Commonwealth Areas which might include *in situ* resources in the Australian Antarctic Territory as well as Antarctica's *ex situ* resources that are stored in government-owned storage facilities on the Australian mainland, but not those held in private facilities within Australia or any facilities outside Australia's jurisdiction.[158] However, the ownership of each collection would need to be considered on its own merits, taking into account a range of factors including ownership prior to entering the repository, the circumstances under which the material passed into the possession of the *ex situ* holder (including contractual agreements), and any relevant legislation.[159]

Temporal complexities arise in the context of the purpose of use. These complexities could be overcome to a certain extent by requiring that if resources extracted from Australian Antarctic Territory waters for a non-commercial purpose are later used for a commercial purpose, a benefit sharing agreement will need to be negotiated with the original provider. Without effective

153 *EPBC Regulation*, reg 8A.04(1) and div 8A.2.
154 *EPBC Regulation*, reg 8A.08(c).
155 *EPBC Regulation*, reg 8A.08(l).
156 *EPBC Regulation*, reg 8A.08(k).
157 See above n 27 and accompanying text.
158 See, eg, John Voumard, *Access to Biological Resources in Commonwealth Areas* (Commonwealth Public Inquiry, July 2000) [8.10] ff.
159 Ibid [4.37].

coordination between *ex situ* facilities though, it may be difficult to determine the original provider and track the benefit sharing obligations connected with the physical sample once the temporal link between *in situ* access and subsequent *ex situ* use is severed (for example, by passing through different private and public facilities that are subject to different ABS laws).

A similar temporal complexity arises in the context of the purpose of extraction. The EPBC Act does not apply to the taking of public resources for collecting broodstock for aquaculture grow-out.[160] In aquaculture, however, it is often difficult to distinguish when the resource is used as a commodity, such as broodstock for grow out, or for its genetic material, such as using the biological resource's antifreeze gene promoters to breed cold tolerant fish, the latter of which does fall within the CBD's[161] and the EPBC Act's ABS regime. Wild broodstock may be collected without an ABS agreement, stored in an *ex situ* facility and subsequently used for a different purpose – for its genetic material – but the opportunity for sharing the benefits in accordance with the Antarctic Treaty System may be lost by the temporal disconnect.

A third temporal and spatial complexity arises if the *ex situ* derivative such as the chemical compounds and the information or knowledge component of the genetic resource (the digital resource) are used independently of the physical sample in Antarctic waters to which the derivative relates. While it is clear that derivatives of the physical genetic resource fall within CBD and Nagoya Protocol obligations, there is legal uncertainty about the type of derivatives to which their obligations apply.[162] The CBD's Group of Legal and Technical Experts on Concepts, Terms, Working Definitions and Sectoral Approaches observed that there was no common understanding of the concept of a derivative but that it could include: (a) derivatives understood as the result of an organism's metabolism (eg natural chemical compounds); (b) derivatives understood as the result of human activity using the genetic resource (eg synthetic compounds); or (c) derivatives understood as information on genetic resources (eg the abstract digital resource).[163] Naturally occurring biochemical compounds clearly fall within the meaning of a derivative,[164] however derivatives accessed independently of genetic resources fall outside of the scope of the obligations.[165] This is because Article 15 of the CBD is limited to the 'utilization of

---

160 *EPBC Regulation*, reg 8A.03(4)(a).

161 Fran Humphries, 'Technology Transfer of Aquatic Genetic Resources under the *Convention on Biological Diversity* and *Nagoya Protocol*: "Sponging" off Patent Law Defences' (2016) 39(1) *University of New South Wales Law Journal* 234, 257.

162 Ibid, 248.

163 Ad Hoc Open-Ended Working Group on Access and Benefit-Sharing, *Report of the Meeting of the Group of Legal and Technical Experts on Concepts, Terms, Working Definitions and Sectoral Approaches* (2008) UNEP/CBD/WG-ABS/7/2, Annex (*Outcome of the Meeting of the Group of Legal and Technical Experts on Concepts, Terms, Working Definitions and Sectoral Approaches*) [20].

164 *Protocol*, Art 2(e).

165 Greiber *et al.*, above n 25, p 71.

genetic resources' and Article 2 of the Nagoya Protocol links utilisation to the genetic and/or biochemical composition of the genetic resources.[166] Further, the CBD's technology transfer obligations under Article 16 are limited to technologies that 'make use' of genetic resources.[167] The criterion therefore for whether other types of derivatives fall within the scope of obligations appears to be the biological origin rather than the biological form.[168] This means that digital resources are likely to fall within the scope because the transfer of genetic information into digital form does not change its genetic character.[169] Whether a synthetic derivative falls within the scope may depend on its link with the original material.[170] The link would be stronger if there has been some use of genetic material in the developmental phase of the synthetic compound.[171]

Complexities for benefit sharing arise where a derivative is derived from the abstract digital resource that relates to an Antarctic genetic resource under an access agreement. In the example above, digital resources are not specifically regulated under the EPBC Act, the ATEP Act or the AMLRC Act. However, the terms of access (mutually agreed terms) might include benefit sharing obligations concerning the digital resource. The issue is how to ensure that subsequent uses of *ex situ* Antarctic digital resources, such as those that are part of the DNA barcode project example above[172] that do not depend on access to the physical sample, are held accountable to benefit sharing obligations for the original accession. The emphasis under the *Antarctic Treaty* of information and knowledge sharing for freedom and cooperation of scientific investigation that 'accords with the interests of science and the progress of all [hu]mankind' demonstrates the value it holds for the digital resource independently of the physical resource. Research results on the original genetic resource can, however, easily be lost in the dissemination process, for example through databases, media and publications.[173] Leaving the ABS of Antarctica's *ex situ* genetic resources up to the bilateral territorial approach undermines the *Antarctic Treaty's* objectives unless this temporal disconnect is effectively addressed.

166 Ibid.
167 CBD, Art 16.
168 Morten Walløe Tvedt and Peter Johan Schei, 'The Term "Genetic Resources": Flexible and Dynamic while Providing Legal Certainty?' in Sebastian Oberthür and G Kristin Rosendal (eds), *Global Governance of Genetic Resources: Access and Benefit Sharing after the Nagoya Protocol* (Routledge, 2014) pp 18 and 21.
169 Ibid.
170 Ibid, p 29.
171 Humphries, above n 161, 251.
172 See above n 107 and accompanying text.
173 Evanson Chege Kamau and Gerd Winter, 'Unbound R & D and Bound Benefit Sharing' in Evanson Chege Kamau, Gerd Winter and Peter-Tobias Stoll, *Research and Development on Genetic Resources: Public Domain Approaches in Implementing the Nagoya Protocol* (Routledge, New York, 2015) pp 1–24 and 21.

Growing awareness of the importance of ABS concerning subsequent uses of the digital resource and the time lag between accessing the original physical resource have led to initiatives such as the *Micro B3 Model Agreement on Access to Marine Microorganisms and Benefit Sharing* (Micro B3 Agreement). This agreement:

> sets out the terms for the access to genetic resources found in/on the Provider State's marine internal waters, territorial sea, exclusive economic zone or continental shelf, for the utilization and transfer to third parties of the accessed genetic resources, for the management and transfer to third parties of associated knowledge and for the sharing of benefits drawn from the same.[174]

While this clause would need modification if it were to apply to Antarctic genetic resources, the Micro B3 Agreement is a good example of how benefit sharing obligations can travel with the digital resource separately from the physical sample. The Commentary on the Micro B3 Agreement explains that it applies to three scenarios – full non-commercial (public domain), hybrid, and full commercial use at the point of access with differing benefit sharing obligations.[175] It allows for changes of intent by both the provider and the recipient of the genetic resource so that conditions are renegotiated at the time of change of intent.[176] Significantly, it sets out the conditions under which the recipient is allowed to transfer the accessed genetic resources and/or the associated genetic knowledge to third parties through a 'viral licence clause'.[177] In other words, subsequent recipients are bound by the same obligations that were imposed on the first recipient in the contract concluded with the provider.[178] The digital resource which may include not only data and information but also knowledge does not need to remain connected with the original sample for the obligations to apply. If a similar model applied to Antarctic genetic and digital resources, there would need to be a way to overcome the reality of the highly migratory nature of aquatic genetic resources where those extracted from the high seas may also be extracted from waters within national jurisdictions.[179] In other words, recipients may claim that the digital resource

---

174 Caroline von Kries *et al.*, *MICRO B3 Model Agreement on Access to Marine Microorganisms and Benefit Sharing* (MICRO B3 WP8, version 1.0, 10 June 2013) (*Micro B3 Agreement*), Art 1.1, available at <https://www.microb3.eu/work-packages/wp8> (accessed 20 August 2017).
175 Caroline von Kries *et al.*, *Commentary to the MICRO B3 Model Agreement on Access to Marine Microorganisms and Benefit Sharing* (MICRO B3 WP8, version 1.0, 10 June 2013) (*Micro B3 Commentary*) p 2 available at <https://www.microb3.eu/work-packages/wp8> (accessed 20 August 2017).
176 *Micro B3 Agreement*, Arts 4.4 and 4.5.
177 *Micro B3 Agreement*, Arts 5; *Micro B3 Commentary*, above n 175, p 14.
178 Ibid.
179 See Paul Oldham *et al.*, *Valuing the Deep: Marine Genetic Resources in Areas Beyond National Jurisdiction, Final Report* (Department of Environment, Food and Rural Affairs UK, 2014) p 17.

originated from a physical sample within national jurisdictions and the benefits may not flow back to Antarctica.

In summary, the CBD's bilateral territorial approach to ABS may regulate Antarctica's *ex situ* genetic resources physically located within national jurisdictions, but not genetic resources and derivatives that were deposited in an *ex situ* facility before the CBD entered into force,[180] in repositories within the jurisdiction of nations that are not party to the CBD, or where the samples were not acquired 'in accordance with' the CBD. Depending on how a country has implemented its CBD obligations, its regulation may extend to Antarctic *ex situ* genetic resources in private facilities. The benefits flow back to the country that has jurisdiction over the *ex situ* facility in which the Antarctic genetic resource is based. Whether or not subsequent uses of the *ex situ* physical and digital resources benefit Antarctica depends on the discretion of the parties negotiating a contract over a particular resource and how they deal with matters like changes of intent and subsequent third parties to the agreement. The tension between the CBD's and Nagoya Protocol's bilateral territorial approach and the Antarctic Treaty System's cooperative commons approach to sharing genetic resources makes it difficult for the former approach to uphold the *Antarctic Treaty*'s overarching principle of cooperation and freedom of scientific investigation.

B. Multilateral cooperative commons approaches

Various multilateral cooperative commons approaches do not yet regulate the use of Antarctic *ex situ* genetic resources but they may provide insights into how an ABS framework could achieve the *Antarctic Treaty*'s overarching principle of cooperation and freedom of scientific investigation. The Nagoya Protocol recognises that 'an innovative solution is required to address the fair and equitable sharing of benefits derived from the utilization of genetic resources and traditional knowledge associated with genetic resources that occur in transboundary situations or for which it is not possible to grant or obtain prior informed consent'.[181] To this end, the Nagoya Protocol requires Contracting Parties to consider the possible development of a global multilateral ABS mechanism for these resources.[182] Such a mechanism may be achieved through the New Instrument under UNCLOS. As it is too early to tell what the final model will be, this section outlines a similar mechanism under the Plant Treaty that might also serve as a guide.

i. UNCLOS implementing agreement for areas beyond national jurisdiction

Some participants of the ATCM have suggested that further regulation under the Antarctic Treaty System to fill ABS gaps should be dealt with under a New

---

180 Glowka *et al.*, above n 130, p 6.
181 *Protocol*, Preamble.
182 *Protocol*, Art 10.

Instrument.[183] The regulatory vacuum for a comprehensive ABS regime under UNCLOS for genetic resources from areas beyond national jurisdictions, or the 'deep sea', is well documented.[184] The deep sea includes the high seas water column[185] and the Area – the seabed and ocean floor and subsoil below the water column.[186] This includes the high seas in the Southern Ocean surrounding Antarctica.[187] The technology transfer obligations under UNCLOS include technological cooperation and collaboration,[188] participation in research activities,[189] information sharing[190] and capacity building.[191] Marine Scientific Research obligations include promoting the flow of data and information and the transfer of knowledge resulting from marine scientific research.[192] The provisions concerning technology transfer and knowledge sharing of deep sea genetic resources do not necessarily override those under the Antarctic Treaty System because UNCLOS:

> shall not alter the rights and obligations of States Parties which arise from other agreements compatible with this [UNCLOS] and which do not affect the enjoyment by other States Parties of their rights or the performance of their obligations under this [UNCLOS].[193]

The New Instrument will, however, fill the regulatory gaps concerning the sharing of benefits of the use of deep sea genetic resources, capacity building and the transfer of marine technology.[194] The Nagoya Protocol would cede to a specialised instrument regarding the specific genetic resources it covers.[195] An important issue to resolve will be whether the New Instrument will deal with *ex situ* high seas resources or only *in situ* resources. It is unclear whether it would apply to all of Antarctica's genetic resources (land and sea). Also, it is

183 *Biological Prospecting in Antarctica*, above n 16, p 5.
184 See, eg, Thomas Greiber, *Access and Benefit Sharing in Relation to Marine Genetic Resources from Areas Beyond National Jurisdiction: A Possible Way Forward*, Study Paper (Federal Agency for Nature Conservation, 2011); Kristina Gjerde *et al.*, *Regulatory and Governance Gaps in the International Regime for the Conservation and Sustainable Use of Marine Biodiversity in Areas Beyond National Jurisdiction*, Environmental Policy and Law Papers (International Union for the Conservation of Nature, 2008).
185 *UNCLOS*, Arts 86–120.
186 *UNCLOS*, Arts 133–191.
187 '[N]othing in the present Treaty shall prejudice or in any way affect the rights, or the exercise of the rights, of any State under international law with regard to the high seas within that area': *Antarctic Treaty*, Art VI.
188 *UNCLOS*, Arts 268(e), 270, 271, 272, 273 and 274.
189 *UNCLOS*, Arts 269 (d) and (e).
190 *UNCLOS*, Art 268(a).
191 *UNCLOS*, Arts 266(2), 268(d) and 269(d).
192 *UNCLOS*, Art 244(2).
193 *UNCLOS*, Art 311(2).
194 *New Instrument Resolution*, above n 7, [2].
195 *Protocol*, Art 4(4).

unclear whether it will tailor the benefits arising from Antarctica's genetic resources to support the *Antarctic Treaty*'s collective purpose 'in the interests of science and the progress of all [hu]mankind'. If the benefits flow toward a purpose (similar to the Plant Treaty framework below), it will be interesting to see if they flow to a broader purpose concerning the whole of the world's oceans under UNCLOS or only the Antarctic Treaty System's more narrow knowledge sharing, conservation and peaceful purposes.

ii. The FAO's Plant Treaty model

The Plant Treaty creates a Multilateral System for a negotiated selection of plant genetic resources used for food and agriculture[196] using a Standard Material Transfer Agreement (SMTA) for all exchanges[197] and removing the need for bilateral negotiations between Contracting Parties for each resource.[198] It does not apply to genetic resources used for other purposes such as pharmaceuticals,[199] which continue to require negotiation on a bilateral basis under the CBD. The Multilateral System does not apply to aquatic animal genetic resources. However, arguably the definition of 'plant genetic resources for food and agriculture' (PGRFA) is broad enough to include aquatic plants.[200] Annex 1 (listing the plants to which the Multilateral System applies) does not currently list aquatic plants but there appears to be no impediment to include other materials[201] and Contracting Parties may decide to provide facilitated access to these resources.[202] Recipients cannot claim intellectual property that limits facilitated access to PGRFA 'in the form' received from the Multilateral System.[203] If a recipient prevents others from using any product they develop using materials from the System they must share a percentage of their commercial benefits with an international fund.[204] Under this cooperative arrangement and through a SMTA, Contracting Parties provide access to each other's PGRFA for research, breeding and training subject to benefit sharing arrangements in the areas of technology transfer, information exchange, capacity building and the benefits of commercialisation.[205] The Governing Body has the power to sanction violators of the SMTA by excluding them from obtaining other resources within the Multilateral System.[206]

---

196 *Plant Treaty*, Art 3.
197 *Plant Treaty*, Art 10.
198 Greiber *et al.*, above n 25, p 34.
199 *Plant Treaty*, Art 12(3)(a).
200 Humphries, above n 61, 86.
201 *Plant Treaty*, Art 11(2).
202 *Plant Treaty*, Arts 15(3) and (4).
203 *Plant Treaty*, Art 12(3)(d).
204 *Plant Treaty*, Art 13(2)(d).
205 *Plant Treaty*, Arts 12(3)(a) and 13(2).
206 *Plant Treaty*, Art 11(4).

Under the Plant Treaty, the benefits 'should flow primarily, directly or indirectly, to farmers in all countries, especially in developing countries and countries with economies in transition, who conserve and sustainably utilize [PGRFA]'.[207] The Multilateral System includes the physical samples as well as certain digital resources,[208] although it does not extend to sharing commercially sensitive knowledge[209] such as that controlled by intellectual property claims. The Multilateral System's Global Information System on Plant Genetic Resources for Food and Agriculture 'integrates and augments existing systems to create the global entry point to information and knowledge for strengthening the capacity for PGRFA conservation, management and utilization'.[210] In other words, it is a 'conglomeration of existing (and future) systems', rather than a single database[211] and is built on cooperation between Contracting Parties to the Plant Treaty.[212] In summary, the Plant Treaty provides a model where *ex situ* resources and their digital components are held in trust and can only be freely accessed for a defined purpose. The benefits from their subsequent use do not flow to the provider *per se* but towards fulfilling a common purpose through a Multilateral Fund created under the Plant Treaty.

Apart from the Plant Treaty which could only potentially apply to Antarctica's *ex situ* plant genetic resources, the CBD's territorial bilateral approach is the norm for ABS rules globally.[213] This bilateral approach has limitations when dealing with Antarctica's *ex situ* genetic resources because it depends on resolving temporal and spatial complexities outlined above for each accession. The collective multilateral approach under the Plant Treaty also has challenges. For example, a similar closed list approach to aquatic genetic resources is limited by the fact that these resources could include thousands of species with many yet to be discovered[214] and the Antarctic Treaty System structure has no governing body capable of holding sanctioning powers for contraventions of ABS rules. However, unlike the territorial bilateral approach where the

---

207 *Plant Treaty*, Art 13(3).
208 *Plant Treaty*, Art 12(3)(c).
209 Charles Lawson, 'Information, Intellectual Property and the Global Information System for Plant Genetic Resources for Food and Agriculture' (2015) 26 *Australian Intellectual Property Journal* 27, 37.
210 Governing Body of the International Treaty on Plant Genetic Resources for Food and Agriculture, *Sixth Session of the Governing Body of the International Treaty on Plant Genetic Resources for Food and Agriculture* (2015) IT/GB-6/15/Report, Appendix A, Annex 1, p 10.
211 Lawson, above n 209, 36.
212 *Plant Treaty*, Art 17.
213 There are other specialised multilateral mechanisms that do not yet apply to Antarctica's *ex situ* genetic resources such as the World Health Assembly, *Pandemic Influenza Preparedness: Sharing of Influenza Viruses and Access to Vaccines and other Benefits* (2011) WHA64/5, Resolution 64.5, Agenda item 13.1 available at <apps.who.int/gb/ebwha/pdf_files/WHA64/A64_R5-en.pdf> (accessed 20 August 2017). The PIP framework only applies to the sharing of H5N1 and other influenza viruses with human pandemic potential: at Art 3.
214 *IWG Intersessional Workshops*, above n 68, [49].

provider is responsible for access as well as being the recipient of benefits that flow from their subsequent use, this purpose driven collective multilateral approach breaks the ABS territorial nexus so that the provider country grants *access* but the *benefits* flow to the collective to achieve a particular goal.

Whether the ABS model to be adopted by the New Instrument will resolve the complex jurisdictional issues surrounding Antarctica's *ex situ* genetic resources remains to be seen. What is clear is that leaving ABS to the current patchwork of ABS regimes runs the risk that the benefits from the use of Antarctica's *ex situ* genetic resources will not flow back to the conservation of the Antarctic Treaty Area or to achieve freedom of scientific investigation as envisaged by the *Antarctic Treaty*. More creative options under the existing frameworks should be explored in the meantime. The following section gives insights into an often overlooked 'multilateral' approach to accessing and sharing the physical and digital genetic resource – the framework of defences for patent infringements under the TRIPS Agreement of the World Trade Organization (WTO).

4.5 A patent solution for regulating Antarctica's *ex situ* resources

While there is much debate about the impacts of patents on the scientific objectives of the *Antarctic Treaty*, there has been less attention on how the framework of defences under TRIPS might offer an existing multilateral approach to sharing knowledge and technology concerning Antarctica's *ex situ* resources in a way that is consistent with the *Antarctic Treaty*'s objectives.[215] TRIPS provides an international framework for national patent laws of WTO Members. Its objective is to promote 'technological innovation and for the transfer and dissemination of technology to the mutual advantage of producers and users of technological knowledge, in a manner conducive to social and economic welfare and to a balance of rights and obligations'.[216] To this end, TRIPS sets out a minimum level of patent protection[217] but leaves it up to each Member to determine the means by which this level of protection is secured in their legal system.[218] Generally, patent holders have exclusive rights over their inventions that are either products or processes,[219] subject to disclosure of their invention.[220]

215 For an analysis of the patent debate, see Julia Jabour-Green and Dianne Nicol, 'Bioprospecting in Areas Outside National Jurisdiction: Antarctica and the Southern Ocean' (2003) 4 *Melbourne Journal of International Law* 76.

216 *TRIPS*, Art 7.

217 *TRIPS*, Art 27.

218 World Trade Organization, *Canada – Patent Protection of Pharmaceutical Products* (2000) WT/DS114/R (17 March 2000), [4.30] (*Canada – Pharmaceutical Products Case*), citing *TRIPS*, Art 1(1).

219 *TRIPS*, Art 28.

220 *TRIPS*, Art 29.

The ATCM has raised questions about whether patents' exclusive rights interfere with freedom of scientific investigation in accordance with the *Antarctic Treaty* and whether the confidentiality required prior to lodgement of a patent claim is compatible with obligations for the free exchange of scientific observations and results.[221] A concern is that broad patent claims relating to Antarctica's genetic resources could restrict access to the physical and digital resource for further research or use by others and direct the benefits towards the patent holder, rather than the provider of the genetic resource on behalf of the Antarctic Treaty System.[222] WTO Members, however, have the option to include exceptions and defences in their national laws that regulate the circumstances in which patented genetic resources and their derivatives can be shared without the authorisation of the patent holder. This defence framework has a multilateral effect because the circumstances for sharing do not depend on bilateral agreements between parties to a given transaction. Patent law defences may explicitly provide that contractual agreements attempting to limit a particular defence are void.[223] While patent laws are national in operation, TRIPS and its defence framework have evolved to manage the globalised use of patented products and processes across multiple national jurisdictions.

Exceptions against infringement must be in accordance with the 'three step test' under Article 30 of TRIPS. They must: (a) be limited in their impact on rights; (b) 'not unreasonably conflict with a normal exploitation of the patent'; and (c) 'not unreasonably prejudice the legitimate interests of the patent owner, taking account of the legitimate interests of third parties'.[224] Examples under national laws include experimental use exceptions,[225] non-commercial use exceptions,[226] breeding exceptions,[227] regulatory review exceptions[228] and innocent bystander exceptions.[229] TRIPS also allows other circumstances where the permission of the patent holder is not required for the use of a patented invention.[230] Examples include the principle of exhaustion,[231] compulsory licensing[232] and temporary presence defences.[233] The purpose of the

---

221 *A Gap Analysis,* above n 26, p 16.
222 See Jabour-Green and Nicol, above n 215, 94.
223 See, eg, *Bundesgesetz über die Erfindungspatente 1954* [Federal Act on Patents for Inventions 1954] (Switzerland), Art 35a(Abis)(4).
224 *TRIPS,* Art 30 as interpreted in *Canada – Pharmaceutical Products Case,* above n 218, [7.20]–[7.21], [7.31] and [7.54].
225 See, eg, Australia's *Patents Act 1990* (Cth) s 119C.
226 See, eg, *Patents Act 1977* (UK) c 37, s 60(5)(a).
227 See, eg, Germany's *Patentgesetz 1980* [Patent Law 1980] § 11(2a).
228 See, eg, Australia's *Patents Act 1990* (Cth) s 119A.
229 See, eg, Switzerland's *Bundesgesetz über die Erfindungspatente 1954* [Federal Act on Patents for Inventions 1954], Art 9(1)(f).
230 The following examples are not restricted by the three step test in above n 224 and accompanying text.
231 See *TRIPS,* Art 6.
232 See TRIPS, Art 31.
233 See *Paris Convention for the Protection of Industrial Property* (1967) 828 UNTS 305, Art 5ter(1) and *TRIPS,* Art 2(1).

following discussion is not to enter the debate about whether TRIPS achieves technology transfer. Rather, the aim is to give insight into how TRIPS-compliant defences approach the sharing of patented Antarctic genetic resource inventions with respect to two of the legal temporal and spatial complexities identified above for the ABS of Antarctica's *ex situ* resources under the CBD and the Nagoya Protocol. These complexities are: first, how to fairly approach changes of intent between commercial and non-commercial uses of the resources; and second, how to overcome the shortcomings of the CBD's geographical origin approach to ABS including the territorial restrictions of national laws, and the extent to which they capture the ABS of digital resources separate to the ABS of physical resources.

A. Change of intent for purpose of use

The ATCM has identified that 'there is a time lag of approximately 8–10 years between developing sufficient knowledge base about an [Antarctic] organism, and a commercial product based on that organism entering the market'.[234] This time lag raises questions about how to deal with situations where the recipient has originally accessed the genetic resource with the intent of non-commercial research but subsequently the recipient or third parties use the genetic resource for a commercial purpose. The distinction between commercial and non-commercial uses is important for the effective operation of several aspects of the CBD and the Nagoya Protocol's ABS regime. The distinction helps to distinguish between the different modalities of ensuring compliance (user measures or contractual enforcement),[235] between the sharing of monetary and non-monetary benefits,[236] and between simplified and normal access conditions as outlined below.

Significantly, countries are obliged to 'create conditions to promote and encourage research which contributes to the conservation and sustainable use of biological diversity … including through simplified measures on access for non-commercial research purposes, taking into account the need to address a change of intent for such research'.[237] This provision links facilitated access with the objective that knowledge should be generated to conserve and sustainably use the resources and some commentators have argued that this requires publicly available knowledge.[238] The requirement for simplified access becomes complicated when Antarctica's *ex situ* genetic resources are in water-based as

234 *Biological Prospecting – A Way Forward*, above n 77, p 12.
235 See Humphries, above n 161, 257.
236 See Caroline von Kries and Gerd Winter, 'Defining Commercial and Non-commercial Research and Development under the Nagoya Protocol and in other Contexts' in Evanson Chege Kamau, Gerd Winter, and Peter-Tobias Stoll (eds), *Research and Development on Genetic Resources: Public Domain Approaches in Implementing the Nagoya Protocol* (Routledge, 2015) pp 60 and 65.
237 *Protocol*, Art 8(a). See also CBD, Art 15(2).
238 See Kries and Winter, above n 236, p 67.

opposed to land-based facilities. Where the resources are held in territorial waters, UNCLOS provides that 'marine scientific research ... shall be conducted only with the express consent of and under the conditions set forth by the coastal State'.[239] Given that the CBD defers to UNCLOS in the case of conflict,[240] this may create an anomalous situation where countries are obliged to create simplified access for non-commercial uses of Antarctic *ex situ* aquatic resources located in land repositories but not for the same resources in facilities located in territorial waters.[241] Given the difficulties with distinguishing between non-commercial or 'pure' research and research whose purpose is to produce a commercial outcome,[242] particularly in the area of biotechnology,[243] this complex array of ABS laws concerning the purpose of use may impede the access and exchange of scientific information about Antarctica's resources contrary to the objectives of the *Antarctic Treaty.*

Patent law can offer insights into how to treat commercial and non-commercial uses of Antarctic *ex-situ* genetic resources to fulfil the objectives of the *Antarctic Treaty.* Many countries have non-commercial use exceptions that only facilitate pure rather than commercial or applied research.[244] However, experimental use exceptions which allow use of a patented genetic resource invention that would otherwise infringe a patent holder's rights differ under national laws in whether they allow uses with ultimately non-commercial as well as commercial uses.[245] For example, the Belgian exception excludes experiments with purely commercial purposes but it applies in cases of mixed commercial and scientific purposes.[246] Emerging norms for experimental use exceptions seek to strike a balance between the two phases of research.[247] For example, the German exception does not distinguish between commercial and

239 *UNCLOS*, Art 245.

240 CBD, Art 22.

241 See Charlotte Salpin, 'The Law of the Sea: A Before and an After Nagoya?' in Elisa Morgera, Matthias Buck and Elsa Tsioumani (eds), *The 2010 Nagoya Protocol on Access and Benefit-Sharing in Perspective: Implications for International Law and Implementation Challenges* (Martinus Nijhoff, 2013) pp 149 and 158.

242 Australian Law Reform Commission, *Genes and Ingenuity: Gene Patenting and Human Health*, Report No 99 (ALRC, 2004) p 329 [13.49].

243 Advisory Council on Intellectual Property, *Patents and Experimental Use* (ACIP, 2005) p 19.

244 See Richard Gold and Yann Joly, *Experts' Study on Exclusions from Patentable Subject Matter and Exceptions and Limitations to the Rights*, World Intellectual Property Organization Standing Committee on the Law of Patents (2010) SCP/15/3, Annex 6 (*The Patent System and Research Freedom: A Comparative Study*) p 40.

245 Ibid, p 41.

246 See Geertrui van Overwalle and Esther van Zimmeren, 'Reshaping Belgian Patent Law: The Revision of the Research Exemption and the Introduction of a Compulsory License for Public Health' (2006) 64 *Chizaiken Forum* 44.

247 Matthew Rimmer, *Intellectual Property and Biotechnology: Biological Inventions* (Edward Elgar, 2008) p 182.

non-commercial uses, as long as the ultimate goal is to promote technical or scientific progress.[248]

ABS laws concerning Antarctica's genetic resources could take a similar pragmatic approach to commercial and non-commercial phases of research that may concern the physical or digital Antarctic *ex situ* genetic resource. This is not inconsistent with the way in which the Antarctic Treaty System regulates Antarctica's *in situ* resources. None of the Antarctic Treaty System treaties explicitly regulate bioprospecting for *in situ* genetic resources of potential value.[249] Bioprospecting, however, is a scientific activity, even if it is ultimately for a commercial purpose, and indirectly falls within the access provisions of the Antarctic Treaty System[250] as well as the benefit sharing provisions of Article III of the *Antarctic Treaty*.[251] The requirement to record the purpose of use at the time of taking the resource does not appear to affect whether access will proceed.[252] The focus of access restrictions under the *Antarctic Treaty's* prior notification and the Madrid Protocol's and the CCAMLR's permit systems[253] is arguably concerned with the accumulation of scientific information for the protection of Antarctica's environment and for the benefit of humankind, rather than with questions of whether the access will result in commercial or non-commercial uses. Unlike under the CBD where the conditions of access may be dependent upon the purpose of use of the genetic resource, a specialised instrument concerning Antarctic genetic resources (such as the New Instrument) could follow the German experimental use exception approach because the *Antarctic Treaty* does not distinguish between the two forms of uses for the purposes of ABS, as long as the ultimate goal is to promote technical or scientific progress.

B. *Geographical origin of the genetic resource*

At the heart of the sovereignty territorial approach to ABS under the CBD is the need to determine the geographical origin of the genetic resources to ascertain from whom permission is required for the resources' access and towards whom the benefits of their use should flow. The preceding sections have argued that because the *Antarctic Treaty* does not apply to *ex situ* genetic resources but the CBD may apply on a case-by case basis, the 'origin' becomes

---

248 *Clinical Trials II*, Bundesgerichtshof [German Federal Court of Justice],X ZR 68/94, 17 April 1997 reported in (1997) 135 BGHZ 217, quoted in Annette Kur and Thomas Dreier, *European Intellectual Property Law: Text, Cases and Materials* (Edward Elgar, 2013) p 120.

249 David Leary, 'Bi-polar Disorder? Is Bioprospecting an Emerging Issue for the Arctic as well as Antarctica?' (2008) 17(1) *Reciel* 41, 44.

250 See above n 29 and accompanying text.

251 Dagmar Lohan and Sam Johnston, *The International Regime for Bioprospecting: Existing Policies and Emerging Issues for Antarctica* (United Nations University Institute of Advanced Studies, 2003) p 11.

252 See above n 61 and accompanying text.

253 See above n 36 and following text.

the repository in which the physical resource is held, which means that the benefits from the physical or digital resource do not automatically flow back to the Antarctic Treaty Area. This is especially problematic for the use of Antarctica's digital resources. If a bilateral contract, similar to the *Micro B3 Agreement*,[254] incorporates benefits from the use of the digital resource derived from an *ex situ* genetic resource, the biological origin is traced through the viral licence clause back to the accession of the geographical location of the physical *ex situ* resource in a national jurisdiction to which the CBD applies and not necessarily the original *in situ* location in Antarctic waters. Derivatives including digital resources that are accessed independently of genetic resources fall outside the scope of the ABS obligations.[255] A key question therefore is how to ensure that subsequent uses of *ex situ* Antarctic digital resources, such as those that are part of the DNA barcode project,[256] and that do not depend on access to the physical samples, are held accountable to information sharing obligations under the *Antarctic Treaty.*

Patent law largely deals with the knowledge component of the genetic resource and can give insights into how to conceptualise and regulate the sharing of the digital resource independently from the physical resource. Instead of using the geographical origin as the link between the physical and the digital resource, emerging norms in Europe incorporate a functional temporal approach for clarifying the point at which a derivative is sufficiently removed from the genetic resource invention on which it is based to no longer be protected under patent law.[257] For example, under patent law, protection generally extends to every plant or animal containing the inventive element or resulting from a patented process.[258] This means that a broad patent claim concerning a fish's gene promoter such as an antifreeze protein may have the same outcome as patenting the fish and a patent holder may be able to prevent others from using it for breeding purposes. The question will come down to the extent to which a new strain may contain the patented inventive element before a user is liable for infringement.[259] For example, would a user be liable for infringement if an antifreeze gene promoter from an initial patented transgenic fish is present, but not expressed or 'switched on' in subsequent fish strains that are the result of a cross between the transgenic fish and another strain incorporating different genetic combinations?[260] An emerging European approach suggests

---

254 See above n 174 and accompanying text.
255 See above n 165 and accompanying text.
256 See above n 107 and accompanying text.
257 *Monsanto Technology LLC v Cefetra BV* (C-428/08) [2010] ECR I-6765, I-6806–7 [50], citing *European Biotechnological Directive* [1998] OJ L 213/13, Art 9.
258 Viola Prifti, 'The Breeding Exemption in Patent Law: Analysis of Compliance with Article 30 of the *TRIPS* Agreement' (2013) 16 *Journal of World Intellectual Property* 218, 218.
259 Fran Humphries, 'Shellfish Patents Krill Experimentation…Defences for Sharing Patented Aquatic Genetic Materials in Aquaculture' (2015) 37(4) *European Intellectual Property Review* 210, 213.
260 Ibid.

that a patented trait may be *present* in material derived from the invention without attracting infringement, but that a patent may only be protected when the patented trait is *performing its function at the time of* the alleged infringement (not merely present but also expressed).[261] This clarifies when functionality is relevant for proprietary interests – at the time of the use that constitutes infringement, rather than at the time of the original accession or some other indefinite time.

Applying patent law's functional temporal approach to an Antarctic *ex situ* digital resource means that the functionality of the *in situ* genetic resource could be a more relevant benchmark than geographical location when determining the biological origin for the purposes of benefit sharing. Under this approach, the subsequent use of an Antarctic digital resource may trigger benefit sharing under Article III of the *Antarctic Treaty* if the characteristics of the original *in situ* resource are merely present in the resulting product or process. However, these benefit sharing obligations could only be limited by legitimate proprietary interests over the resulting patented product that expresses the *functional* characteristics of the original resource at the time of its use. In this way, subsequent uses of *ex situ* Antarctic digital resources that are acquired independently of the physical sample could fulfil information sharing obligations under the *Antarctic Treaty* while not offending TRIPS obligations.

Several commentators suggest how territorial limitations of the CBD's ABS concept could be overcome using multilateral models such as the Plant Treaty.[262] The present chapter highlights how patent laws are similarly evolving to overcome the limitations of the territorial approach for sharing patented genetic resource inventions that span multiple jurisdictions in the globalised market. The way in which the principle of exhaustion and temporary vessel defences can achieve multilateral objectives within national regimes has been argued elsewhere.[263] Another example of a cooperative multilateral approach is the framework for compulsory licensing as amended by the 2001 *Doha Ministerial Declaration on TRIPS* (Doha Declaration)[264] that may prove insightful in the way it promotes technology transfer and benefit sharing to fulfil a global objective.

Compulsory licensing is a type of non-voluntary authorisation to use a patent holder's intellectual property without their permission but in return for a reasonable set fee.[265] It may also operate as a defence, for example, for a

261 *Monsanto Technology LLC v Cefetra BV* (C-428/08) [2010] ECR I-6765, I-6806–7 [50], citing *European Biotechnological Directive* [1998] OJ L 213/13, Art 9.
262 See above n 196 and accompanying text.
263 See Humphries, above n 161, 266.
264 World Trade Organisation, *Declaration on the TRIPS Agreement and Public Health* (2001) WT/MIN(01)/DEC/2 (*Doha Declaration*).
265 Coenraad Visser, *Experts' Study on Exclusions from Patentable Subject Matter and Exceptions and Limitations to the Rights*, World Intellectual Property Organization Standing Committee on the Law of Patents (2010) SCP/15/3, Annex 5 (*Patent Exceptions and Limitations in the Health Context*) pp 10–11.

breeder using a patented aquatic genetic resource to create new strains[266] or a researcher using the resource to create a new drug subject to reasonable remuneration to the patent holder. The requirements for compulsory licences are generally standard in all patent laws[267] in accordance with the minimum requirements under Article 31 of TRIPS.[268] One of the minimum requirements is that the licence must be primarily for the supply of the domestic market.[269] This effectively limited the ability of countries that could not make pharmaceutical products from importing cheaper generics from countries where pharmaceuticals are patented.[270] In response to paragraph 6 of the Doha Declaration,[271] the WTO's General Council decided to waive Article 31(f). This waiver effectively allows generic copies made under compulsory licences to be exported to countries that lack production capacity if certain procedures and conditions are followed.[272] Eligible importing and exporting WTO Members 'are encouraged to use the system set out in [the] Decision in a way which would promote' the 'transfer of technology and capacity building in the pharmaceutical sector'.[273]

A similar cooperative approach to technology transfer that achieves a particular purpose could be applied to the ABS of Antarctica's *ex situ* genetic resources. If an *in situ* Antarctic genetic resource was originally acquired in accordance with the CBD so that a jurisdiction's national ABS laws apply to a given Antarctic genetic resource located within its national repository, that country has the sovereign right to restrict other countries or people from using it for research, breeding or other purposes. The Nagoya Protocol's innovative 'user measures' require Contracting Parties to take measures to comply with the provider country's access requirements, to address non-compliance with those requirements, and to cooperate with other Contracting Parties in cases

---

266 Humphries, above n 259, 217.
267 Visser, above n 265, p 10.
268 For example, each case must be considered on its merits; the applicant must generally have attempted to obtain a licence from the patentee; a licence must be limited in scope and duration to the purpose for which it is granted, may not be exclusive, may not be assigned, must be primarily for the supply of the domestic market, may be terminated if circumstances leading to it cease to exist, subject to the licensee's legitimate interests; and the patent holder must receive adequate remuneration; *TRIPS*, Art 31.
269 *TRIPS*, Art 31(f).
270 'Decision Removes Final Patent Obstacle to Cheap Drug Imports' (World Trade Organization Press Release, Doc no. 03–4558, PRESS/350 30 August 2003) p 1, available at <https://www.wto.org/english/news_e/pres03_e/pr350_e.htm> (accessed 20 August 2017).
271 'WTO members with insufficient or no manufacturing capacities in the pharmaceutical sector could face difficulties in making effective use of compulsory licensing under the TRIPS Agreement'; Doha Declaration, [6].
272 *Implementation of paragraph 6 of the Doha Declaration on the TRIPS Agreement and Public Health* (World Trade Organization General Council Decision, 30 August 2003) [2]–[3].
273 Ibid [7].

of alleged non-compliance.[274] However, using the compulsory licensing approach, by collective agreement either through the Conference of the Parties to the CBD or by membership in the Antarctic Treaty System, countries could recognise the sovereign right to regulate genetic resources within their jurisdictions but waive access obligations, including compliance with user measures, in relation to those genetic resources within their repositories that originated from Antarctic waters. As mentioned above, there is precedent under the Nagoya Protocol for allowing more simplified or relaxed ABS procedures for using genetic resources but only in relation to non-commercial purposes.[275] The compulsory licensing approach above, however, recognises that even requirements that protect commercial interests can be relaxed to fulfil a global purpose, in that case, to ensure poorer countries have access to affordable medicine which indirectly benefits all of humankind.

Under this approach, while the provider would not be able to limit the exchange or use of an Antarctic *ex situ* genetic resource that it provides, it would receive a reasonable set fee from the recipient at the time of its provision. The unlimited exchange or use of an Antarctic *ex situ* genetic resource in the form received from the recipient would mean that the benefits of using the genetic resource are not directed back to the nation granting access but are instead fulfilling the *Antarctic Treaty*'s primary benefit sharing requirement of freedom of scientific investigation, including the exchange and free availability of scientific observations and results of Antarctica's resources for the benefit of all of humankind.[276] This approach is also consistent with the technology transfer obligations under the CBD (as distinct from its ABS provisions) for the transfer of information and technologies that make use of genetic resources, not only towards the provider of the resource but towards all CBD Parties, particularly least-developed ones.[277]

4.6 Conclusion

There is a mounting argument that leaving regulation of Antarctic *ex situ* genetic resources to the complex matrix of ABS systems outside the Antarctic Treaty Area undermines the *Antarctic Treaty*'s principles including international cooperation and freedom of scientific investigation that 'accords with the interests of science and the progress of all [hu]mankind.' The complexity of ABS rules is not surprising when considering the unique governance arrangements in Antarctica where sovereign rights are on hold and the regulation of *ex situ* resources is beyond the reach of the Antarctic Treaty System. What is surprising is the extent of uncertainty relating to the status of Antarctica's *ex situ* physical and digital resources under the CBD's and the Nagoya Protocol's

---

274 *Protocol*, Arts 15 and 16.
275 *Protocol*, Art 8(a).
276 *Antarctic Treaty*, Art III.
277 CBD, Arts 16 and 19.

bilateral territorial ABS system. The status needs to be determined on a case-by-case basis depending on the timing and circumstances of the original extraction from Antarctic waters as well as a temporal link between the physical and digital resource. This determination is almost impossible without effective coordination between *ex situ* facilities. Unfortunately however, information repositories often contain data in forms that are not easily shared with each other's systems, and coordination of aquatic gene banks is lagging behind similar repositories holding terrestrial germplasm. The result is a complicated *ad hoc* global exchange system based on the territorial origin of the genetic resource where the benefits flow to the provider country and not the Antarctic Treaty Area to meet the *Antarctic Treaty*'s objectives and principles.

Trying to find a fair and equitable solution that supports the *Antarctic Treaty*'s principles of cooperation and freedom of scientific investigation requires a search for a common ground between the CBD's bilateral territorial approach and the *Antarctic Treaty*'s cooperative commons approach to ABS. One option is a multilateral approach similar to the Plant Treaty that breaks the ABS territorial nexus so that the provider country grants access but the benefits flow to the collective to achieve a particular goal. Whether the New Instrument under UNCLOS will incorporate an approach similar to the Plant Treaty framework for aquatic genetic resources remains to be seen. A multilateral model that already applies to Antarctica's *ex situ* patented genetic resource inventions is the framework of TRIPS-compliant patent law defences, which offers existing practical solutions to the territorial regulation of increasingly global genetic resource inventions. This chapter has offered insights into how the defence framework approaches two of the challenges of ABS systems: effectively overcoming the blurred practical distinction between commercial and non-commercial uses that differentiate ABS rules; and overcoming the shortcomings of the geographical origin approach to ABS including the territorial restrictions of national laws and the extent to which they capture the ABS of digital resources separate to the ABS of physical resources.

At the time of writing it is too early to tell whether the scope of the New Instrument under UNCLOS will include Antarctica's *ex situ* genetic resources. Despite the flaws of leaving the increasing use of Antarctica's genetic resources up to national bilateral ABS laws based on the CBD, ATCM Consultative Parties appear to be taking a wait-and-see approach in the hope of riding out the regulatory storm that is brewing. In the meantime, there is ample scope for investigating creative TRIPS-compliant solutions for sharing *ex situ* resources that support the *Antarctic Treaty*'s objective of free exchange of information and resources in the 'interests of science and the progress of all [hu]mankind.'

5 Nomenclature as a standardised metadata system for ordering and accessing information about plants[*]

Charles Lawson

5.1 Introduction

Biological taxonomy involves ordering organisms into groupings and has a number of purposes – identifying an unfamiliar organism, a convenient and practical way to know what is being discussed, an orderly system for storing and retrieving information, showing kinship relationships between organisms, constructing classes about which inductive generalisations might be made, and so on.[1] The organism once ordered into a particular grouping, however, then needs a classification identifier (a name) so that individuals in a particular grouping can be distinguished from individuals in other groupings: '[t]he botanist is distinguished from the layman in that [s/]he can give a name which fits one particular plant and not another, and which can be understood by anyone the world over'.[2] A name is, therefore, fundamental to being able to communicate about organisms[3] (especially in commerce)[4] and as an anchor for mobilising, serving, integrating and exchanging information[5] – 'names are

* The research assistance of Dr Clare Morrison is acknowledged and appreciated.

1 See Frederick Warburton, 'The Purpose of Classifications' (1967) 26 *Systematic Zoology* 241, 241–242. See also Ernst Mayr, *The Growth of Biological Thought: Diversity, Evolution and Inheritance* (Harvard University Press, 1982) pp 148–149.

2 Carl Linnaeus, *Critica Botanica* (Leyden, 1737) No 210, cited in William Stern, 'The Background of Linnaeus's Contribution to the Nomenclature and Methods of Systematic Biology' (1959) 8 *Systematic Biology* 4, 7–8.

3 See Roger Spence, Rob Cross and Peter Lumley, *Plant Names: A Guide to Botanical Nomenclature* (3rd edition, CSIRO Publishing, 2007) p 1; Sandra Knapp, Gerardo Lamas, Eimear Nic Lughadha and Gianfranco Novarino, 'Stability or Stasis in the Names of Organisms: The Evolving Codes of Nomenclature' (2004) 359 *Philosophical Transactions of the Royal Society of London B: Biological Sciences* 611, 611–612; H W Rickett, 'The Status of Botanical Nomenclature' (1959) 8 *Systematic Zoology* 22, 23–24.

4 See Staffan Müller-Wille, 'Nature as a Marketplace: The Political Economy of Linnaean Botany' (2003) 35 *History of Political Economy* 154, 157–158.

5 Charles Hussey, Yde de Jong and David Remsen, 'Actual Usage of Biological Nomenclature and its Implications for Data Integrators; A National, Regional and Global Perspective' (2008) 1950 *ZooTaxa* 5, 5.

mere cyphers which are easier to use than lengthy descriptions'.[6] This also means that along with the development of taxonomy goes the important development of naming or nomenclature, being the technique of naming:[7]

> A *taxonomic system* is an integrated set of conventions specifying how taxonomies are to be constructed; a *nomenclatural system* is an integrated set of conventions specifying how names are to be applied – that is, for naming taxa and regulating the use of those names. These two kinds of methodological systems should not be confused with one another, though a given nomenclatural system might be considered part of a more comprehensive taxonomic system.[8]

Over the centuries nomenclature has evolved from local common names into a highly regulated and formal process based around naming codes.[9] The *International Code of Nomenclature for algae, fungi and plants* (*Plant Code*)[10] addresses the scientific needs of botanists and taxonomists and the *International Code of Nomenclature for Cultivated Plants* (*Cultivated Plant Code*)[11] addresses the special requirements for plants in cultivation including horticulture, forestry, agriculture and silviculture.[12] These codes address the problems of the same plant having many names (such as *Caltha palustris* having 90 common names in the United Kingdom, 140 in Germany and 60 in France) and many different plants having the same name (such as commonly named bluebells being named *Wahlenbergia saxicola* in New Zealand, *Phacelia*

---

6 D Gledhill, *The Names of Plants* (Cambridge University Press, 1985) p 3.

7 See Werner Greuter, 'Recent Developments in International Biological Nomenclature' (2004) *Turkish Journal of Botany* 17, 18. See also Mark Costello, Robert May and Nigel Stork, 'Can We Name Earth's Species Before They Go Extinct?' (2013) 339(6118) *Science* 413.

8 Kevin de Queiroz, 'The Linnaean Hierarchy and the Evolutionization of Taxonomy, with Emphasis on the Problem of Nomenclature' (1997) 15 *Aliso* 125, 126.

9 For general historical accounts of naming see, for examples, Anna Pavord, *The Naming of Names: The Search for Order in the World of Plants* (Bloomsbury, 2005); G Perry, 'Nomenclature Stability and the Botanical Code: A Historical Review' in D Hawksworth (ed) *Improving the Stability of Names: Needs and Options* (Koeltz Scientific Books, 1991) pp 79–93; Gledhill, above n 6, pp 5–22; and so on.

10 J McNeill, F Barrie, W Buck, V Demoulin, W Greuter, D Hawksworth, P Herendeen, S Knapp, K Marhold, J Prado, W Prud'Homme Van Reine, G Smith and J Wiersema, *International Code of Nomenclature for algae, fungi and plants (Melbourne Code) adopted by the Eighteenth International Botanical Congress Melbourne, Australia, July 2011* (Koeltz Scientific Books, 2012) (*International Code of Nomenclature for algae, fungi and plants*).

11 C Brickell, C Alexander, J David, W Hetterscheid, A Leslie, V Malecot, X Jin and J Cubey, *International Code of Nomenclature for Cultivated Plants* (CABI, 2009) (*International Code of Nomenclature for Cultivated Plants*).

12 See Roger Spencer and Robert Cross, 'The *International Code of Botanical Nomenclature* (ICBN), the *International Code of Nomenclature for Cultivated Plants* (ICNCP), and the Cultigen' (2007) 56 *Taxon* 938, 938.

whitlavia in the United States and *Hyacinthoides non-scripta* in the United Kingdom).[13] The purposes of these codes, therefore, is to regulate the form of naming so that a plant only has one name and that name remains the same over long periods of time.[14] This is critically important because the name of a plant represents 'the backbone upon which virtually all biological information is organised'.[15] And as biological information is increasingly being collected, stored, searched, retrieved and integrated in computers these names can be a standardised metadata system for ordering and accessing that information.[16] In the sense used here: '[m]etadata is structured information that describes, explains, locates, or otherwise makes it easier to retrieve, use, or manage an information resource'.[17] Putting this slightly differently, '[m]etadata is ... data about data or information about information'.[18] So, for example, the plant name *Phaius australis* is a metadata structure for information about the plant addressing its legal status as a threatened species, its distribution, population dynamics, habitats, lifecycle, threat abatement and recovery plans, newsletters, and so on.[19]

This chapter is about the important role of naming plants – of tethering names to plants.[20] The purpose of this chapter is to address the developing

13 Gledhill, above n 6, pp 2–4. See also Spence, Cross and Lumley, above n 3, p 9. Some estimates are that there are approximately 2 million described species and the current Global Names Index contains approximately 20 million distinct name strings: see R Pyle, 'Towards a Global Names Architecture: The Future of Indexing Scientific Names' (2016) 550 *ZooKeys* 261, 269–270 and the references therein.

14 See the various contributions in Hawksworth, above n 9, pp 17–208.

15 Richard Pyle and Ellinor Michel, 'ZooBank: Developing a Nomenclature Tool for Unifying 250 Years of Biological Information' (2008) 1950 *ZooTaxa* 39, 40.

16 See David Patterson, Dmitry Mozzherin, David Peter Shorthouse and Anne Thessen, 'Challenges with Using Names to Link Digital Biodiversity Information' (2016) 4 *Biodiversity Data Journal* e8080 (doi: 10.3897/BDJ.4.e8080), 1–2; Pyle, above n 13, 267–273; David Patterson, Sarah Faulwetter and Alexey Shipunov, 'Principles for a Names-based Cyberinfrastructure to Serve All of Biology' (2008) 1950 *ZooTaxa* 153, 154–155. Although, notably, this is not without some problems: see David Remsen, 'The Use and Limits of Scientific Names in Biological Informatics' (2016) 550 *ZooKeys* 207.

17 See National Information Standards Organization, *Understanding Metadata* (National Information Standards Organization, 2004) p 1.

18 See ibid.

19 Department of Environment, '*Phaius australis* – Lesser Swamp-orchid', available at <http://www.environment.gov.au/cgi-bin/sprat/public/publicspecies.pl?taxon_id=5872#distribution> (accessed 18 May 2017).

20 Noting that nomenclature is important in other areas of the scientific endeavour: zoology – International Commission on Zoological Nomenclature, *International Code of Zoological Nomenclature* (4th Edition, International Trust for Zoological Nomenclature, 1999); bacteria – Stephen Lapage, Peter Sneath, Erwin Lessel, V Skerman, H Seeliger and W Clark, *International Code of Nomenclature of Bacteria: Bacteriological Code* (ASM Press, 1992); viruses – Andrew King, Michael Adams and Elliot Lefkowitz, *Virus Taxonomy: Classification and Nomenclature of Viruses*, Ninth Report of the International Committee on Taxonomy of Viruses

challenges for a suitable metadata structure for organising biological information under the access and benefit sharing (ABS) arrangements for genetic resources. The generalised international ABS regulatory scheme covering *all* genetic resources (except human genetic resources)[21] is set out under the United Nations' *Convention on Biological Diversity* (CBD)[22] and the *Nagoya Protocol on Access to Genetic Resources and the Fair and Equitable Sharing of Benefits Arising from their Utilization to the Convention on Biological Diversity* (Nagoya Protocol).[23] There are then ABS specific compatible schemes now directed to some agricultural plants under the Food and Agriculture Organization of the United Nations' *International Treaty on Plant Genetic Resources for Food and Agriculture* (Plant Treaty),[24] and human pandemic influenza virus under the World Health Organization's (WHO) *Pandemic Influenza Preparedness Framework for the Sharing of Influenza Viruses and Access to Vaccines and Other Benefits* (PIP Framework).[25] There are also schemes developing under the United Nations' *Law of the Sea Convention*,[26] and for various classes of organisms like microorganisms, livestock and forestry, although these are in the very early stages of negotiation.[27] The founding principle of each of these regulatory forms is recognition that Nation States have sovereignty over the genetic resources within their jurisdictions and the

(Elsevier, 2011); plant communities or 'syntaxa' – H Weber, J Moravec and J-P Theurillat, 'International Code of Phytosociological Nomenclature, 3rd Edition' (2000) 11 *Journal of Vegetation Science* 739; genes and proteins – Julia White, Hester Wain, Elspeth Bruford and Sue Povey, 'Promoting a Standard Nomenclature for Genes and Proteins' (1999) 402 *Nature* 347; and so on.

21 See Conference of the Parties to the Convention on Biological Diversity, *Access to Genetic Resources and Benefit Sharing: Legislation, Administrative and Policy Information* (1995) UNEP/CBD/COP/2/13, pp 15–18. See also Conference of the Parties to the Convention on Biological Diversity, *Report of the Sixth Meeting of the Conference of the Parties to the Convention on Biological Diversity* (2002) UNEP/CBD/COP/6/20, pp 60–62 and 253–269 (Bonn Guidelines, cl 19).

22 [1993] ATS 32 (CBD).

23 Conference of the Parties to the Convention on Biological Diversity, *Report of the Tenth Meeting of the Conference of the Parties to the Convention on Biological Diversity* (2010) UNEP/CBD/COP/10/27, [103] and Annex (Decision X/1, Annex 1 (Nagoya Protocol) pp 89–109).

24 [2006] ATS 10 (Plant Treaty).

25 World Health Organization, *Pandemic Influenza Preparedness: Sharing of Influenza Viruses and Access to Vaccines and Other Benefits* (2011) A64/8, Attachment 2 (PIP Framework). This was adopted by the Member States of the World Health Organization: World Health Organization, *Pandemic Influenza Preparedness: Sharing of Influenza Viruses and Access to Vaccines and Other Benefits*, Sixty-fourth World Health Assembly (2011) WHA64.5, [1].

26 See United Nations General Assembly, *Letter Dated 13 February 2015 from the Co-Chairs of the Ad Hoc Open-ended Informal Working Group to the President of the General Assembly* (2015) A/69/780.

27 See Charles Lawson, *Regulating Genetic Resources: Access and Benefit-sharing in International Law* (Edward Elgar, 2012) pp 241–246.

authority to determine the terms and conditions for their access.[28] Each of the existing schemes then enables (or facilitates) access to genetic resources in exchange for benefit sharing, either through an individually negotiated contract between a resource holder and a bioprospector under the CBD and the Nagoya Protocol,[29] or through a Standard Material Transfer Agreement (SMTA) with fixed terms and conditions under the Plant Treaty[30] and the PIP Framework.[31] In addition to the SMTA, the PIP Framework, in particular, provides for an annual contribution from influenza vaccine, diagnostic and pharmaceutical manufacturers using a framework that is based on a formula determined by the WHO.[32] Notably, national laws implementing these schemes are either still to be implemented[33] or only cover some genetic resources within a jurisdiction.[34] Biological information about genetic resources is an important benefit under each of these schemes,[35] and naming is becoming increasingly important as the demands of information, and ordering information, about plants escalate in responding to climate change and habitat loss, and the flood of results from the massive increase in biology and environmental research.[36] While the vast majority of this information is not easily accessible or interconnected, names provide an intriguing possibility for cross-linking and seamlessly integrating this disparate information.[37] This chapter argues that names provide a metadata

28 See CBD, Arts 3 and 15; Plant Treaty, Art 10; PIP Framework, Art 1 (Principle PP11).
29 See CBD, Art 15; Nagoya Protocol, Art 6.
30 See Plant Treaty, Art 12.4.
31 See PIP Framework, Art 5.4.
32 See PIP Framework, Art 6.14.3. See also World Health Assembly, *Pandemic Influenza Preparedness: Sharing of Influenza Viruses and Access to Vaccines and Other Benefits* (2014) A67/36 Add.1, Annex ([7]-[14]).
33 The CBD has 196 parties of which only 57 have implemented some type of law, measures or instruments to regulate ABS: J C Medaglia *et al., Overview of National and Regional Measures on Access and Benefit Sharing: Challenges and Opportunities in Implementing the Nagoya Protocol* (CISDL Biodiversity & Biosafety Law Research Programme, 2014) p 9.
34 So, for example, in Australia the Commonwealth scheme only applies to genetic resources collected in 'Commonwealth areas' (*Environment Protection and Biodiversity Conservation Act 1999* (Cth), s 525; *Environment Protection and Biodiversity Conservation Regulations 2000* (Cth), reg 8A.02), and the State and Territory schemes (where they exist) only apply to some State or Territory lands ('State land or Queensland waters': *Biodiscovery Act 2004* (Qld), ss 5 and 10 and Sch; 'Commonwealth areas' in the Territory: *Biological Resources Act 2006* (NT), s 9), with the remaining lands in Commonwealth, State and Territory jurisdictions, predominately privately owned lands, subject to no formal ABS obligations, and on these privately owned lands the landholder determines the terms and conditions of access and benefit sharing according to existing land and other laws: see John Voumard, *Access to Biological Resources in Commonwealth Areas* (Commonwealth of Australia, 2000) pp 41–49.
35 See CBD, Art 17.1; Plant Treaty, Art 13.2(a); PIP Framework, Arts 6.1.2(i) and (ii).
36 See H Godfray, B Clark, I Kitching, S Mayo and M Scoble, 'The Web and the Structure of Taxonomy' (2007) 56 *Systematic Biology* 943, 943–945.
37 Pyle, above n 13, 268–269.

structure for ordering and accessing all this information, and that naming remains preferable to various disembodied metadata structures. This is because names retain the human dimension of being understandable, memorable and easily communicated that makes them widespread, stable and popular schemes.

This chapter is structured as follows: Part 2 addresses the evolving naming practices from the time of the Ancients and up to recent formal naming codes; Part 3 addresses the current formal naming codes, including the specific issues of authorship, priority, publication and types; Part 4 addresses proposals for alternative codes; and Part 5 sets out a discussion and conclusion that the current naming codes maintain their links to earlier developments with the key elements of a binomial name linked to a published description, and that the name remains a vital metadata structure for organising information about that plant despite some of the inherent problems with the naming codes.

5.2 The evolving naming practices

For modern science formal plant taxonomy really started with Theophrastus and his works *Historia Plantarum* and *De Causis Plantarum*[38] and followed the earlier work of Aristotle's *Historia Animalium* classifying animals.[39] These works trace back to the earlier metaphysics of natural kinds and essences starting from Plato's ideas about distinguishing between things we can see and their universal forms, and the conception that things could be grouped into their natural kinds that might reveal their ideal form or essence.[40] Adopting this approach meant that the essence could be identified applying intellectual intuition with the thing being named and described using words, now called methodological essentialism by philosophers[41] and typology by taxonomists[42] – 'that natural kinds have real essences which can be defined by a set of properties which are severally necessary and jointly sufficient for membership'.[43] Aristotle's great advance was to reject Plato's method of dichotomy and to consider

---

38 Noting that there remains some contest about the form of Theophrastus' works: see, for example, Benedict Einarson, 'The Manuscripts of Theophrastus' *Historia Plantarum*' (1976) 71 *Classical Philology* 67. See also Jason Tipton, *Philosophical Biology in Aristotle's Parts of Animals* (Springer, 2014); Alan Morton, *History of Botanical Science: An Account of the Development of Botany from Ancient Times to the Present Day* (Academic Press, 1981); Erwin Stresemann, *Ornithology: From Aristotle to the Present* (Harvard University Press, 1975); Geoffrey Lloyd, 'The Development of Aristotle's Theory of the Classification of Animals' (1961) 6 *Phronesis* 59.

39 See also Werner Greuter, 'The Ancient Greek Roots of Biological Sciences' (2002) 12 *Flora Mediterranea* 5.

40 See Karl Popper, *The Open Society and Its Enemies* (Princeton, 1950) p 31.

41 Ibid, pp 31–32.

42 See Robert Sokal, 'Typology and Empiricism in Taxonomy' (1962) 3 *Journal of Theoretical Biology* 230, 234–250.

43 David Hull, 'Contemporary Systematic Philosophies' (1970) 1 *Annual Review of Ecology and Systematics* 19, 38.

multiple differences at the outset: '[n]o single differentia ... either by itself or with its antecedents, can possibly express the essence of a species'.[44] Aristotle also established the concept that a species was a grouping of individuals with a common specific form so that all members of that species possess universal attributes (multiple differentia) common to all the individuals:

> The individuals comprised within a species, such as Socrates and Coriscus, are the real existences; but inasmuch as these individuals possess one common specific form, it will suffice to state that universal attributes of the species, that is, the attributes common to all its individuals, once for all, as otherwise there will be endless reiteration.[45]

Aristotle then recognised larger groupings consisting of many species with shared universal attributes that have a universal nature: 'to treat generically the universal attributes of the groups that have a common nature and contain closely allied subordinate forms'.[46] The result was that Aristotle recognised three kinds of likeness: first, the likeness or identity within a species where the differences were only between individuals where the whole and the parts were the same ('one man's nose or eye resembles another man's nose or eye');[47] secondly, a likeness of the genus where the differences are between the species such as a property ('such as colour and shape')[48] or extra parts ('for instance, some have spurs and others not');[49] and thirdly, likeness by analogy where there is a homology between the parts ('nail to hoof, hand to claw, and scale to feather').[50]

Thus Aristotle's logic was based on there being a true form and an ability to define the essence of a thing – the necessary and permanent conditions or characters of a thing that make it that thing.[51] According to this ideal, the inherent essence or nature of a thing is its definition and the word or phrase of its name designates the essence of the thing defined.[52] In the language of the predicables – genus, differentia, definition (species), property

44 Aristotle, *De Partibus Animalium*, 644 a 3–5 in William Ross (ed), *The Works of Aristotle Translated into English*, Volume 5 (translated by William Ogle; Clarendon Press, 1965). Noting, of course, that Aristotle and his contemporaries were using 'species' in the vernacular or technical logical sense rather than as a biological term that didn't arise until the end of the sixteenth century: see John Wilkins, *Species: A History of the Idea* (University of California Press, 2009) pp 231–232.

45 Aristotle, ibid, 644 a 22–28.

46 Ibid, 644 b 1–4.

47 Aristotle, *Historia Animalium*, 486 a 18 in William Ross (ed), *The Works of Aristotle Translated into English*, Volume 4 (translated by D'Arcy Wentworth Thompson; Clarendon Press, 1967).

48 Ibid, 486 b 6.

49 Ibid, 486 b 13.

50 Ibid, 486 b 20–21.

51 Aristotle, *Topica*, Book I, 4–5 in William Ross (ed), *The Works of Aristotle Translated into English*, Volume 1 (translated W Pickard-Cambridge; Oxford University Press, 1971).

52 See Karl Popper, *Conjectures and Refutations* (Basic Books, 1962) p 19.

and accident – that Aristotelian logic applied to every premise and every problem,[53] the genus 'is predicated in the category of essence of a number of things exhibiting differences in kind'[54] and the definition (species) 'is a phrase signifying a thing's essence',[55] with each genus made up of many species (definitions).[56] Using this logic, a genus and differentia taken together identifies and distinguishes one true form from another, and the definition (species) comprising the genus together with the differentia captures the essence of the thing, enabling a real (natural) classification.[57] Aristotle's lasting contribution was to define a taxon ('species') by its attributes to a higher-ranking taxon ('genus') and contrast the differences through diagnosis ('differentia') within that higher-ranking taxon ('genus').[58]

Theophrastus in *De Causis Plantarum* records that most 'wild kinds' of plants had no names and that the cultivated kinds had simple vernacular names, such as 'vine, fig, pomegranate, apple, pear, bay, [and] myrtle'.[59] Up until Carl Linnaeus applied linguistic rules (albeit just recommendations rather than strict rules),[60] nomenclatures proceeded on the basis that the non-vernacular name defined the plant or animal and this usually involved a single word for a known kind of plant (a generic word, such as Chestnut), and then an additional word or words if two or more kinds were known (a specific word with a generic word, such as Red Oak, Pin Oak, and so on).[61] As the number of known species increased 'the specific names developed into long descriptive phrases'[62] that were 'just sufficient to distinguish a given species unambiguously from all others included within the same genus'.[63] These polynomial

53　Aristotle, above n 51, 101 a 17–25. Noting there remains debate about the form of the predicables and their applications: see, for examples, Christos Evangeliou, 'Aristotle's Doctrine of Predicables and Porphyry's *Isagoge*' (1985) 23 *Journal of History of Philosophy* 15; David Ross, *Aristotle* (Methuen and Co, 1966) pp 57–58.

54　Aristotle, ibid, 102 a 32–33.

55　Ibid, 101 b 39–40.

56　Aristotle, above n 57, 644 a 34–35 and 644 b 1–9.

57　For a discussion of this logic applied to taxonomy see A Cain, 'Logic and Memory in Linnaeus's System of Taxonomy' (1958) 169 *Proceedings of the Linnaean Society of London* 144, 145–156.

58　Greuter, above n 7, 18.

59　Theophrastus, *De Causis Plantarum*, Book I, xiv, 3–5 in Arthur Hort (ed), *Theophrastus Enquiry into Plants and Minor Works on Odours and Weather Signs* (translated by Arthur Hort; Heinmann, 1916) p 101.

60　See Benoît Dayrat, 'Celebrating 250 Dynamic Years of Nomenclatural Debates' in Andrew Polaszek, *Systema Naturae 250: The Linnaean Ark* (CRC Press, 2010) pp 189–190. See also T Sprague, 'The Plan of Species Plantarum' (1955) 165 *Proceedings of the Linnaean Society of London* 151.

61　Helen Choate, 'The Origin and Development of the Binomial System of Nomenclature' (1912) 15 *Plant World* 257, 257. See also Knapp *et al.*, above n 3, 611–612; William Stearn, 'The Background of Linnaeus's Contributions to the Nomenclature and Methods of Systematic Biology' (1959) 8 *Systematic Zoology* 4, 5–7.

62　Choate, ibid, 257. See also Stearn, ibid, 6.

63　John Heller, 'The Early History of Binomial Nomenclature' (1964) 1 *Huntia* 33, 34 and the references therein.

phrase-names reflected the Aristotelian ideal that an organism could be identified and distinguished according to a statement in words of a 'genus' together with the 'differentia' to render a definition (species).[64] In Aristotelian terminology, the genus being 'the category of essence all such things as it would be appropriate to mention in reply to the question, "What is the object before you?"', and the definition (species) being 'a phrase signifying a thing's essence'.[65] Examples set out by Linnaeus's *Flora svecica* (1745) for the species grouped in the genus *Veronica* illustrate the polynomial name description: *Veronica floribus spicatis, foliis ternis; Veronica floribus spicatis, foliis oppositis, caule erecto; Veronica floribus racemosis lateralibus, foliis linearibus integerrimis;* and so on.[66]

A key development in biological taxonomy was recognising that the essence of a thing may not be knowable[67] because the essences and properties could not necessarily be distinguished,[68] and therefore the taxonomy was arbitrary and convenient: 'these boundaries of species are as men, and not as Nature, makes them'.[69] While maintaining the language of Aristotle, this was a significant advance because this recognised that the name was not a definition of the essence (the 'real essence') but rather a signifier of the notional idea of the grouping of organisms (the 'nominal essence').[70] As John Locke stated:

> The measure and boundary of each sort or species, whereby it is constituted that particular sort, and distinguished from others, is that we call its essence, which is nothing but that abstract idea to which the name is annexed; so that everything contained in that idea is essential to that sort. This, though it be all the essence of natural substances that we know, or by which we distinguish them into sorts, yet I call it by a peculiar name, the nominal essence, to distinguish it from the real constitution of

64 Aristotle, above n 51, 101 b 17–25.
65 Ibid, 101 b 39–40.
66 Heller, above n 63, 48.
67 See Phillip Sloan, 'John Locke, John Ray, and the Problem of the Natural System' (1972) 5 *Journal of the History of Biology* 1, 14–26. This is the entry into the debates about the distinctions between artificial and natural systems and essentialism that are not addressed here: see S Müller-Wille, 'Systems and How Linnaeus Looked at them in Retrospect' (2013) 70 *Annals of Science* 305, 307–316 and the references therein.
68 See Cain, above n 57, 146–147 and the references therein.
69 John Locke, *An Essay Concerning Human Understanding* (A Fraser (ed), Dover Publications, 1959) p 81 (Book III, iv, 30).
70 By extension this leads to thinking about meaning and definition of species as individuals where they are diagnosed rather than defined exhibiting part–whole relations and their names are proper names of individual rather than collective names of groupings: see Roberto Keller, Richard Boyd and Quentin Wheeler, 'The Illogical Basis of Phylogenetic Nomenclature' (2003) 69 *Botanical Review* 93, 95–97 and the references therein.

substances, upon which depends this nominal essence, and all the properties of that sort; which, therefore, as has been said, may be called the real essence.[71]

The starting point for the modern linguistic rules of binomial naming are generally traced to Linnaeus's *Species Plantarum* (1753)[72] that named the genus to which the species belonged followed by the name of the species within the genus.[73] These practices were articulated as aphorisms in *Philosophia Botanica* (1751):[74] 'A plant is completely named if it is provided with a generic name and a specific one'.[75] The generic name covered all species living and extinct in the same genus and the specific name applied only to all the individuals within the species.[76] These generic names and specific names were then linked to descriptions of the genera and species.[77] Importantly, Linnaeus didn't invent the binomial nomenclature or abandon the polynomial system (the use of several words or phrases).[78] Rather 'he introduced a dual system of nomenclature which led to the replacement of diagnostic polynomials by merely designating binomials'.[79] It may be that Linnaeus adopted the binomial naming system more broadly just to assist his students who were confused by the existing long form naming methods and needed something simpler.[80] This is certainly consistent with Linnaeus' view that

71 Locke, above n 69, p 57 (Book III, iv, 2).
72 See, for example, N Britton, 'Nomenclature at the Vienna International Botanical Congress' (1905) 22(555) *Science* 217, 219.
73 See Stern, above n 2, 5 and 10–14. See also Heller, above n 63.
74 See Frans Stafleu, *Linnaeus and the Linnaeans: The Spreading of Their Ideas in Systematic Botany (1735–1789)*, *Regnum Vegetabile* Volume 79 (International Association for Plant Taxonomy, 1971).
75 Carl Linnaeus, *Philosophia Botanica* (1751) (translated by Stephen Freer, Oxford University Press, 2003) p 219 (Aphorism No 256). See also Stearn, above n 61, 7–8.
76 See Stern, above n 2, 5.
77 See Dayrat, above n 60, pp 188–189; Stern, above n 2, 5.
78 See Choate, above n 61, 258. Analyses of earlier pre-Linnaean works show that the binomial names were in earlier use: see, for examples, Gledhill, above n 6, p 15; Heller, above n 63; Stearn, above n 61; E Greene, 'Botanical Literature Old and New' (1888) 1 *Pittonia* 176. Interestingly Carl Linnaeus, 'Species Orchidum et Affinium Plantarum' [1740] *Acta Societatis Regiae Scientiarum Upsaliensis* 137 uses polynomial names for his account of orchids.
79 Stern, above n 2, 6. Notably Linnaeus also expanded monomials into binomials: Stern, above n 2, 13. One account provides 'Linnaeus's main contribution to botany was his method of naming plants, in which he combined Bauhin's and Belleval's use of binomials with Tournefort's and Boerhaave's concepts of the genus': Gledhill, above n 6, p 16. See also Stafleu, above n 74.
80 See Pehr Olsson-Seffer, 'On the Place of Linnaeus in the History of Botany' (1904) 42 *Journal of Botany* 262, 267. See also Stearn, above n 61, 10. For another account of 'motivations' see Marc Ereshefsky, *The Poverty of the Linnaean Hierarchy: A Philosophical Study of Biological Taxonomy* (Cambridge University Press, 2000) pp 204–206.

memory was a critical part of any botanist's and zoologist's taxonomy.[81] In all his work naming, Linnaeus was, however, still well within the realm of Aristotle,[82] although not a strict version of that logic:[83]

> The concept of a species consists of an essential feature, by which alone it is distinguished from all others in the same genus ... A specific definition contains features in which the species differs from those in the same genus. But the specific name contains the essential features of the definition ... Therefore the specific name is the essential definition.[84]

Perhaps Linnaeus's contribution is best described as separating the binomial designatory name (such as *Phlomis fruticosa*) from the Aristotelian polynomial diagnostic name (such as *Plomis foliis subrotundis tomentosis creates, involucris lanceolatis*)[85] – separating the name from the description[86] – and minimising classification.[87] Thus, '[w]here Linnaeus would read, *Rosa Carolina*, the pre-Linnaeans would, exhaustively, say *Rosa Carolina fragrans, follis medio tenis serratus*. The name said it all. Literally'.[88]

While Linnaeus's language and form of naming attracted some interest among a number of other proposals around that time,[89] it is probably a much more pedestrian history that accounts for our modern naming practices. To counter the 'radical reformers' wanting to rename and destabilise existing conventions (particularly energised by the colonial bounty of new organisms from the empires[90] and the 'new curiosity ... if not to discover the science of

81 See Cain, above n 57, 156–157.
82 See ibid, 145–156; Henry Svenson, 'On the Descriptive Method of Linnaeus' (1945) 47 *Rhodora* 273. Although this is a much contested perspective: see Mary Winsor, 'Linnaeus's Biology was not Essentialist' (2006) 93 *Annals of the Missouri Botanic Gardens* 2, 3–4 and the references therein; Mary Winsor, 'Non-essentialist Methods in Pre-Darwinian Taxonomy' (2003) 18 *Biology and Philosophy* 387, 388–391 and the references therein; Peter Stevens, 'Why do We Name Organisms? Some Reminders from the Past' (2002) 51 *Taxon* 11, 14–15 and the references therein.
83 See Scott Atran, *Cognitive Foundations of Natural History: Towards an Anthropology of Science* (Cambridge University Press, 1990) p 84.
84 Linnaeus, above n 75, pp 219–220.
85 Knapp *et al.*, above n 3, 611; Stern, above n 2, 13.
86 Gerry Moore, 'Should Taxon Names be Explicitly Defined?' (2003) 69 *Botanical Review* 2, 5.
87 Knapp *et al.*, above n 3, 611.
88 Gordon McOuat, 'Species, Rules and Meanings: The Politics of Language and the Ends of Definitions in 19th Century Natural History' (1996) 27 *Studies in the History and Philosophy of Science* 473, 479.
89 See Dayrat, above n 60, pp 190–193.
90 McOuat, above n 88, 479 and 481–493 and the references therein. See also Adrian Desmond, 'The Making of Institutional Zoology in London 1822–1836: Part I' (1985) 23 *History of Science* 153; Adrian Desmond, 'The Making of Institutional Zoology in London 1822–1836: Part 2' (1985) 23 *History of Science* 223. For an example of one of the alternative schemes see Aaron Novick, 'On the

life, at least to give them a hitherto unsuspected scope and precision'),[91] the 'gentleman-naturalist establishment' in England[92] sought control over their preferred naming practices.[93]

The 'gentleman-naturalist establishment' adopted a strategic approach to developing their rules – '[r]ules should govern the social parameters of naming, not naming itself'[94] – and formed a nomenclature committee to develop the first naming code (the Strickland Code).[95] These rules were set out in the report of the nomenclature committee in the 1842 British Association for the Advancement of Science meeting report.[96] The committee's justification for the rules was to 'lead to sufficient uniformity of method in future to rescue the science from becoming a mere chaos of words'.[97] Interestingly, the committee considered Linnaeus's binomial naming 'admirable' and that '[i]f zoologists had paid more attention to the principles of that code, the present attempt at reform would perhaps have been unnecessary'.[98] Their main reason appears to have been the convenience of Linnaeus's approach: '[p]revious to [Linnaeus], naturalists were wont to indicate species not by a name comprised of one word, but by a definition which occupied a sentence, the extreme verbosity of which method was productive of great inconvenience'.[99] The committee's nomenclature was divided between rectifying the existing names and setting the conventions for future names.[100] The characteristic of this naming code was to use a binomial of genus and species[101] (with the species being 'what competent (read: institutional, published, gentlemanly,

Origins of the Quinarian System of Classification' (2016) 49 *Journal of the History of Biology* 95.

91 Michel Foucault, *The Order of Things: The Archaeology of the Human Sciences* (Routledge Classics, 2002) p 136.
92 McOuat, above n 88, 507. See also Gordon McOuat, 'Cataloguing Power: Delineating "Competent Naturalists" and the Meaning of Species in the British Museum' (2001) 34 *British Journal for the History of Science* 1; Harriet Ritvo, 'The Power of the Word: Scientific Nomenclature and the Spread of Empire' (1990) 77 *Victorian Newsletter* 5.
93 See McOuat, above n 88, 494–504 and the references therein. For an early articulation and discussion of possible rules see Hugh Strickland, 'Rules for Zoological Nomenclature' (1837) 1 *Magazine of Natural History and Journal of Zoology, Botany, Mineralogy, Geology, and Meteorology* 173.
94 McOuat, ibid, 505.
95 L Rookmaaker, 'The Early Endeavours by Hugh Edwin Strickland to Establish a Code for Zoological Nomenclature in 1842–1843' (2011) 68 *Bulletin of Zoological Nomenclature* 29, 30–38; McOuat, ibid, 504–511 and the references therein.
96 British Association for the Advancement of Science, *Report of the Twelfth Meeting of the British Association for the Advancement of Science* (John Murray, 1843) pp 105–121.
97 Ibid, p 108.
98 Ibid, p 108 (footnote).
99 Ibid, p 109.
100 Ibid, p 108.
101 Ibid. p 110.

conservative) naturalists said they were'),[102] to use Latin,[103] and to 'be *amply* defined, and *extensively* circulated' meaning published with a full description in book form.[104] Most importantly, however, the committee's rules formally embraced the Lockean break between the name and the definition:[105]

> It being admitted on all hands that words are only the conventional signs of ideas, it is evident that language can only attain its end effectually by being permanently established and generally recognized. This consideration ought, it would seem, to have checked those who are continually attempting to subvert the established language of zoology by substituting terms of their own coinage. But, forgetting the true nature of language, they persist in confounding the *name* of a species or group with its *definition*; and because the former often falls short of the fullness of expression found in the latter, they cancel without hesitation, and introduce some new term which appears to them more characteristic, but which is utterly unknown to science, and is therefore devoid of all authority.[106]

Another key feature of the nomenclature committee's code was the recognition of authorship and rules dealing expressly with priority.[107] The concern appears to have been the 'injustice of erasing the name originally selected by the person to whose labours we owe our first knowledge of the object' and 'pretenders ... dragging themselves into notice at the expense of original observers'.[108] As a direct consequence, the nomenclature committee proposed a priority that the name originally given 'should be permanently retained'.[109] There were, however, some concessions 'necessary' to apply this priority in practice: priority applied from Linnaeus onwards and not to earlier 'authors'; genus names should never be cancelled; subdivided genera should retain the original name in one of the subdivisions; in compounded genera the earliest named genus should take precedence; and so on.[110] The

102 McOuat, above n 88, 512.
103 British Association, above n 96, pp 114 and 116.
104 McOuat, above n 88, 512.
105 See also the reports of a meeting to consider the system of trinomial nomenclature advocated by American zoologists and the arguments against mixing naming and meaning: Editor, 'Zoological Nomenclature' (1884) 30 *Nature* 256.
106 British Association, above n 96, pp 108–109. The footnote then sets out: 'Linnaeus says on this subject, "Abstinendum ab hac innovation quae nunquant cessaret, quin indies aptiora detegerentur ad infinitum"'.
107 British Association, ibid, pp 109 and 119. This appears to have been the first time authorship was addressed: Dan Nicolson, 'A History of Botanical Nomenclature' (1991) 78 *Annals of the Missouri Botanic Garden* 33, 34. Although see Strickland, above n 93, 174.
108 British Association, ibid, p 109.
109 Ibid, pp 109–110.
110 Ibid, pp 109–114.

nomenclature committee's code was circulated widely and formed the template for later codes, being the basis for later zoological codes and the format for the later botanical codes.[111]

The effect of the nomenclature committee's code was to normalise the Linnaean binomial and initiate the break between the botanical and zoological nomenclatures.[112] The break was from the recognition that the Linnaean approach had been developed fairly well for botanical nomenclature but not for zoology nomenclature, and that the latter required more certainty.[113] The history of these evolving botanical and zoological nomenclatures is long, complex and well documented by others.[114] The most significant problem for plants, however, was that the ideals of priority conflicted with increasing numbers of new plants that didn't fit the genera established by Linnaeus and the other early systematists.[115] This crystallised as a need to modify the existing practices that led eventually, and after many 'conflicts and compromises',[116] to the modern-day *Plant Code.*[117]

A significant early milestone in these developments was Alphonse de Candolle's proposed nomenclature rules submitted to the International Botanic Congress in 1867 that sought to bring back some order to the then fragmenting botanical research and naming.[118] The earlier 'gentleman-naturalist establishment' nomenclature committee's naming code (the Strickland Code) was a guiding

111 McOuat, above n 88, 509–510. See also Rookmaaker, above n 95, 38–39.
112 Alessandro Minelli, 'Zoological vs Botanical Nomenclature: A Forgotten "Bio-Code" Experiment from the times of the Strickland Code' (2008) 1950 *ZooTaxa* 21, 22; Nicolson, above n 107, 34.
113 British Association, above n 96, p 121. See also R Melville, *Towards Stability in the Names of Animals: A History of the International Commission on Zoological Nomenclature 1895–1995* (ICZN, 1995).
114 See Dayrat, above n 60, pp 186–240 and the references therein; Otto Kraus, 'The Linnaean Foundations of Zoological and Botanical Nomenclature' (2008) 1950 *ZooTaxa* 9 and the references therein; Knapp *et al.*, above n 3, and the references therein; Melville, ibid; Nicolson, above n 107 and the references therein; M Green, 'History of Plant Nomenclature' [1927] *Bulletin of Miscellaneous Information* 403; and so on.
115 See Knapp *et al.*, above n 3, 612–615; T Cheeseman, 'Notes on Botanical Nomenclature; with Remarks on the Rules Adopted by the International Botanical Congress of Vienna' (1907) 40 *Transactions and Proceedings of the Royal Society of New Zealand* 447, 448–449.
116 Rickett, above n 3, 22. See also Will Blackwell, 'One-Hundred-Year Code Déjà Vu?' (2002) 51 *Taxon* 151.
117 McNeill *et al.*, above n 10.
118 See Alphonse de Candolle, *Laws of Botanical Nomenclature adopted by the International Botanical Congress held at Paris in August 1867, together with an Historical Introduction and Commentary by Alphonse de Candolle* (translated by Hugh Weddell; Reeve & Company, 1868) pp 8–9. See also Nicolson, above n 107, 34–35; Cheeseman, above n 115, 449–450; Asa Grey, 'Laws of Botanical Nomenclature adopted by the International Botanical Congress held at Paris in August 1867, together with an Historical Introduction and Commentary by Alphonse de Candolle' (1868) 46 *American Journal of Science and Arts* 63, 74–75.

source for de Candolle.[119] The significance of de Candolle's proposed nomenclature rules was to confirm that each species should only have one name,[120] each valid name should have a priority set from the earliest publication from 1753 (Linnaeus's *Species Plantarum*),[121] the publication of the name should include a description and diagnosis,[122] and the citation of the author's name should follow the plant's name.[123] Most interestingly, much of de Candolle's original nomenclature still remains in the *Plant Code*, albeit re-phrased, expanded or modified.[124]

The de Candolle nomenclature attracted criticism over the following decades and various other proposals addressed a number of unresolved issues with at least five rival codes being developed and used.[125] The main dispute was about the priority of genus and species names.[126] To again bring back some order to naming, the International Botanic Congress in 1905 distilled the various proposals and agreed to impose a binding code for botanical nomenclature.[127] Subsequent congresses have addressed the remaining controversies and refined the code,[128] including the priority of names,[129] the application of a name determined by reference to a type specimen,[130] publication requirements,[131] the development and adoption of a separate *Cultivated*

---

119 de Candolle, ibid, pp 10–11.

120 Ibid, p 17 (Art 3).

121 Ibid, pp 21–22 (Art 15).

122 Ibid, pp 29–30 (Arts 41–47).

123 Ibid, pp 30–32 (Arts 48–52).

124 See C Weatherby, 'Botanical Nomenclature Since 1867' (1949) 35 *American Journal of Botany* 5, 7.

125 See Nicolson, above n 107, 35–38; Weatherby, ibid, 6–7; Green, above n 114, 411–414.

126 Weatherby, ibid. See also J Britten, 'The Berlin Rules of Nomenclature' (1897) 35 *Journal of Botany* 305.

127 See Cheeseman, above n 115; Britton, above n 72; A Rendle, 'The Botanical Congress at Vienna' (1905) 72 *Nature* 272. See also Nicolson, above n 107, 38–39.

128 See Nicolson, ibid, 38–42 and the references therein; P Parkinson, 'The International Code of Botanical Nomenclature: An Historical Review and Bibliography' (1975) 21 *TANB Journal of the Auckland University Field Club* 153, 153–161 and the references therein; Weatherby, above n 124, 6–7.

129 Rickett, above n 3, 25–26; Knapp *et al.*, above n 3, 613–614.

130 H Rickett and F Stafleu, 'Nomina Generica Conservanda et Rejicienda Spermatophytorum' (1959) 8 *Taxon* 213, 216; Rickett, above n 3, 24–25. That this remains contentious see Joeri Witteveen, 'Suppressing Synonym with a Homonym: The Emergence of the Nomenclatural Type Concept in Nineteenth Century Natural History' (2016) 49 *Journal of the History of Biology* 135; Joeri Witteveen, '"A Temporary Oversimplification": Mayr, Simpson, Dobzhansky, and the Origins of the Typology/Population Dichotomy' (2015) 54 *Studies in History and Philosophy of Science Part C* 20; Paul Faber, 'The Type-Concept in Zoology During the First Half of the Nineteenth Century' (1976) 9 *Journal of the History of Biology* 93; A Hitchcock, 'Nomenclatural Type Specimens of Plant Species' (1905) 21(543) *Science* 828.

131 Knapp *et al.*, above n 3, 616–617. See also Sandra Knapp and Debbie Wright, 'e-Publish or Perish?' in Andrew Polaszek, *Systema Naturae 250: The Linnaean Ark* (CRC Press, 2010) pp 83–93 and the references therein.

Plant Code,[132] and the institutional form of the International Association for Plant Taxonomy with official journals *Taxon* and *Regnum Vegetabile* and the International Bureau of Plant Taxonomy and Nomenclature as advocates for botanical nomenclature.[133] There is also an arrangement for resolving disputes about names relying on binding rulings after guidance from a committee of taxonomic experts.[134] The International Botanic Congress now meets every six years and endorses resolutions from the Nomenclature Section of the Congress about the *Plant Code* that have previously been published in the journal *Taxon* and subject to a postal ballot among members of the International Association of Plant Taxonomy.[135] The separate *Cultivated Plant Code* is modified and approved by the International Union of Biological Sciences' Commission on the Nomenclature of Cultivated Plants with some members also being involved with the International Botanic Congress to maintain a consistency between the codes.[136] Both codes remain voluntary agreements among practising scientists with non-compliance sanctioned by a disregard in establishing the priority of a name.[137]

In current naming the strict Aristotelian origins of name definitions have been clouded, the Lockean break between the name and the definition has been confirmed, and the Linnaean binomial name has been entrenched. For example, the current *Plant Code (Melbourne Code)* provides, in part:

> Biology requires a precise and simple system of nomenclature that is used in all countries, dealing on the one hand with the terms that denote the ranks of taxonomic groups or units, and on the other hand with the scientific names that are applied to the individual taxonomic groups. The purpose of giving a name to a taxonomic group is not to indicate its characters or history, but to supply a means of referring to it and to indicate its taxonomic rank.[138]

132 See William Stearn, 'Historical Survey of the Naming of Cultivated Plants' (1986) 182 *Acta Horticulturae* 19.

133 Editors, 'International Association for Plant Taxonomy' (1951) 1 *Taxon* 5.

134 *International Code of Nomenclature for algae, fungi and plants*, Arts 38.4 and 53.5. See, for example, Manuel Crespo and Gea Zijlstra, 'Request for a Binding Decision on Whether *Lerouxia* Mérat (*Primulaceae*) and *Lerrouxia* Caball. (*Plumbaginaceae*) are Sufficiently Alike to be Confused' (2012) 61 *Taxon* 1335; Fred Barrie, 'Report of the General Committee' (2011) 60 *Taxon* 1212; Lorelei Norvell, 'Report of the Nomenclature Committee for Fungi' (2010) 59 *Taxon* 292; and so on.

135 *International Code of Nomenclature for algae, fungi and plants*, Division III. See also Knapp *et al.*, above n 3, 615.

136 *International Code of Nomenclature for Cultivated Plants*, Division VI. See also Knapp *et al.*, above n 3, 615. For a brief description of the differences between the codes see David Spooner, Wilbert Hetterscheid, Ronald van den Berg and Willem Brandenburg, 'Plant Nomenclature and Taxonomy' (2003) 28 Horticultural Reviews 1, 39–45.

137 Knapp *et al.*, above n 3, 615. Notably there is a resistance to govern and manage naming codes in any different ways: see, for example, Richard Brummitt, 'The *BioCode* is Unnecessary and Unwanted' (1997) 22 *Systematic Botany* 182.

138 McNeill *et al.*, above n 10, Preamble 1 (p 21).

The Aristotelian origins remain, however, through the requirement for valid publication of the name that includes a description that 'distinguishes the taxon from other taxa'[139] capturing the essence of the thing. This is the link between the name and the definition, although the name and the definition are no longer the same word (or words) following Linnaeus's binomial naming separating the species name from the species description.[140] Perhaps surprisingly, earlier codes suggested names indicate something of the appearance, the characters or the properties of the species,[141] while the latest code merely requires letters in the form of two words.[142] Similarly, the Linnaean origins for naming though the link between taxon names and Linnaeus's taxa rank hierarchy (Kingdoms, Classes, Orders, Genera and Species) and the modern hierarchy (Kingdom, Phylum, Class, Order, Family, Genus and Species) have parted ways,[143] although the link between taxon names and a hierarchy of taxa ranks remains (despite recent attempts to introduce a truly phylogenetic code).[144] In other words, the name is more than just a tag because the form and the content of the name describe the relationship of the named plant in a classification system. The detailed descriptions, however, are removed to another place through publications. The codes now establish conventions posited as a set of principles, binding rules, and non-binding recommendations and illustrative examples that are scientifically neutral and independent of the scientific opinion used to decide the taxonomy.[145] The effect of this binomial genus and species naming is to serve the two critical functions: to generically name a genus to signify a believed relationship; and, to uniquely identify a species with a specific name.[146] This effectively facilitates comprehension and communication.[147] The next part addresses the forms of the modern plant naming in the codes.

5.3 The current codes

The International Botanical Congress, with the International Association for Plant Taxonomy acting as the secretariat, made the current *Plant Code* (called the *International Code of Botanical Nomenclature* before 2011).[148] Essentially,

---

139 *International Code of Nomenclature for algae, fungi and plants*, Arts 38.1 and 38.2. See also *International Code of Nomenclature for Cultivated Plants*, Art 25.1.
140 Moore, above n 86, 5.
141 de Candolle, above n 118, p 26 (Art 32).
142 See *International Code of Nomenclature for algae, fungi and* plants, Art 23.
143 de Queiroz, above n 8, 127 and 132–133. See also Moore, above n 86, 4–7.
144 Kevin de Queiroz and Jacques Gauthier, 'Toward a Phylogenetic System of Biological Nomenclature' (1994) 9 *Trends in Ecology and Evolution* 27.
145 Although there remain competing nomenclature practices and conventions: see, for examples, Greuter, above n 7, 23–24.
146 Ernst Mayr, 'Notes on Nomenclature and Classification' (1954) 3 *Systematic Zoology* 86, 86.
147 Stevens, above n 82, 11 and 17.
148 See McNeill *et al.*, above n 10, Preface.

the code has been developed through practice ('conflicts and compromises')[149] and applies to 'all organisms traditionally treated as algae, fungi, or plants, whether fossil or non-fossil, including blue-green algae (*Cyanobacteria*), chytrids, oomycetes, slime moulds, and photosynthetic protists with their taxonomically related non-photosynthetic groups (but excluding *Microsporidia*)'.[150] The principle ranks of taxa are 'kingdom (regnum), division or phylum (divisio or phylum), class (classis), order (ordo), family (familia), genus (genus), and species (species)'[151] with various secondary and sub-divisions available, including subspecies (*subspecies*), variety (*varietas*) and form (*forma*) below species.[152] Names can then be formulated for the ranks according to the rules,[153] so that 'each species is assignable to a genus, each genus to a family, etc.'[154] – boxes within boxes.[155]

Applying the code rules, the name of a species is 'a binary combination consisting of the name of the genus followed by a single specific epithet in the form of an adjective, a noun in the genitive, or a word in apposition, or several words',[156] such as '*Cornus sanguinea*'.[157] And to maintain the Linnaean binomial naming and to prevent a return to the Aristotelian origins there are express restrictions against '[d]escriptive designations consisting of a generic name followed by a phrase name (Linnaean "*nomen specificum legitimum*") of one or more descriptive nouns and associated adjectives in the ablative'.[158] A range of rules then apply to impose stability on the names by requiring: *publication* of a name with a circumscription (description) to diagnose the type specimen so that a legitimate name will continue in force and displace another later name for the same species,[159] and also to impose a measure of consensus and review before a name becomes formally accepted;[160] *priority* to the first name to address synonyms (the same plant having different names) and homonyms (different plants having the same name);[161] *authorship* may also be

---

149 Rickett, above n 3, 22.
150 *International Code of Nomenclature for algae, fungi and plants*, Preamble 8.
151 *International Code of Nomenclature for algae, fungi and plants*, Art 3.1.
152 *International Code of Nomenclature for algae, fungi and plants*, Arts 4 and 5.
153 *International Code of Nomenclature for algae, fungi and plants*, Arts 16–17 (above the rank of family), 18–19 (families and subfamilies, tribes and sub-tribes), 20–22 (genera and subdivisions of genera), 23 (species) and 24–27 (taxa below the rank of species (infra-specific taxa)).
154 *International Code of Nomenclature for algae, fungi and plants*, Art 3.1.
155 Although this is itself a controversial proposition: see, for example, McOuat, above n 88 and the references therein.
156 *International Code of Nomenclature for algae, fungi and plants*, Art 23.1.
157 *International Code of Nomenclature for algae, fungi and plants*, Art 23.2 (Example 1).
158 *International Code of Nomenclature for algae, fungi and plants*, Art 23.6(a).
159 *International Code of Nomenclature for algae, fungi and plants*, Arts 6.1–6.3 and 29–45.
160 See *International Code of Nomenclature for algae, fungi and plants*, Arts 29–50.
161 *International Code of Nomenclature for algae, fungi and plants*, Arts 11–12. See also Alessandro Minelli, 'The Status of Taxonomic Literature' (2003) 18 *Trends in Ecology and Evolution* 75.

recorded as the person(s) first naming and describing the plant;[162] and, *types* so that a name is associated with a physical type specimen, generally held in a herbarium or culture collection, for species rank and below, or associated with a genus rank and above.[163] The type specimen also has the effect of distinguishing nomenclature from taxonomy,[164] as a change in the circumscription (description) of the type in a revised taxonomy does not (necessarily) change the name, so maintaining the stability of the name.[165]

The *Cultivated Plant Code* is directed to plants under cultivation accepting the naming by the *Plant Code* and merely adding extra parts to those names to differentiate lower level variations (below species level).[166] This is because cultivation selects for desirable character traits and against undesirable character traits[167] so that a cultivated plant generally shows a rapid divergence from the wild plants through an increased number of desired parts, an increased size of desired parts, and a loss of undesirable morphological, chemical and defence traits.[168] Over time this can mean significant differences between the wild varieties of organisms and those in cultivation, and a dramatic variation across closely related organisms in cultivation. This reflects the power of cultivation (and breeding in cultivation) to select desired characters and reveals the potential genetic diversity within the wild varieties that can be applied for human utility. This expanded variation, however, poses problems for naming because the taxonomic genus and species grouping remain the same while the characters (morphology) may be dramatically different.[169] Accordingly the existing *Plant Code* is not sufficient,[170]

162 *International Code of Nomenclature for algae, fungi and plants*, Arts 46–50.
163 *International Code of Nomenclature for algae, fungi and plants*, Arts 7–10. For an historical account of the development of the type see, for example, Gerry Moore, 'A Comparison of Traditional and Phylogenetic Nomenclature' (1998) 47 *Taxon* 561, 564–566 and the references therein; Nicolson, above n 107, 39–40.
164 Although there may be a measure of correspondence between taxonomy and naming codes: see de Queiroz, above n 8, 127.
165 See Dan Nicolson, 'Stone, Plant, or Animal' (2002) 51 *Taxon* 7, 9; Moore, above n 163, 564–566; Dan Nicolson, 'Typification of Names vs Typification of Taxa: Proposals on Article 48 and Reconsideration of Mitracarpus hirtus vs M. villosus (Rubiaceae)' (1977) 26 *Taxon* 569. Although those favouring a phylogenetic nomenclature point to the name instability when a taxon's name changes because new information brings about a change in its hierarchy position, from one genus to another: see, for examples, Dayrat, above n 60, pp 230–231; Philip Cantino, Richard Olmstead and Steven Wagstaff, 'A Comparison of Phylogenetic Nomenclature with the Current System: A Botanical Case Study' (1997) 46 *Systematic Biology* 313, 314 and the references therein.
166 *International Code of Nomenclature for Cultivated Plants*, Preamble 8, Principle 2 and Art 1.
167 See *International Code of Nomenclature for Cultivated Plants*, Preamble 1 (footnote).
168 See Franz Schwanitz, *The Origin of Cultivated Plants* (Harvard University Press, 1966) pp 30 and 42.
169 See L Bailey, 'The Indigen and Cultigen' (1918) 47(1213) *Science* 306.
170 See William Stearn, 'Proposed International Code of Nomenclature for Cultivated Plants' (1952) 77 *Journal of the Royal Horticultural Society* 77. Even Linnaeus

and the *Cultivated Plant Code* introduces the 'cultivar' names below the level of species to distinguish cultivated varieties without disrupting the traditional binomial naming system.[171] The *Cultivated Plant Code* also serves the function of providing a different kind of name to suit the requirements of economically important cultivated plants as opposed to the taxonomical naming for scientific purposes, and so avoids the Latin names in favour of simpler name forms that are more appealing in commerce.[172] Thus, the code provides an additional and simple non-Latin name for commercial or ornamental plants (so-called 'fancy' names)[173] complimenting the Latin taxonomic genus-species name with a cultivar,[174] group,[175] and grex[176] epithet.[177] The cultivar is defined as a grouping selected for characters that are distinct, uniform and stable in these characters and retains those characters on propagation.[178] The group is essentially any useful characters that can define cultivars or individual plants, and might be used to identify a grouping of different cultivars according to any kind of shared character, such as a growing condition.[179] And for orchids alone, a special formal naming category exists called the grex – such as *Cymbidium* Alexanderi grex[180] – that identifies plants with a specified parentage.[181] These grex names are maintained as separate and unique names starting from 1 January 1858[182] and are applied to artificial hybrids with at least one known parent.[183] The *Cultivated Plant Code* also allows the 'unambiguous common name' of the plant to be combined with the epithet for

was conscious of this likely problem: see W Hetterscheid, R Berg and W Brandenburg, 'An Annotated History of the Principles of Cultivated Plant Classification' (1996) 45 *Acta Botanica Neerlandica* 123, 124.

171 *International Code of Nomenclature for Cultivated Plants*, Principle 2. See also J McNeill, 'Nomenclature of Cultivated Plants: A Historical Botanical Standpoint' (2004) 634 *Acta Horticulturae* 29; P Trehane, '50 Years of the International Code of Nomenclature for Cultivated Plants: Future Prospects for the Code' (2002) 634 *Acta Horticulturae* 17; Stearn, above n 132.

172 See Spencer and Cross, above n 12, 938. See Gledhill, above n 6, p 41.

173 See an account of the historical origins of these names: Stearn, above n 170. Interestingly this was also the approach recommended by the International Botanic Congress in 1905: see also de Candolle, above n 118, pp 49–50.

174 *International Code of Nomenclature for Cultivated Plants*, Art 4.1; *International Code of Nomenclature for Cultivated Plants*, Arts 2 and 21.

175 *International Code of Nomenclature for Cultivated Plants*, Arts 3 and 22.

176 *International Code of Nomenclature for Cultivated Plants*, Arts 4 and 23.

177 See *International Code of Nomenclature for Cultivated Plants*, Art 7.1. The code also provides for graft-chimeras formed from grafting the tissues of two or more plants belonging to different taxonomic groupings (Art 5).

178 *International Code of Nomenclature for Cultivated Plants*, Art 2.3.

179 *International Code of Nomenclature for Cultivated Plants*, Art 3.

180 *International Code of Nomenclature for Cultivated Plants*, Arts 4 and 16.

181 *International Code of Nomenclature for Cultivated Plants*, Art 4.1.

182 *International Code of Nomenclature for Cultivated Plants*, Arts 4.3 and 18.2.

183 *International Code of Nomenclature for Cultivated Plants*, Arts 4.1 and 27.

the cultivar,[184] group[185] or grex.[186] The form of names under the *Cultivated Plant Code* is best illustrated by examples:

a   Cultivars – The cultivar name is composed of the correct name according to the *Plant Code* followed by a cultivar epithet (such as *Achillea millefolium* 'Cerise Queen' or *Achillea millefolium* cv. Cerise Queen), or the unambiguous common name followed by a cultivar epithet (such as yarrow 'Cerise Queen').[187]

b   Groups – The group name is composed of the correct name according to the *Plant Code* (or abbreviated to just the genus) followed by a group epithet (such as *Allium cepa* Aggregatum Group or *Allium* Aggregatum Group) or the unambiguous common name followed by a group epithet and the word 'Group' (such as shallot Aggregatum Group).[188]

c   Grexes – The grex name is composed of the correct name according to the *Plant Code* followed by a grex epithet (such as *Dendrobium speciosum* Maddison) or the unambiguous common name followed by a grex epithet and the word 'grex' (such as *Paphiopeddilum* Greenteaicecreamandraspberries grex).[189]

The naming can get a little more complex depending on the way the cultivated plant has been created. The following illustrates the complexity demonstrating the interaction between the *Plant Code* and the *Cultivated Plant Code* using orchids as an illustration:

a   *Orchids from the wild* – Orchids from the wild have the traditional *Plant Code* names, such as *Dendrobium specialis*, and might be more specifically described by a variety or form epithet such as *Dendrobium specialis* var. *grandiflora*.[190]

b   *Orchids brought into cultivation* – Orchids brought into cultivation and subject to selection have a standard *Plant Code* name, such as *Dendrobium specialis*,[191] and can have additional cultivar, group or grex names according to the *Cultivated Plant Code*, such as (the cultivar) *Dendrobium specialis* 'Blue Fire'.[192]

c   *Interspecific hybrids* – Interspecific hybrids (so hybrids within a genus) have, according to the *Plant Code*, a genus name, an 'x' (or the prefix

184 *International Code of Nomenclature for Cultivated Plants*, Art 21.1.
185 *International Code of Nomenclature for Cultivated Plants*, Art 22.1.
186 *International Code of Nomenclature for Cultivated Plants*, Art 23.1.
187 See *International Code of Nomenclature for Cultivated Plants*, Art 21.1 (Ex 1).
188 See *International Code of Nomenclature for Cultivated Plants*, Art 22.1 (Ex 1).
189 See *International Code of Nomenclature for Cultivated Plants*, Art 23.3 (Ex 1).
190 See *International Code of Nomenclature for algae, fungi and plants*, Art 23.
191 See *International Code of Nomenclature for algae, fungi and plants*, Art 23.
192 See *International Code of Nomenclature for Cultivated Plants*, Arts 2–4 and 21–23.

'notho-') and then a collective name, such as *Dendrobium* x *liberia*.[193] The hybrid can also be listed as a hybrid formula such as *Sarcochilus fitzgeraldi* x *Sarcochilus hartmannii*.[194] The hybrid name may also include a cultivar, group or grex name according to the *Cultivated Plant Code*, such as (the cultivar) *Dendrobium* x *liberia* 'New Tarzan'.[195]

d   *Intergeneric hybrids* – Intergeneric hybrids between at least two different genus have, according to the *Plant Code*, an 'x' followed by a combination of the genus names for combinations of up to three genuses, such as x *Brassocattleya* being a hybrid between *Brassavola* and *Cattleya*, and the name of a person followed by '-ara' for combinations of three or more gensus, such as x *Qwertare* for a hybrid between *Brassavola*, *Cattleya*, *Doritis* and *Phalaenopsis*.[196] The name may also include a cultivar, group or grex name according to the *Cultivated Plant Code*, such as (the cultivar) x *Brassocattleya* 'Old Tarzan'.

The key point about the cultivar, group or grex names is that the cultivar provides a way to identify breeding characteristics among a population of plants, the group provides a way of identifying some other useful grouping that may be unrelated to breeding or parentage, and the grex identifies orchid plants based on knowing at least one parent. Significantly, the name captures the taxonomic relationship within the classification system and sometimes information about the breeding heritage. In this sense, the name is more than just a (Lockean) tag and includes a partial (Aristotelian) description.

Names under the *Cultivated Plant Code* must also be published through the 'distribution of printed or similarly duplicated material' being 'publication reproduced by any mechanical or graphical process whereby a number of identical, legible, and identifiable copies are made'.[197] Names under the *Cultivated Plant Code* may also be registered with an 'International Cultivar Registration Authority' appointed by the International Society for Horticultural Science (ISHS) Commission for Nomenclature and Cultivar Registration.[198] While neither publication nor registration establishes a legal right to the names, they provide a mechanism for implementing the naming norms set out in the codes and a means of establishing a name as a convention for that plant. This is essentially a self-regulating arrangement whereby the ISHS Commission for

---

193 See *International Code of Nomenclature for algae, fungi and plants*, Appendix I (Art H.3). See also *International Code of Nomenclature for Cultivated Plants*, Div III.

194 See *International Code of Nomenclature for algae, fungi and plants*, Appendix I (Art H.2).

195 See *International Code of Nomenclature for Cultivated Plants*, Arts 2–4 and 21–23.

196 See *International Code of Nomenclature for algae, fungi and plants*, Appendix I (Art H.6). See also *International Code of Nomenclature for Cultivated Plants*, Div III.

197 *International Code of Nomenclature for Cultivated Plants*, Art 25.1 (Note 1).

198 *International Code of Nomenclature for Cultivated Plants*, Principle 8 and Div IV.

Nomenclature and Cultivar Registration appoints an 'International Cultivar Registration Authority' for a particular grouping of plants. For example, for orchids the Royal Horticultural Society has been appointed and provides a listing for the *Orchidaceae*.[199] The registration process operates to limit the problems of instability – from the same plant having multiple names (synonyms), different plants having the same names (homonym) and the same plant having different names under different codes (ambiregnal taxa).[200] The *Cultivated Plant Code* also provides for priority through criteria for establishment that includes a date of publication,[201] authorship (although this is not mandatory),[202] and recognition of a type (nomenclature standard) as a reference point against which the name can be assessed.[203]

There remain some tensions in applying the *Plant Code* and the *Cultivated Plant Code*.[204] And there remains a fundamental incompatibility between the codes because the *Plant Code* is restricted to nomenclature while the *Cultivated Plant Code* addresses nomenclature, classification and registration.[205] Despite these differences, the codes provide for a single name for a species,[206] publication (including type specimens for named plants under the *Plant Code*),[207] and priority (and authorship).[208] The development of these elements is considered next because they demonstrate that the name and associated description remain central to an effective naming code – that plants with the same name have the same descriptions and diagnoses and with a particular plant description everyone will give the plant the same name.

199 See *International Code of Nomenclature for Cultivated Plants*, Appendix I. See also Royal Horticultural Society, *Plant Registration*, available at <https://www.rhs.org.uk/plants/plantsmanship/plant-registration> (accessed 18 May 2017).

200 See D Hawksworth, 'The Need for a More Effective Biological Nomenclature for the 21st Century' (1992) 109 *Botanical Journal of the Linnean Society* 543, 560–561.

201 *International Code of Nomenclature for Cultivated Plants*, Arts 25.1, 26 and 27.1.

202 *International Code of Nomenclature for Cultivated Plants*, Art 28.

203 *International Code of Nomenclature for Cultivated Plants*, Div V.

204 See Spence, Cross and Lumley, above n 3, pp 58–61; J Ochsmann, 'Current Problems in Nomenclature and Taxonomy of Cultivated Plants' (2004) 634 *Acta Horticulturae* 53. See also B Pickersgill, M Chacón Sánchez and D Debouck, 'Multiple Domestications and their Taxonomic Consequences: The Example of *Phaseolus vulgaris*' (2003) 22 *Schriften zu Genetischen Ressourcen* 71.

205 See W Brandenburg and F Schneide, 'Cultivar Grouping in Relation to the International Code of Nomenclature for Cultivated Plants' (1988) 37 *Taxon* 141, 141. See also W Hetterscheid and W Brandenburg, 'The Culton Concept: Setting the Stage for an Unambiguous Taxonomy of Cultivated Plants' (1994) 413 *Acta Horticulturae* 29.

206 *International Code of Nomenclature for algae, fungi and* plants, Principle IV; *International Code of Nomenclature for Cultivated Plants*, Principle 3.

207 *International Code of Nomenclature for algae, fungi and* plants, Principle III, Arts 7–10 and 32–45; *International Code of Nomenclature for Cultivated Plants*, Principle 3, Arts 7 and 25.

208 *International Code of Nomenclature for algae, fungi and* plants, Principle III, Art 11–12 (and Arts 46–50); *International Code of Nomenclature for Cultivated Plants*, Principle 3, Art 27 (and Art 28).

A Authorship

Both the *Plant Code* and the *Cultivated Plant Code* provide discretion for the author of a valid plant name to be recorded in the name.[209] Authorship is closely tied to priority and can be traced back to the original International Botanic Congress in 1867 that provided for the citation of the author's (abbreviated) name following the plant's name.[210] At the time there was controversy about whether the recorded name should be that of the person originally naming the genus or the species, and this was resolved by adopting the practice that the author be the person who first described and named the species.[211] This choice probably reflected ideals of justice and that a person's labour has value that requires recognition, as Locke detailed in the *Two Treaties of Government*:[212] 'the improvement of labour makes a far greater part of the value [of land]. I think it will be but a very modest computation to say, that of the products of the Earth useful to the Life of Man nine tenths are the effects of labour'.[213] This ideal was almost certainly captured in the 'gentleman-naturalist establishment' nomenclature committee's naming code (the Strickland Code) that appears to have influenced the International Botanic Congress in 1867:[214]

> No one person can subsequently claim an authority equal to that possessed by the person who is the first to define a new genus or describe a new species; and hence it is that the name originally given, even though it may be inferior in point of elegance or expressiveness to those subsequently proposed, ought as a general principle to be permanently retained. To this consideration we ought to add the injustice of erasing the name originally selected by the person to whose labours we owe our first knowledge of the object; and we should reflect how much the permission of such a practice opens a door to obscure pretenders for dragging themselves into notice at the expense of original observers.[215]

A more utilitarian justification might be that citing the author is 'an orderly measure' to distinguish plants with the same names and to enable the priority

---

209 See *International Code of Nomenclature for algae, fungi and plants*, Arts 46–50; *International Code of Nomenclature for Cultivated Plants*, Art 28.
210 de Candolle, above n 118, pp 30–32 (Arts 48–52).
211 Ibid, pp 51–63. Although the debate continued in the context of whether preserving the species name, and consequently the author, was paramount: see Cheeseman, above n 115, 450–452.
212 See Adam Mossoff, 'Saving Locke from Marx: The Labor Theory of Value in Intellectual Property Theory' (2012) 29 *Social Philosophy and Policy* 283.
213 John Locke, *Two Treaties of Government* (Peter Laslett (ed), Cambridge University Press, 2005) p 296 (Chapter IV, paragraph 40).
214 See de Candolle, above n 118, p 52.
215 British Association, above n 96, p 110.

to be properly settled.[216] The issue of authorship remained contentious and was tied up with the question of priority and whether well-accepted species names should be overturned when the species was moved to another genus to reflect an updated taxonomy.[217] The International Botanic Congress in 1905 essentially resolved these contentions determining that the species name should be retained when transferring from one genus to another.[218] This agreement also settled the basic rules of authorship: the first author publishing the name should be quoted in the name (such as *Simaruba laevis* Grisebach and *Simaruba amara* Aublet *var. opaca* Engler);[219] author names are abbreviated unless short;[220] and, when a species is moved to a new genus the author is the one that effects the change and the earlier author can be cited in parenthesis (such as *Chieranthus tristis* L. when moved becomes *Matthiola tristis* R. Br., or *Matthiola tristis* (L.) R. Br.).[221] So for example, '*Veronica spicata* L. subsp. *hybrida* (L.) E F Warburg' means that Warburg reduced Linnaeus's *V. hybrida* to a subspecies of *V. spicata*.[222]

Significantly, at the International Botanic Congress in 1905 the authorship requirement was mandatory: '[f]or the indication of the name or names of a group to be accurate and complete, and in order that the date may be readily verified, it is necessary to quote the author who first published the name or combination of names in question'.[223] This requirement became discretionary at the International Botanic Congress in 1999,[224] and has remained discretionary up to the present with the requirement in the *Plant Code* that '[i]n publications ... it may be desirable ... to cite the author(s) of the name concerned'.[225] The reason for the change from mandatory to discretionary appears to have been that 'author citation is quite unnecessary in many publications and leads

216 de Candolle, above n 118, p 57. See also T Caruel, 'Botanical Nomenclature' (1877) 15 *Journal of Botany* 282, 282.

217 For examples of this dispute see: Edward Greene, 'The Permanency of Specific Names' (1887) 25 *Journal of Botany* 301, 301–303; Asa Gray, 'Botanical Nomenclature' (1887) 25 *Journal of Botany* 353, 353–355; Asa Gray, 'The Citation of Botanical Authorities' (1882) 20 *Journal of Botany* 173, 173–174; Caruel, ibid, 282; H Trimen, 'Botanical Nomenclature' (1877) 15 *Journal of Botany* 242, 242–243; H Trimen, 'Some Points in Botanical Nomenclature' (1877) 15 *Journal of Botany* 189, 198–190. See also Nicolson, above n 107, 35 and the references therein.

218 See B Robinson, 'On the Rules of Botanical Nomenclature Adopted by the Vienna Congress' (1907) 9 *Rhodora* 30, 48 (Art 48). See also Weatherby, above n 124, 6; Britton, above n 72, 219; C B, 'The Vienna Congress' (1905) 40 *Botanical Gazette* 68, 72.

219 Robinson, ibid, 45 (Art 40).

220 Ibid, 45 (Recommendation 25).

221 Ibid, 45 (Art 43).

222 See Gledhill, above n 6, p 30.

223 Robinson, above n 218, 45 (Art 40).

224 See Piers Trehan, 'Twelve Miscellaneous Proposals to Amend the Code' (1998) 47 *Taxon* 941, 941.

225 *International Code of Nomenclature for algae, fungi and plants*, Art 46.1.

to cumbersome presentation'.[226] The *Cultivated Plant Code* adopts the same discretionary approach.[227] This change may reflect the improvements in recording names and descriptions in accessible forms, whereas in the past the author name was essentially the only link between a named specimen and its description for the purposes of taxonomy and nomenclature (and avoiding the scourge of synonym).

B Priority

The 'gentleman-naturalist establishment' in England was eager 'to have checked those who are continually attempting to subvert the established language of zoology by substituting terms of their own coinage'.[228] As a consequence they proposed that the first name given 'should be permanently retained, to the exclusion of all subsequent synonyms'.[229] To make this work they also proposed that the priority of names dates from the 12th edition of Linnaeus's *Systema Naturae* in 1766 to 1768.[230] The effect was to exclude all earlier synonyms and confirm Linnaeus's renaming as a starting point even though his practice had been criticised as arbitrary.[231] The de Candolle nomenclature in 1867 adopted the same proposition applied more broadly to Linnaean binomial naming generally.[232] Subsequent proposals then established the priority date from Linnaeus's *Species Plantarum* in 1753, the most recent being a series of dates depending on the organism with most from 1 May 1753,[233] and some exceptions for names that must be retained even though they post-date Linnaeus.[234] The simple principle has, however, gained some complexity over time recognising certain alternative names,[235] fossil names,[236] various conserved names,[237] and so on.[238] The over-riding objective, however, appears to be to retain the stability of naming by recognising the first incident of the name.[239] The effect of priority is to place the first designated name with a description as the authoritative name and description, and that later modifications to the

226 Trehan, above n 211, 941.
227 *International Code of Nomenclature for Cultivated Plants*, Art 28.1.
228 British Association, above n 96, p 108.
229 Ibid, p 109.
230 Ibid, pp 109–110.
231 See de Candolle, above n 118, pp 43–44.
232 See, ibid pp 21–22 (Art 15) and 43–44.
233 *International Code of Nomenclature for algae, fungi and plants*, Art 13.
234 See, for example, Robinson, above n 218, 36 (Art 20).
235 *International Code of Nomenclature for algae, fungi and plants*, Art 11.1.
236 *International Code of Nomenclature for algae, fungi and plants*, Art 11.7.
237 See *International Code of Nomenclature for algae, fungi and plants*, Art 14.
238 See *International Code of Nomenclature for algae, fungi and plants*, Arts 11.7, 15, 19.4, 56 and 57.
239 For an early expression of this sentiment see Lester Ward, 'The Nomenclature Question' (1895) 22 *Bulletin of the Torrey Botanical Club* 308.

description (circumspection) can then be traced so that the name and the description remain tightly linked.

C Publication

For de Candolle's proposed nomenclature publication set the priority date.[240] To be validly published, however, the plant name needed to include a genus and species together with 'information as to its characters'.[241] The same principle carries through to the current code although developments in technology continue to challenge what constitutes a valid publication.[242] The current *Plant Code* provides:[243]

> Publication is effected, under this Code, by distribution of printed matter (through sale, exchange, or gift) to the general public or at least to scientific institutions with generally accessible libraries. Publication is also effected by distribution on or after 1 January 2012 of electronic material in Portable Document Format ... in an online [accessible electronically via the World Wide Web] publication with an International Standard Serial Number (ISSN) or an International Standard Book Number (ISBN).[244]

To be validly published under the *Plant Code* the name must 'be accompanied by a description or diagnosis of the taxon' or 'by a reference to a previously and effectively published description or diagnosis'.[245] Further the description cannot include statements about 'purely aesthetic features, economic, medicinal or culinary use, cultural significance, cultivation techniques, geographical origin, or geological age'.[246] The diagnosis is essentially distinguishing between the newly named species and other species.[247] In this sense these words signify different concepts: a description being 'an account of a plant's habit, morphology and periodicity' and a diagnosis being 'an author's definitive statement of the plant's diagnostic features, and circumscribes the limits outside which plants do not pertain to that named species'.[248] The *Cultivated*

---

240 de Candolle, above n 118, p 29 (Art 41).
241 Ibid, pp 29–30 (Art 46).
242 See Sandra Knapp, John McNeill and Nicholas Turland, 'Changes to Publication Requirements Made at the XVIII International Botanical Congress in Melbourne – What Does e-Publication Mean for You?' (2011) 167 *Botanical Journal of the Linnean Society* 133.
243 See also Arthur Chapman, Nicholas Turland and Mark Watson, 'Report of the Special Committee on Electronic Publication' (2010) 59 *Taxon* 1853.
244 *International Code of Nomenclature for algae, fungi and plants*, Arts 29.1 and 29.2.
245 *International Code of Nomenclature for algae, fungi and plants*, Art 38.1(a).
246 *International Code of Nomenclature for algae, fungi and plants*, Art 38.3.
247 *International Code of Nomenclature for algae, fungi and plants*, Art 38.2.
248 Gledhill, above n 6, p 24.

Plant Code also requires publication.[249] Interestingly, publication here for cultivars and groups requires the name 'be accompanied by a description or a reference to a previously published description'[250] where the description is 'a word or words that (a) indicate one or more recognisable characters ... or (b) distinguishes ... from one whose name has been previously or is simultaneously being established'.[251] Orchids do not require a description,[252] although the parentage, history and the breeder 'should be stated where known'.[253] For both codes there are not set formats for descriptions and diagnoses. Various formats have, however, been proposed[254] and there is recourse to reviewing doubtful description and diagnosis statements in establishing validity.[255] The importance of publication, however, is to provide the description (and diagnosis) that is linked to the name so that others can determine that plants with the same name will have the same descriptions and diagnoses and with a particular plant description everyone will give the plant the same name.

D Types

The type concept was well known in zoology in the 1800.[256] The Botanical Society of America first formally proposed the idea of nomenclature types for plants in 1910 and this wasn't formally accepted until 1918[257] following protracted discussions about the idea over the previous decades.[258] This was in

---

249 *International Code of Nomenclature for Cultivated Plants*, Arts 7 and 25.
250 *International Code of Nomenclature for Cultivated Plants*, Art 27.1(d)
251 *International Code of Nomenclature for Cultivated Plants*, Art 27.2.
252 *International Code of Nomenclature for Cultivated Plants*, Art 27.3.
253 *International Code of Nomenclature for Cultivated Plants*, Recommendation 27D.2.
254 See, for examples, Zlatko Kvaček, 'The Role of Types in Palaeobotanical Nomenclature' (2008) 64 *Acta Musei National Pragae, Series B, Historia Naturalis* 89; W Punt, 'Format of Descriptions of New Taxa of Fossil Plants (Genera, Species)' (1994) 80 *Review of Palaeobotany and Palynology* vii; and so on.
255 See *International Code of Nomenclature for algae, fungi and plants*, Art 38.4.
256 See Witteveen, above n 130; Paul Farber, 'The Type-concept in Zoology During the First Half of the Nineteenth Century' (1976) 9 *Journal of the History of Biology* 93.
257 A Hitchcock, 'Report of the Committee on Generic Types of the Botanical Society of America' (1919) 49(1266) *Science* 333, 333. See also Hawksworth, above n 200, 555.
258 See, for examples, O Cook, 'Terms Relating to Generic Types' (1914) 48 *American Naturalist* 308; Walter Swingle, 'Types of Species in Botanical Taxonomy' (1913) 37(962) *Science* 864; Lancaster Burling, 'The Nomenclature of Types' (1912) 2 *Journal of the Washington Academy of Sciences* 519; A Hitchcock, 'Nomenclatorial Type Specimens of Plant Species' (1905) 21(543) *Science* 828; O Cook, 'Types and Synonyms' (1902) 15(382) *Science* 646; O Cook, 'The Method of Types in Botanical Nomenclature' (1900) 12(300) *Science* 475; O Marsh, 'The Value of Type Specimens and Importance of their Preservation' (1898) 6 *American Journal of Science* 548; O Cook, 'The Method of Types' (1898) 8(198) *Science* 513; C Merriam, 'Type Specimens in Natural History' (1897) 5(123) *Science*

part a reaction to the International Botanical Congress in 1905 and the earlier nomenclature code from 1867 requiring 'a simpler set of rules' based on 'the method of establishing and maintaining botanical names by the method of types'.[259] This was asserted to be a method of referencing a type specimen rather than a 'method of concepts' referencing a description (in Latin).[260] The fundamental principle was: '[t]he application of generic names shall be determined by type species' and '[t]he type species shall be the species or one of the species included in the genus when originally published' dating from the issue of Linnaeus's *Species Plantarum* in 1753.[261] This development was to replace the 'concept embodied in a description or definition associated with a name' with a type specimen as a 'representative of the group that became known to science'.[262] The effect is that the type fixes a reference to the name without actually having to define the distinguishing features.[263] The International Botanical Congress finally adopted the type specimen in the code at the congress in 1930.[264] And the requirement to designate a nomenclature type for publication was then adopted in 1958.[265]

The *Plant Code* now provides that '[t]he application of names of taxa of the rank of family or below is determined by means of nomenclatural types (types of names of taxa)' and '[t]he application of names of taxa in the higher ranks is also determined by means of types when the names are ultimately based on generic names'.[266] The type specimen can be a specimen plant, parts of a plant, or an illustration,[267] or 'cultures of algae and fungi, if preserved in a metabolically inactive state'.[268] Importantly, however, the type is merely representative of the features of the species and marked a transition from description to a

731; Charles Schuchert, 'What is a Type in Natural History' (1897) 5(121) *Science* 636; Ward, above n 239. For a much earlier discussion of types see William Whewell, *The Philosophy of the Inductive Sciences*, Volume 1 (John Parker, 1847) pp 74–78.

259 Nomenclature Commission of the Botanical Club of the American Association for the Advancement of Science, 'American Code of Botanical Nomenclature' (1907) 34 *Bulletin of the Torrey Botanical Club* 167, 167. See also A Hitchcock, 'The Type Concept in Systematic Botany' (1921) 8 *American Journal of Botany* 251.

260 Cook, 'The Method of Types', above n 258, 513.

261 Hitchcock, above n 257, 333.

262 Cook, 'Terms Relating to Generic Types', above n 258, 308.

263 See Joeri Witteveen, 'Naming and Contingency: The Type Method of Biological Taxonomy' (2015) 30 *Biology and Philosophy* 569, 570.

264 A Rendle, 'International Rules of Botanical Nomenclature adopted by the Fifth International Botanical Congress' (1934) 72 *Journal of Botany (supplement)* 1, 6 (Art 18). See also Nicolson, above n 107, 39–40.

265 J Lanjouw, C Baehni, W Robyns, R Ross, J Rousseau, J Schopf, G Schulze, A Smith, R de Vilmorin and F Stafleu, *International Code of Botanical Nomenclature, Adopted by the Ninth International Botanical Congress* (International Association for Plant Taxonomy, 1961) Art 37(1).

266 *International Code of Nomenclature for algae, fungi and plants*, Art 7.1.

267 *International Code of Nomenclature for algae, fungi and plants*, Arts 8.1 and 8.2.

268 *International Code of Nomenclature for algae, fungi and plants*, Art 8.4.

physical representation of the species with a fixed (priority) name rather than the traditional logic of an abstract idea linked to a name.[269] The ideal is that the type provides a link between the name, a physical plant and an objective standard to distinguish between a named plant and another *different* plant. Framed this way a type provides a reference point as part of the mechanics of classification making up for inadequate descriptions or illustrations and as the model species for the name.[270] This also allows later verification to recognise previously unrecognised determinative details.[271] Under the *Cultivated Plant Code* the type, called a 'nomenclatural standard',[272] is not required although it is 'strongly encouraged'.[273] This probably reflects the variable characteristics within their circumscription making a type of little authority as a reference standard.[274]

Perhaps more intriguingly the type acknowledges a fundamental underpinning of the taxonomy and naming schemes.[275] In theory, a natural classification would take into account every feature of a plant, and by describing every part of every plant, the essential and distinguishing features would become apparent. This is, however, an impossible task. A compromise is to select a limited number of features and use those in determining the taxonomy.[276] The type also means that a description does not need to define the essential features and make up for inadequate descriptions and diagnoses.[277] This was Linnaeus's approach and accounts for his favouring floral characters (*methodus propria*)[278] and, as he readily acknowledged, rendered his classification an artificial (non-natural) system.[279] While the type was implicit in most early classification and naming,[280] its formal adoption as a part of taxonomy and nomenclature remains contentious.[281] In linking the name to the description

---

269 See Lorraine Daston, 'Type Specimens and Scientific Memory' (2004) 31 *Critical Inquiry* 153, 158–165. For an early discussion of types and their problems see Schuchert, above n 258.

270 Farber, above n 256, 95.

271 Charles Santos, Dalton Amorim, Bruna Klassa, Diego Fachin, Silvio Nihei, Claudio Carvalho, Rafaela Falaschi, Cátia Mello-Patiu, Márcia Couri, Sarah Olieira, Vera Silva, Guilherme Ribeiro, Renato Capellari and Carlos Lamas, 'On Typeless Species and the Perils of Fast Taxonomy' (2016) 41 *Systematic Entomology* 511, 512.

272 *International Code of Nomenclature for Cultivated Plants*, Div 5.

273 *International Code of Nomenclature for Cultivated Plants*, Preamble 9 and Div 5.

274 *International Code of Nomenclature for Cultivated Plants*, Div 5 (Note 2).

275 See Foucault, above n 91, pp 150–158.

276 See ibid, pp 150–158.

277 See Witteveen, above n 263, 570.

278 Lisbet Koerner, 'Carl Linnaeus in his Time and Place' in N Jardine, J Secord and E Spary (eds), *Cultures of Natural History* (Cambridge University Press, 1966) pp 146–150.

279 See Müller-Wille, above n 67, 311 (footnote 25).

280 See Farber, above n 256, 94–95.

281 Phillip Honenberger, 'Greene and Hull on Types and Typological Thinking in Biology' (2015) 50 *Studies in History and Philosophy of Science Part C: Studies in*

(and diagnosis) the type specimen effectively substitutes for a determinative description (and diagnosis) becoming a proxy for the description and anchoring the name to a physical plant.[282] Again the idea was to avoid the different judgements of taxonomists giving different names to the same plants (or synonyms).[283]

5.4 Alternative code proposals

While the *Plant Code* and the *Cultivated Plant Code* remain the codes used in practice for plants, there are other alternative proposals. These codes presently co-exist with the plant codes and various comparable codes including the *International Code of Zoological Nomenclature*, the *International Code of Nomenclature of Bacteria* and the *Classification and Nomenclature of Viruses.*[284] The main alternative proposals are the *International Code of Biological Nomenclature* (or *BioCode*) and the *PhyloCode.*[285] The *BioCode* seeks to harmonise the existing codes[286] and the *PhyloCode* relies on the rank-based codes for the name and seeks to apply those names from the rank-based codes according to phylogenetically determined clades.[287] The *BioCode* was proposed to address the concern that taxonomists were having to distinguish between generic names legitimately used under animal and plant codes, and the problem of naming organisms that might legitimately be named under plant, animal or bacterial codes.[288] This resulted in a proposal to harmonise the

History and Philosophy of Biological and Biomedical Sciences 13, 14–18 and the references therein.

282 Importantly, the flaw in type specimens reasoning was that the first specimen collected became the type without a better knowledge and understanding of the diversity within the species so that the type specimens may not actually be representatives of the named species – 'an atypical type': Daston, above n 269, 161.

283 See Witteveen, 'Suppressing Synonyms' above n 130, 178–180.

284 Zoology – International Commission on Zoological Nomenclature, above n 20; bacteria – Lapage *et al.*, above n 20; viruses – King, Adams and Lefkowitz, above n 20.

285 See W Greuter, G Garrity, D Hawksworth, R Jahn, P Kirk, S Knapp, J McNeill, E Michel, D Patterson, R Pyle and B Tindall, 'Draft BioCode (2011): Principles and Rules Regulating the Naming of Organisms' (2011) 60 *Taxon* 201; P Cantino and K de Queiroz, *PhyloCode: International Code of Phylogenetic Nomenclature*, Version 4c (Committee on Phylogenetic Nomenclature, 2010) available at <https://www.ohio.edu/phylocode> (accessed 18 May 2017).

286 David Hawksworth, 'Introducing the Draft BioCode (2011)' (2011) 3 *Bionomics* 24, 24. See also David Hawksworth (ed), *The New Bionomenclature: The BioCode Debate*, Special Issue No 34 (IUBS, 1997).

287 Kevin de Queiroz and Jacques Gauthier, 'Towards a Phylogenetic System of Biological Nomenclature' (1994) 9 *Trends in Ecology and Evolution* 27, 28–30. See also Kevin de Queiroz and Jacques Gauthier, 'Phylogenetic Taxonomy' (1992) 23 *Annual Review of Ecology and Systematics* 449.

288 A Orchard, W Anderson, M Gilbert, D Sebsebe, W Stearn and E Voss, 'Harmonized Bionomenclature: A Recipe for Disharmony' (1996) 45 *Taxon* 287, 287.

codes.[289] The *BioCode* had an unpopular reception,[290] and has not been adopted despite some keen advocates.[291]

The *PhyloCode* was proposed to address the specific concern that the ideals of the current nomenclatures were developed before the widespread acceptance of common descent so that the codes are 'Linnaean rather than evolutionary in that their most fundamental concepts and principles are based on Linnaean taxonomic categories'.[292] The main flaws that the *PhyloCode* was to address were the practices of unification and division (called 'lumping' and 'splitting') of rank-based categories leading to taxon names changing evolutionary meaning based on judgements about the degrees of difference necessary to be within a category rather than true evolutionary (cladistics) groupings.[293] Put simply, the *PhyloCode* was to provide stability of names and promote more certain communication.[294] The reception of the *PhyloCode* has not, however, been favourable with critiques concerned about the 'radical consequences for biology' and 'a fundamental misunderstanding of the difference between a phylogeny (which is real) and a classification (which is utilitarian)'.[295]

5.5 Discussion and conclusions

Classifying (or ordering), naming, and then controlling are a fundamental objective of law so that the world is reordered for the benefit of humans. This is because a technological mode of revealing is necessary for science that 'demands that nature be orderable as standing-reserve' and that 'nature reports itself in some way or other that is identifiable through calculation and that it remain orderable as a system of information'.[296] As such, naming systems are a

See also Werner Greuter, 'On a New *BioCode*, Harmony and Expediency' (1996) 45 *Taxon* 291.

289 See Werner Greuter, John McNeill and Fred Barrie, 'Report on Botanical Nomenclature: Yokohama 1993. XV International Botanical Congress, Tokyo: Nomenclature Section, 23 to 27 August 1993' (1994) 14 *Englera* 1, 193.

290 See, for examples, Brummitt, above n 137; Orchard *et al.*, above n 288.

291 See Greuter *et al.*, above n 285.

292 de Queiroz and Gauthier, above n 287, 27. See also Benoît Dayrat, Philip Cantino, Julia Clarke and Kevin de Queiroz, 'Species Names in the *PhyloCode*: The Approach Adopted by the International Society for Phylogenetic Nomenclature' (2008) 57 *Systematic Biology* 507 and the references therein.

293 de Queiroz and Gauthier, above n 287, 27–28.

294 Ibid 28.

295 Michael Benton, 'Stems, Nodes, Crown Clades, and Rank-free Lists: Is Linnaeus Dead?' (2000) 75 *Biological Reviews of the Cambridge Philosophical Society* 633, 633. See also Quentin Wheeler, 'Taxonomic Triage and the Poverty of Phylogeny' (2004) 359 *Philosophical Transactions of the Royal Society of London B: Biological Sciences* 571, 577–578 and the references therein; Peter Forey, '*PhyloCode* – Pain, No Gain' (2002) 51 *Taxon* 43 and the references therein; Moore, above n 163 and the references therein.

296 Martin Heidegger, *The Question Concerning Technology and Other Essays* (translated William Lovitt; Garland Publishing, 1977) p 23.

common human hierarchical thought and language scheme that also aids communication, comprehension and memory.[297] This appears to have been a widespread human endeavour with ethno-botanists finding a similar consensus about the groupings of plants across cultures, although there remained strong disagreement about particular descriptions.[298] So, for example, German mosses have been subjected to 12 successive classifications over some 70 years and only 13 per cent of the names and circumspections (descriptions) remained consistent over that time.[299] This reflects the element of judgement in deciding the features that are significant even though the 'overall resemblances' or 'general likeness' are readily agreed.[300] The *Plant Code* and the *Cultivated Plant Code* provide, as the analysis in this chapter outlines, the mode of revealing and the heritage of naming shows that this has now evolved into a sophisticated form of controlling.

As a means of controlling there has been general acceptance that taxonomy is artificial (and not natural) since at least Linnaeus's time, and just a system for our understanding of relationships among existing and extinct organisms.[301] The debates about the form of a classification to properly reflect the natural systems continue, perhaps best illustrated by the advocates of the *PhyloCode* and the distinction between the traditional rank-based nomenclature and their proposed phylogenetic nomenclature.[302] This is because bringing together the various science disciplines in recent times to provide an account of evolution (known as the 'Modern Synthesis')[303] has definitely posed a problem for identifying and naming in that a species is not a stable concept,[304] and there is no one true form or type, but rather an evolving gene pool in a population.[305]

297 Stevens, above n 82, 12. See also H Gleason, 'The Individualistic Concept of Plant Association' (1926) 53 *Bulletin of the Torrey Botanical Club* 7.
298 See Brent Berlin, *Ethno-biological Classification: Principles of Categorization of Plants and Animals in Traditional Societies* (Princeton University Press, 1992) pp 53–96.
299 Marc Geoffroy and Walter Berendsohn, 'The Concept Problem in Taxonomy: Importance, Components, Approaches' (2003) 39 *Schriftenreihe Vegetationsk* 14.
300 See A Cain and G Harrison, 'An Analysis of the Taxonomic Judgment of Affinity' (1958) 131 *Proceedings of the Zoological Society of London* 85, 85.
301 Müller-Wille, above n 67, 310–311.
302 See, for example, Kevin de Queiroz, 'The PhyloCode and the Distinction between Taxonomy and Nomenclature' (2006) 55 *Systematic Biology* 160.
303 See Julian Huxley, *Evolution: The Modern Synthesis* (Allen and Unwin, 1942); Ernst Mayr, *Systematics and the Origin of Species* (Columbia University Press, 1942); Theodosius Dobzhansky, *Genetics and the Origin of Species* (Columbia University Press, 1937).
304 There are presently 27–29 species concepts: M Casiraghi, A Galimberti, A Sandionigi, A Bruno and M Labra, 'Life With or Without Names' (2016) *Evolutionary Biology* 1 (DOI: 10.1007/s11692-016-9384-5); John Wilkins, 'Philosophically Speaking, How Many Species Concepts are There?' (2011) 2765 *Zootaxa* 58.
305 There is a large and comprehensive literature about the definition of species, with probably the best definition being 'what a community of taxonomists says it is': see, for highlights, Richard Richards, *The Species Problem: A Philosophical Analysis*

This presents a fundamental challenge for a stable taxonomy as a means of classification and naming – '[i]f species aren't real, then "species" has no reference and classification is completely arbitrary'.[306] This might not, however, be so grim if species are considered from the bottom-up, and inductively generalised from individuals keeping lineages distinct, rather than a top-down logic of classification that treats species as natural kinds.[307] Further, the Aristotelian ideals of precise definition requiring a description have been moved from being a part of the name to another place, the name is theoretically now just the Lockean tag so that the Linnaean binomial functions merely as a convenient and unique identifier. Put slightly differently, the naming ideal has been developed into a scheme with simple names (tags) linked to published descriptions and diagnoses so that plants with the same name will have the same descriptions and diagnoses and with a particular plant description everyone will give the plant the same name. Therefore, '[t]he plant is thus engraved in the material of the language into which it has been transposed, and recomposes its pure form before the reader's very eyes'.[308] In this sense nomenclature is a standardised metadata system for ordering information about plants so that it can be collected, stored, searched, retrieved and integrated. It is a little more complex, however, as the analysis of the naming codes in this chapter shows, because the names also convey information about the plant's relationship to other plants in a classification system, and sometimes information about a plant's parentage or hybridity. This then raises the fundamental challenge in finding meaning where a word or words represent a concept or thing.

The conventional understanding of language and meaning is that a word represents a thing and the interposition of a concept or meaning: '[b]esides articulate sounds, therefore, it was further necessary that he [man] should be able to use these sounds as signs of internal conceptions; and to make them stand as marks for the ideas within his own mind, whereby they might be made known to others, and the thoughts of men's minds be conveyed from one to

---

(Cambridge University Press, 2010); Wilkins, above n 44; John Wilkins, *Defining Species: A Sourcebook from Antiquity to Today* (Peter Lang International, 2009); Mayr, above n 1; David Hull, 'The Effect of Essentialism on Taxonomy: Two Thousand Years of Stasis' (1965a) 15 *British Journal for the Philosophy of Sciences* 314; David Hull, 'The Effect of Essentialism on Taxonomy: Two Thousand Years of Stasis' (1965b) 16 *British Journal for the Philosophy of Sciences* 1; George Simpson, *Principles of Animal Taxonomy* (Columbia University Press, 1961); Arthur Cain, *Animal Species and their Evolution* (Princeton Legacy, 1954); Theodosius Dobzhansky, 'A Critique of the Species Concept in Biology' (1935) 2 *Philosophy of Science* 244; and so on.

306 Hull (1965a), ibid, 320. See also Hull, above n 43.

307 Wilkins, above n 44, pp 233–234. See also John Boodin, 'The Discovery of Form' (1943) 4 *Journal of the History of Ideas* 177, 185 ('Aristotle started with a large universal, a genus, and by division and adding of differences tried to "approach" the individual').

308 Foucault, above n 91, p 147.

another'.[309] According to this understanding a word represents and expresses meaning so that giving a thing a name gives that thing a meaning and a medium to communicate that meaning: '[t]he use, then, of words, is to be sensible marks of ideas; and the ideas they stand for are their proper and immediate significance':[310]

> I would not here be thought to forget, much less to deny, that Nature, in the production of things, makes several of them alike: there is nothing more obvious, especially in the races of animals, and all things propagated by seed. But yet I think we may say, the sorting of them under names is the workmanship of the understanding, taking occasion, from the similitude it observes amongst them, to make abstract general ideas, and set them up in the mind, with names annexed to them, as patterns or forms, (for, in that sense, the word form has a very proper signification,) to which as particular things existing are found to agree, so they come to be of that species, have that denomination, or are put into that classic. For when we say this is a man, that a horse; this justice, that cruelty; this a watch, that a jack; what do we else but rank things under different specific names, as agreeing to those abstract ideas, of which we have made those names the signs? And what are the essences of those species set out and marked by names, but those abstract ideas in the mind; which are, as it were, the bonds between particular things that exist, and the names they are to be ranked under?[311]

This conception of naming presumes that there is a pre-existing reality that can be described by appropriate naming. Ferdinand de Saussure challenged this ideal positing that the concept (signified) and the word corresponding with the concept (signifier) together make a sign, and that the relationship between the concept and the word is arbitrary or not natural.[312] According to this schema, meaning is the product of, and constructed from, the relationship between the word (signifier) and the concept (signified). And the concept associated with the word is then derived from what it is not:

> Instead of pre-existing ideas, then, we find ... values emanating from the system. When they are said to correspond to concepts, it is understood that the concepts are purely differential and defined not by their positive content but negatively by their relations with the other terms of the system. Their most precise characteristic is in being what the others are not.[313]

---

309 Locke, above n 69, p 3 (Book III, i, 2).
310 Ibid, p 9 (Book III, ii, 1).
311 Ibid, pp 23–24 (Book III, iii, 13).
312 Ferdinand de Saussure, *Course in General Linguistics* (New York Philosophical Library, 1959) pp 114–120.
313 Ibid, p 117.

The importance of this proposition is that it disrupts the conventional understanding of language and meaning as being based on a thing that pre-existed the representation: '[w]hether we take the signified or the signifier, language has neither ideas nor sounds that existed before the linguistic system, but only conceptual and phonic differences that have issued from the system. The idea or phonic substance that a sign contains is of less importance than the other signs that surround it'.[314] In short, the naming of a plant is not the name representing the plant, but rather the name that constitutes the plant within the subliminal system of understanding the name and its function. And then the understanding of that name is according to all the things that it is not. So, *Diuris magnifica* has a meaning by knowing its differences from related species *Diuris micrantha*, *Diuris ochroma* and *Diuris oporina*, and within the genera *Diuris* that are different from the *Orchidaceae* genera *Disperis*, *Distylodon*, *Domingoa*, *Dossinia*, and so on. Despite this apparently confronting proposition, really this just means that the way we think about plants is situated in the discourse about plants and that this does not have an independent existence. Perhaps surprisingly, a long time ago Linnaeus readily accepted that his naming and classification was arbitrary (and not natural).[315] And similarly, the quest to define a non-arbitrary species concept continues unfulfilled even though a species is at the heart of our current classification and naming codes,[316] and this has not rendered classification unworkable. Unlike Linnaeus, and probably the vast majority of modern taxonomist questing for a classification and naming system that represents real natural relationships (phylogenetics), de Saussure's proposition leads to the conclusion that naming in a classification system will always be arbitrary because the naming takes place within a discourse about classification that does not have a natural existence. In this sense, names are a perfect metadata structure because they constitute the plant within the data structures.

Following on from this structuralist ideal about naming, the post-structuralists (deconstructionists) posit that the name has a subjective interpretation and meaning: '[l]anguage is so organised that it permits each speaker to *appropriate to himself* an entire language by designating himself as *I*'.[317] This means that there is no definitive interpretation, but instead a multitude of interpretations:

> We know now that a text is not a line of words releasing a single 'theological' meaning (the 'message' of the Author-God) but a multidimensional space in which a variety of writings, none of them original, blend and clash. The text is a tissue of quotations drawn from the innumerable centres of culture.[318]

---

314 Ibid, p 120.
315 Müller-Wille, above n 67, 311 (footnote 25).
316 See Wilkins, above n 44, pp 227–234.
317 Émile Benveniste, *Problems in General Linguistics* (University of Miami Press, 1971) p 227.
318 Roland Barthes, *Image Music Text* (Fontana Press, 1977) p 146.

This is not the destruction of meaning. Rather this acknowledges that there is complexity in agreeing to a meaning. Most importantly, however, this also suggests that there is not a direct relationship between the concept (signified) and the word corresponding with the concept (signifier). As Jacques Derrida points out, in attempting to define or identify the essential characters of a concept we are trying to fix a meaning.[319] Unfortunately, in finding meaning for the concept (signified) there are two concerns: first, the meaning is deferred (or postponed) as words attempting to define the meaning rely on more words to define those words, and so on;[320] and secondly, the process of finding meaning relies on differences that are continuously assessed and reassessed.[321] The consequence of these propositions is that the interpretation leading to meaning is determined from the context, and this depends on the context at each interpretation. The consequences of deconstruction (or post-structuralism) in considering naming codes are questioning and reconstructing the fundamental ideas embedded in the codes. There remains, however, some hesitation about the methodology, as Derrida also accepts:

> This is why, especially in the United States, the motif of deconstruction has been associated with 'post-structuralism' (a word unknown in France until its 'return' from the States). But the undoing, decomposing, and desedimenting of structures, in a certain sense more historical than the structuralist movement it called into question, was not a negative operation. Rather than destroying, it was also necessary to understand how an 'ensemble' was constituted and to reconstruct it to this end. However, the negative appearance was and remains much more difficult to efface than is suggested by the grammar of the word (de-), even though it can designate a genealogical restoration [*remonter*] rather than a demolition. That is why the word, at least on its own, has never appeared satisfactory to me (but what word is), and must always be girded by an entire discourse. It is difficult to effect it afterward because, in the work of deconstruction, I have had to, as I have to here, multiply the cautionary indicators and put aside all the traditional philosophical concepts, while reaffirming the necessity of returning to them, at least under erasure. Hence, this has been called, precipitately, a type of negative theology (this was neither true nor false but I shall not enter into the debate here).[322]

Put slightly differently, interpretation remains somewhat predictable because even though each context cannot be exhaustively determined, and the writing

319 Jacques Derrida, *Of Grammatology*, (translated by Gayatri Chakravorty Spivak; John Hopkins University Press, 1974) p 12.
320 Ibid, p 158.
321 Jacques Derrida, *Margins of Philosophy* (translated by Alan Bass; Harvester Press, 1982) pp 7–8.
322 Jacques Derrida, 'Letter to A Japanese Friend' in Julian Wolfreys (ed), *Literary Theories: A Reader and Guide* (New York University Press, 1999) p 284.

context is almost always removed from the reading of that writing context,[323] the iteration may be less ambiguous in its particular context so that the meaning is more likely revealed.[324] Communication happens when, in the particular context(s), there is congruence or consensus of interpretation and the readers agree to a particular meaning. With an appropriate process, there may be a general congruence or consensus, and a preferable meaning will be apparent because controlling the context reduces the possible ambiguity (different meanings). In other words, among a community of taxonomists[325] using the rules in the *Plant Code* and the *Cultivated Plant Code*, controlling the format and content of communication with a name and a description and diagnosis, agreeing to a forum conforming to the practices and values of taxonomy peer reviewing their taxonomic and naming decisions through publication, and with the potential to formally adjudicate different interpretations through binding rulings after guidance from a committee of taxonomic experts, there is the potential for shared common meanings (congruence or consensus). The success of the *Plant Code* and the *Cultivated Plant Code* in establishing this context for a less ambiguous meaning must be their ongoing adoption and use, even in the face of alternatives like the *BioCode* and the *PhyloCode*.

Framed this way the ongoing challenge for taxonomy and nomenclature is to establish the context that reduces the potential for ambiguity, even though complete knowledge is unknowable and unattainable.[326] The present codes reduce ambiguity well, and as the analyses in this chapter show, authorship, priority, publication, types and registration each work to confer a context for meaning and remove ambiguity in matching a name to a plant. What is important, however, is that the name exists within a context. The particular context for the naming codes is placing a plant into a classification system that orders its relationship with all other plants, and then distinguishes that plant from others according to a type specimen (*Plant Code*) or a definition and diagnoses (*Cultivated Plant Code*). And in some cases the name can also detail aspects of the plant's parents and breeding where there is a hybridisation, and so on. This suggests that despite the developments from Aristotle, Linnaeus, Locke and the Strickland Code detailed in this chapter, there remains some meaning in the name and it is more than just a tag. What about the context for metadata systems?

323 Derrida notes that 'a context is never absolutely determinable': Jacques Derrida *Limited Inc* (Northwestern University Press, 1988) pp 3 and 9.
324 Ibid, p 2 ('massively reduced') and the subsequent pages.
325 See S Knapp, 'Taxonomy as a Team Sport' in Quentin Wheeler, *The New Taxonomy* (CRC Press, 2008) pp 33–53.
326 See Richard Ladle and Joaquín Hortal, 'Mapping Species Distribution: Living with Uncertainty' (2013) 5 *Frontiers of Biogeography* 8, 8–9. See also Joaquín Hortal, Francesco de Bello, José Alexandre Diniz-Filho, Thomas Lewinsohn, Jorge Lobo and Richard Ladle, 'Seven Shortfalls that Beset Large-scale Knowledge of Biodiversity' (2015) 46 *Annual Review of Ecology, Evolution, and Systematics* 523.

Names do provide a standardised metadata system for collecting, storing, searching, retrieving and integrating information about plants. This is because a consensus about a plant's name is useful for linking all manner of information about that plant to that plant.[327] Current projects such as *LifeWatch*,[328] *Atlas of Living Australia*,[329] *Encyclopaedia of Life*,[330] *Global Names Architecture*,[331] *Catalogue of Life*,[332] and so on, all use names as a metadata structure for ordering their content. There are, however, some problems with relying on names for these metadata structures: many names for the same plant (synonyms) and many plants with the same name (homonyms),[333] vernacular or surrogate names,[334] alternative (mis-)spellings (and orthographic variants)[335] or format errors,[336] emendation (ongoing process of revision),[337] circumscription changes (changing the description but not the name such as geographical distributions),[338] alternative nomenclature combinations (the species epithet combined with different generic and other epithets),[339] and so on.[340] The consequence is that either the name identifies information that is not relevant to that name (a false positive), or information that is relevant to that name is not identified (a false negative).[341] In both instances the name and the related information are not correctly linked.

At the heart of this is the process of matching a name to a concept to a thing.[342] In the language of informatics, semantic refers to the relationship

---

327 See Pyle, above n 13, 268–269; D Patterson, J Cooper, P Kirk, R Pyle and D Remsen, 'Names are Key to the Big New Biology' (2010) 25 *Trends in Ecology and Evolution* 686.

328 *LifeWatch* available at <http://www.lifewatch.eu> (accessed 18 May 2017).

329 *The Atlas of Living Australia* available at <http://www.ala.org.au> (accessed 18 May 2017).

330 *Encyclopaedia of Life* available at <http://eol.org> (accessed 18 May 2017).

331 *Global Names Architecture* available at <http://globalnames.org> (accessed 18 May 2017).

332 *Catalogue of Life* available at <http://www.catalogueoflife.org> (accessed 18 May 2017).

333 Patterson *et al.*, above n 16, 2–3; Remsen, above n 16, 214–219; Pyle, above n 13, 270; Denis Lepage, Gaurav Vaidya and Robert Guralnick, 'Avibase – A Database System for Managing and Organizing Taxonomic Concepts' (2014) 420 *ZooKeys* 117, 118; Patterson *et al.*, above n 327, 687.

334 Patterson *et al.*, ibid, 687.

335 Patterson *et al.*, above n 16, 3; Remsen, above n 16, 214; Pyle, above n 13, 270; Lepage *et al.*, above n 333, 118; Patterson *et al.*, above n 327, 688.

336 See Paula Zermoglio, Robert Guralnick and John Wieczorek, 'A Standardized Reference Data Set for Vertebrate Taxon Name Resolution' (2016) 11 *PLoS One* e0146894, 3.

337 Lepage *et al.*, above n 333, 118.

338 Ibid 118.

339 Patterson *et al.*, above n 16, 3; Pyle, above n 13, 270.

340 See Zermoglio, Guralnick and Wieczorek, above n 336, 2.

341 See Remsen, above n 16, 212.

342 See Remsen, ibid, 210. See also Nico Franz and Beckett Sterner, 'Taxonomy – For Computers' (2015) *bioRxiv* 022145.

between the sign (name) and the thing (plant), and syntactics refers to the relationship between signs (names) within a data structure (such as a database).[343] The same post-structuralists' (deconstructionists') concern about fixing meaning is apparent – that the meaning of a name depends on the context in which it is being interpreted – so that, again in the language of informatics, the names communicate meaning because the name evokes congruence between the referent (the thing such as a plant) and the symbol (such as a name), accepting that 'whether partial [communication] is good enough is contingent on context-specific inference needs that the reciprocal concept alignment must fulfil'.[344] So:

> two persons look at the same avocado and one declares it a fruit, because it is derived from floral ovaries, while another declares it is not a fruit because it is not sweet. This conflict occurs when there is no congruency in the concepts invoked through the use of the name. Similar issues occur within taxonomy. In the simple case above, the term 'fruit' is associated with two definitions, or, more formally, the *cardinality* between syntax and semantics is one-to-two, or more generally, one-to-many (1:N). The same object evokes the same name but refers to two concepts according to two individuals. It is the relationship between the name and the concept that is important. Cardinality between syntax and semantics has a direct impact on the use and limits of scientific names as identifiers in biological informatics.[345]

The solution to this problem is developing unique identifiers. In other words, there must be a one to one (1:1) relationship between the semantics and the syntax so that the name corresponds with the thing (plant) and *only* that thing: '[u]nless the semantic relations across all phases in the transition model are indeed stable and congruent, the services [asking computers to represent and reason over taxonomic (provenance) knowledge] cannot reliable materialize'.[346] The binomial name according to the *Plant Code* and the *Cultivated Plant Code* cannot deliver this cardinality between syntax and semantics because of the inherent instability in naming from synonyms, homonyms, changed circumscriptions, taxonomic modifications and developments, different taxonomic philosophies, and so on.[347] There are two apparent solutions to this problem: (1) developing systems to address and correct/remove the synonyms, homonyms, incorrect spellings, and so on, to render names as unique identifiers (one plant, one name);[348] or (2) developing systems that capture the ontologies of names, being the hierarchical (taxonomic), non-hierarchical and arbitrary

343 See Remsen, ibid, 210.
344 Ibid, 210–211.
345 Ibid, 211.
346 Ibid, 212; Franz and Sterner, above n 342.
347 See Remsen, ibid, 214–219.
348 See Patterson *et al.*, above n 327, 688–690 (Global Names Architecture).

relationship between concepts captured by the name.[349] The former approach of developing systems to correct anomalies (such as name-processing tools) has been relatively successful with various approaches available to reduce and remove the variations towards one name to one plant.[350] For example, the various names and variants might be collected as a catalogue of all name strings together with a reconciliation group and a query starting with any of the names can then exploit the reconciliation group and address the query.[351] Meanwhile, the latter ontological approach has some potential but there are significant limitations as there are many more taxonomic concepts than names that each requires definitions and interpretations (and pairwise comparisons grow exponentially) making processing concepts potentially (much) more ambiguous than names.[352] This is a problem common to all attempts to reduce quantitative and qualitative data to be both computer-readable and interoperable.[353] Perhaps the major impediment, however, is that a solution relying on purely computational logic might be more efficient but will lack the basic requirement of being usable by humans because the symbols used need not relate to communicating a recognisable and readable name, and would probably be 128-bit strings that are not easily read and communicated by humans.[354] In short, traditional Linnaean names still retain their elegance in their simplicity and their ability to communicate. So rather than developing new metadata structures to manage the increasing volumes of information about plants, the solution is undoubtedly to improve the current naming practices in the context of their role as metadata structures. This is because they provide a universal biological standard that has an agreed process developed over a very long time for making names together with the ability to revise

349 See N Franz and R Peet, 'Perspectives: Towards a Language for Mapping Relationships Among Taxonomic Concepts' (2009) 7 *Systematics and Biodiversity* 5, 6–11.
350 See, for examples, Patterson *et al.*, above n 16; Edward Berghe, Gianpaolo Coro, Nicolas Bailly, Fabio Fiorellato, Caselyn Aldemita, Anton Ellenbroek and Pasquale Pagano, 'Retrieving Taxa Names from Large Biodiversity Data Collections Using a Flexible Matching Workflow' (2015) 28 *Ecological Informatics* 29; Zermoglio, Guralnick and Wieczorek, above n 336; Brad Boyle, Nicole Hopkins, Zhenyuan Lu, Juan Antonio Raygoza Garay, Dmitry Mozzherin, Tony Rees, Naim Matasci, Martha Narro, William Piel, Sheldon Mckay, Sonya Lowry, Chris Freeland, Robert Peet and Brian Enquist, 'The Taxonomic Name Resolution Service: An Online Tool for Automated Standardization of Plant Names' (2013) 14 *Bioinformatics* 14; and so on.
351 Patterson, Faulwetter and Shipunov, above n 16, 156.
352 Lepage *et al.*, above n 333, 119.
353 See Andrew Deans, Suzanna Lewis, Eva Huala, Salvatore Anzaldo, Michael Ashburner, James Balhoff, David Blackburn *et al.*, 'Finding Our Way through Phenotypes' (2015) 13 *PLoS Biology* e1002033, 2.
354 Franz and Sterner, above n 342, 8. For another possibility see J Kennedy, R Hyam, R Kukla and T Paterson, 'Standard Data Model Representation for Taxonomic Inforamtion' (2006) 10 *Journal of Integrative Biology* 220.

and resolve disputes, and the proven potential for names as a link across the many sources and forms of information.[355]

There are also various initiatives to reduce synonyms, homonyms, ambiregnals, mis-spellings and so on. Perhaps the best advance has been the development of name registries, indexes and lists.[356] The *Cultivated Plant Code* already provides for name registration with an 'International Cultivar Registration Authority'.[357] This provides a mechanism for implementing the naming norms set out in the codes and operates to limit the problems of instability – from the same plant having multiple names (synonyms), different plants having the same names (homonym), and so on.[358] The same registration is not presently required under the *Plant Code*.[359] This is probably because starting to register names without the existing names means that the register will include very few names as a proportion of all named plants effectively duplicating and replacing existing systems.[360] The latest iteration of this code, however, provided for newly named fungi, on or after 1 January 2013, 'the citation in the protologue of the identifier issued by a recognized repository for the name' for valid publication.[361] Instead of registration, there also exist a range of indexes and lists for plant names (other than protected names under the codes),[362] such as the *International Plant Names Index* (merging *Index Kewensis, Gray Herbarium Index* and the *Australian Plant Names Index*)[363] that tracks and records names.[364] These indexes and lists are just a compilation of available information

355 See Godfray *et al.*, above n 36, 944.
356 See Lyubomir Penev, Alan Paton, Nicola Nicolson, Paul Kirk, Richard Pyle, Robert Whitton, Teodor Georgiev *et al.*, 'A Common Registration-to-publication Automated Pipeline for Nomenclatural Acts for Higher Plants (International Plant Names Index, IPNI), Fungi (Index Fungorum, MycoBank) and Animals (Zoo-Bank)' (2016) 550 *ZooKeys* 23 and the references therein.
357 *International Code of Nomenclature for Cultivated Plants*, Principle 8 and Div IV.
358 See Hawksworth, above n 200, 561–562.
359 See Urs Eggli, 'Why We Don't Need Registration' (1998) 47 *Taxon* 963; William Anderson and William Buck, 'Registration of Names' (1998) 50 *Brittonia* 428; Nicholas Turland and Gerrit Davidse, 'Registration of Plant Names: Undesirable, Unnecessary, and Unworkable' (1998) 47 *Taxon* 957; Werner Greuter, 'Proposals on Registration of Plant Names: A New Concept for the Nomenclature of the Future' (1986) 35 *Taxon* 816. See also A Polaszek, D Agosti, M Alonso-Zarazaga, G Beccaloni, P Bjørn, P Bouchet, D Brothers, G Cranbrook, N Evenhuis, H Godfray, N Johnson, F Krell, D Lipscomb, C Lyal, G Mace, S Mawatari, S Miller, A Minelli, S Morris, P Ng, D Patterson, R Pyle, N Robinson, L Rogo, J Taverne, F Thompson, J van Tol, Q Wheeler, E Wilson, 'A Universal Register for Animal Names' (2005) 437 *Nature* 477.
360 Turland and Davidse, ibid, 958.
361 *International Code of Nomenclature for algae, fungi and plants*, Art 42.1.
362 See Hawksworth, above n 200, 558–560.
363 *International Plant Names Index* available at <http://www.ipni.org> (accessed 18 May 2017).
364 See, for example, J Croft, N Cross, S Hinchcliffe, E Nic Lughadha, P Stevens, J West and G Whitbread, 'Plant Names for the 21st Century: The International Plant Names Index, A Distributed Data Source of General Accessibility' (1999) 48

about names, synonyms, homonyms and so on.[365] Perhaps the most famous list is the *Index Animalium* that provided an alphabetical listing of species together with the genus, species and author, abbreviated title of the publication, and the critical date and page specifics.[366] This has now been digitised,[367] and together with a number of other lists,[368] they all provide a demonstration of the kinds of compilations that can assist in clarifying the current names through addressing synonyms, homonyms, and so on. The modern examples are databases such as the *Global Names Architecture* that is 'a system of web-services which helps people to register, find, index, check and organize biological scientific names and interconnect on-line information about species'.[369]

Together with the consideration of registration, indexes and lists, there has also been the development of standards. Perhaps the most significant of these has been the *Darwin Core* that articulates a formal set of standard terms including names 'to create a common language for sharing biodiversity data that is complementary to and reuses metadata standards from other domains wherever possible'.[370] The other initiatives that are significant for interoperability include those directed towards unique identifiers – Globally Unique Identifier (GUIDs), LifeScience Identifiers (LSIDs) and Digital Object Identifiers (DOIs).[371] This is a rapidly developing area and the likely standards that take precedence over time remain unclear.

Taxon 317. See also for a discussion about ways to improve nomenclature: D Hawksworth, 'Proposals to Streamline Botanical (including Mycological) Nomenclature Thwarted' (2000) 104 *Mycology Research* 5; John McNeill, 'Naming the Groups: Developing a Stable and Efficient Nomenclature' (2000) 49 *Taxon* 705.

365 See Jun Wen, Stefanie Ickert-Bond, Marc Appelhans, Laurence Dorr and Vicki Funk, 'Collections-based Systematics: Opportunities and Outlook for 2050' (2015) 53 *Journal of Systematics and Evolution* 477; Eimear Lughadha, 'Towards a Working List of All Known Plant Species' (2004) 359 *Philosophical Transactions of the Royal Society of London B: Biological Sciences* 681; and so on. See also Hawksworth, above n 200, 560–561.

366 See Neal Evenhuis, 'Charles Davies Sherborn and the "Indexer's Club"' (2016) 550 *ZooKeys* 13, 18.

367 See Smithsonian Institution Libraries, *INDEX ANIMALIUM/Charles Davies Sherborn* available at <http://www.sil.si.edu/digitalcollections/indexanimalium> (accessed 18 May 2017). See also Suzanne Pilsk, Martin Kalfatovic, Joel Richard, 'Unlocking Index Animalium: From Paper Slips to Bytes and Bits' (2016) 550 *ZooKeys* 153.

368 See Pyle, above n 13.

369 *Global Names Architecture* available at <http://globalnames.org> (accessed 18 May 2017). See also Pyle, ibid.

370 John Wieczorek, David Bloom, Robert Guralnick, Stan Blum, Markus Döring, Renato Giovanni, Tim Robertson and David Vieglais, 'Darwin Core: An Evolving Community-Developed Biodiversity Data Standard' (2012) 7 *PLoS One* e29715, 2.

371 International DOI Foundation, *The DOI® System* available at <https://www.doi.org> (accessed 18 May 2017). See also Godfray *et al.*, above n 36, 948; Roderic Page, 'Taxonomic Names, Metadata and the Semantic Web' (2006) 3 *Biodiversity Informatics* 1, 3–4.

What is apparent, and demonstrated by the analysis in this chapter, is that plant names (or their unique associated identifiers, such as GUIDs, LSIDs or DOIs) are still linked to a type or a description and diagnosis that enables a plant to be distinguished from other similar plants. These names retain the echoes of Aristotle and the heritage of developments that have been traced through this chapter. And intriguingly, and coming full circle, the Aristotelian predicables and the development of these sophisticated naming codes have a direct application to names (or even GUIDs, LSIDs or DOIs) as data structures – a genus and differentia taken together identifies and distinguishes one true form from another, and the definition (species) comprising the genus together with the differentia captures the essence of the thing, enabling a real (natural) classification.[372] Metadata structures are in essence just another form of classification, and being able to use these structures requires that the structure be defined and described, fixing a meaning (within a context) with a congruence or consensus of interpretation.

Turning now to the suitability of plant names as a metadata structure for organising and accessing biological information under the ABS arrangements in the CBD, the Nagoya Protocol, the Plant Treaty, the PIP Framework and developing ABS schemes. There are already a number of frameworks that have been developed to deal with information about genetic resources, including the Global Biodiversity Informatics Outlook,[373] Digital Seed Bank,[374] European Search Catalogue for Plant Genetic Resources (Eurisco),[375] Global Gateway to Genetic Resources (GeneSys),[376] World Information Sharing Mechanism for the implementation of the Global Plan of Action (WISM-GPA),[377] and so on. Each of these frameworks identifies the importance of collecting and understanding information about biodiversity, although not actually resolving the effect and consequences of how this information is best structured. The database global standards are, however, emerging. The Germplasm Resource Information Network (GRIN-Global) for plants (with similar systems for animal, microbial and invertebrate germplasm), that originated with the United States Department of Agriculture's Agricultural Research Service and has since been modified with the assistance of the Global Crop Diversity Trust and Bioversity International to apply more generally to germplasm collections useful to agriculture,[378] and the Diversity Seek (DivSeek), bringing together a large number of public organisations and private partners from around the

---

372 For a discussion of this logic applied to taxonomy see Cain, above n 57, 145–156.
373 See <www.biodiversityinformatics.org> (accessed 18 May 2017).
374 See <www.globalplantcouncil.org> (accessed 18 May 2017).
375 See <www.ecpgr.cgiar.org> (accessed 18 May 2017).
376 See <www.genesys-pgr.org> (accessed 18 May 2017).
377 See <www.fao.org/pgrfa-gpa-archive/selectcountry.jspx> (accessed 18 May 2017).
378 See <www.ars-grin.gov> (accessed 18 May 2017).

globe to mine information on plant genetic resources,[379] are establishing metadata structures. There is, for example, an existing practice at GRIN-Global to use the *Plant Code* and the *Cultivated Plant Code* names for accessions[380] and active discussions about the kinds of metadata structures for DivSeek,[381] with the focus being '[t]o develop a common standard for Permanent Unique Identifiers applied to [plant genetic resources for food and agriculture] and an operational mechanism to promote the adoption of DOIs'.[382] Similarly, the Plant Treaty secretariat recently released the data requirements for the assignment of unique identifiers for germplasm (being DOIs) in the Plant Treaty's Global Information System.[383] These requirements expressly include a plant 'scientific name' as a mandatory value to be included in the descriptors for all plant samples maintained under the Plant Treaty.[384]

While DOIs will undoubtedly be useful in these circumstances because they have a standard certification (ISO 26324) that is centrally managed (International DOI Foundation) and have a flexible and extensible metadata structure,[385] plant names remain important. The plant name remains valuable because of their uses across many and diverse information collections resulting from the massive increase in biology and environmental research and the long association of plants groupings with a name. The naming codes also provide a standard for naming and the critical linkage (metadata structure) to access most plant information held around the world. And at the heart of the ABS arrangements in the CBD, the Nagoya Protocol, the Plant Treaty, the PIP Framework and developing ABS schemes, is benefit sharing that depends on the disclosed data and information about the genetic resources. As such, accessing and sharing information is a major shared benefit and a feature of the information obligations under these ABS arrangements. While these GUIDs, LSIDs and DOIs do have a role in addition to plant names to distinguish the

---

379 See <www.divseek.org> (accessed 18 May 2017).
380 For example, the US National Plant Germplasm System accession detail unique identifiers together with a name consistent with the naming codes, such as 'Clor 1344 *Oryza sativa* L. "Fortuna"' available at <https://npgsweb.ars-grin.gov/gringlobal/accessiondetail.aspx?id=1013133> (accessed 18 May 2017).
381 See Governing Body of the International Treaty on Plant Genetic Resources for Food and Agriculture, *Sixth Session of the Governing Body of the International Treaty on Plant Genetic Resources for Food and Agriculture* (2015) IT/GB-6/15/Report, [31] and Appendix A.3 (Resolution 3/2015).
382 Ibid, Appendix A.3 (Annex 2, item 3(a)).
383 Secretariat of the International Treaty on Plant Genetic Resources for Food and Agriculture, *Guidelines for the Optimal Use of Digital Object Identifiers as Permanent Unique Identifiers for Germplasm Samples – v.2* (FAO, 2017) available at <http://www.fao.org/3/a-bt114e.pdf> (accessed 14 December 2017)
384 Data Required, ibid, p 5.
385 See International Organization for Standardization, *Information and documentation – Digital Object Identifier (DOI)* (International Organization for Standardization, 2008).

various biological entities within the named plant grouping (and especially below the species level as part of the management of plant collections, such as seeds), it is the plant names that are a vital linkage between the various repositories of data and information. Plant naming also remains preferable to various disembodied metadata structures because names retain the human dimension of being understandable, memorable and easily communicated.

6 Free prior informed consent – mere politics or meaningful change?

Paul Martin

Introduction

Two things drive the view that Australia should comprehensively embrace a principle of 'free, prior and informed consent' (FPIC) by Indigenous Peoples for decisions that will affect their interests. One is that this principle has been advocated through international policy, and then incorporated to a limited degree into law in Australia. The second, which underpins the first, is the belief that First Nations Peoples (will) benefit substantially from legally obligatory Indigenous engagement provisions.[1] FPIC is founded in

---

1 I use 'engagement' as the broad term for consultation and participation processes in this chapter. There are many different philosophies, purposes and processes of engagement, and the outcomes that are expected from engagement vary widely: see Bruce Lindsay, 'Public Participation, Litigation and Adjudicative Procedure in Water Resources Management' (2016) 33 *Environmental and Planning Law Journal* 325; Kylie Lingard and Paul Martin, 'Strategies to Support the Interests of Aboriginal and Torres Strait Islander Peoples in the Commercial Development of Gourmet Bush Food Products' (2016) 23 *International Journal of Cultural Property* 33; Tanya Howard, 'The "Rules of Engagement": A Socio-legal Framework for Improving Community Engagement in Natural Resource Governance' (2015) 5 *Oñati Socio-legal Series* 1209; Tanya Howard, 'From International Principles to Local Practices: A Socio-legal Framing of Public Participation Research' (2015) 17 *Environment, Development and Sustainability* 747; Emma Dudley, Diaan-Yi Lin, Matteo Mancini and Jonathan Ng, Implementing a Citizen-centric Approach to Delivering Government Services (2015) available at <http://www.mckinsey.com/industries/public-sector/our-insights/implementing-a-citizen-centric-approach-to-delivering-government-services> (accessed 5 May 2017); Margherita Pieraccini, 'Rethinking Participation in Environmental Decision-Making: Epistemologies of Marine Conservation in South-East England' (2015) 27 *Journal of Environmental Law* 45; A Curtis, H Ross, G Marshall, C Baldwin, J Cavaye, C Freeman, A Carr and G Syme, 'The Great Experiment with Devolved NRM Governance: Lessons from Community Engagement in Australia and New Zealand since the 1980s' (2014) 21 *Australasian Journal of Environmental Management* 175; National Water Commission, *A Review of Indigenous Involvement in Water Planning, 2013* (National Water Commission, 2014) available at <http://www.healthinfonet.ecu.edu.au/uploads/resources/27638_27638.pdf> (accessed 30 July 2017); Robyn Bartel, 'Vernacular Knowledge and Environmental Law: Cause and Cure for Regulatory Failure' (2013) 19 *Local Environment* 891; Sue

international human rights law with the aim of ensuring more effective
bottom-up participation of Indigenous Peoples in decision making, for

Jackson, Poh-Ling Tan, Carla Mooney, Suzanne Hoverman and Ian White,
'Principles and Guidelines for Good Practice in Indigenous Engagement in Water
Planning' (2012) 474 *Journal of Hydrology* 57; Poh-Ling Tan, K Bowmer and C
Baldwin, 'Continued Challenges in the Policy and Legal Framework for Colla-
borative Water Planning' (2012) 478 *Journal of Hydrology* 84; Kylie Lingard, 'The
Impact of the Law on Consultation Practices and Purpose: A Case Study of
Aboriginal Cultural Heritage Consultations' (2012) 1 *International Journal of
Rural Law and Policy* 1; Elizabeth Kirk and Kirsty Blackstock, 'Enhanced Deci-
sion Making: Balancing Public Participation Against "Better Regulation" in British
Environmental Permitting Regimes' (2011) 23 *Journal of Environmental Law* 97;
Brian Wampler and Stephanie McNulty, *Does Participatory Governance Matter?
Exploring the Nature and Impact of Participatory Reforms* (Woodrow Wilson
International Center for Scholars, 2011) available at <https://www.wilsoncenter.
org/sites/default/files/CUSP_110108_Participatory%20Gov.pdf> (accessed 5
May 2017); Lyndal Thompson, Nyree Stenekes, Heleen Kruger and Anna Carr,
Engaging in Biosecurity: Literature Review of Community Engagement Approaches
(Bureau of Rural Sciences, 2009); Michael Christie, Patricia Rowe and David
Pickernell, 'Unpacking a Wicked Problem: Enablers/Impediments to Regional
Engagement' (2009) 68 *Australian Journal of Public Administration* 83; Jon
Altman and David Martin (eds), *Power, Culture, Economy: Indigenous Australians
and Mining*, CAEPR Monograph No 30 (ANU E-press, 2009); Mark Reed, Anil
Graves, Norman Dandy, Helena Posthumus, Klaus Hubacek, Joe Morris, Chris-
tina Prell, Claire Quinn and Lindsay Stringer, 'Who's In and Why? A Typology of
Stakeholder Analysis Methods for Natural Resource Management' (2009) 90
Journal of Environmental Management 1933; Tanya King and Kristina Murphy,
'Procedural Justice and Australian Environment: The Case of the Wonthaggi
Water Desalination Plant' (2009) 4 *Public Policy* 105; Mark Reed, 'Stakeholder
Participation for Environmental Management: A Literature Review' (2008) 141
Biological Conservation 2417; John Tibby, Marcus Lane and Peter Gell, 'Local
Knowledge and Environmental Management: A Cautionary Tale from Lake Ains-
worth, New South Wales, Australia' (2007) 34 *Environmental Conservation* 334;
Archon Fung, 'Varieties of Participation in Complex Governance' (2006) 66
Public Administration Review 66 (issue Supplement 1); Marcus Lane and Tony
Corbett, 'The Tyranny of Localism: Indigenous Participation in Community-
based Environmental Management' (2005) 7 *Journal of Environmental Policy and
Planning* 141; Judith Innes and David Booher, 'Reframing Public Participation:
Strategies for the 21st Century' (2004) 5 *Planning Theory and Practice* 419;
Samuel Brody, David Godschalk and Raymond Burby, 'Mandating Citizen Parti-
cipation in Plan Making: Six Strategic Planning Choices' (2003) 69 *Journal of the
American Planning Association* 245; Peter Oliver and James Whelan, *Literature
Review: Regional Natural Resource Governance, Collaboration and Partnerships*,
Technical Report 45 (Cooperative Research Centre for Coastal Zone, Estuary &
Waterway Management, 2003) available at <http://www.ozcoasts.gov.au/pdf/
CRC/45-reg_natural_res_governance_lit_rev.pdf> (accessed 5 May 2017); Jürgen
Grote and Bernard Gbikpi, *Participatory Governance: Political and Societal Impli-
cations* (Springer, 2002); Jeff Smith, *The Changing Nature of Environmental Law:
Recent Developments in Public Participation* (Environmental Defender's Office,
1999) available at <http://d3n8a8pro7vhmx.cloudfront.net/edonsw/pages/
677/attachments/original/1381976394/publicpartic.pdf?1381976394>

example, by establishing an obligation to consult and to obtain the consent of Indigenous Peoples before legal obligations affecting their interests are implemented.[2]

The history of other international politico/legal principles ratified by Australia demonstrates that there is a rocky path from political aspiration to useful application, and the outcomes have not been unambiguously successful.[3] The social justice and sustainable development aims of the United Nations' *Convention on Biological Diversity* (CBD),[4] in particular, have not been fully addressed. This is clearly reflected in the following statement from the United Nations Conference on Sustainable Development, Rio+20:

We recognize that the twenty years since the Earth Summit in 1992 have seen uneven progress, including in sustainable development and poverty eradication. We emphasize the need to make progress in implementing previous commitments.[5]

(accessed 5 May 2017); National Water Commission, *First Peoples' Water Engagement Council (FPWEC)* (National Water Commission, n.d.) available at <http://webarchive.nla.gov.au/gov/20160615062343/http://www.nwc.gov.au/organisation/partners/fpwec> (accessed 30 July 2017); First Peoples' Water Engagement Council, *Advice to The National Water Commission* (National Water Commission, 2012) available at <http://content.webarchive.nla.gov.au/gov/wayback/20160615062343/http://www.nwc.gov.au/__data/assets/pdf_file/0004/22576/FPWEC-Advice-to-NWC-May-2012.pdf> (accessed 30 July 2017); Paul Martin, *Expert Review from a Social and Economic Perspective: Appendix J2* (Murray Darling Basin Authority, 2010).

2 See, for examples, Martin Papillon and Thierry Rodon, 'Proponent-Indigenous Agreements and the Implementation of the Right to Free, Prior, and Informed Consent in Canada' (2017) 62 *Environmental Impact Assessment Review* 216; Lorenza and Jean Grugel, 'The Politics of Indigenous Participation Through "Free Prior Informed Consent": Reflections from the Bolivian Case' (2016) 77 *World Development* 249; Robert Goodland, 'Free, Prior and Informed Consent and the World Bank Group' (2004) 4 *Sustainable Development Law and Policy* 66; and so on.

3 Demonstrated clearly with the Precautionary Principle – see Jacqueline Peel, *The Precautionary Principle in Practice: Environmental Decision-making and Scientific Uncertainty* (Federation Press, 2005); Evan Hamman, Katie Woolaston, Rana Koroglu, Hope Johnson, Bridget Lewis, Brodie Evans and Rowena Maguire, 'The Effectiveness of the Precautionary Principle in Protecting Australia's Endangered Species' in Paul Martin, Ben Boer and Lydia Slobodian (eds), *Framework for Assessing and Improving Law for Sustainability: A Legal Component of a Natural Resource Governance Framework*, IUCN Environmental Policy and Law Paper No 87 (International Union for Conservation of Nature, 2016); David Freestone and Ellen Hey (eds) *The Precautionary Principle and International Law: The Challenge of Implementation* (Kluwer Law International, 1996).

4 [1993] ATS 32 (CBD).

5 United Nations, *The Future We Want*, A/CONF.216/L.1(2012) [19] available at <https://rio20.un.org/sites/rio20.un.org/files/a-conf.216l-1_english.pdf.pdf> (accessed 5 May 2017).

The Secretary General of the Organization of American States has referred to the implementation of environmental governance instruments as 'the greatest challenge of our century'.[6] Literature from around the world point to the very many risks of failure or of perverse effects in the implementation of international law principles at a national level.[7]

Many things are unknown about how FPIC will translate into Australian jurisprudence and governance processes, and what practical impacts this will have. The eventual costs, benefits and outcomes will be determined by legal and administrative details, by the specific issues that are the focus of application and contestation, and by context. Given the uncertainty of these variables, risk management is justified so that positive outcomes become likely for Indigenous Australians from adopting FPIC through law and public policy.

A rationale for managing policy risk

Formalised risk management is used where failure may have a substantial impact on public welfare. Corporate governance and technical design standards and processes, for example, institutionalise increasingly sophisticated risk management processes. When supported by statutory or civil accountability these processes create a strong impetus to use best-available technologies and methods, and they direct attention to protecting the interests of those who may be vulnerable. This purposefully pessimistic analysis helps to improve the reliability of strategies, technologies and innovations.

If the scholarly literature, media and political rhetoric are to be believed, public policy (particularly when it concerns Indigenous Peoples' welfare) often results in failures and unanticipated undesirable impacts on the people it is meant to benefit.[8] However, despite this known potential for failure, and even though regulatory impact and benefit-cost analysis are widely used to test the

---

6 Organization of American States, *OAS and UNEP Sign Agreement on Environmental Rule of Law and Sustainable Development. Organization of American States*, Press Release E-506/14 (2014) available at <http://www.oas.org/en/media_center/press_release.asp?sCodigo=E-506/14> (accessed 5 May 2017).
7 Michael Howes, Liana Wortley, Ruth Potts, Aysin Dedekorkut-Howes, Silvia Serrao-Neumann, Julie Davidson, Timothy Smith and Patrick Nunn, 'Environmental Sustainability: A Case of Policy Implementation Failure?' (2017) 9 *Sustainability* 165.
8 Christine Parker, *Reducing the risk of policy failure: challenges for regulatory compliance* (OECD, 2000) available at <https://www.oecd.org/gov/regulatory-policy/1910833.pdf> (accessed 5 May 2017); Richard Trudgen, *Djambatj Mala: Why Warriors Lie Down and Die: Towards an Understanding of Why the Aboriginal People of Arnhem Land Face the Greatest Crisis in Health and Education Since European Contact* (Aboriginal Resource & Development Services Inc, 2000); Kate Crowley and Ken J Walker, *Environmental Policy Failure: The Australian Story* (The University Press, 2012).

feasibility of new laws, an explicit risk analysis of proposed laws and policies is not part of conventional public governance.[9] Accountability for failure is not systematised and a lack of objective performance evaluation and risk accountability limits what can be learned through experience to help improve the reliability of public governance.

A few risk analysis methods are available that could be applied to the management of public policy risk, though public policy risk analysis is not a well-developed discipline.[10] The Policy Risk Analysis approach developed by this

---

9 For public policy risk issues see: Australian National Audit Office, *Public Sector Governance: Strengthening Performance Through Good Governance*, Better Practice Guide (Australian National Audit Office, 2014); Allan Dale, Karen Vella, Robert Pressey, Jon Brodie, Hugh Yorkston and Ruth Potts, 'A Method for Risk Analysis Across Governance Systems: A Great Barrier Reef Case Study' (2013) 8 *Environmental Research Letters* 015037; P Martin and J Williams, 'Water Governance: A Policy Risk Perspective' (2013) 171 *Water Resources Management* 73; Elodie Gal, 'The Effects of Institutional Path Dependence, Political Dynamics and Transaction Costs on the Potential for "Smart" Regulatory Innovation: An Illustration with the Biofuel Weed Risk Case Study' (2012) 15 *Australasian Journal of Natural Resources Law and Policy* 219; Mark Frigo and Richard Anderson, 'What is Strategic Risk Management?' (2011) *Strategic Finance* 21 (April 2011); Ian Goldin and Tiffany Vogel, 'Global Governance and Systemic Risk in the 21st Century: Lessons from the Financial Crisis' (2010) 1 *Global Policy* 4; Chris McGrath, *Does Environmental Law Work? How to Evaluate the Effectiveness of an Environmental Legal System* (Lambert Academic Publishing, 2010); J Ruhl, 'The Political Economy of Climate Change Mitigation Policies' (2012) 97 *Minnesota Law Review* 206; International Risk Governance Council, *Risk Governance Deficits. An Analysis and Illustration of the Most Common Deficits in Risk Governance* (IRGG, 2009) available at <http://www.irgc.org/IMG/pdf/IRGC_rgd_web_final.pdf> (accessed 5 May 2017); Marie Florin and Christopher Bunting, 'Risk Governance Guidelines for Bioenergy Policies' (2009) 17 *Journal of Cleaner Production* S106–S108; Grant Kirkpatrick, 'The Corporate Governance Lessons from the Financial Crisis' (2009) 1 *OECD Journal: Financial Market Trends* 1, available at <http://search.oecd.org/finance/financial-markets/42229620.pdf> (accessed 5 May 2017); Ortwin Renn, 'White Paper on Risk Governance: Towards an Integrative Approach' in Ortwin Renn and Katherine Walker, *Global Risk Governance: Concept and Practice Using the IRGC Framework* (Springer, 2008) pp 3–73; Robert Stavins, *Introduction to the Political Economy of Environmental Regulations* (Resources for the Future, 2004) available at <http://ageconsearch.tind.io//bitstream/10876/1/dp040012.pdf> (accessed 5 May 2017); Christine Parker, *Reducing the Risk of Policy Failure: Challenges for Regulatory Compliance* (OECD, 2000) available at <https://www.oecd.org/gov/regulatory-policy/1910833.pdf> (accessed 5 May 2017); Paul Martin and Jacqueline Williams, *Policy Risk Assessment*, Technical Report No. 03/10 (CRC for Irrigation Futures, 2010).

10 See International Risk Governance Council, *An Introduction to the IRGC Risk Governance Framework* (IRGC, 2008) available at <https://www.irgc.org/IMG/pdf/An_introduction_to_the_IRGC_Risk_Governance_Framework.pdf> (accessed 5 May 2017); International Standards Association Australia, *Risk Management*, AS/NZS 4360:2004 (Standards Australia, 2004); Paul Martin and Jacqueline Williams, *Policy Risk Assessment*, Technical Report No. 03/10 (CRC for Irrigation Futures, 2010).

author to particularly address water and other natural resource policy failures[11] focuses on three categories of risk: political risk, instrument and implementation risk, and the risk of spill overs. Two main categories of adverse possibilities are considered under this approach: the risk that a policy will fail to efficiently achieve its intended results, or that it will cause undesirable unexpected consequences.

History suggests that the implementation of FPIC will involve three activities with each of these having some form of risk. These include the risks that may arise while translating a politically negotiated principle from international agreements into binding local law and practice; the risks of failures of citizen engagement (of which FPIC is a particular type); and the general risks of public policy failure which has been demonstrated to be substantial for Indigenous justice and welfare. For obligatory engagement and consent to reliably deliver value to Indigenous Peoples and to Australian society will require far more than good intentions and new legal instruments. Substantially better institutional arrangements and supports than are currently available will be needed to manage the possibility that FPIC approaches will not work and/or become oppressive in themselves.

Relevant principles and instruments

Legally, FPIC in relation to Indigenous interests in natural resources is a potential procedural principle and substantive right that was specified in the CBD.[12] Though the principle has a history in other contexts, in the CBD context it concerns the intersection between Indigenous Peoples' interests in biological ecosystem services, traditional knowledge and culture. The Preamble recognises:

> the close and traditional dependence of many Indigenous and local communities embodying traditional lifestyles on biological resources, and the desirability of sharing equitably benefits arising from the use of traditional knowledge, innovations and practices relevant to the conservation of biological diversity and the sustainable use of its components.[13]

Article 8(j) of the CBD creates obligations on its Contracting Parties, subject to their national legislation:

11 Paul Martin and Jacqueline Williams, *Policy Risk Assessment*, Technical Report No. 03/10 (CRC for Irrigation Futures, 2010).
12 CBD, Arts 8(j) and 15(5). While Art 8(j) refers to 'Indigenous and local communities' and Art 15(5) only refers to 'prior informed consent' of the Contracting Parties, this has been expansively interpreted as FPIC following the United Nations *Declaration on the Rights of Indigenous Peoples*, 61/295, 107th Plenary Meeting, 13 September 2007 (UN, 2007) Arts 10, 11, 19, 28 and 29.
13 CBD, Preamble.

to respect, preserve and maintain knowledge, innovations and practices of Indigenous and local communities embodying traditional lifestyles relevant for the conservation and sustainable use of biological diversity and promote their wider application with the approval and involvement of the holders of such knowledge, innovations and practices and encourage the equitable sharing of the benefits arising from the utilization of such knowledge, innovations and practices.[14]

These obligations are further linked to the rights and obligations of the Contracting Parties under Article 15(5) which specifies that '[a]ccess to genetic resources shall be subject to prior informed consent of the Contracting Party providing such resources, unless otherwise determined by that Party'.[15] To become binding in law requires ratification by the signatory State, and thus the legal content of the concept depends on the legal instrument used by the signatory State to implement the principle.

Principle 22 of the *Rio Declaration* broadens the emphasis of the principle:

Indigenous People(s) and their communities and other local communities have a vital role in environmental management and development because of their knowledge and traditional practices. States should recognize and duly support their identity, culture and interests and enable their effective participation in the achievement of sustainable development.[16]

Other international instruments have complicated the interpretation of the scope and meaning of the principle whilst attempting to strengthen its use.[17]

14 CBD, Art 8(j).
15 CBD, Art 15(5).
16 The rationale is outlined by the United Nations Educational, Scientific and Cultural Organization, *Links Between Biological and Cultural Diversity: Report of an International Workshop* (UNESCO, 2007) available at <http://unesdoc.unesco.org/images/0015/001592/159255E.pdf> (accessed 5 May 2017).
17 *International Covenant on Economic, Social, and Cultural Rights* [1976] ATS 5; *Indigenous and Tribal Peoples Convention* (1989) ILO 169; International Covenant on Civil and Political Rights [1980] ATS 23; Conference of the Parties to the Convention on Biological Diversity, *Report of the Seventh Meeting of the Conference of the Parties to the Convention on Biological Diversity* (2000) UNEP/CBD/COP/7/21, [292] and Annex (Decision VII/16, Annex (Akwé: Kon Voluntary Guidelines for the Conduct of Cultural, Environmental and Social Impact Assessment regarding Developments Proposed to Take Place on, or which are Likely to Impact on, Sacred Sites and on Lands and Waters Traditionally Occupied or Used) pp 261–276); United Nations General Assembly, *United Nations Declaration on the Rights of Indigenous Peoples*, 61/295, 107th Plenary Meeting, 13 September 2007 (UN, 2007); Stakeholder Forum for a Sustainable Future, *Review of Implementation of the Rio Principles: Detailed review of implementation of the Rio Principles* (Sustainable Development in the 21st century, 2011) available at <https://sustainabledevelopment.un.org/content/documents/1127rioprinciples.pdf> (accessed 30 July 2017).

Some commentators may believe that the ratification of the CBD creates a right for Indigenous Australians to be consulted and that their consent should be required for a spectrum of development, land use, natural resources, culture, knowledge or other actions that will, or may, impact on their interests or sensitivities. The CBD in itself does not create such a legal right. It is explicit in the CBD and related documents that the focus of the CBD provisions on FPIC is State-to-State governance of biological material, not the creation of a new human right. How the obligations of the signatory States to the CBD are acquitted is left to the States, with a clear affirmation of State sovereignty in these matters.[18]

Politically, FPIC issues are interwoven with two other areas of internationally developed rights/obligations: citizen rights to participation and human rights. These also depend on state ratification and legalisation for their legal effect though some human rights interests may be applied through international law.[19] The political interleaving of participatory requirements and environmental and social interests in the matrix structure of the CBD and the *Rio Declaration* is illustrated by Principle 10:

> Environmental issues are best handled with the participation of all concerned citizens, at the relevant level. At the national level, each individual shall have appropriate access to information concerning the environment that is held by public authorities, including information on hazardous materials and activities in their communities, and the opportunity to participate in decision-making processes. States shall facilitate and encourage public awareness and participation by making information widely available. Effective access to judicial and administrative proceedings, including redress and remedy, shall be provided.[20]

Other human rights instruments (beyond those I have listed) are potentially relevant[21] but I will not focus on these. International politics has a principle

18 CBD, Preamble and Arts 3 and 15(1).
19 For aspects of the rights dialogues see Megan Davis, 'To Bind or Not to Bind: The United Nations Declaration on the Rights of Indigenous Peoples Five Years On' (2012) 19 *Australian International Law Journal* 17; A Wood, 'Why Australia Won't Recognise Indigenous Customary Law', *The Conversation* (2016) available at <http://theconversation.com/why-australia-wont-recognise-indigenous-customa ry-law-60370> (accessed 5 May 2017); Philippe Sands, *Principles of International Environmental Law* (Cambridge University Press, 2003); Tim Wilson, *Opening Minds to 'Forgotten Freedoms'* (The Australian, 8 May 2014) available at <http://www.tim wilson.com.au/articles/opening-minds-to-forgotten-freedoms-the-australian> (accessed 30 July 2017); Tim Wilson, *Rights and Responsibilities: Consultation Report* (Australian Human Rights Commission, 2015) available at <http://www.huma nrights.gov.au/sites/default/files/document/publication/rights-and-responsibili ties-report-2015.pdf> (accessed 30 July 2017).
20 United Nations General Assembly, *Report of the United Nations Conference on Environment and Development – Rio Declaration on Environment and Development* (1992) A/CONF.151/26 (Vol. I), [10].
21 See, for example, *International Convention on the Elimination of All Forms of Racial Discrimination* [1975] ATS 40; *International Covenant on Civil and Political Rights*

that embeds confusion between individual rights, procedural requirements, and State sovereignty.

Australia's legal position – informed consent and biological resources

Australian governments have not taken an expansionary approach to engagement, informed consent or human rights. Australia and three other countries opposed the ambitious United Nations *Declaration on the Rights of Indigenous Peoples*, with its proposed Indigenous Peoples' rights to self-determination (Article 3 and others); including Article 19 which proposes that:

> States shall consult and cooperate in good faith with the Indigenous Peoples concerned through their own representative institutions in order to obtain their [FPIC] before adopting and implementing legislative or administrative measures that may affect them.

Australia has not legislated human rights, nor adopted overall engagement rules such as the *Aarhus Convention*.[22]

Though an underlying strategy (if one could be said to exist) is not explicit it would however be inaccurate to represent Australia's position as antagonistic to expanding obligatory engagement and citizen rights. It would be more accurate to report the approach as cautious. Engagement (and to a lesser degree consent) requirements permeate Australia's national and state laws and policies, and these advance incrementally. Obligations to consult, and procedural or other rights for Australians as a whole or for Aboriginal Australians as a special class, can be found in many laws and administrative rules.

Australia has signed but not yet ratified the 2010 *Nagoya Protocol on Access To Genetic Resources and the Fair and Equitable Sharing of Benefits Arising from their Utilization under to the Convention on Biological Diversity* (Nagoya Protocol).[23] Article 7 of the Protocol states that:

[1980] ATS 23; *International Covenant on Economic, Social and Cultural Rights* [1976] ATS 5 and associated Optional Protocols; Principles concerning women's (CBD and United Nations General Assembly, *Report of the United Nations Conference on Environment and Development – Rio Declaration on Environment and Development* (1992) A/CONF.151/26 (Vol. I), [20]) and youth (United Nations General Assembly, *Report of the United Nations Conference on Environment and Development – Rio Declaration on Environment and Development* (1992) A/CONF.151/26 (Vol. I), [21]) interests; and linking environmental protection and poverty reduction (United Nations General Assembly, *Report of the United Nations Conference on Environment and Development – Rio Declaration on Environment and Development* (1992) A/CONF.151/26 (Vol. I), [5]).

22 A Andrusevych, T Alge and C Konrad (eds.), *Case Law of the Aarhus Convention Compliance Committee, 2004–2011* (2nd ed, RACSE, Lviv 2011).

23 Conference of the Parties to the Convention on Biological Diversity, *Report of the Tenth Meeting of the Conference of the Parties to the Convention on Biological*

In accordance with domestic law, each Party shall take measures, as appropriate, with the aim of ensuring that traditional knowledge associated with genetic resources that is held by Indigenous and local communities is accessed with the prior and informed consent or approval and involvement of these Indigenous and local communities, and that mutually agreed terms have been established.[24]

Subordinate to the sovereignty of signatory States means that the Nagoya Protocol (if ratified by Australia) does not *per se* create rights for Indigenous Peoples. It is best understood as a political framework for the subsequent creation of legal rights by signatory States at their discretion. The Nagoya Protocol only deals with issues such as access, bioprospecting, biodiscovery, transfer of genetic material, and the like. FPIC under the CBD though also subject to State sovereignty is far broader in its potential application, and is coming into use primarily around land rights and land access (for example mining on Aboriginal or Torres Strait Islander land) under a variety of national and state laws. There are many proposals to expand the application of FPIC.[25]

This chapter is concerned only with FPIC in relation to access to biological resources and related cultural products. The many proposals concerning the Indigenous Peoples' FPIC suggest that as society's understanding of economic and political interests in nature and culture continues to expand, the concept is likely to be applied to many decisions and activities involving land, land-use

Diversity (2010) UNEP/CBD/COP/10/27, [103] and Annex (Decision X/1, Annex 1 (*Nagoya Protocol on Access to Genetic Resources and the Fair and Equitable Sharing of Benefits Arising from their Utilization to the Convention on Biological Diversity*) pp 89–109) (Nagoya Protocol).

24 Nagoya Protocol, Art 7.
25 See, for examples, Judith Preston, 'Valuing Indigenous Knowledge in Sustainable Resource Management in Australia' and Johnnie Aseron, Kylie Anne Lingard, Chris McLaughlin, Jacqueline Williams, Paul Martin and Neyooxet Greymorning, 'Asserting Cultural Interests Through the Law: Issues and Innovations' in Natalie Stoianoff (ed.), *Indigenous Knowledge Forum – Comparative Systems for Recognising and Protecting Indigenous Knowledge and Culture* (LexisNexis, 2016) pp 565–581 and 69–96 respectively; Paul Martin and Michael Jeffery, 'Using a Legally Enforceable Knowledge Trust Doctrine to Fulfil the Moral Obligation to Protect Indigenous Secrets' (2007) 7 *New Zealand Journal of Environmental Law* 1; Terri Janke, *Our Culture: Our Future – Report on Australian Indigenous Cultural and Intellectual Property* (Michael Frenkel and Co, 1998); Jon Altman and David Martin (eds), *Power, Culture, Economy: Indigenous Australians and Mining*, CAEPR Monograph No 30 (ANU E-press, 2009); Jon Altman and Michelle Cochrane, *Indigenous Interests in Water: A Comment on the "Water Property Rights – Report to COAG from the Water CEOs Group"*, Discussion Paper ANU, 2003 available at <https://www.researchgate.net/publication/251775121_Indigenous_Interests_in_Water_A_Comment_on_the_%27Water_Property_Rights-Report_to_COAG_from_the_Water_CEOs_Group%27_Discussion_Paper> (accessed 7 May 2017). Kylie Lingard and Paul Martin, 'Strategies to Support the Interests of Aboriginal and Torres Strait Islander Peoples in the Commercial Development of Gourmet Bush Food Products' (2016) 23 *International Journal of Cultural Property* 33.

and natural resource development projects; human and non-human biological research and products or processes; and traditional knowledge about such matters. The boundaries of the application of the Indigenous Peoples' FPIC will be formed by political and economic dynamics and advances in knowledge, but ultimately will be defined through its embodiment in statute and other law and policy instruments, and through interpretation and contestation. It seems likely that the process of lawmaking of the Nagoya Protocol, reforms to Indigenous land management (including mining approvals), and attempts to govern the exploitation of Indigenous Peoples' culture, food systems or knowledge, will expand the use of the FPIC concept.

Section 301 of the *Environment Protection and Biodiversity Conservation Act 1999* (Cth) (the EPBC Act) gives the Commonwealth power to control access to biological materials on Commonwealth lands and to create a permit system, which explicitly incorporates prior informed consent. Part 8A of the *Environment Protection and Biodiversity Conservation Regulations 2000* (Cth) specifies the details of this permitting approach, which has been in operation for some time.

Consultation on 'A Model for Implementing the Nagoya Protocol in Australia' ended in May 2014. The model that was circulated for consultation is a refinement and an extension of the existing approach for Commonwealth lands, and was explicitly concerned with scientific biodiscovery.[26] Along with new regulations under the EPBC Act this model proposed that Australia would:

- Implement compliance measures only for genetic resources and associated traditional knowledge acquired after the Nagoya Protocol came into effect;
- Put jurisdictional limits on the application of bio-resource trade measures;
- Emphasise co-regulation as the means of implementation, through codes of conduct negotiated with specialist sectors; and
- Require agreements between users of traditional knowledge and related Indigenous Peoples.

Some Australian states have bioprospecting/biodiscovery laws and administration approaches that endeavour to implement their obligations under the CBD. The *Biodiscovery Act 2004* (Qld) reiterates the sovereign interests of the State in biodiscoveries under the CBD, and creates a permit system akin to that of the Commonwealth. In the Northern Territory, the *Biological Resources Act*

26 No longer found on the Department website. The relevant document now states: 'The Australian Government is consulting with the research community, Indigenous people, industry partners and state and territory governments to find the best way to implement the [Nagoya] Protocol in Australia': Department of Sustainability, Environment, Water, Population and Communities, The Nagoya Protocol in Australia (2017) available at <http://www.environment.gov.au/system/file s/pages/9fc06ac0-f5af-4b47-a80f-d9378088d743/files/nagoya-factsheet.pdf> (accessed 7 May 2017). Ambiguity allows free reign to speculative interpretation and politics.

2006 (NT) regulates bioprospecting, which is restrictively defined in section 5. The law creates a permit system. Part 4 that deals with benefit sharing requires an agreement with a 'resource access provider' which is specified under section 6 to encompass owners or managers of the land, including Aboriginal land-holders. These statutory schemes also only apply to Commonwealth and State lands and waters leaving privately held lands unregulated.

Costs, risks and Indigenous engagement

A diverse mosaic of State and Commonwealth legal arrangements creates engagement, human rights and FPIC procedural obligations or citizen rights. These include human rights,[27] heritage protection,[28] commercialisation and cultural protection,[29] and 'rules for engagement' under many laws. It is beyond the scope of this chapter to canvass all of these. However, specifically Indigenous Peoples' rights are not the only sources of legal rights to be consulted and (in limited instances) to consent to actions that may impact on their interests. As Australian citizens Aboriginal and Torres Strait Peoples benefit from (or are sometimes oppressed by) many consultation or consent requirements. As Aboriginal and Torres Strait Islander Peoples (particularly as land-holders) they are also embraced by other more targeted engagement processes. Many organisations have rules or standards for aspects of citizen engagement or FPIC.[30] However, none of the current or proposed legal rules and administrative arrangements for FPIC provide binding frameworks that legally

27 Discussed in Allan Hawke, *Independent Review of the Environment Protection and Biodiversity Conservation Act 1999: Summary of Public Submissions* (Australian Government Department of the Environment, Water, Heritage and the Arts, 2009) available at <https://www.environment.gov.au/system/files/resources/d2231053-0cb1-4670-aea8-09458a5ea8a0/files/public-submissions-summary.pdf> (accessed 30 July 2017).

28 Kylie Lingard, 'The Impact of the Law on Consultation Practices and Purpose: A Case Study of Aboriginal Cultural Heritage Consultations' (2012) 1 *International Journal of Rural Law and Policy* 1.

29 Kylie Lingard and Paul Martin, 'Strategies to Support the Interests of Aboriginal and Torres Strait Islander Peoples in the Commercial Development of Gourmet Bush Food Products' (2016) 23 *International Journal of Cultural Property* 33.

30 Including, for examples, CRC Remote Economic Participation Guidelines including on Informed Consent: Ninti One Limited, *What is Free Prior Informed Consent?* Briefing Paper No 7, available at <https://crc-rep.com/sites/default/files/upload/bp7_free-prior-informed-consent.pdf> (accessed 7 May 2017); National Health and Medical Research Council, the Australian Research Council and Universities Australia, *Australian Code for the Responsible Conduct of Research* (NHMRC, 2007) available at <https://www.nhmrc.gov.au/_files_nhmrc/file/research/research-integrity/r39_australian_code_responsible_conduct_research_150811.pdf> (accessed 7 May 2017); National Health and Medical Research Council and the Australian Research Council, *The Australian Research Integrity Committee Framework* (NHMRC, 2011) available at <https://www.nhmrc.gov.au/_files_nhmrc/file/research/research-integrity/aric_framework_update_130604.pdf> (accessed 7 May 2017); National Health and Medical Research

guarantee the quality of processes for consultation and engagement. These rules and arrangements do not also create safeguards for the integrity of the implementation of engagement rules for Indigenous Peoples.

FPIC is a strategy to reduce social disadvantage through the engagement of Indigenous Peoples in decisions that affect their interests. Citizen engagement can be specified as process requirements or citizen rights with the former being more likely to be used in Australia. Obligations to engage citizens (regardless of race) exist in processes such as those for planning and development approvals, or obligations or rights can be applicable to members of classes defined by situation, identity or vulnerability. Indigenous Peoples thus are affected by obligatory engagement requirements: (1) as Australian citizens who must be engaged because of process requirements; (2) as beneficiaries of the rights of Australian citizens *per se*; (3) as Australians with particular rights due to membership of specific categories (such as rural or disadvantaged people); and (4) as Australian Aboriginal or Torres Strait Islander Peoples.

To be effective, efficient and fair, FPIC like any other policy should: (1) deliver decisions that lead to social or economic benefits with low cost (at least less than the value of the benefits); and (2) distribute the benefits and costs consistent with social expectations of equity. However, experience suggests that effective community engagement is often a contested and vexed area of policy which leaves many expectations unsatisfied.

Indigenous engagement processes seem sometimes to reflect a view that Indigenous consultation is a panacea or an end in itself, or to be driven by bureaucratic or legal obligations, or based on a questionable belief that consultation *per se* is a benefit to Indigenous Peoples. Public-spirited Indigenous Peoples who are (as a class) disadvantaged can invest a lot of time and can suffer significant disadvantages through their participation in processes that may not result in any tangible benefit to themselves or other Indigenous Peoples. The investment of time, energy and limited resources will be effective, efficient or fair only if it leads to tangible or psychic benefits from the process that more than offsets their costs of engaging. The transaction costs may be justified if there are net benefits to Indigenous stakeholders and the broader community. If this is not so these costs may add the experience of oppression that obligatory engagement is meant to redress. Even if value is delivered in

Council, Australian Research Council and Australian Vice-Chancellors' Committee, *National Statement on Ethical Conduct in Human Research* (NHMRC, 2007 and updated to 15 May 2015) available at <http://www.nhmrc.gov.au/guidelines/publications/e72> (accessed 7 May 2017); Australian Institute of Aboriginal and Torres Strait Islander Studies, *Guidelines for Ethical Research in Indigenous Studies* (AIATSIS, 2012) available at <https://aiatsis.gov.au/sites/default/files/docs/research-and-guides/ethics/gerais.pdf> (accessed 7 May 2017); Australian Anthropological Society, *Code of Ethics* (AAS, 2012) available at <http://www.aas.asn.au/wp-content/uploads/2013/05/AAS_Code_of_Ethics-20121.pdf> (accessed 7 May 2017); Australian Sociological Association, *Ethics Guidelines for Research* (ASA, 2010) available at <https://www.tasa.org.au/wp-content/uploads/2008/12/Ethical-Guidelines_August-2015.pdf> (accessed 7 May 2017).

some situations (for example, mining approval on Aboriginal lands), this may be merely a redistribution of inequity if the transaction costs to some Indigenous Peoples are greater than the benefits to them.

It is not clear that there is a causal connection between Indigenous engagement and beneficial outcomes in many instances, or for Indigenous Peoples' engagement overall. In some instances, that I discuss below, well intended Indigenous policies, including mandatory engagement, have the potential to cause harm to Indigenous Peoples' interests and, if there is no tangible benefit to the intended beneficiaries of the policy, a wasteful cost to society. More than laws, policies and administrative arrangements are needed to ensure that implementation costs and risks, and the likelihood and extent of tangible benefits, do result in a net positive risk/reward outcome to Indigenous Peoples and to society.

Public policy failure and spill over risks

Public policies, including laws and other interventions, can fail to achieve their intended purposes (wholly or partially) or produce undesirable adverse effects (negative spill overs) that can range from trivial to catastrophic. The potential causes of failure or adverse spill overs create risks, which should be managed to ensure reliable policy. The explanations of underperformance are generically labelled as poor implementation, but more specific diagnoses are needed for effective risk management. More specific causes include poor analysis of the policy problem, defective design of solutions, weak implementation strategy, gaps in the platform of economic or human resources for implementation, weak commitment, political issues that cause non-implementation or opposition, or adverse contingencies.[31] Specific risks need to be identified if they are to be managed effectively. The risk management approach for potential political opposition, for example, is fundamentally different to managing risks of staff capacity to implement, or information deficits.

The importance of effective meta-governance (the governing of governance)[32] to guide the implementation of environmental, social or other international

---

31 Other categories are proposed in Michael Howes, Liana Wortley, Ruth Potts, Aysin Dedekorkut-Howes, Silvia Serrao-Neumann, Julie Davidson, Timothy Smith and Patrick Nunn, 'Environmental Sustainability: A Case of Policy Implementation Failure?' (2017) 9 *Sustainability* 165.

32 See Jan Kooiman and Svein Jentoft, 'Meta-governance: Values, Norms and Principles, and the Making of Hard Choices' (2009) 87 *Public Administration* 818; Stephen Bell and Alex Park, 'The Problematic Metagovernance of Networks: Water Reform in New South Wales' (2006) 26 *Journal of Public Policy* 63; Bob Jessop, 'The Rise of Governance and the Risk of Failure: The Case of Economic Development' (1998) 50 *International Social Science Journal* 29; Michael Lockwood, Julie Davidson, Allan Curtis, Elaine Stratford and Rod Griffith, 'Multi-level Environmental Governance: Lessons from Australian Natural Resource Management' (2009) 40 *Australian Geographer* 169; Louis Meuleman, *Public Management and the Metagovernance of Hierarchies, Networks and Markets: The Feasibility*

commitments is under-appreciated in Australia.[33] In the absence of integrity safeguards, governments and their agencies can make political commitments and create policies and laws, without being accountable for non-implementation, failure or spill over consequences. A systematic risk analysis which addresses distributional consequences and reliable empirical evaluation of outcomes of policy instruments could contribute to greater accountability and provide an impetus for more reliable laws and policies.[34]

History demonstrates that there are many risks in the translation of politically negotiated principles or goals from international agreements to effective law and policy. These include delays and a partial adoption of the agreed principles into law, their limited effectiveness, and spill overs that arise with the implementation of policies. Specifically, there are four aspects of the implementation of international instruments where failure may arise: (1) while translating international agreements into Australian legal and administrative instruments; (2) while implementing the instruments that are created; (3) in the course of achieving required behaviour changes for the principle to work; and (4) in the achievement of desired outcomes, which may be frustrated by many things including misdiagnosis of the issues or changes to context.[35] The implementation of the Precautionary Principle illustrates the risks. The Precautionary Principle was adopted into Australian national environmental law with the EPBC Act in

---

of Designing and Managing Governance Style Combinations (Springer Science & Business Media, 2008).

33 Paul Martin, Marcia Dieguez Leuzinger and Solange Teles da Silva, 'Improving the Effectiveness of Legal Arrangements to Protect Biodiversity: Australia and Brazil' (2016) 13 *Brazilian Journal of International Law* 25; Tabatha Wallington and Geoffrey Lawrence, 'Making Democracy Matter: Responsibility and Effective Environmental Governance in Regional Australia' (2008) 24 *Australia. Journal of Rural Studies* 277; Ross Colliver, 'Community-based Governance in Social-ecological Systems: An Inquiry into the Marginalisation of Landcare in Victoria' (Murdoch University, 2011) available at <https://core.ac.uk/download/pdf/11236988.pdf?repositoryId=343> (accessed 7 May 2017). M Leach, G Bloom, A Ely, P Nightingale, I Scoones, E Shah and A Smith, *Understanding Governance: Pathways to Sustainability*, STEPS Working Paper No 2 (STEPS Working Paper, 2007) available at <http://steps-centre.org/wp-content/uploads/final_steps_gov ernance.pdf> (accessed 7 May 2017).

34 Paul Martin, Robyn Bartel, Jack Sinden, Niel Gunningham and Ian Hannam, *Developing a Good Regulatory Practice Model for Environmental Regulations Impacting on Farmers* (Land and Water, 2007) available at <http://www.inside cotton.com/xmlui/bitstream/handle/1/1623/pk071355.pdf?sequence=2&isAl lowed=y> (accessed 7 May 2017).

35 Identified from a series of international case studies in Paul Martin, Ben Boer and Lydia Slobodian (eds), *Framework for Assessing and Improving Law for Sustainability: A Legal Component of a Natural Resource Governance Framework*, IUCN Environmental Policy and Law Paper No 87 (International Union for Conservation of Nature, 2016); See also Michael Howes, Liana Wortley, Ruth Potts, Aysin Dedekorkut-Howes, Silvia Serrao-Neumann, Julie Davidson, Timothy Smith and Patrick Nunn, 'Environmental Sustainability: A Case of Policy Implementation Failure?' (2017) 9 *Sustainability* 165.

1999, but had previously been incorporated in other laws and policies. In her book *The Precautionary Principle in Practice: Environmental Decision-making and Scientific Uncertainty* in 2005 Jacqueline Peel assessed the legal implementation of this principle. She concluded:

> To date the achievements of precaution, in terms of promoting decision-making processes which are responsive to issues of scientific uncertainty, have been less spectacular than the breadth of the principle's adoption in policy and legal instruments.[36]

After almost two decades, the outcomes of the Precautionary Principle are far less than required for good environmental governance, and the implementation of many actions in pursuit of the CBD principles, such as the protection of native vegetation, is still the subject of intense political contests.

The risk of policy failure for FPIC is high. The complexity of issues concerning Indigenous Peoples' welfare, culture and other interests is notorious, and history demonstrates that policy in this area has proven to have a high risk of failing, causing perverse outcomes, or doing both. This has been recently demonstrated by the Northern Territory Emergency Response[37] that was introduced in 2007 in five pieces of legislation.[38] This legislation aims to address the serious disadvantages that the Aboriginal Peoples in Northern Australia face and that have been documented in the *Little Children are Sacred* report by the Northern Territory Government.[39] The interventions included the involvement of the army in housing and other work, changes to policing and enforcement, land ownership, and funding and welfare programmes. The intervention initially had cross-party political support in Parliament but over time criticisms increased. There were competing claims that the effect of the intervention was alternatively disastrous or desirable, and it seems likely that it was either, depending on the particular issue being debated, the specific context as effects seem to have varied across communities, and the perspective of

---

36 Jacqueline Peel, *The Precautionary Principle in Practice: Environmental Decision-making and Scientific Uncertainty* (Federation Press, 2005) p 219;
37 See Northern Territory Emergency Response Review Board, *Northern Territory Emergency Response: Report of the NTER Review Board* (Department of Families, Housing, Community Services and Indigenous Affairs, 2008) available at <http://apo.org.au/node/551> (accessed 8 May 2017).
38 The *Northern Territory National Emergency Response Bill 2007* (Cth) contained the legislative package, available at <http://parlinfo.aph.gov.au/parlInfo/search/display/display.w3p;adv=yes;orderBy=customrank;page=0;query=Northern%20Territory%20National%20Emergency%20Response%20Bill%202007%20Dataset%3AbillsPrevParl;rec=3;resCount=Default> (accessed 7 May 2017).
39 Northern Territory Board of Inquiry into the Protection of Aboriginal Children from Sexual Abuse, *Mekarle, Ampe Akelyernemane Meke 'Little Children are Sacred': Report of the Northern Territory Board of Inquiry into the Protection of Aboriginal Children from Sexual Abuse* (Northern Territory Government, 1992) pp 197–248.

the critic. The replacement *Stronger Futures Policy* maintains many of the initiatives but criticism of the policy seems to have become stronger.[40] It is difficult to judge the balance of positive and negative outcomes, given highly polarised and politicised views and disagreements about the evidence. It is however reasonable to say that the failures and spill over effects have undermined the intentions of the policy, and this is not an outcome that is unique to this particular policy. The chilling book *Why Warriors Lie Down and Die: Towards an Understanding of Why the Aboriginal People of Arnhem Land Face the Greatest Crisis in Health and Education Since European Contact: Djambatj mala*[41] documents a depressing history of often well-intentioned policies undermining the morale and welfare of Australian Aboriginal communities.

Making engagement requirements reliable?

International agreements, Australian law and institutional policies advocate public participation, consultation or engagement for both Indigenous and non-Indigenous citizens, in many situations. It has become conventional wisdom that a mandatory consultation with Aboriginal and Torres Strait Islander Peoples is key to effective, efficient and fair outcomes for Indigenous citizens. But is a mandatory consultation a reliable prescription for improved outcomes?

An important variable is the extent of Indigenous Peoples' empowerment that is required by the law or embedded in the processes that are used. Arnstein's 'ladder of participation' is often used to discuss this spectrum of consultative empowerment.[42] Consultation can be, and often is, a passive process of

40 Jack Ah Kit, *Building stronger regions – stronger futures,* Address to the Local Government Association of the Northern Territory. Alice Springs (Minister for Community Development, 14 May 2003).

41 Richard Trudgeon, *Why Warriors Lie Down and Die: Towards an Understanding of Why the Aboriginal People of Arnhem Land Face the Greatest Crisis in Health and Education Since European Contact: Djambatj mala* (Aboriginal Resource and Development Services, 2000).

42 Sherry Arnstein, 'A Ladder of Citizen Participation' (1969) 35 *Journal of the American Institute of Planners* 216. For illustrative discussions see Judith Innes and David Booher, 'Reframing Public Participation: Strategies for the 21st Century' (2004) 5 *Planning Theory and Practice* 419; Mark Reed, 'Stakeholder Participation for Environmental Management: A Literature Review' (2008) 141 *Biological Conservation* 2417; Kylie Lingard, 'The Impact of the Law on Consultation Practices and Purpose: A Case Study of Aboriginal Cultural Heritage Consultations' (2012) 1 *International Journal of Rural Law and Policy* 1; Tanya Howard, 'The "Rules of Engagement": A Socio-legal Framework for Improving Community Engagement in Natural Resource Governance' (2015) 5 *Oñati Socio-legal Series* 1209; Paul Martin, 'Creating the Next Generation of Water Governance' (2016) 33 *Environmental and Planning Law Journal* 388; Peter Oliver and James Whelan, 'Regional community-based planning: the challenge of participatory environmental governance' (2003) 12 *Australasian Journal of Environmental Management* 126–135.

informing stakeholders (weak empowerment), or it can mean information gathering from stakeholders, a dialogue where proposals are canvassed, consensus decision-making, or more rarely processes of stakeholder decision-making authority, perhaps with accountability to stakeholders (substantial empowerment).

Some form of engagement is obligatory under many laws and policies. Community consultation (and less commonly consent) requirements are mandated for Environmental Impact Assessment of development projects, for statutory land use management and planning processes, for the approval of mining projects, in heritage protection, and by the policies and management instruments of public agencies. These requirements can require public and private actors to carry out engagement, with the specifics of how this is conducted depending on the matters that are involved. Private industry will, for example, have engagement requirements for the approval of development projects, or when dealing with cultural heritage. It is also important to note that Environmental Impact Assessment often involves some form of public consultation. Public agencies must comply with engagement requirements when developing and implementing plans and strategies. They vary in what is legally required and what implementation approaches are used. Often the rules do not specify the purposes, processes or the outcomes, merely specifying 'public consultation' which can mean many different things. Even when instruments prescribe consultation in similar terms or for similar issues the processes and/or the outcomes can vary because of many variables that are intrinsic to engagement processes, stakeholder characteristics and contexts.

The term 'consultation' in Australian public policy often signifies a relatively weak (un-empowered) form of engagement, typically interpreted as requiring that information is provided to the community and that stakeholders have the opportunity to respond, but carrying no legal obligation other than to conduct the process. FPIC of Indigenous Peoples is an ethnically specific seemingly strong empowerment version of obligatory engagement. Within the concept of FPIC, the term 'consent' indicates an intention to transfer authority to stakeholders, as they are free to withhold consent. This suggests that the principle is meant to institutionalise a hybrid governance model to the management of biological resources, though the literature does not discuss the intent in these co-management terms.[43] Due to a lack of specification of what constitutes FPIC and given the paramount status of State sovereignty under the CBD

43 Hybrid governance is increasingly evident in Australia's land management system, including co-management of some national parks, and large areas of country designated as Indigenous Protected Areas: see Jon Altman, Kirrily Jordan, Sean Kerins, Geoff Buchanan, Nicholas Biddle, Emilie-Jane Ens, and Katherine May, *Indigenous interests in land & water* (Department of Infrastructure, Transport, Regional Development and Local Government, 2009) pp 1–56. And for Indigenous Protected Areas (IPA's) see Lee Godden and Stuart Cowell, 'Conservation Planning and Indigenous Governance in Australia's Indigenous Protected Areas' (2016) 24 *Restoration Ecology* 692. See also Department of the Environment and

(including the Nagoya Protocol), signatory States have an unconstrained freedom to define what this means within their jurisdiction. States determine the processes that may or must be used to obtain consent, which stakeholders will be involved, what authority community stakeholders will have, how they will be restricted or enabled in the process, how decisions will be implemented, how accountability would be considered for the implementation of decisions, and where consent will be required. How this unfettered State discretion is exercised will determine what the 'consent' requirement means in practice (for example qualifying its common meaning or limiting when or how it can be exercised), and could introduce spill over risks, for example, by creating inequitable or non-feasible transaction costs for some citizens or conflicts over legitimacy of participation or consent authority.

Within the concept of FPIC, the terms 'free', 'prior' and 'informed' indicate that there is a concern for process integrity, but do not, for example, specify the key matters that will dictate how Indigenous Peoples will be engaged and the real degree of empowerment. These terms: do not on their own make it mandatory that the process must be carried out in good faith; indicate the quality or forms of process; the evidence required to enable effective engagement or to demonstrate compliance, competence of those managing the process; or enablement of participation, appeal or other integrity mechanisms and other matters that will determine the outcomes. These are all left to the discretion of the signatory State.

Though many consultation and engagement approaches are used in public consultation, there are no widely accepted 'best management practices' in Australia against which the integrity and quality of the implementation of such requirements can be tested. Unlike signatory countries to the *Aarhus Convention*,[44] Australia does not have any meta-governance structures to oversee the integrity of the implementation of legal or administrative requirements, and citizen appeal rights for the implementation of the obligations are not available.[45]

It is not unusual for Australian laws that mandate engagement to place severe limits on the authority allowed to citizens who participate, in effect, prohibiting more empowered approaches. For example, the *Water Act 2007* (Cth) requires consultation with Aboriginal and other stakeholders in the development of water plans for the Murray-Darling Basin but the Minister

Energy, *Australia's Fifth National Report under the Convention on Biological Diversity* (Department of the Environment and Energy, 2014) pp 1–84.

44 United Nations Economic Commission for Europe, *Convention on Access to Information, Public Participation in Decision-making and Access to Justice in Environmental Matters* (Adopted on 25 June 1998 in Aarhus, Denmark and entered into force on 30 October 2001) available at <http://ec.europa.eu/envir onment/aarhus/> (accessed 30 July 2017).

45 Court oversight being a strong metagovernance mechanism: A Andrusevych, T Alge and C Konrad (eds.), *Case Law of the Aarhus Convention Compliance Committee, 2004–2011* (2nd ed, RACSE, Lviv 2011).

must make decisions based on other specified considerations, meaning that the outcomes of consultation must have a limited ability to guide the eventual decisions.[46] I will discuss Aboriginal engagement in water policy below, to illustrate some contingencies that could affect the implementation of FPIC rules.

Failures of obligatory engagement

The 'myth' – a story that is widely believed – that underpins the conventional wisdom is that Indigenous Peoples benefit from law and administrative requirements that they be consulted about decisions that may affect their interests. Like many myths, this is not devoid of truth but its validity is not universal. The causal link between obligatory requirements for Indigenous engagement in matters that affect them, and beneficial outcomes for Indigenous Peoples, is unproven. Further, often Indigenous consultation requirements impose a significant burden on the Aboriginal and Torres Strait Peoples who take on the responsibilities of engagement, for little or no benefit to Indigenous Peoples, adding to the oppression that these requirements are intended to reduce.

Aboriginal Australians as a class have the unenviable status of being severely disadvantaged on most statistical measures, despite the rhetoric of inclusion and many policy initiatives. Australian Aboriginal and Torres Strait Islander Peoples as a whole exhibit lamentable characteristics of severe disadvantage and disruption through colonisation that are seen around the world: high levels of imprisonment, drug and alcohol use, intra-community conflict and conflict with authorities, and many other phenomena of oppression.[47] However, despite impediments many Aboriginal and Torres Strait Islander Peoples actively strive to improve the situation of their communities through engagement at many levels, including participation in collaborative governance and consultative structures. This can involve overcoming personal disadvantages that non-Indigenous peoples are not aware of.

The experiences when I was the Chairman of a New South Wales (NSW) Catchment Management Board (CMB), a regional natural resource management organisation caused me to question the reliability and fairness of obligatory consultation as it is currently configured.[48] CMBs were made up of government and community representatives, including Aboriginal stakeholders, and they conducted many engagement meetings, discussions and other activities

46 Paul Martin and Amanda Kennedy, 'Water Management in Rural Australia: The Human Rights Dimension' (2011) 20 *Human Rights Defender* 12.

47 For a summary see Steering Committee for the Review of Government Service Provision, *Overcoming Indigenous Disadvantage: Key Indicators 2014*, Report (Productivity Commission, 2014) available at <http://www.pc.gov.au/research/ongoing/overcoming-indigenous-disadvantage/key-indicators-2014/key-indicators-2014-report.pdf> (accessed 7 May 2017) pp 1.1–13.5.

48 Regional natural resource management structure described in Lisa Robins and Stephen Dovers, 'Community-based NRM Boards of Management: Are They Up To the Task?' (2007) 14 *Australasian Journal of Environmental Management* 111.

involving Aboriginal Peoples. Some excellent Aboriginal-led projects were supported through the CMB. However, the degree to which consultation contributed significantly, or was merely 'noise' or a source of unproductive transaction costs, is impossible to say. Decision-making authority was not transferred through these processes.

It is hard to adequately explain the unique challenges that some Aboriginal participants in consultation had to overcome. Statistics can only indicate the economic difficulties, which become tangible as things like the lack of a computer or a motor car, which did result in Aboriginal representatives having to forego a day's work to attend a meeting, or having to make difficult arrangements to get to and participate in meetings or other events. I became increasingly aware of the engagement burden carried by some Aboriginal Peoples. A task that might take a couple of hours for someone with ample resources would take a day or more for someone without. Social research can also only hint at the political complexities that Aboriginal representatives sometimes face. From time to time community tensions and the perception by some that their representatives should be in a position to deliver tangible or political benefits made the task particularly difficult for Aboriginal representatives. Information about the complexities of Aboriginal cultures can barely hint at the difficulties and personal stresses that can be involved in dealing with, for example, culturally sensitive knowledge.

The complexities when dealing with Aboriginal and Torres Strait Islander Peoples' cultural links to nature cannot be overstated. There can be sensitive norms and relationships involved even when considering seemingly straightforward things, and these become more difficult when different Indigenous groups are thrown together given tribal, clan, family, 'skin' or language groups, complex moiety arrangements and diverse cultural secrets and authority arrangements. Using bush-food issues as an example, the obvious complexity is the identification of matters as men's business or women's business. But over and above this are the difficulties of determining the distinct norms and relationships to nature and associated knowledge for the many different groups who may have a relationship with species or products, or the ecosystems within which these exist. Delving deeper, within each tribal group or community, sophisticated totemic relationships can affect what knowledge, often in the form of stories, might be associated with the products, who has rights to products, stories, and other interests, and what parts of the cultural system are accessible to what people. Cultural complexities can become a minefield for those who strive to honestly represent Indigenous Peoples' interests. It should thus not be surprising that Aboriginal consultative roles can involve stress, potential conflict and damage to relationships, sometimes leading to high personal economic and other costs.

Legislating FPIC obligations will not *per se* make these issues any easier. Given the hope of economic gains from bioprospecting that the CBD and the Nagoya Protocol aims to promote, and the complexity of potential rights claims, some of these difficulties may increase. Conflicts over economic opportunity can reasonably be expected given the economic circumstances of many Aboriginal and Torres Strait Islander Peoples.

Creating conditions to ensure the voices of Indigenous Peoples are heard and understood, so that consent truly is 'free' and 'informed', may be difficult. Even decisions about the language(s) of engagement, or for providing information, involve risks to genuine informed consent.[49] Colonisation and subsequent developments have created many forms of social exclusion that may prejudice achieving genuine FPIC. The dimensions of exclusion include political disempowerment, individual loss of confidence, language and modes of communication, limited opportunities for education, and the like. Modes of engagement that may seem to be fair and effective from a dominant cultural perspective may provide a deceptive sense of understanding, dialogue and agreement that can undermine the base tenets of FPIC, even whilst giving the appearance of satisfying them.

It has been proposed that 'culturally safe' settings and rules are needed for effective and fair Indigenous Peoples' engagement:

'Cultural safety' exists when people from the non-dominant (Indigenous) culture are free from the risk of disrespect or misunderstanding of the unique and subtle aspects of their culture, and where they feel free from this risk. The achievement of true cultural safety involves adjusting power relations between the dominant and the repressed culture, to overcome the disempowering effects of dominant language, received background understanding, and other sources of risk or discomfort. Thus cultural safety is not theoretical; it results from conditions and processes that ensure equality when participating in dialogue with cultural content and in dealing with the practical consequences of that dialogue. It involves an intersection between legal, cultural and environmental adjustments. A safe cultural 'space' thus refers to physical or psychic circumstances where First Nations Peoples are able with justification to feel culturally safe.[50]

Some of the difficulties of engagement leading to consent, which involves determining which Indigenous Peoples have what rights or obligations to nature and nature-related intellectual property, are demonstrated in the protection of Indigenous Peoples' heritage.[51] From an examination of Aboriginal

---

49 Canvassed in Johnnie Aseron, Kylie Anne Lingard, Chris McLaughlin, Jacqueline Williams, Paul Martin and Neyooxet Greymorning, 'Asserting Cultural Interests Through the Law: Issues and Innovations' in Natalie Stoianoff (ed.), *Indigenous Knowledge Forum – Comparative Systems for Recognising and Protecting Indigenous Knowledge and Culture* (LexisNexis, 2016) pp 69–96.
50 Ibid, p 92.
51 Kylie Lingard, 'The Impact of the Law on Consultation Practices and Purpose: A Case Study of Aboriginal Cultural Heritage Consultations' (2012) 1 *International Journal of Rural Law and Policy* 1.

stakeholders' views on heritage protection laws in NSW and other states, Kylie Lingard concludes that:

> The design of the [*National Parks and Wildlife Regulation 2009* (NSW)] duty to consult ensures the decision-maker has sufficient information on the archaeological value of objects, and the economic interests at stake. However, even perfect compliance with the consultation requirements fails to provide the decision-maker with sufficient Aboriginal information on each decision-making criterion. This provides support for the argument that statutory duties to consult are ill-designed to fulfil the purpose of the consultation.[52]

She suggests that the legalisation of engagement obligations can in itself generate perverse effects:

> … consultation requirements may in effect defeat the purpose of the duty to consult … Previous research assumes that key consultation issues relate to good or bad procedures and practices. Evidence related to the case study in this article suggests that the source of consultation issues may be the law. The case study consultation requirements were shown to lack the standards and specifications necessary to ensure the implementation of effective practices. The duty to consult was found to be ill-designed to fulfil the purpose of the consultation. These results suggest that statutory consultation requirements and purposes must be taken seriously for consultation to be more than a mere token gesture.[53]

Further risks of ineffectiveness and/or perverse effects from obligatory consultation can be seen by examining how the interests of Aboriginal Australians under the Commonwealth *Water Act 2007* (Cth) have been managed in developing the Murray-Darling Basin Plan. The legal mandate to accommodate the interests of Aboriginal Peoples exists through the *Water Act 2007* (Cth) and in policy statements.[54] Developing the Murray-Darling Basin plan involved extensive consultation including with Aboriginal Peoples in the Basin catchment.[55]

52 Ibid, p 5.
53 Ibid, p 25.
54 National Water Commission, *Position Statement: Indigenous access to water resources* (National Water Commission, 2012) available at <http://webarchive.nla. gov.au/gov/20160615060726/http://www.nwc.gov.au/nwi/position-statem ents/indigenous-access> (accessed 30 July 2017) First Peoples' Water Engagement Council, *Advice to The National Water Commission* (National Water Commission, 2012) available at <http://content.webarchive.nla.gov.au/gov/wayba ck/20160615062343/http://www.nwc.gov.au/__data/assets/pdf_file/0004/ 22576/FPWEC-Advice-to-NWC-May-2012.pdf> (accessed 30 July 2017).
55 Murray-Darling Basin Authority, *Stakeholder Engagement Strategy: Involving Australia in the Development of the Murray-Darling Basin Plan* (Murray-Darling Basin Authority, 2009) available at <https://www.mdba.gov.au/sites/default/

Particular Aboriginal citizen engagement initiatives were commenced.[56] Many aspects of the engagement approach were laudable.

Indigenous citizens (430) and Indigenous organisations (21)[57] suggested that the cultural interests of Aboriginal Peoples should be recognised through 'cultural flows', to be developed on a basis that is distinct from environmental or economic concerns.[58] A 'First Peoples' Engagement Council' convened a First Peoples' National Water Summit. The summit proposed that: (1) Aboriginal water allocations be a legal right; (2) Aboriginal water engagement and decision-making approaches be more effective; (3) capacity building and targeted scientific support be extended; and (4) that a sufficiently funded national Aboriginal water strategy be implemented.[59] Unfortunately a commitment to consult is not a commitment to act on that consultation, nor does it create a capacity to act effectively.[60]

These outcomes point to policy risks from the intersection of institutional arrangements. Section 21(4)(c)(v) of the *Water Act 2007* (Cth) requires the Minister to have regard to 'social, cultural, Indigenous and other public benefit issues' in making decisions and section 10(2)(h)(vii) provides that the Authority's rules must take into account 'the economic and social wellbeing of

files/pubs/Stakeholder-Engagement-Strategy-brochure_0.pdf> (accessed 30 July 2017); Murray-Darling Basin Authority, *Fact Sheet 4: Basin Community Committee* (Murray Darling Basin Authority, 2009) available at <http://www.south westnrm.org.au/sites/default/files/uploads/ihub/bcc-fact-sheet-41.pdf> (accessed 30 July 2017).

56 National Water Commission, *First Peoples' Water Engagement Council (FPWEC)* (National Water Commission, n.d.) available at <http://webarchive.nla.gov.au/gov/20160615062343/http://www.nwc.gov.au/organisation/partners/fpwec> (accessed 30 July 2017); Murray Lower Darling Rivers Indigenous Nations, *Home* available at <http://www.mldrin.org.au> (accessed 30 July 2017).

57 National Water Commission, *A Review of Indigenous Involvement in Water Planning* (National Water Commission, 2014) p 8 available at <http://www.hea lthinfonet.ecu.edu.au/uploads/resources/27638_27638.pdf> (accessed 30 July 2017).

58 For background literature see Australian Cultural Heritage Management, *National Cultural Flows Research Project Component 1* (Australian Cultural Heritage Management, 2014) available at <http://culturalflows.com.au/~culturalflowscom/images/documents/Component%201_Desktop%20Literature%20Review.pdf> (accessed 30 July 2017).

59 National Water Commission, *A Review of Indigenous Involvement in Water Planning* (National Water Commission, 2014) p 6 available at <http://www.hea lthinfonet.ecu.edu.au/uploads/resources/27638_27638.pdf> (accessed 30 July 2017).

60 Sherry Arnstein, 'A Ladder of Citizen Participation' (1969) 35 *Journal of the American Institute of Planners* 216. In the case of Australian water policy, citizen power is limited in practice: see Poh-Ling Tan, 'Learning from Water Law Reform in Australia' in Philippe Cullet, Alix Gowlland-Gaultieri, Roopa Madhav and Usha Ramanathan (eds.), *Water Governance in Motion: Towards Socially and Environmentally Sustainable Water Laws* (Cambridge University Press, 2010) pp 447–476.

the communities in the Murray Darling Basin'.[61] However, the Minister was bound more tightly by the requirement in the legislation that decisions be based upon 'best available scientific knowledge and socio-economic analysis'.[62] This legal commitment to science-based decisions is a constraint to what other information and analysis the Minister could legitimately use. To date 'there has been no substantial increase in water allocations for Indigenous purposes – social, economic or cultural. The challenges in Indigenous water allocation and access remain largely the same as in 2010'.[63] At this stage the practical benefit from extensive Aboriginal commitment of time and effort, and emotional capital, to consultations seem to have fallen well short of everyone's aspirations.

The proposed strategy to deal with this is to reshape 'non-science' knowledge and methods to fit science conventions. The Authority reports that the Murray-Darling Basin Authority is working with relevant stakeholders:

> … and the National Cultural Flows Planning and Research Committee to investigate appropriate scientifically robust tools to help Indigenous People(s) articulate their cultural perspectives on particular sites in a systematic way. To date, the Cultural Health Index for Streams and Waterways developed by New Zealand Māori scientists has been carefully considered. Plans are underway to develop trials for these methodologies in the basin.[64]

Even this well-intentioned approach has risks of unreliability and cultural, and perhaps functional, oppressiveness. Fundamental to science is that: (1) knowledge should be derived and tested empirically; (2) knowledge is free of subjectivity and it is transparent and open to all; and (3) scientific theories and explanations should be universal, regardless of race or religion or other social artifacts. Science(s) use a common technically precise language, with known and repeatable methods. Indigenous knowledge and culture often involves beliefs that cannot be empirically tested. Even when dealing with the same phenomena, issues or species knowledge and beliefs vary between tribes, sexes and totemic groups. Access to knowledge can be limited to those who meet certain (sometimes secret) requirements, and important information is often secret and arcane. A requirement that the epistemologies, cosmologies and traditional

---

61 Note, however, that economic theory suggests that multi-objective optimisation may lead to suboptimal policy, compared to the use of distinct instruments: see Lin Crase, 'A Cautionary Note on the Use of Socio-Economic Analyses in Water Planning' (2010) 29 *Economic Papers* 41.

62 *Water Act 2007* (Cth) s 21(4).

63 National Water Commission, *A Review of Indigenous Involvement in Water Planning, 2013* (National Water Commission, 2014) available at <http://www.hea lthinfonet.ecu.edu.au/uploads/resources/27638_27638.pdf > (accessed 7 May 2017) p 5.

64 Ibid, p 9. The Cultural Flows research project, due for completion in 2016, is another attempt to bridge the gap.

knowledge of Indigenous Peoples must be reshaped to fit the expectations of science carries a risk of altering and removing what is unique and valued by the communities that the FPIC requirements are meant to advantage. The approach is intrinsically colonialist, even if well intentioned. There is a risk that it will not deal adequately with the rich trove of beliefs, knowledge, norms and relationships that would properly inform decisions intended to protect Indigenous interests.

Systematic evaluation of the risks

The discussion above demonstrates that substantial risks do exist for the three aspects of FPIC – the translation of politically endorsed principles into implemented laws and policies, the effectiveness and effects of obligatory engagement, and the implementation of Indigenous Peoples' policies. The existence of risks, and the extent of harm that can arise if potential adverse contingencies do arise, indicate that systematic management of this policy risk should be a priority. This section considers possible approaches to risk evaluation and management, and identifies some specific issues and possible risk management approaches. However, systematic risk evaluation and risk management strategies require a detailed analysis involving Indigenous Peoples, which is beyond the scope of this chapter. Such a policy risk analysis would strengthen any proposed approach to implementing FPIC as a national framework.

A few methods are available for such a structured policy risk analysis. The International Standards Organization *Risk Management Standard* provides one approach and the International Risk Governance Council (IRGC) provides its IRGC framework.[65] Based on these and other inputs we developed a Policy Risk Framework, which has been applied to various public policies.[66] That framework considers three generic categories of risk. The first category is political risk, with politics defined broadly to include formal politics of governance systems, involving the Parliamentary system and identifiable political actors, but also the less formal politics involved in corporate and community life. This category also encompasses the responses of affected stakeholders such as agency capture, opposition and the operations of the market for political power. The second category is instrumental and consequent implementation risks. That there are many risks to the effective, efficient and fair implementation of FPIC under the CBD and the Nagoya Protocol is suggested by the foregoing discussion and examples. The final category is perverse spill overs, and again the foregoing discussion suggests that these risks are present.

65 International Risk Governance Council, *An Introduction to the IRGC Risk Governance Framework* (IRGG, 2008) available at <https://www.irgc.org/IMG/p df/An_introduction_to_the_IRGC_Risk_Governance_Framework.pdf> (accessed 7 May 2017);

66 Paul Martin and Jacqueline Williams, *Policy Risk Assessment*, Technical Report No. 03/10 (CRC for Irrigation Futures, 2010).

The issue of who has power/authority, including FPIC, is a central consideration in all engagement processes and is particularly important when dealing with Aboriginal and Torres Strait Islander engagement, given the ongoing effects of colonisation. If choices about authority are implied in governance arrangements rather than explicit as they traditionally are in Australia, those who control the processes can design these to meet their needs and priorities, or institutionalise processes that they are comfortable and do not have to necessarily take into account the special requirements of Indigenous Peoples. The motivation, knowledge and skills of those in charge will determine whether these design choices are suitable, and this is a risk that should be managed. A starting point might be for measurable empowerment objective to be made explicit in the legislation, supporting policies or project objectives. For example, the FPIC process should result in Indigenous People(s) effectively co-managing the use of the genetic material or resource. Coupling clear empowerment objectives with post-process (formative and summative) evaluation and transparent reporting would provide a stronger impetus for empowerment than would be provided by broad legal requirements alone.

FPIC deliberations may require consideration of information that is sensitive within Indigenous communities, and disclosures that may be outside their cultural norms. This raises the risk either that the process will be frustrated by non-disclosure, that the disclosure will be a violation of those cultures, or that the process (regardless of disclosure or non-disclosure) will be culturally and perhaps socially costly to the individuals and communities concerned. Cultural safety involves a risk that probably can only ultimately be addressed by Indigenous Peoples themselves, but without support it is hard to see how it can be properly managed. New consultative processes are likely to be part of any effective management of these risks.

The quality of engagement processes, and the integrity and skill of those leading their implementation, will be critical to the outcomes. Australia's lack of engagement process standards and integrity safeguards creates a risk to the successful implementation of FPIC principles. The complications specific to Indigenous Peoples' engagement and consent indicate the need for processes that are different to those that may be suitable for general consultation and decision-making. Designing and implementing these processes is a difficult but important challenge. Sophisticated methods of engagement, objective feedback and continuing improvement, with strong integrity safeguards, such as rights of review and appeal over engagement processes, would be a partial means to address the risk of process failures.

Many people or organisations will have roles in FPIC processes. The examples discussed above suggest that their involvement will draw on capabilities and resources that include cultural knowledge and skills, tangible resources, and trustful relationships. The outcomes of FPIC processes may be determined by the capacity of the 'weakest link' in the chain of consultation, engagement and consent, suggesting that capacity to engage effectively is an important risk management issue. To address this risk requires FPIC processes to involve a thorough analysis of the necessary capability platform, to identify gaps that must be filled, and to devise effective strategies to implement FPIC principles. Specialist support and additional resources are needed, particularly for Indigenous Peoples who retain a close connection to traditional culture, who live traditional lives, or who are severely disadvantaged.

Finally, given all of the considerations discussed above, it should be anticipated that there will be failures. There will be times when the consent that is given is not truly 'free and informed', where the consent is tainted by process failures or by issues of legitimacy whether innocent or otherwise, or where the outcomes cause unanticipated harms. Recognising that failures are probably inevitable requires consideration of what remediation and improvement approaches will be built into the implementation plans. This is particularly important if the damaging impacts of colonisation are not to be carried forward even in the implementation of a principle that is intended to reduce these effects.

The engagement processes for achieving FPIC of Indigenous Australians do involve particular challenges for cultural, economic and political reasons. These require *sui generis* solutions. However, we should also remain aware that all Australians, including Indigenous citizens, should be able to benefit from more general engagement processes and that the integrity and the effectiveness of these processes are far from ideal. Every day processes are being undertaken that are meant to ensure better-informed decisions and/or citizen empowerment in decisions that affect them. Australia does not yet have a management regime, including standards, evaluation and continuing improvement, to manage the risks of failure or perverse outcomes from these processes. The challenges of implementing Indigenous Peoples' engagement in the management of biological material under the CBD and the Nagoya Protocol thus also points to a broader problem of Australia's lack of reliable integrity mechanisms for the engagement requirements that we already have to make engagement requirements effective, efficient and fair. Addressing the general problems of citizen engagement would also help reduce some problems of the more specific Indigenous Peoples consultation, to the benefit of all citizens, leaving a smaller 'space' where *sui generis* reform would be required.

7 The *Trans-Pacific Partnership* and sustainable development
Access to genetic resources, informed consent, and benefit sharing

Matthew Rimmer

7.1 Introduction

The *Trans-Pacific Partnership* (TPP) is a mega-regional agreement, spanning the Pacific Rim.[1] The trade deal includes Australia, Brunei, Canada, Chile, Japan, Malaysia, Mexico, New Zealand, Peru, Singapore, and Vietnam. The United States of America (US) was a key member of the trade negotiations under President Barack Obama – but has withdrawn from the discussions under President Donald Trump. Significantly, the agreement excludes the BASIC/BRICS countries, namely Brazil, China, India, Russia and South Africa.[2] Curiously, in spite of its name, the TPP also does not include Pacific Island States.[3] The agreement also does not involve a number of countries of the Association of Southeast Asian Nations (ASEAN) such as Cambodia and Indonesia.

Despite the exclusion of a number of countries of different trade blocs and regions, the TPP is considered ambitious not only in terms of its membership but also in respect of its subject matter. The agreement is not merely confined

---

1 The Department of Foreign Affairs and Trade, *The Trans-Pacific Partnership*, available at <http://dfat.gov.au/trade/agreements/tpp/official-documents/Pa ges/official-documents.aspx> (accessed 15 August 2017). For commentary see Jane Kelsey (ed.), *No Ordinary Deal: Unmasking the Trans-Pacific Partnership Free Trade Agreement* (Bridget Williams Books Inc, 2010); Tania Voon (ed.), *Trade Liberalisation and International Co-operation: A Legal Analysis of the Trans-Pacific Partnership Agreement* (Edward Elgar, 2013); Chin Leng Lim, Deborah Elms and Patrick Low (eds.), *The Trans-Pacific Partnership: A Quest for a Twenty-First Century Trade Agreement* (Cambridge University Press, 2012); Jane Kelsey, *Hidden Agendas: What We Need to Know about the Trans-Pacific Partnership Agreement (TPPA)* (Bridget Williams Books Limited, 2013); Scott Sinclair and Stuart Trew (eds.), *The Trans-Pacific Partnership and Canada: A Citizen's Guide* (James Lorimer & Company Ltd, 2016); and Thilo Rensmann, *Mega-Regional Agreements* (Springer, 2017).
2 The BASIC Group includes Brazil, South Africa, India, and China. The BRICS Group includes Brazil, Russia, India, and China.
3 The *Pacific Agreement on Closer Economic Relations (PACER) Plus* 2017 covers Australia, New Zealand, and eight Pacific island countries – Cook Islands, Kiribati, Nauru, Niue, Samoa, Solomon Islands, Tonga and Tuvalu.

to matters of trade and market access. The TPP also covers regulatory topics, such as intellectual property, electronic commerce and investment. The Pacific Rim trade agreement also considers other issues, such as the environment, sustainable development and access to genetic resources.

In negotiating the TPP, there was a contentious debate over the treatment of Indigenous intellectual property, biodiversity and sustainable development. Hans Morten Haugen observed of the negotiations over the TPP:

> It might not be surprising that Australia and the United States have positions that seek to place upon themselves the least onerous duties with regard to Indigenous Peoples, while Peru seems most concerned for the rights of Indigenous People. It is, however, somewhat surprising that a country like Chile sides with the Australian and USA position.[4]

The final text revealed a complex web of provisions on Indigenous intellectual property, access to genetic resources and sustainable development.

This paper considers the impact of the regional trade agreement – the TPP – upon the United Nations' (UN) *Sustainable Development Goals* (SDGs).[5] The TPP text was the result of years of negotiations on trade ties between nations around the Pacific Rim. The UN's SDGs aim to eradicate poverty and reduce inequality by addressing critical issues such as food security, health care, access to education, clean and affordable water, clean energy and climate action. Unfortunately the TPP and the SDGs are incompatible. Several chapters of the TPP impinge upon the SDGs, potentially undermining the UN's efforts to promote sustainable development and equality throughout the Pacific region. Moreover, many developing countries, least-developed countries and small island states in the Pacific region are excluded from the TPP's preferential trade deal. Such concerns are particularly evident in the debate over access to genetic resources, informed consent and benefit sharing.

While Obama was champion of the TPP, his successor has been an opponent of the mega-regional agreement. The new US President Donald Trump has withdrawn the US from the negotiations and the agreement.[6] Nonetheless, a number of other participants – including Australia and New Zealand – are considering the possibility of implementing the agreement without the

---

4 Hans Morten Haugen, 'How are Indigenous and Local Communities' Rights Over Their Traditional Knowledge and Genetic Resources Protected in Current Free Trade Negotiations? Highlighting the Draft Trans-Pacific Partnership Agreement' (2014) 17 *The Journal of World Intellectual Property* 81, 92.
5 United Nations, *Sustainable Development Goals*, available at <http://www.un.org/sustainabledevelopment/sustainable-development-goals> (accessed 15 August 2017).
6 The White House, 'Presidential Memorandum Regarding Withdrawal of the United States from the Trans-Pacific Partnership Negotiations and Agreement', Press Release, 23 January 2017, available at <https://www.whitehouse.gov/the-press-office/2017/01/23/presidential-memorandum-regarding-withdrawal-united-states-trans-pacific> (accessed 15 August 2017).

participation of the US.[7] The Australian Prime Minister Malcolm Turnbull has mooted the possibility of other countries joining the TPP to compensate for the departure of the US.[8] The last New Zealand Prime Minister Bill English has argued: 'In the case of TPP, I think there is a sense there that among the remaining 11 countries, it would be quite beneficial for Australia and New Zealand to show some confidence that this could be moved forward'.[9] Many of the other TPP participants, however, remain hesitant to commit themselves to the agreement, without the inclusion of the US. As such, the fate of the TPP remains uncertain at the time of writing in August 2017.

This chapter considers a number of key chapters of the TPP relating to access to genetic resources, informed consent, and benefit sharing. Part 2 looks at the TPP Chapter on Intellectual Property and focuses on access to genetic resources, informed consent, and benefit sharing. In particular, this part considers Indigenous intellectual property in the context of a challenge under the *Treaty of Waitangi* between the New Zealand government and the Māori. This conflict has raised larger questions about Indigenous sovereignty, investor-state dispute settlement and plant intellectual property. Part 3 considers the TPP Chapter on the Environment, and its treatment of access to genetic resources. Part 4 focuses on the TPP Chapter on Development, and considers its relevance and implications for biodiversity. The conclusion in Part 5 considers the future of the TPP, and the rival regional agreement, the *Regional Comprehensive Economic Partnership* (RCEP).[10] The conclusion contends that trade agreements in the Pacific Rim should seek to strengthen the regional institutions, networks, and rules in respect of access to genetic resources, informed consent and benefit sharing.

7.2 The TPP: Indigenous intellectual property, access to genetic resources and biodiversity

There have long been significant concerns about how international trade agreements affect Indigenous rights, particularly in respect of Indigenous

7 Radio New Zealand, 'NZ and Australia to Work Together to Salvage TPP – English', *Radio New Zealand*, 17 February 2017, available at <http://www.ra dionz.co.nz/news/political/324729/nz-and-australia-to-work-together-to-salva ge-tpp-english> (accessed 15 August 2017).

8 'PM Malcolm Turnbull says China could join the TPP after the US and Donald Trump opted out', News.com.au, 25 January 2017, available at <http://www. news.com.au/national/politics/prime-minister-malcolm-turnbull-says-china -could-join-the-tpp-after-donald-trump-opted-out/news-story/bbb12eb9cf8ba d68acdf364bf31c2043> (accessed 15 August 2017).

9 Radio New Zealand, 'NZ and Australia to Work Together to Salvage TPP – English', *Radio New Zealand*, 17 February 2017, available at <http://www.ra dionz.co.nz/news/political/324729/nz-and-australia-to-work-together-to-salva ge-tpp-english> (accessed 15 August 2017).

10 Department of Foreign Affairs and Trade, *The Regional Comprehensive Economic Partnership*, available at <http://dfat.gov.au/trade/agreements/rcep/Pages/ regional-comprehensive-economic-partnership.aspx> (accessed 15 August 2017).

intellectual property. There has been an ongoing conversation about the relationship between Indigenous communities, intellectual property and trade.[11] Such discussions have traditionally taken place in multilateral fora like the World Trade Organization (WTO), the World Intellectual Property Organization (WIPO), the UN Environment Programme, international climate talks and the UN Permanent Forum on Indigenous Peoples. Of late, the debate has also arisen in the context of bilateral trade agreements such as the *Australia-United States Free Trade Agreement* 1994 and mega-regional trade agreements like the TPP.

Writing in 2008, Megan Davis, the Director of the Indigenous Law Centre at the University of New South Wales, and the current Chair of the UN Permanent Forum on Indigenous Peoples, expressed concerns about how the *Australia-United States Free Trade Agreement* would impact upon Indigenous communities in Australia.[12] She commented that '[Free Trade Agreements] have the potential to encroach upon laws, regulations and policy making with respect to culture, education, health, environment and heritage and this would have a disproportionately negative impact upon Indigenous communities'.[13]

There has been much general controversy over the TPP. In the context of Indigenous rights, there has been trepidation about how the trade deal will affect Indigenous communities. There have been concerns that the TPP has been secretly negotiated without the participation or consent of Indigenous communities. Moreover, there have been complaints that the TPP falls far short of the standards set by the United Nations *Declaration for the Rights of Indigenous Peoples* (UNDRIP).[14]

In New Zealand there has been a heated debate over the process of the negotiations of the TPP and the final outcomes.[15] A particular concern is whether the New Zealand government had respected the *Treaty of Waitangi* while negotiating the TPP.[16] There are a range of procedural and substantive

11 See Matthew Rimmer (ed.), *Indigenous Intellectual Property: A Handbook of Contemporary Research* (Edward Elgar, 2015).
12 Megan Davis, 'Indigenous Australia and the Australia-United States Free Trade Agreement' (2008) 2 *Ngoya: Talk the Law* 76 available at <http://www.austlii. edu.au/au/journals/NgiyaTLaw/2008/8.pdf> (accessed 15 August 2017).
13 Ibid, p 76.
14 *United Nations Declaration on the Rights of Indigenous Peoples* (2007) A/RES/ 61/295 available at <http://www.un.org/esa/socdev/unpfii/documents/ DRIPS_en.pdf> (accessed 15 August 2017) (UNDRIP).
15 Amokura Kawharu, 'Process, Politics and the Politics of Process: The *Trans-Pacific Partnership* in New Zealand', (2016) 17 *Melbourne Journal of International Law* 1, available at <http://law.unimelb.edu.au/__data/assets/pdf_file/0011/ 2214479/02-Kawharu.pdf> (accessed 15 August 2017).
16 *Treaty of Waitangi* 1840, English version and Māori version. For the English version, the Māori version and a literal translation by Sir Hugh Kawharu of the Treaty, see Te Puni Kokiri (Ministry of Māori Development) at <http://www.tpk. govt.nz/en/search/?q=literal+translation+treaty+of+waitangi> (accessed 15 August 2017).

issues involved in this matter[17] with Māori communities bringing an action against the TPP under the *Treaty of Waitangi*.[18] Musician and film-maker Moana Maniapoto commented about the action:

> Māori have been struggling to protect our culture in the face of an [intellectual property] system that has never been a good fit for our people and culture. The experience of having my name trademarked by a company in Germany brought it home in a very personal way how much our language, culture and music is being appropriated left, right and center by companies. The WAI262 Claim reiterated that. There's been no movement by the government to undo existing agreements or legislation that fail to protect our culture. Yet the government wants to haul us all into a hefty – and very secret – international agreement that will disempower Māori even more? I am very concerned about this – especially given the track record of the key player, the USA.[19]

The claimants have been concerned that the New Zealand Crown's actions in relation to the *Trans-Pacific Partnership Act 2015* (NZ) that implemented the TPP commitments may negatively affect Māori health, education and culture, and will impinge on Māori rights to self-government as guaranteed by the principles of the *Treaty of Waitangi* and UNDRIP.[20] On the 5 May 2016, the Waitangi Tribunal handed down its report on the TPP and the *Treaty of Waitangi*.[21] The Waitangi Tribunal addressed a number of important issues – including the exception clause relating to the *Treaty of Waitangi*, investor-state dispute settlement and Indigenous intellectual property.

A The Treaty of Waitangi General Exceptions Clause

The primary issue for Waitangi Tribunal was whether or not the *Treaty of Waitangi* exception clause is an effective protection of Māori interests. In the

---

17 Carwyn Jones, Claire Charters, Andrew Erueti, and Jane Kelsey, 'Māori Rights, Te Tiriti O Waitangi and the Trans-Pacific Partnership Agreement', 2015, available at <https://tpplegal.files.wordpress.com/2015/12/ep3-tiriti-paper.pdf> (accessed 15 August 2017).

18 TPP Legal – Waitangi Tribunal at <https://tpplegal.wordpress.com/waitangi-tribunal> (accessed 15 August 2017). This site contains the affidavits, evidence, hearing transcripts and closing submissions.

19 'High Profile Māori File Waitangi Tribunal Claim over TPPA', 25 June 2015, available at <https://www.maoritelevision.com/news/politics/high-profile-ma ori-file-waitangi-tribunal-claim-over-tppa> (accessed 15 August 2017).

20 TPP Legal – Waitangi Tribunal available at <https://tpplegal.wordpress.com/wa itangi-tribunal> (accessed 15 August 2017); *United Nations Declaration on the Rights of Indigenous Peoples* 2007, 61st sess, UN Doc A/61/L.67, adopted by General Assembly Resolution 61/295 on 13 September 2007

21 Waitangi Tribunal, *Report on the Trans-Pacific Partnership Agreement*, WAI 252, Waitangi Tribunal Report, 2016, available at <https://forms.justice.govt.nz/sea rch/Documents/WT/wt_DOC_104833137/Report%20on%20the%20TPPA% 20W.pdf> (accessed 15 August 2017).

General Exceptions Chapter, Article 29.6 of the TPP deals with the *Treaty of Waitangi* providing, in part:

> 1. Provided that such measures are not used as a means of arbitrary or unjustified discrimination against persons of the other Parties or as a disguised restriction on trade in goods, trade in services and investment, nothing in this Agreement shall preclude the adoption by New Zealand of measures it deems necessary to accord more favourable treatment to Māori in respect of matters covered by this Agreement, including in fulfilment of its obligations under the *Treaty of Waitangi*.
> 2. The Parties agree that the interpretation of the *Treaty of Waitangi*, including as to the nature of the rights and obligations arising under it, shall not be subject to the dispute settlement provisions of this Agreement. Chapter 28 (Dispute Settlement) shall otherwise apply to this Article. A panel established under Article 28.7 (Establishment of a Panel) may be requested to determine only whether any measure referred to in paragraph 1 is inconsistent with a Party's rights under this Agreement.[22]

The Waitangi Tribunal found: 'We conclude that the exception clause will be likely to operate in the [TPP] substantially as intended and therefore can be said to offer a reasonable degree of protection to Māori interests'.[23] The Waitangi Tribunal added: 'We have come to this view even though the clause as drafted only applies to measures that the Crown deems necessary to accord more favourable treatment to Māori'.[24]

I have my doubts as to whether this General Exceptions clause will be effective in the TPP. Moreover, it is notable that Indigenous communities in other Pacific Rim countries outside New Zealand involved in the TPP do not have any particular special protection in trade disputes. This is problematic. In other TPP nations, there are a range of processes underway designed to enhance Indigenous self-determination. For instance, in Australia, Indigenous leaders have called for a representative body and a treaties process after the Uluru Convention.[25] Meanwhile, in Canada, Justice Trudeau has said that 'it is time for a renewed, nation-to-nation relationship with Indigenous Peoples,

22 *Trans-Pacific Partnership*, Art 29.6, available at <https://ustr.gov/trade-agreem ents/free-trade-agreements/trans-pacific-partnership/tpp-full-text> (accessed 15 August 2017) (TPP).

23 Waitangi Tribunal, *Report on the Trans-Pacific Partnership Agreement*, WAI 252, Waitangi Tribunal Report, 2016, x, available at <https://forms.justice.govt.nz/ search/Documents/WT/wt_DOC_104833137/Report%20on%20the%20TPPA% 20W.pdf> (accessed 15 August 2017).

24 Ibid, p x.

25 Bridget Brennan and Stephanie Zillman, 'Indigenous Leaders Call for Representative Body and Treaties Process After Uluru Convention', *ABC News*, 26 May 2017 <http://www.abc.net.au/news/2017-05-26/constitutional-recognition-re jected-by-indigenous-leaders-uluru/8563928> (accessed 15 August 2017).

based on recognition of rights, respect, co-operation, and partnership'.[26] It is unclear how the TPP would take into account the outcomes of such domestic processes. UNDRIP emphasises that 'Indigenous Peoples have the right to self-determination' and that, 'by virtue of that right they freely determine their political status and freely pursue their economic, social, and cultural development'.[27] The TPP does not recognise the fundamental right of self-determination of Indigenous Peoples in terms of its architecture.

B *Investor-state dispute settlement*

Second, the Waitangi Tribunal did express reservations and caveats about the inclusion of an investor-state dispute settlement regime in the TPP. There has been much controversy over the investor-state dispute settlement mechanism proposed for the TPP.[28] Investor-state dispute settlement is a mechanism which enables foreign investors to seek compensation from national governments at international arbitration tribunals.[29] There has been a particular concern that the investor-state dispute settlement mechanism is being used and exploited by fossil fuel companies and natural resource entities.[30] There have been larger concerns about the impact of Investor-State Dispute Settlement upon the rule of law, the position of judiciary[31] and the role of Parliament.[32]

The Waitangi Tribunal observed: 'From the evidence before us, it seems the most likely source of risk to Māori under the [TPP] will be investor-state claims in respect of domestic measures which place Māori at a relative advantage in comparison to a foreign investor'.[33] The Waitangi Tribunal commented: 'In

---

26 Ravi de Costa, 'Trudeau Launches Canada Into A Radically New Approach to Indigenous Affairs', *The Conversation*, 26 January 2016 <https://theconversation. com/trudeau-launches-canada-into-a-radically-new-approach-to-indigenous-affa irs-53159> (accessed 15 August 2017)
27 UNDRIP, Art. 3.
28 TPP, Ch 9.
29 United Nations Conference on Trade and Development, 'Recent Developments in Investor-State Dispute Settlement: Updated for the Multilateral Dialogue on Investment', April 2014, available at <http://unctad.org/en/PublicationsLibra ry/webdiaepcb2014d3_en.pdf> (accessed 15 August 2017).
30 Kyla Tienhaara, *The Expropriation of Environmental Governance: Protecting Foreign Investors at the Expense of Public Policy* (University of Cambridge Press, 2009)
31 Chief Justice Robert French, 'Investor-State Dispute Settlement – A Cut Above the Courts?', Supreme and Federal Courts Judges' Conference, 9 July 2014, available at <http://www.hcourt.gov.au/assets/publications/speeches/curren t-justices/frenchcj/frenchcj09jul14.pdf> (accessed 15 August 2017).
32 The Hon. Melissa Parke, 'The Trans-Pacific Partnership', the House of Representatives, Australian Parliament, 10 February 2016, available at <http://parlinfo. aph.gov.au/parlInfo/search/display/display.w3p;query=Id%3A%22chamber% 2Fhansardr%2Fef9bd10-ec92-4de4-9372-a92d6a12d7ef%2F0293%22> (accessed 15 August 2017).
33 Waitangi Tribunal, *Report on the Trans-Pacific Partnership Agreement*, WAI 252, Waitangi Tribunal Report, 2016, x, available at <https://forms.justice.govt.nz/

these instances we think the exception clause should operate to provide a reasonable degree of protection'.[34] Despite this finding, the Waitangi Tribunal still harboured concerns, noting: 'The protections and rights given to foreign investors under the [TPP] are extensive'.[35] The Waitangi Tribunal commented: 'The rights foreign investors have to bring claims against the New Zealand Government in our view raise a serious question about the extent to which those claims, or the threat or apprehension of them, may have a chilling effect on the Crown's willingness or ability to meet its [*Treaty of Waitangi*] obligations or to adopt otherwise Treaty-consistent measures'.[36] The Waitangi Tribunal observed: 'This issue and the appropriate text for a [*Treaty of Waitangi*] exception clause for future free trade agreements are matters about which there should, in our view, be further dialogue between Māori and the Crown'.[37]

In my opinion, the Waitangi Tribunal still gravely underestimates the risks posed to Indigenous communities by investor-state dispute settlement mechanisms. Gus van Harten from Osgoode Hall Law School at York University has highlighted the lack of consent by Indigenous communities for Investor-State Dispute Settlement clauses in his latest book, *Sold Down the Yangtze*.[38] Likewise, Jane Kelsey from the University of Auckland has demonstrated that pro-corporate investor clauses are toxic for Indigenous rights in respect of land, water, the environment and Traditional Knowledge.[39]

C Indigenous intellectual property

Third, the Waitangi Tribunal considered the question of the treatment of Indigenous intellectual property under the TPP. In the Waitangi Tribunal, New Zealand has provided for strong recognition of Indigenous intellectual property in the 'Wai 262' decision.[40] In a research handbook on *Indigenous*

    search/Documents/WT/wt_DOC_104833137/Report%20on%20the%20TPPA%
    20W.pdf> (accessed 15 August 2017).
34 Ibid.
35 Ibid.
36 Ibid.
37 Ibid.
38 Gus van Harten, *Sold Down the Yangtze: Canada's Lopsided Investment Deal with China* (IIAP, 2015).
39 Jane Kelsey, 'Trans-Pacific Partnership's Toothless Environment Chapter Gets the Wikileaks Treatment', *The Conversation*, 23 January 2014, available at <https://theconversation.com/trans-pacific-partnerships-toothless-environment-chapter-gets-the-wikileaks-treatment-22135> (accessed 15 August 2017).
40 Waitangi Tribunal, *Ko Aotearoa Tenei: A Report into Claims Concerning New Zealand Law and Policy Affecting Māori Culture and Identity – Te taumata tuatahi* (Wai 262 Waitangi Tribunal Report 2 July 2011), available at <http://www.waitangitribunal.govt.nz/scripts/reports/reports/262/05AC7023-0EEA-4ECC-8B6E-A B136A2EA7F8.pdf> (accessed 15 August 2017). See also Fleur Adcock, 'Diluted Control: A Critical Analysis of the Wai 262 Report on Māori Traditional Knowledge and Culture' in Matthew Rimmer (ed.), *Indigenous Intellectual Property: A*

Intellectual Property, Fleur Adcock and Sarah Rosanowski explore various dimensions of the landmark ruling in the 'Wai 262' decision.[41] Jessica Christine Lai has also been analysing the significance of the decision.[42]

The Waitangi Tribunal cited with approval the statement in the 'Wai 262' decision that 'it is for Māori to say what their interests are, and to articulate how they might best be protected – in this case, in the making, amendment, or execution of international agreements'.[43] Building upon the 'Wai 262' decision, the Waitangi Tribunal observed: 'In accordance with the [*Treaty of Waitangi*], then, the Crown must work out a level of protection for Māori interests, as identified and defined by Māori, that is reasonable when balanced where necessary against other valid interests, and in the sometimes constrained international circumstances in which it must act'.[44] In its report on the TPP, the Waitangi Tribunal reiterated its support for the findings in the 'Wai 262' decision: 'Māori interests are entitled to a reasonable degree of protection when those interests are affected by international instruments entered into by the New Zealand Government'.[45]

There has been a long historical debate over the protection of plant intellectual property.[46] The TPP has sought to provide protection in respect of plant breeders' rights. Nonetheless, for New Zealand, that raises cross-over issues with Indigenous intellectual property and Traditional Knowledge. Article 18.16 of the TPP provides for cooperation in respect of Traditional Knowledge:

1. The Parties recognise the relevance of intellectual property systems and traditional knowledge associated with genetic resources to each

Handbook of Contemporary Research, (Edward Elgar, 2015) p 497 and Sarah Rosanowski, 'Protection of Traditional Cultural Expressions within the New Zealand Intellectual Property Framework: A Case Study of the *Ka Mate* Haka', in Matthew Rimmer (ed.), *Indigenous Intellectual Property: A Handbook of Contemporary Research,* (Edward Elgar, 2015) p 264; Jessica Christine Lai, *Indigenous Cultural Heritage and Intellectual Property Rights: Learning from the New Zealand Experience?* (Springer, 2014).

41 Fleur Adcock, 'Diluted Control: A Critical Analysis of the Wai 262 Report on Māori Traditional Knowledge and Culture' in Matthew Rimmer (ed.), *Indigenous Intellectual Property: A Handbook of Contemporary Research,* (Edward Elgar, 2015) p 497 and Sarah Rosanowski, 'Protection of Traditional Cultural Expressions within the New Zealand Intellectual Property Framework: A Case Study of the *Ka Mate* Haka', in Matthew Rimmer (ed.), *Indigenous Intellectual Property: A Handbook of Contemporary Research,* (Edward Elgar, 2015) p 264.

42 Jessica Christine Lai, *Indigenous Cultural Heritage and Intellectual Property Rights: Learning from the New Zealand Experience?* Cham: Springer, 2014.

43 Waitangi Tribunal, *Report on the Trans-Pacific Partnership Agreement,* WAI 252, Waitangi Tribunal Report, 2016, 11, available at <https://forms.justice.govt.nz/search/Documents/WT/wt_DOC_104833137/Report%20on%20the%20TPPA%20W.pdf> (accessed 15 August 2017).

44 Ibid, p 12.

45 Ibid, p 13.

46 Jay Sanderson, *Plants, People and Practices: The Nature and History of the UPOV Convention* (Cambridge University Press, 2017).

other, when that traditional knowledge is related to those intellectual property systems.

2. The Parties shall endeavour to cooperate through their respective agencies responsible for intellectual property, or other relevant institutions, to enhance the understanding of issues connected with traditional knowledge associated with genetic resources, and genetic resources.

3. The Parties shall endeavour to pursue quality patent examination, which may include:

    (a) that in determining prior art, relevant publicly available documented information related to traditional knowledge associated with genetic resources may be taken into account;
    (b) an opportunity for third parties to cite, in writing, to the competent examining authority prior art disclosures that may have a bearing on patentability, including prior art disclosures related to traditional knowledge associated with genetic resources;
    (c) if applicable and appropriate, the use of databases or digital libraries containing traditional knowledge associated with genetic resources; and
    (d) cooperation in the training of patent examiners in the examination of patent applications related to traditional knowledge associated with genetic resources.[47]

Such language, though, is weak. It seems left open to individual States to determine at their own discretion whether or not they take action to provide Indigenous intellectual property.

The Annex to Article 18.7.2 in the Intellectual Property Chapter of the TPP provides some specific commentary on New Zealand:

1. Notwithstanding the obligations in Article 18.7.2 (International Agreements), and subject to paragraphs 2, 3 and 4 of this Annex, New Zealand shall:

    (a) accede to the [*International Union for the Protection of New Varieties of Plants* (UPOV)] 1991 within three years of the date of entry into force of this Agreement for New Zealand; or
    (b) adopt a *sui generis* plant variety rights system that gives effect to the UPOV 1991 within three years of the date of entry into force of this Agreement for New Zealand.

2. Nothing in paragraph 1 shall preclude the adoption by New Zealand of measures it deems necessary to protect indigenous plant species in fulfilment of its obligations under the *Treaty of Waitangi*, provided

47 TPP, Art 18.6.

that such measures are not used as a means of arbitrary or unjustified discrimination against a person of another Party.

3. The consistency of any measures referred to in paragraph 2 with the obligations in paragraph 1 shall not be subject to the dispute settlement provisions of this Agreement.

4. The interpretation of the *Treaty of Waitangi*, including as to the nature of the rights and obligations arising under it, shall not be subject to the dispute settlement provisions of this Agreement. Chapter 28 (Dispute Settlement) shall otherwise apply to this Annex. A panel established under Article 28.7 (Establishment of a Panel) may be requested to determine only whether any measure referred to in paragraph 2 is inconsistent with a Party's rights under this Agreement.[48]

The Waitangi Tribunal noted that 'the Crown is still developing its process for engagement' in 'respect of changes to be made to the plant variety rights regime and whether or not New Zealand should accede to UPOV [1991]'.[49] Justice Doogan commented: 'On that issue, we adjourn our inquiry with a view to assessing what (if any) further steps may be necessary once further information is available'.[50]

Overall, in my view, the regime for Indigenous intellectual property in the TPP falls far short of the standards established in UNDRIP.[51] Article 31(1) of UNDRIP provides:

Indigenous Peoples have the right to maintain, control, protect and develop their cultural heritage, traditional knowledge and traditional cultural expressions, as well as the manifestations of their sciences, technologies and cultures, including human and genetic resources, seeds, medicines, knowledge of the properties of fauna and flora, oral traditions, literatures, designs, sports and traditional games and visual and performing arts. They also have the right to maintain, control, protect and develop their intellectual property over such cultural heritage, traditional knowledge, and traditional cultural expressions.[52]

Article 31(2) further provides: 'In conjunction with Indigenous Peoples, States shall take effective measures to recognize and protect the exercise of these

48 TPP, Art 18.7.2.
49 Waitangi Tribunal, *Report on the Trans-Pacific Partnership Agreement*, WAI 252, Waitangi Tribunal Report, 2016, x, available at <https://forms.justice.govt.nz/search/Documents/WT/wt_DOC_104833137/Report%20on%20the%20TPPA%20W.pdf> (accessed 15 August 2017).
50 Ibid.
51 For commentary see Mauro Barelli, *Seeking Justice in International Law: The Significance and Implications of the UN Declaration on the Rights of Indigenous Peoples* (Routledge, 2016).
52 UNDRIP, Art 31(1).

rights'.[53] This would seem to be a much higher standard than that provided for by the TPP. Moreover, there remain larger issues about New Zealand's implementation of international laws in respect of access to genetic resources, informed consent, and benefit sharing.[54]

In process and substance, the TPP has shown little respect or recognition for the rights and interests of Indigenous communities in the Pacific Rim. It had been hoped that the challenge by Māori claimants against the TPP would raise such larger questions about Indigenous sovereignty, self-determination and rights. Unfortunately, the report of the Waitangi Tribunal on the TPP seems to be rather blasé about the relationship between trade agreements and Indigenous rights. The Waitangi Tribunal seems to be of the view that the exception clause for the *Treaty of Waitangi* will be sufficient to protect Indigenous interests in the TPP. The then New Zealand Prime Minister John Key says Māori communities should embrace the TPP (even though they were not properly consulted).[55] Likewise, the New Zealand Trade Minister welcomed the Waitangi Tribunal report.[56]

For their part, the Māori Council were disappointed by the Waitangi Tribunal ruling. Council Chair Sir Edward Durie commented:

> The New Zealand Māori Council welcomes the Waitangi Tribunal *Trans-Pacific Partnership Report*. The report provides helpful advice on how to move matters forward in protecting Māori interests in international trade agreements. The Council considers that Māori were entitled to a positive finding that a clause which purports to protect Māori interests does not in fact provide such protection, and the report is disappointing in that respect. In particular the clause provides for affirmative policies to bring Māori achievement into line with national standards but it fails to protect Māori property interests. It will be disappointing in that respect for those iwi with significant water and geothermal interests. However, given that the TPP proposal has passed beyond the negotiation stage, the Tribunal has helpfully proposed that Māori and the Crown should now engage in perfecting the clause for the future, and in developing the New Zealand approach to the application of the clause in the event of a dispute where the clause may be invoked.[57]

53   UNDRIP, Art 31(2).
54   Sarah Macindoe, 'Managing Plant Genetic Resources for Food and Agriculture: International Efforts and Lessons from the New Zealand Experience', in Lloyd Davis and Robert Patman (eds.), *Science Diplomacy: New Day or False Dawn?* (World Scientific Publishing Co, 2015) pp 45–68.
55   'John Key says Māori Should "Embrace" TPP', *NewsHub*, 6 May 2016, available at <http://www.newshub.co.nz/home/new-zealand/2016/05/john-key-says-maori-should-embrace-tpp.html> (accessed 15 August 2017).
56   The Hon. Todd McClay, 'Trade Minister Welcomes Tribunal TPP Report', 6 May 2016, available at <http://www.scoop.co.nz/stories/PA1605/S00102/tra de-minister-welcomes-tribunal-tpp-report.htm> (accessed 15 August 2017).
57   Māori Council, 'Māori Council response to the Waitangi Tribunal', Press Release, 6 May 2016, available at <http://www.scoop.co.nz/stories/PO1605/

In my view, though, there remain outstanding issues of concern as to how the TPP will affect Indigenous rights. The General Exceptions clause seems quite limited – both in terms of its scope and its focus on New Zealand. The investor-state dispute settlement regime poses a serious and real danger to Indigenous sovereignty, self-determination and decision-making. The Intellectual Property Chapter of the TPP falls far short of both the 'Wai 262' decision and UNDRIP. In future, Indigenous communities should not be excluded or marginalised in trade agreements, as they have been in the TPP. Indigenous Peoples should have a much greater say in the negotiation of trade agreements, investor clauses and intellectual property rights.

There has been further work undertaken about policy solutions if the TPP comes into force. Burcu Kilic has considered the development of 'a resolution that can properly protect the rights of Māori under the Treaty of Waitangi whilst meeting New Zealand's obligations under the TPP, should that agreement come into force'.[58] She has made a number of recommendations for 'establishing a plant variety protection system that is supportive of, or at least not detrimental to Indigenous rights and tāonga of Māori'.[59] Kilic concludes: 'The effective implementation of a sui generis system depends on the Crown's commitment to take a legislative approach that delivers to Māori their rights'.[60]

7.3 The TPP: the environment, biodiversity and access to genetic resources

The multilateral framework for access to genetic resources, informed consent and benefit sharing that the United Nations' *Convention on Biological Diversity* (CBD) establishes has only been unevenly implemented in the Pacific Rim. As Charles Lawson has documented, there has been concern about the rigour and the efficacy of the multilateral framework for the protection of biodiversity.[61] As demonstrated by the Sorcerer II Expedition, regional biodiscovery projects can cut across the Nation States of the Pacific Rim, and the wide diversity of rules and institutions in those jurisdictions.[62] The Pacific Rim lacks an effective regional mechanism in respect of access to genetic resources, informed consent and benefit sharing.

S00082/maori-council-response-to-the-waitangi-tribunal.htm> (accessed 15 August 2017).
58 Burcu Kilic, 'The Trans-Pacific Partnership Agreement Annex 18-A, Māori and the Treaty of Waitangi' (New Zealand Law Foundation, May 2017).
59 Ibid.
60 Ibid.
61 Charles Lawson, *Regulating Genetic Resources: Access and Benefit Sharing in International Law* (Edward Elgar Publishing, 2012).
62 Matthew Rimmer, 'The Sorcerer II Expedition: Intellectual Property and Bio-discovery' (2009) 6 *Macquarie Journal of International and Comparative Environmental Law* 147.

A The Convention on Biological Diversity 1992 and the Nagoya Protocol 2010

With the outstanding exception of the US, the CBD in the Pacific Rim has been widely subscribed to amongst TPP countries (Table 7.1). However, the implementation of the regime has been patchy, with a variety of different models of regulation adopted across the Pacific Rim. Unfortunately, there have been only a few countries amongst the TPP States, which have implemented the *Nagoya Protocol on Access to Genetic Resources and the Fair and Equitable Sharing of Benefits Arising from their Utilization to the Convention on Biological Diversity* (Nagoya Protocol)[63] (Table 7.2). There has been ongoing debate about whether the Nagoya Protocol represents a higher order of obligation or merely recapitulates existing norms and requirements.[64]

There has been a longstanding concern about whether such regimes provide adequate protection in respect of Indigenous intellectual property and Traditional Knowledge. Peter Drahos has contended that 'the international regime for Indigenous knowledge delivers symbolic recognition while preserving the sovereignty of [S]tates over their property orders'.[65]

Table 7.1 TPP Parties to the *Convention on Biological Diversity*

Party/Member	Signed	Ratification	Party
Australia	1992-06-05	1993-06-18	1993-12-29
Brunei Darussalam		2008-04-28	2008-07-27
Canada	1992-06-11	1992-12-04	1993-12-29
Chile	1992-06-13	1994-09-09	1994-12-08
Japan	1992-06-13	1993-05-28	1993-12-29
Malaysia	1992-06-12	1994-06-24	1994-09-22
Mexico	1992-06-13	1993-03-11	1993-12-29
New Zealand	1992-06-12	1993-09-16	1993-12-29
Peru	1992-06-12	1993-06-07	1993-12-29
Singapore	1992-06-12	1995-12-21	1996-03-20
United States	1993-06-04		
Vietnam	1993-05-28	1994-11-16	1995-02-14

63 Conference of the Parties to the Convention on Biological Diversity, *Report of the Tenth Meeting of the Conference of the Parties to the Convention on Biological Diversity* (2010) UNEP/CBD/COP/10/27, [103] and Annex (Decision X/1, Annex 1 (Nagoya Protocol) pp 89–109).

64 Achmad Gusman Siswandi, 'The *Nagoya Protocol*: Unfinished Business Remains Unfinished', in Matthew Rimmer (ed.), *Indigenous Intellectual Property: A Handbook of Contemporary Research* (Edward Elgar 2015) p 334.

65 Peter Drahos, *Intellectual Property, Indigenous People and their Knowledge* (Cambridge University Press, 2014) p 135.

Table 7.2 TPP Parties to the Nagoya Protocol

Party/Member	Signed	Ratification	Party
Australia	2012-01-20		
Brunei Darussalam			
Canada			
Chile			
Japan	2011-05-11	2017-05-22	2017-08-20
Malaysia			
Mexico	2011-02-24	2012-05-16	2014-10-12
Peru	2011-05-04	2014-07-08	2014-10-12
New Zealand			
Singapore			
United States			
Vietnam		2014-04-23	2014-10-12

In terms of empirical evidence, there has been significant debate about the extent to which biopiracy has been a problem in the Pacific Rim. In the context of Australia, Daniel Robinson has sought to document relevant cases and controversies of biopiracy that exploits Traditional Knowledge without appropriate consent and benefit sharing arrangements.[66] In New Zealand, there has also been ongoing debate over the protection of access to genetic resources in light of the 'Wai 262' case. More broadly, similar controversies continue around the Pacific Rim.

In the US, there has been raging litigation over gene patents, intellectual property and biotechnology.[67] Canada has faced complex questions in respect of Traditional Knowledge governance.[68] Mexico's intellectual property regime has been affected by regional trade agreements.[69] Chile has been a focal point for debates over access to genetic resources.[70] Peru has been prominent in the

66 Daniel Robinson and Margaret Raven, 'Identifying and Preventing Biopiracy in Australia: Patent Landscapes and Legal Geographies for Plants with Indigenous Australian Uses' (2017) 48 *Australian Geographer* 311. See also Daniel Robinson, *Biodiversity, Access and Benefit-Sharing: Global Case Studies* (Routledge, 2014).

67 Shobita Parthasarathy, *Patent Politics: Life Forms, Markets and the Public Interest in the United States and Europe* (University of Chicago Press, 2017).

68 Jeremy de Beer and Daniel Dylan, 'Traditional Knowledge Governance Challenges in Canada' in Matthew Rimmer, *Indigenous Intellectual Property: A Handbook of Contemporary Research*, (Edward Elgar, 2015) p 517; Chidi Oguamanam, *Intellectual Property in Global Governance: A Development Question* (Routledge, 2012).

69 Blayne Haggart, *Copyfight: The Global Politics of Digital Copyright Reform* (University of Toronto Press, 2014).

70 Simon Wilson Cortijo, 'The Successes and Drawbacks of Peru's Fight Against Biopiracy', *Latin Correspondent*, 7 March 2016, available at <http://latincorresp

debate over Indigenous intellectual property, access to genetic resources, informed consent and benefit sharing.[71]

As the host of the Nagoya Protocol, Japan has deployed rhetoric about the importance of access to genetic resources. Singapore has a national biodiversity strategy and plan.[72] There has been debate in Malaysia, Brunei and Vietnam as to whether biodiversity projects will support local development, biodiversity and Indigenous knowledge. These various concerns establish that the CBD and the Nagoya Protocol remain contentious and unresolved despite their apparent favour among the Pacific Rim states.

There has been further debate over the extent to which the CBD has realised its goal of protecting and conserving biodiversity – in light of the challenges of urbanisation, rapid capitalist development and runaway climate change.

B Drafting the text of the TPP on trade and biodiversity

The TPP has a controversial Chapter on the Environment.[73] The agreement was intended to give force to multilateral international agreements on the environment.

The Pacific Rim features a rich and diverse environment, with ecosystems such as the Great Barrier Reef,[74] the Amazon and a third of all the threatened species on earth. Obama's second US Trade Representative, Michael Froman, argued that the TPP would be a boon for biodiversity:

> Through our negotiations, we are seeking to address conservation challenges that are particularly prevalent in the Asia-Pacific region. Our TPP partners include many 'biodiversity hotspots' some of which have served as conduits for illegal trade and smuggling in threatened animal, timber, plant and marine species. This makes TPP a unique opportunity to

ondent.com/2016/03/the-successes-and-drawbacks-of-perus-fight-against-biop iracy> (accessed 15 August 2017).

71 See Brendan Tobin, *Indigenous Peoples, Customary Law and Human Rights – Why Living Law Matters* (Routledge, 2014); Brendan Tobin, 'Traditional Knowledge Sovereignty: The Fundamental Role of Customary Law in the Protection of Traditional Knowledge', in Matthew Rimmer (ed.), *Indigenous Intellectual Property: A Handbook of Contemporary Research*, (Edward Elgar, 2015), 565.

72 Singapore, *Conserving Our Biodiversity: Singapore's National Biodiversity Strategy and Action Plan*, 2009, available at <https://www.nparks.gov.sg/biodiversity/ our-national-plan-for-conservation//~/media/nparks-real-content/biodiversity/ national-plan/nbsap_2009.pdf> (accessed 15 August 2017).

73 TPP, Ch 20; Matthew Rimmer, 'Greenwashing the Trans-Pacific Partnership: Fossil Fuels, the Environment, and Climate Change' (2016) 14 *Santa Clara Journal of International Law* 488.

74 Iain McCalman, *The Reef: A Passionate History* (Penguin Books, 2013), Charlie Veron, *A Life Underwater* (Penguin Books, 2017), Terry Hughes *et al.*, 'Global Warming and Recurrent Mass Bleaching of Corals' (2017) 543 *Nature* 373, and Terry Hughes *et al.*, 'Coral Reefs in the Anthropocene', (2017) 546 *Nature* 82–90.

improve regional cooperation and enforcement of the rules of the *Convention on International Trade in Endangered Species* (CITES), from the islands of Southeast Asia to the interior of Vietnam, from the forests of Chile and Peru to the plains of Australia. Whether protecting big-leaf mahogany or tigers, sharks and chinchillas, stronger legal frameworks, more cooperation, and better enforcement will improve the chances that these species survive.[75]

Froman has maintained: 'Similarly, the broader US proposals on conservation, also detailed in our Green Paper, would elevate other TPP countries' commitments toward our own congressionally-set standards on issues such as the conservation of wildlife, forests, and protected areas'.[76]

In 2012, members of the US Congress – including Senator Ron Wyden (D-OR), Olympia Snowe (R-ME), John Kerry (D-MA) – emphasised the need for biodiversity protection and environmental conservation:

An agreement that is good for American businesses, good for the environment, creates jobs, and keeps the playing field across the Pacific region can only be achieved by strengthened the legal and sustainable trade of natural resources and combating trade in illegal timber, fish, and wildlife. Without such provisions, the rich biodiversity of the Pacific Rim and the legitimate businesses and good jobs it sustains will continue to be threatened, ultimately undermining legal trade and the USA economy.[77]

Draft Article SS 13 of the Environment Chapter of the TPP addressed the topic of trade and biodiversity.[78] The language provided a minimalist recapitulation of some of the key principles in the CBD,[79] the *Bonn Guidelines on Access to Genetic Resources and Fair and Equitable Sharing of the Benefits Arising out of their Utilization* (Bonn Guidelines)[80] and the Nagoya Protocol.

75 Michael Froman, 'A Values-Driven Trade Policy: Remarks by Ambassador Froman at the Center for American Progress', Office of the United States Trade Representative, 18 February 2014, available at <http://www.ustr.gov/about-us/p ress-office/press-releases/2014/February/A-Values-Driven-Trade-Policy_Rema rks-by-USTR-Froman-at-Center-for-American-P> (accessed 15 August 2017).
76 Ibid.
77 Ron Wyden and others, 'A Letter to the Honourable Ron Kirk, United States Trade Representative', 17 October 2012, available at <http://www.sierraclub. org/trade/downloads/Wyden-Snowe-TPP-Enviro-Lette-Oct%202012.pdf> and <http://sierraclub.typepad.com/compass/2012/10/senator-tpp-letter.html> (archived at the Internet archive, accessed 15 August 2017).
78 WikiLeaks, 'WikiLeaks Release of Secret Trans-Pacific Partnership: Environment Chapter Consolidated Text', 24 November 2013, available at <https://wikileaks. org/tpp-enviro> (accessed 15 August 2017).
79 *Convention on Biological Diversity* 1992, opened for signature 5 June 1992, 1760 U.N.T.S. 79 (entered into force 29 December 1993).
80 Conference of the Parties to the Convention on Biological Diversity, *Report of the Sixth Meeting of the Conference of the Parties to the Convention on Biological Diversity* (2002) UNEP/CBD/COP/6/20, pp 60–62 and 253–269 (Bonn Guidelines)

Draft Article SS 13(1) of the TPP recognised the 'importance of conservation and sustainable use of biological diversity and their key role in achieving sustainable development'.[81] The text promotes access to genetic resources, benefit sharing, and the protection of Indigenous knowledge. Draft Article SS 13(2) provided that 'the Parties are committed to promoting and encouraging the conservation and sustainable use of biological diversity and sharing in a fair and equitable way the benefits arising from the utilization of genetic resources'.[82]

Draft Article SS 13(3) emphasised that: 'the Parties reiterate their commitment to, subject to national legislation, respecting, preserving and maintaining the knowledge, innovations, and practices of Indigenous and local communities embodying traditional lifestyles relevant for the conservation and sustainable use of biological diversity, and encourage the equitable sharing of the benefits arising from the utilization of such knowledge, innovations and practices'.[83] Draft Article SS 13(4) emphasised that: 'The Parties recognize the sovereign rights of States over their natural resources, and that the authority to determine access to genetic resources rests with the national governments and is subject to national legislation'.[84]

Draft Article SS 13(5) stressed: 'The Parties recognize that, subject to national legislation, access to genetic resources for their utilization, where granted, should be subject to the prior informed consent of the Party providing such resources, unless otherwise determined by that Party'.[85] The provision maintains: 'The Parties further recognize that benefits arising from the utilization of these genetic resources should be shared in a fair and equitable way'. It stressed that 'Such sharing should be upon mutually agreed terms'.[86]

Draft Article SS 13(6) maintained that: 'The Parties also recognize the importance of public participation and consultations, as provided for by domestic law or policy, on matters concerning the conservation and sustainable use of biological diversity'.[87] It suggests: 'Each Party should make publicly available information about its programs and activities, including cooperative programs, related to the conservation and sustainable use of biological diversity'.[88]

Draft Article SS 13(7) promoted cooperative activity: 'The Parties are committed to enhance their cooperative efforts in areas of mutual interest related to biological diversity, including through Article SS 10 (Cooperation). Cooperation may include, but is not limited to, exchanging information and

---

81 WikiLeaks, 'WikiLeaks Release of Secret Trans-Pacific Partnership: Environment Chapter Consolidated Text', 24 November 2013, available at <https://wikileaks. org/tpp-enviro> (accessed 15 August 2017).
82 Ibid.
83 Ibid.
84 Ibid.
85 Ibid.
86 Ibid.
87 Ibid.
88 Ibid.

experiences in areas related to: (a) the conservation and sustainable use of biological diversity; (b) the protection and maintenance of ecosystem and ecosystem services; and (c) the fair and equitable sharing of the benefits arising out of the utilisation of genetic resources, including by appropriate access to genetic resources'.[89]

Under the leadership of President Barack Obama, the US had provided opposition to this text on the basis that it was not a Contracting Party of the CBD.

On the topic of biodiversity, Jane Kelsey from the University of Auckland was critical of the failure of the Environment Chapter of the TPP to properly address Indigenous rights.[90] She commented: 'Prior consent to accessing genetic resources and fair and equitable sharing of the benefits in paragraph 5 relates to the [S]tate, not to Indigenous Peoples or local communities'.[91] In her view, the approach taken in the TPP was inferior to what was required under the CBD, the Bonn Guidelines and the Nagoya Protocol. Moreover, Kelsey commented that the regime of the TPP showed little respect of international rights of Indigenous communities: 'This falls far short of [UNDRIP]'.[92] The problem is further compounded by the final version of the Intellectual Property Chapter of the TPP.[93] The final text has weak and soft language about cooperation by Nation States in respect of the protection of Traditional Knowledge. This may help explain the grievances of Māori groups and communities about the TPP under the *Treaty of Waitangi*.[94]

In a letter to the US Trade Representative in July 2015, a group of 19 House Democrats led by Earl Blumenauer expressed concerns about the Environment Chapter of the TPP.[95] The group observed that the 'TPP countries represent some of the most resource-rich regions in the world'.[96] The House Democrats warned that the TPP would have a significant impact upon a range of delicate ecosystems: 'From Vietnam's Mekong Delta to the Peruvian Amazon to Chile's Patagonia wilderness to the rich Pacific Ocean that ties all TPP countries together, we cannot forego an opportunity to improve

89 Ibid.
90 Jane Kelsey, 'TPPA Environment Chapter and Chair's Commentary Posted by Wikileaks – Issues for NZ', 16 January 2014, available at <http://www.itsourfu ture.org.nz/wp-content/uploads/2014/01/TPPA-Environment-Chapter.pdf> (accessed 15 August 2017).
91 Ibid.
92 Ibid.
93 WikiLeaks, 'TPP Treaty: Intellectual Property Rights Chapter', 5 October 2015, available at <https://wikileaks.org/tpp-ip3> (accessed 15 August 2017).
94 TPP Legal, 'Waitangi Tribunal Claim', 23 August 2015, available at <https://tpp legal.wordpress.com/2015/08/23/waitangi-tribunal-claim> (accessed 15 August 2017).
95 Earl Blumenauer and others, 'Letter to Ambassador Michael Froman on the TPP Environment Chapter', 29 July 2015, available at <http://blumenauer.house. gov/images/pdf/072915_letter_TPP.pdf> (accessed 15 August 2017).
96 Ibid.

environmental protections, enforce conservation standards, and prohibit the illegal trade in wildlife, forest, and living marine resources to a degree that no level of foreign aid could accomplish'.[97] However, this plea for greater protection of biodiversity in the Pacific Rim was not heeded by the Obama White House and the US Trade Representative.

C The final text of the TPP on trade and biodiversity

The final text of the TPP does contain language on trade and biodiversity in Article 20.13.[98] Article 20.13.1 provides: 'The Parties recognise the importance of conservation and sustainable use of biological diversity and their key role in achieving sustainable development'.[99] Article 20.13.2 states: 'Accordingly, each Party shall promote and encourage the conservation and sustainable use of biological diversity, in accordance with its law or policy'.[100]

Article 20.13.3 provides: 'The Parties recognise the importance of respecting, preserving and maintaining knowledge and practices of Indigenous and local communities embodying traditional lifestyles that contribute to the conservation and sustainable use of biological diversity'.[101] It is noticeable here that there is a limited reference to Indigenous rights in respect of access to genetic resources. There is no guarantee, though, of full recognition and protection of Indigenous intellectual property.

Article 20.13.4 states: 'Parties recognise the importance of facilitating access to genetic resources within their respective national jurisdictions, consistent with each Party's international obligations'.[102] Moreover, 'The Parties further recognise that some Parties require, through national measures, prior informed consent to access such genetic resources in accordance with national measures and, where such access is granted, the establishment of mutually agreed terms, including with respect to sharing of benefits from the use of such genetic resources, between users and providers'.[103] Article 20.13.5 provides: 'The Parties also recognise the importance of public participation and consultation, in accordance with their respective law or policy, in the development and implementation of measures concerning the conservation and sustainable use of biological diversity'.[104] Thus, there could be a wide diversity of approaches to access genetic resources under the TPP.

Article 20.13.5 is a clause about information sharing: 'Each Party shall make publicly available information about its programmes and activities, including cooperative programmes, related to the conservation and sustainable use of

97 Ibid.
98 TPP, Art 20.13.
99 TPP, Art 20.13.1.
100 TPP, Art 20.13.2.
101 TPP, Art 20.13.3.
102 TPP, Art 20.13.4.
103 TPP, Art 20.13.4.
104 TPP, Art 20.13.5.

biological diversity'.[105] Article 20.13.6 observes that 'the Parties shall cooperate to address matters of mutual interest' – including '(a) the conservation and sustainable use of biological diversity; (b) the protection and maintenance of ecosystems and ecosystem services; and (c) access to genetic resources and the sharing of benefits arising from their utilization'.[106]

In 2016, the Environmental Defenders Offices of Australia addressed an Australian Parliamentary Committee on the TPP and the environment.[107] The submission maintained that Australia needed to improve its national environmental laws under Chapter 20 (Environment) of the TPP. It raised concerns about access to justice. The Environmental Defenders Offices warned of the potential adverse impact of Investor-State Dispute Settlement provisions of the TPP.

There has been deep justified cynicism about the promises of the TPP to do much to promote the conservation of biodiversity in the Pacific Rim. Writing from a Canadian perspective, Jacqueline Wilson bluntly concludes:

> The TPP environment chapter will not protect the environment. The requirements of the parties with respect to protection of the environment are vague and discretionary, frequently only requiring governments to take measures to address environmental problems. The scope of the environment chapter is also restricted by its limited application to the laws of the central government of each TPP country. The mechanisms to enforce the environment chapter are also flawed.[108]

She concludes that 'the TPP at best represents the status quo for environmental protection, and will not offer any safeguard against environmentally destructive provisions found elsewhere in the agreement'.[109]

Reviewing the Environment Chapter, Rafael Leal-Arcas comments:

> The TPP's Environment Chapter demonstrates a lack of clarity with regard to the environment and sustainability. Even though the TPP's main purpose is trade liberalization and investment protection, there is less focus on environment and sustainability in the chapter that especially aims to protect the environment. While the TPP's Environment Chapter touches

---

105 TPP, Art 20.13.5.
106 TPP, Art 20.13.6.
107 Environmental Defenders Offices of Australia, 'Proposed Trans-Pacific Partnership Agreement', 28 October 2016, <https://d3n8a8pro7vhmx.cloudfront.net/edonsw/pages/3316/attachments/original/1478148084/Proposed_Trans-Pacific_Partnership_Agreement_EDOs_of_Australia_Submission_October_2016.pdf? 1478148084> (accessed 15 August 2017).
108 Jacqueline Wilson, 'The TPP and the Environment', in Scott Sinclair and Stuart Trew (ed.), *The Trans-Pacific Partnership and Canada: A Citizen's Guide* (James Lorimer & Company Ltd, 2016) p 92.
109 Ibid, p 93.

upon crucial areas of environmental protection that can pave the way for future talks, it does not inspire.[110]

Leal-Arcas regrets that '[Regional Trade Agreements], while conducive to greater trade liberalization, face the same concerns as multilateral trade agreements when it comes to the environment and sustainable development'.[111] He 'hoped that the human race as a whole will eventually learn to move beyond short-term gains'.[112]

With the departure of Barack Obama as President, and the unravelling of the TPP, the model of the Environment Chapter in the TPP is unlikely to be followed. The new President Donald Trump is promising to engage in an aggressive dismantling of environmental laws in US laws.[113] Moreover, he has shown a great antipathy to international law in respect of the environment, biodiversity and climate change. Thus, even though the TPP could well collapse, the position of the environment, biodiversity and climate in the Pacific Rim is not necessarily going to be better off under the rule of Trump.[114]

7.4 The TPP, intellectual property and sustainable development

There has been a perennial debate over intellectual property and sustainable development – spanning the Rio and Rio+20 negotiations.[115] There has also been significant discussion in multilateral bodies such as WIPO.[116] Such concerns have percolated into geopolitical negotiations over regional mega-agreements, such as the TPP and the RCEP.

---

110 Rafael Leal-Arcas, 'Mega-Regionals and Sustainable Development: The Transatlantic Trade and Investment Partnership and the Trans-Pacific Partnership' (2015) 6 *Renewable Energy Law and Policy Review* 248.
111 Ibid.
112 Ibid.
113 Naomi Klein, *No is Not Enough: Defeating the New Shock Politics* (Allen Lane, 2017).
114 Bill McKibben, 'The Planet Can't Stand This Presidency', *The New York Times*, 21 April 2017, available at <https://www.nytimes.com/2017/04/21/opinion/the-planet-cant-stand-this-presidency.html> (accessed 15 August 2017); Bill McKibben, 'Trump's Stupid and Reckless Climate Decision', *The New York Times*, 1 June 2017, available at <https://www.nytimes.com/2017/06/01/opinion/trump-paris-climate-accord.html> and Bill McKibben, 'The Trump Administration's Solution to Climate Change: Ban the Term', *The Guardian*, 8 August 2017, available at <https://www.theguardian.com/commentisfree/2017/aug/08/trump-administration-climate-change-ban-usda> (accessed 15 August 2017),
115 Matthew Rimmer, 'The World Indigenous Network: Rio+20, Intellectual Property, Sustainable Development, and the Future We Want', in Matthew Rimmer (ed), *Indigenous Intellectual Property: A Handbook of Contemporary Research*, (Edward Elgar, 2015) p 106.
116 Daniel Robinson, Ahmed Abdel-Latif and Pedro Roffe (eds), *Protecting Traditional Knowledge: the WIPO Intergovernmental Committee on Intellectual Property and Genetic Resources, Traditional Knowledge and Folkore* (Routledge, 2017).

The long-awaited release of the TPP text was the product of years of negotiations on trade ties between nations around the Pacific Rim.[117] Some six
weeks earlier, another set of deliberations came to an end as the UN unveiled
its 17 SDGs. The SDGs aim to eradicate poverty and reduce inequality
through resolving critical issues such as food security, health care, access to
education, clean and affordable water, clean energy, and climate change.[118]
Jeffrey Sachs has reflected: 'Sustainable development argues that economic
policy works best when it focuses simultaneously on three big issues: first, promoting economic growth and decent jobs; second, promoting social fairness to
women, the poor, and minority groups; and third, promoting environmental
sustainability'.[119] Like his predecessor Ban Ki-moon, the new UN Secretary-
General Antonio Guterres has said that he will support the 2030 Agenda for
Sustainable Development.[120]

There has been a significant discussion about the relationship between
intellectual property and the SDGs. WIPO Director-General Francis Gurry has
highlighted the relevance of intellectual property to SDG 9, dealing with
industry, innovation, and infrastructure.[121] He has also noted that innovation
in practice can play a role in the achievement of other SDGs, dealing with food
security (SDG 2), good health and well being (SDG 3), clean water and sanitation
(SDG 6), SDG 7 (affordable and clean energy), decent work and economic
growth (SDG 8), sustainable cities and communities (SDG 11), and climate action
(SDG 13). Gurry also maintains that innovation as a policy setting can assist in the
realisation of other SDGS – no poverty (SDG 1), decent work and economic
growth (SDG 8), life below water (SDG 14), and life on land (SDG 15).

A The TPP and development

Chapter 23 of the TPP considers the topic of development.[122] The US Trade
Representative has boasted that the TPP's Chapter on Development will be a

---

117 Jean-Paul Gagnon, 'TPP Revealed: At Last We Have the Details – and A Demo-
cratic Deficit to Be Fixed', *The Conversation*, 9 November 2015, available at <http
s://theconversation.com/tpp-revealed-at-last-we-have-the-details-and-a-democra
tic-deficit-to-be-fixed-50232> (accessed 15 August 2017).
118 John Thwaites, 'Explainer: The World's New Sustainable Development Goals',
The Conversation, 22 September 2015, available at <https://theconversation.
com/explainer-the-worlds-new-sustainable-development-goals-47262> (accessed
15 August 2017).
119 Jeffrey Sachs, *Building the New American Economy: Smart, Fair, and Sustainable*
(Columbia University Press, 2017) p 6.
120 UN, 'Antonio Guterres and the Sustainable Development Goals', 2017, available
at <http://www.un.org/sustainabledevelopment/secretary-general/> (accessed
15 August 2017).
121 Francis Gurry, 'WIPO and the Sustainable Development Goals', World Intellectual Property Organization, 9 February 2017, <http://www.wipo.int/export/
sites/www/about-wipo/en/dgo/speeches/pdf/wipo_sdgs_022017.pdf> (accessed 15 August 2017).
122 TPP, Ch 23.

boon for developing Pacific nations, and that it will 'focus attention on major development goals including inclusion of women, micro-enterprise, poverty reduction, and education, science, and technology'.[123] However, critics have doubted whether the agreement is really animated by such a concern for poverty and development in the Pacific Rim. While the chapter is laden with aspiration, the agreement lacks firm commitments or hard obligations. The TPP Development Chapter comments:

> The Parties affirm their commitment to promote and strengthen an open trade and investment environment that seeks to improve welfare, reduce poverty, raise living standards and create new employment opportunities in support of development.[124]

Article 23.2 deals with the promotion of development.[125] There is reference to 'leadership in implementing development policies'.[126] There is recognition of the need to take into account 'the different levels of economic development of the Parties'.[127] There is also recognition that 'transparency, good governance and accountability contribute to the effectiveness of development policies'.[128]

The Development Chapter discusses broad-based economic growth.[129] The Parties 'acknowledge that broad-based economic growth reduces poverty, enables sustainable delivery of basic services, and expands opportunities for people to live healthy and productive lives'.[130] Article 23.4 of the TPP discusses women and economic growth.[131] There is text on economic growth with regard to women (despite the fact that the Sydney TPP talks were an all-male affair).[132] However, in terms of its substance, the TPP does not address gender inequality.

Article 23.5 of the TPP focuses on education, science and technology, research and innovation.[133] Article 23.6 of the TPP considers joint development activities.[134] Article 23.7 provides a pledge to replicate in miniature the

---

123 United States Trade Representative, 'TPP Made in America – Chapter 23, Development', available at <https://ustr.gov/sites/default/files/TPP-Chapter-Summary-Development.pdf> (accessed 15 August 2017).
124 TPP, Art 23.1.1.
125 TPP, Art 23.2.
126 TPP, Art 23.2.1.
127 TPP, Art 23.2.2.
128 TPP, Art 23.2.3.
129 TPP, Art 23.3.
130 TPP, Art 23.3.1.
131 TPP, Art 23.4.
132 TPP Ministerial Meeting, Sydney, 25–27 October 2014, available at <http://trademinister.gov.au/photos/pages/displayalbum.aspx?w=O%2F%2FeXE%2BIYc3HpsIRhVl0XA%3D%3D&album=TPP%20Ministerial%20Meeting%20Sydney%2025%2D27%20October#1308> (accessed 15 August 2017).
133 TPP, Art 23.5.
134 TPP, Art 23.6.

existing United Nations Development Programme (UNDP); although the UNDP itself has criticised the TPP.[135] The text, however, contains a give-away statement that reveals the insignificance of the TPP's development provisions:

> In the event of any inconsistency between this Chapter and another Chapter of this Agreement, the other Chapter shall prevail to the extent of the inconsistency.[136]

The US journalist Dylan Matthews has argued that the Development Chapter is hollow and vapid:

> The 'development chapter' of the deal is almost embarrassingly content-less. It's like a parody of a treaty, using various formalities to dress up the fact that it does absolutely nothing. It mostly consists of the parties 'acknowledging' and 'recognizing' various banalities.[137]

Matthews says of the unenforceable chapter: 'It's 1,200 words, full of pomp and circumstance, ultimately signifying nothing'.[138]

B The neglect of the SDGs

Several other chapters in the TPP reinforce yet more problems with meeting the SDGs. The Intellectual Property Chapter does not promote the WIPO Development Agenda.[139] The copyright provisions undermine efforts to promote access to knowledge and educational initiatives.[140] Likewise, the patent measures for pharmaceutical drugs and biotechnology will hamper access to affordable and essential medicines.[141] There has also been a concern about the

135 TPP, Art 23.7.
136 TPP, Art 23.8.
137 Dylan Matthews, 'How Trade Deals like TPP Fail the Global Poor', *Vox*, 6 November 2015, available at <http://www.vox.com/policy-and-politics/2015/11/6/9680538/tpp-development-trade-poverty> (accessed 15 August 2017).
138 Ibid.
139 TPP, Ch 18.
140 Kimberlee Weatherall, 'Intellectual Property in the TPP: Not "The New TRIPS"' (2016) 17 *Melbourne Journal of International Law* 257.
141 Hazel Moir, Brigette Tenni, Deborah Gleeson and Ruth Lopert 'The Trans Pacific Partnership Agreement and Access to HIV Treatment in Vietnam' (2016) *Global Public Health* 1, available at < http://dx.doi.org/10.1080/17441692.2016.1256418> (accessed 15 August 2017). See also Ruth Dreifuss and others, *Report of the United Nations Secretary-General's High Level Panel on Access to Medicines: Promoting Innovation and Access to Health Technologies*, September 2016, available at <http://static1.squarespace.com/static/562094dee4b0d00c1a3ef761/t/57d9c6ebf5e231b2f02cd3d4/1473890031320/UNSG+HLP+Report+FINAL+12+Sept+2016.pdf> (accessed 15 August 2017).

impact of plant breeders' rights and other forms of plant intellectual property on food security and farm-saved seed.[142] Criminal penalties and procedures for trade secrets will clash with open innovation.[143]

The Environment Chapter of the TPP has been criticised by environmental advocates and climate activists for its limited coverage, toothless enforcement measures, and denial of climate change.[144] Australia's then trade minister Andrew Robb has retorted that the TPP does not need to address climate change: 'This is not a climate change policy. It's not an agreement to do with climate change, it's a trade agreement'.[145] Yet trade and climate change are intimately related. If we want to reduce global carbon emissions, it is essential to move to a low-carbon economy. In her 2014 book *This Changes Everything* the Canadian author and activist Naomi Klein comments that we can no longer think about trade and climate change in two solitudes.[146] In her view, trade deals need to promote climate action – rather than facilitate the export and import of fossil fuels.

The Labor Rights Chapter is also a disappointment.[147] It has been criticised by unions who say that it fails to protect jobs, wages, freedom of association, workers' rights and human rights more generally.[148]

Moreover, the Investment Chapter empowers foreign investors to challenge government decisions and regulations in international tribunals.[149] There has been much disquiet about the creative and innovative use of investor clauses by multinational corporations.

The now former UN right to food rapporteur Olivier De Schutter and his Columbia University colleague Kaitlin Cordes have raised concerns about how

---

142 Hannah Brennan and Burcu Kilic, 'Freeing Trade at the Expense of Local Crop Markets? A Look at the Trans-Pacific Partnership's New Plant Related Intellectual Property Rights from a Human Rights Perspective', *Harvard Human Rights Journal*, April 2015, available at <http://harvardhrj.com/2015/04/freeing-tra de-at-the-expense-of-local-crop-markets-a-look-at-the-trans-pacific-partnership s-new-plant-related-intellectual-property-rights-from-a-human-rights-perspective> (accessed 15 August 2017).
143 TPP, Ch 18, Art. 18.78.
144 TPP, Ch 20; Matthew Rimmer, 'Greenwashing the Trans-Pacific Partnership: Fossil Fuels, the Environment, and Climate Change' (2016) 14 *Santa Clara Journal of International Law* 488.
145 Michael Brissenden, 'Andrew Robb: TPP is a Trade Agreement, not a Climate Change Agreement', *ABC AM*, 6 November 2015, available at <http://www.abc. net.au/am/content/2015/s4346466.htm> (accessed 15 August 2017).
146 Naomi Klein, *This Changes Everything: Capitalism vs The Climate* (Simon & Schuster, 2014).
147 TPP, Chapter 19 <http://dfat.gov.au/trade/agreements/tpp/official-docum ents/Documents/19-labour.pdf>
148 AFL-CIO, 'Trans-Pacific Partnership Free Trade Agreement' <http://www.aflcio. org/Issues/Trade/Trans-Pacific-Partnership-Free-Trade-Agreement-TPP
149 TPP, Chapter 9 <http://dfat.gov.au/trade/agreements/tpp/official-documents/ Documents/9-investment.pdf>

the TPP will affect food security.[150] De Schutter has expanded upon his ideas upon how trade may operate in the service of sustainable development, and promote labour rights and environmental standards.[151] As Director General of the World Health Organization, Margaret Chan warned of the impact of trade agreements and investor clauses in respect of public health.[152] The UN Secretary General's High Level Panel on Access to Medicines has highlighted the potential impact of regional agreements such as the TPP upon public health, human rights and sustainable development.[153] The Hon. Michael Kirby has stressed how public health is an integral part of the SDGs.[154]

Maude Barlow of the Council of the Canadians has warned that investor clauses in trade agreements will undermine water rights, the protection of the environment, and climate action.[155] This demonstrates there is widespread concern about whether the value placed on the investment rights of foreign corporations will conflict with the SDGs.

150 Olivier De Schutter and Kaitlin Cordes, 'Trading Away Human Rights', *Project Syndicate*, 7 January 2014, available at <https://www.project-syndicate.org/ commentary/olivier-de-schutter-and-kaitlin-y–cordes-demand-that-the-trans-pa cific-partnership-s-terms-be-subject-to-a-human-rights-impact-assessment?ba rrier=accessreg> (accessed 15 August 2017).
151 Olivier de Schutter, *Trade in the Service of Sustainable Development: Linking Trade to Labour Rights and Environmental Standards* (Hart Publishing and Bloomsbury Publishing, 2015).
152 Margaret Chan, 'The Changing Development Landscape: What Will It Mean for Specialized Agencies in a Post-2015 Era with Focus on Sustainable Development', UN Economic and Social Council, 25 February 2014, available at <http://www. who.int/dg/speeches/2014/economic-social-council/en> (accessed 15 August 2017); Margaret Chan, 'Health Has an Obligatory Place on Any Post-2015 Agenda', Address to the Sixty-Seventh World Health Assembly, Geneva, Switzerland, 19 May 2014, available at <http://www.who.int/dg/speeches/2014/wha -19052014/en> (accessed 15 August 2017); Margaret Chan, 'Governance: Global Health's 21st Century Challenge', Global Futures Initiative, Georgetown University, Washington DC, USA, 30 September 2015, available at <http:// www.who.int/dg/speeches/2015/georgetown-university-lecture/en> (accessed 15 August 2017); Margaret Chan, 'Opening Remarks at a Joint WHO/WIPO/ WTO Technical Symposium on Public Health, Intellectual Property and TRIPS at 20', Geneva, Switzerland, 28 October 2015, available at <http://who.int/dg/sp eeches/2015/intellectual-property-trips/en> (accessed 15 August 2017).
153 Ruth Dreifuss and others, *Report of the United Nations Secretary-General's High Level Panel on Access to Medicines: Promoting Innovation and Access to Health Technologies*, September 2016, available at <http://static1.squarespace.com/static/562094de e4b0d00c1a3ef761/t/57d9c6ebf5e231b2f02cd3d4/1473890031320/UNSG +HLP+Report+FINAL+12+Sept+2016.pdf> (accessed 15 August 2017).
154 The Hon. Michael Kirby, 'Human Rights meets Global Pharma', the Australian Centre for Health Law Research – 5th Annual Oration, 6 March 2017, available at <https://www.youtube.com/watch?v=hl_pa2siVzk> (accessed 15 August 2017).
155 Maude Barlow, 'UN Climate Change Agreement Must Address Corporate Right to Sue Countries', *The Huffington Post*, 22 September 2015, available at <http:// www.huffingtonpost.ca/maude-barlow/corporations-un-climate-change_b_ 8179118.html> (accessed 15 August 2017).

C Trade and sustainable development

It is clear that much of the TPP is at odds with key elements of the global sustainable development agenda. There needs to be a thorough human rights assessment of the whole agreement. Considering this package of measures, Columbia University economist Jeffrey Sachs laments the lack of substance in the Development Chapter of the TPP, writing:

> Perhaps most disappointing is the lack of creativity in the development, labour, and environmental chapters. Yes, they rhetorically defend global economic development, labor standards, and environmental sustainability, but they do so without specific enforcement powers. Why is it that companies can force arbitration tribunals to defend their investor rights, but workers have no such power? Why is climate change not even considered in the draft, despite the fact that it represents the most important environmental threat of the 21st century, and may have strong implications for future trade rules?[156]

His concern was that the TPP would undermine the SDGs.[157] Sachs has reflected that 'the potential for expanded trade to benefit all parts of the economy – as long as winners compensate losers – is built into the [SDGs], which embrace the potentially beneficial effects of an open global trading system'.[158]

Meanwhile, his colleague from Columbia University, Nobel Laureate, Joseph Stiglitz, is concerned about the TPP exacerbating poverty and inequality.[159] In 2017, Dean Baker, Arjun Jayadev and Joseph Stiglitz have written a policy paper on innovation, intellectual property and development in order to forge a better set of approaches for the twenty-first century.[160] The writers consider the basic logic of intellectual property and alternative systems of research and development. The writers express concern about the pathologies of intellectual property. Baker, Jayadev and Stiglitz consider the intellectual property challenges of developing countries – particularly in respect of food, agriculture and plant genetic resources, climate change, and education.

156 Jeffrey Sachs, 'TPP is Too Flawed for a Simple "Yes" Vote', *The Boston Globe*, 8 November 2015, available at <http://www.bostonglobe.com/opinion/2015/11/08/jeffrey-sachs-tpp-too-flawed-for-simple-yes-vote/sZd0nlnCr18RurX1n549GI/story.html?event=event25> (accessed 15 August 2017).
157 Jeffrey Sachs, *Building the New American Economy: Smart, Fair, and Sustainable* (Columbia University Press, 2017).
158 Ibid, p 55.
159 Joseph Stiglitz, 'The Secret Takeover', *Project Syndicate*, 31 January 2017, available at <https://www.project-syndicate.org/commentary/us-secret-corporate-takeover-by-joseph-e–stiglitz-2015-05?barrier=accessreg> (accessed 15 August 2017).
160 Dean Baker, Arjun Jayadev, and Joseph Stiglitz, 'Innovation, Intellectual Property, and Development: A Better Set of Approaches for the 21st Century', *AccessIBSA*, July 2017. Available online: <http://ip-unit.org/wp-content/uploads/2017/07/IP-for-21st-Century-EN.pdf> (accessed 15 August 2017).

Baker, Jayadev and Stiglitz pay particular attention to the issue of intellectual property and biodiversity. They stress that biodiversity is critically important to food security and sustainable development, noting: 'A diverse biological gene pool increases the resilience of crops to disease and natural disasters, and their adaptability to a changing climate'.[161] Target 2.5 of SDGs requires Nation States 'to maintain the genetic diversity of seeds, cultivated plants and farmed and domesticated animals and their related wild species'. The authors lament that 'the current design of the patent system makes it difficult, on the one hand, for developing countries to provide protections for traditional knowledge and genetic material preserved through developing countries' efforts at maintaining biodiversity, but on the other hand, also makes it difficult for them to prevent multinationals from obtaining patents on this traditional knowledge and genetic material in their own countries'.[162] Baker, Jayadev and Stiglitz contend: 'IPRs promote the advancement of global knowledge, but under current rules, at the expense of genetic diversity; and the lack of diversity can give rise to systemic problems – there is a large externality'.[163] The policy writers note that the success of the Nagoya Protocol is contingent upon national implementation.

This analysis highlights that access to genetic resources, benefit sharing and informed consent should not be treated in a purely technocratic fashion. There is a need to connect the debate over intellectual property and biodiversity to a larger conversation about SDGs.

Baker, Jayadev and Stiglitz recommend that Nation States make use of existing intellectual property flexibilities. The authors stress that there is a need to use national patent laws to prevent weak patents, and maximise the opportunity to context patents. Baker, Jayadev and Stiglitz also advocate the use of compulsory licensing, public sector licensing, knowledge commons, and alternative mechanisms of research and development, such as prizes, gifts and dedications to the public domain. Baker, Jayadev and Stiglitz conclude: 'A substantial recalibration of the international approach to Intellectual Property Rights is required to ensure the advancement of the standards of living and well-being of the entire world – and to ensure consistency with development objectives and obligations and to support those innovations that have the highest value in terms of their contribution to addressing the challenges facing our global society'.[164]

United Nations Conference on Trade and Development (UNCTAD) has called for new innovation approaches to support the implementation of SDGs.[165] In order to facilitate collaboration and cooperation, UNCTAD called for 'flexible intellectual property rules that do not discourage users from

---

161 Ibid, p 44,
162 Ibid, p 38.
163 Ibid, p 44.
164 Ibid, p 71.
165 UNCTAD, 'New Innovation Approaches to Support the Implementation of the Sustainable Development Goals' (United Nations, 2017) <http://unctad.org/

contributing to projects, and that allow fair use of their contributions'.[166] UNCTAD also observed that 'inappropriate intellectual property frameworks, must be reformed'.[167]

Accordingly, there is a need to develop a new kind of trade agreement – one that respects and supports the world's SDGs. In particular, it is essential that future trade deals promote human development, access to knowledge, public health, human development and climate action.

Howard Mann of the International Institute for Sustainable Development argues that 'there is a need to fundamentally re-consider the role that trade and investment agreements make to supporting inclusive and sustainable growth'.[168]

Todd Tucker of the Roosevelt Institute has articulated the 'Sustainable Equitable Trade Doctrine' as a means of improving US policy.[169] He suggests that such an approach 'gives progressives their own long game by changing the nature of delegation to semi-judicial actors, rescuing international cooperation from regressive distortions, and opening up space for selective industrial policy to address persistent worker-harming imbalances'.[170]

The Sierra Club has called for the development of a climate-friendly trade policy.[171] The report lamented: 'For decades, multinational corporations have disproportionately shaped US trade deals, resulting in pacts that cater to their profit-making interests over society's needs'.[172] The Sierra Club was hopeful for a future reform of the trade process: 'If trade policy objectives could be aligned with the interests of the majority, trade pacts could help society tackle some of its biggest challenges'.[173] The Sierra Club contended: 'With the halting of the TPP, we have the responsibility to ensure that the next trade model is one centered on people and planet'.[174]

en/pages/PublicationWebflyer.aspx?publicationid=1775> (access 15 August 2017).

166 Ibid, p 25.

167 Ibid, p 30.

168 Howard Mann, 'The TPP: A Deal Too Far', International Institute for Sustainable Development, January 2016, available at <http://www.iisd.org/sites/default/files/publications/tpp-part-i-deal-too-far-commentary_1.pdf> (accessed 15 August 2017).

169 Todd Tucker, 'The Sustainable Equitable Trade Doctrine', the Roosevelt Institute, 13 March 2017, available at <http://rooseveltinstitute.org/wp-content/uploads/2017/03/The-Sustainable-Equitable-Trade-Doctrine.pdf> (accessed 15 August 2017).

170 Ibid, p 31.

171 Sierra Club, *Discussion Paper: A New, Climate-Friendly Approach to Trade*, Oakland and Washington DC, November 2016, available at <http://www.sierraclub.org/sites/www.sierraclub.org/files/uploads-wysiwig/climate-friendly-trade-model.pdf> (accessed 15 August 2017).

172 Ibid, p 14.

173 Ibid, p 14.

174 Ibid.

7.5 Conclusion

As former New Zealand Prime Minister and past chief of the UNDP, Helen Clark contends: 'Human development for everyone is not a dream, it is attainable'.[175] The argument of this paper has been that the TPP does little to address the concerns of the Pacific Rim region in relation to access to genetic resources, informed consent and benefit sharing. The agreement represents a missed opportunity to provide a regional approach to protecting biodiversity in the region. The TPP certainly falls short of the standards and norms established by the CBD, the Bonn Guidelines and the Nagoya Protocol. This is problematic if the TPP goes ahead, even without the involvement and the participation of the US. Moreover, the TPP raises fundamental issues in respect of UNDRIP – both in terms of its negotiating process, and outcomes for Indigenous communities. The tenth anniversary of UNDRIP in 2017 has highlighted shortfalls in the implementation of the declaration.[176]

While US President Donald Trump has been hostile to the TPP, his objections were not based on the grounds that the agreement would adversely impact the environment, biodiversity and climate change. Indeed, he seemed hostile to stronger international and global rules for the protection of the environment, biodiversity and climate agreements. President Trump has complained that 'environmentalism is out of control'.[177] The new Trump administration has sought to diminish the domestic role of the Environmental Protection Agency, and cut back regulations in respect of clean air, clean water and clean land.[178] The Chief Environment Justice Officer has resigned from the Environmental Protection Agency, expressing concern about the impact of environmental deregulation upon American communities.[179]

175 Helen Clark, 'Speech at the Launch of the 2016 Human Development Report', United Nations Development Programme, 20 March 2017 available at <http://www.undp.org/content/undp/en/home/presscenter/speeches/2017/03/20/helen-clark-speech-at-the-launch-of-the-2016-human-development-report.html> (accessed 15 August 2017).

176 United Nations, 'High-Level Event Marked the 10th Anniversary of UNDRIP Adoption', 13 April 2017 <https://www.un.org/development/desa/indigenouspeoples/news/2017/04/high-level-event-to-mark-the-10th-anniversary-of-the-adoption-of-the-undrip/> (accessed 15 August 2017).

177 Ed King, 'Donald Trump: Environmentalism is "Out of Control"', *Climate Change News*, 24 January 2017, available at <http://www.climatechangenews.com/2017/01/24/trump-environmentalism-is-out-of-control> (accessed 15 August 2017).

178 Jeremy Symons, '5 Chilling Ways Trump Has Declared War on the EPA', *Ecowatch*, 25 March 2017, available at <http://www.ecowatch.com/trump-pruitt-war-on-epa-2328049842.html> (accessed 15 August 2017).

179 Phil McKenna, 'Chief Environmental Justice Official at EPA Resigns, With Plea to Pruitt to Protect Vulnerable Communities', *Inside Climate News*, 9 March 2017, available at <https://insideclimatenews.org/news/09032017/epa-environmental-justice-mustafa-ali-flint-water-crisis-dakota-access-pipeline-trump-scott-pruitt> (accessed 15 August 2017).

The appointment of former Exxon CEO Rex Tillerson as Secretary of State is an indication that the Trump administration will want to boost the export of fossil fuels. Furthermore, there has been much discussion about the approach of the new US President to the CBD and other multilateral environmental and climate agreements. Notably, President Donald Trump has withdrawn the United States from the *Paris Agreement*.[180] Gloria Dickie has commented on the impact of such a stance in the context of the CBD: 'The country's refusal to ratify the agreement could weaken biodiversity conservation both at home and abroad'.[181] Naomi Klein has observed that the Trump administration has been engaged in the deconstruction of regulations designed to protect the environment, biodiversity, and the climate.[182]

There have been threats by the new Trump administration to dramatically reduce funding to the UN.[183] David Victor has observed that the Trump administration will suffer reputational damage if it withdraws from the international framework of environmental and climate law: 'Unlike earlier administrations – such as George W Bush's, which abandoned the Kyoto Protocol before the US tried to ratify the agreement, or George H W Bush's, which never submitted the [CBD] for US ratification – the Trump administration will soon find that it is very difficult and diplomatically costly to abandon existing treaty commitments'.[184]

In this context, the biodiversity of the Pacific Rim seems to be under immense challenges and threats, with weak global rules providing little in the way of protection. The implementation of the UN SDGs will also be challenging in the age of Trump.

180 The White House, 'Statement by President Trump on the Paris Climate Accord', Office of the Press Secretary, The White House, 1 June 2017, available at <https://www.whitehouse.gov/the-press-office/2017/06/01/statement-president-trump-paris-climate-accord> (accessed 15 August 2017) and *Paris Agreement* [2016] ATNIF 31.

181 Gloria Dickie, 'The US is the Only Country That Hasn't Signed on to a Key International Agreement to Save the Planet', *Quartz*, 25 December 2016, available at <https://qz.com/872036/the-us-is-the-only-country-that-hasnt-signed-on-to-a-key-international-agreement-to-save-the-planet> (accessed 15 August 2017).

182 Naomi Klein, *No is Not Enough: Defeating the New Shock Politics* (Allen Lane, 2017).

183 Rachael Revesz, 'Donald Trump to Sign Executive Order to Dramatically Reduce Funding of United Nations', *Independent*, 26 January 2017, available at <http://www.independent.co.uk/news/world/americas/donald-trump-united-nations-funding-cuts-abortion-israel-settlements-president-executive-order-a7546486.html> (accessed 15 August 2017); Max Fisher, 'Trump Administration Holds off on Issuing U.N. Funding Order', *The New York Times*, 28 January 2017, available at <https://www.nytimes.com/2017/01/28/world/americas/trump-un-funding-order.html?_r=0> (accessed 15 August 2017).

184 David Victor, 'What a Trump Win Means for the Global Climate Fight', *Yale Environment 360*, 11 November 2016, available at <http://e360.yale.edu/features/what_donald_trump_win_means_for_global_climate_fight> (accessed 15 August 2017).

The remaining members of the TPP attended a meeting in Chile in March 2017 to discuss the future prospects of the agreement.[185] Australia and New Zealand have promoted a model of the TPP without the further participation of the US. A number of the other countries – such as Canada and Japan – have hesitated at the continuation of the TPP, without the participation of the US. A number of the Latin American and Central American countries have promoted and put forward the lesser option of a Pacific Alliance. In August 2017, Australia's Trade Minister Steve Ciobo has observed that the remaining countries are commited to the TPP-11 – 'Australia, New Zealand, Japan – All of us – are especially focused on trying to secure the benefits of the TPP'.[186] His preference is for there to be few revisions to the original agreement: 'We personally believe the more it reflects the original agreement, the better'.[187] Ciobo said that the option is open for the US to rejoin the agreement at a later date. Canada's Justin Trudeau, though, has sought to revise the TPP.

If the TPP collapses, similar issues may well arise in respect of the RCEP – a rival regional trade agreement. With the fall of the TPP, the ASEAN-led RCEP has become a much more prominent regional agreement for South-East Asia. RCEP is one of the leading potential economic frameworks for the Asia-Pacific region. The proposed membership of RCEP is based upon ASEAN nations – including Lao PDR, Myanmar, Indonesia, the Philippines, Thailand, Cambodia, Brunei, Malaysia, Singapore and Vietnam. The negotiations involve BRICS/ BASIC nations – such as the People's Republic of China, and India. ASEAN trading partners – such as the Republic of Korea, Australia, Japan and New Zealand – are also involved in the RCEP negotiations. A draft of the Intellectual Property Chapter of the agreement has been leaked to Knowledge Ecology International.[188] There is text in RCEP on plant breeder's rights, access to genetic resources, Traditional Knowledge and the environment. This will have larger public policy considerations in respect of food security, biodiversity and climate change. The relationship between the TPP and RCEP will be a complex matter – and will depend upon whether Australia, New Zealand and Japan are successful in importing TPP-style standards in RCEP.

For all these regional battles over trade, there remains a larger global need to implement UNDRIP, fulfil the SDGs and take action to protect biodiversity and the climate. In August 2017, UN Special Rapporteur Victoria Tauli-Corpuz highlighted the central importance of significance of UNDRIP:

185 'Joint Statement by TPP Partners', 16 March 2017, available at <https://www.na tional.org.nz/joint_statement_by_tpp_partners#.WMoMC29zp6U.twitter> (accessed 15 August 2017).
186 Kaori Takahasi, 'Australia Ready to Move Forward on "TPP 11": Trade Minister', *Nikkei*, 9 August 2017, <http://www.bilaterals.org/?australia-ready-to-move-forward-on> (accessed 15 August 2017).
187 Ibid.
188 Knowledge Ecology International, 'Intellectual Property Chapter of the Regional Comprehensive Economic Partnership', 15 October 2015, available at <http:// keionline.org/node/2472> (accessed 15 August 2017).

It is a framework for justice and reconciliation between Indigenous Peoples and states, and applies international human rights standards to the specific historical, cultural, social and economic circumstances of Indigenous Peoples. The Declaration is a standard-setting resolution of profound significance as it reflects a wide consensus at the global level on the minimum content of the rights of Indigenous Peoples. It is a remedial tool which addresses the need to overcome and repair the historical denial of the fundamental human rights of Indigenous Peoples, and affirms their equality to all other members of society.[189]

In particular, Tauli-Corpuz stressed the importance of free, prior and informed consent. She remained concerned about lack of implementation of UNDRIP. Tauli-Corpiz warned: 'If Indigenous Peoples' rights are not secured and protected, it will be impossible for the world to deliver on the promises of the Paris Agreement and the [SDGs]'.[190] Tauli-Corpuz emphasised: 'Secure land rights for Indigenous Peoples is a proven climate change solution, and denying Indigenous land rights and self-determination is a threat to the world's remaining forests and biodiversity'.[191]

189 David Hill, 'Indigenous Peoples are the Best Guardians of World's Biodiversity', *The Guardian*, 8 August 2017, <https://www.theguardian.com/environment/a ndes-to-the-amazon/2017/aug/09/indigenous-peoples-are-the-best-guardia ns-of-the-worlds-biodiversity?CMP=share_btn_tw> (accessed 15 August 2017).
190 Ibid.
191 Ibid.

8 The limits of ABS laws

Why Gumbi Gumbi and other bush foods and medicines need specific indigenous knowledge protections

Daniel Robinson, Margaret Raven and John Hunter

8.1 Introduction

The Australian system of access and benefit sharing (ABS) relating to biological resources provides inadequate protection to Indigenous knowledge (IK). This chapter explores a number of Australian examples where IK associated with endemic species has been utilised for research and/or commercialisation, and where patents have been obtained relating to such uses. The examples that we present in this chapter highlight issues and gaps that exist with the current Australian ABS regime. The chapter is also a collaborative response that reflects common community-based Indigenous voices which are communicating deep concerns about the cultural and spiritual integrity of IK and how their knowledge is being unfairly appropriated for commercial gains using patents (and other intellectual property rights):

> It is commonly expressed by Aboriginal communities that they are concerned about their knowledge being stolen and it is our personal responsibility as professional Aboriginal people to support our communities.[1]

From these perspectives, we make suggestions for how these issues might be rectified.

After ratifying the United Nations' *Convention on Biological Diversity* (CBD) in 1993, Australia started to discuss and develop a system of laws and procedures that regulate access to biological resources for research and development (R&D) and that provide for a mechanism of benefit sharing between the users and providers of the resources and associated IK. Australia began in earnest to attempt to fulfil its obligations under the CBD through the introduction of the *Environment Protection and Biodiversity Act 1999* (Cth) (EPBC

---

1 Gerry Turpin, Aboriginal ethnobotanist (personal communication) Mbabaram and Tablelands Yidinji People, North Queensland, Friday 17 March 2017, Cairns, James Cook University, CSIRO.

Act) – a consolidation of a number of disparate pieces of environmental legislation. As a federated state, however, Australia distributes the power over biodiversity conservation and environmental protection to its six States and its Territories.[2] Because of variable State and Territory objectives, Australia has a patchy landscape of biodiversity conservation policies and laws. Some States and Territories, like the Northern Territory,[3] Queensland,[4] and also the Commonwealth, have a longer history of attempts to regulate access to biological and genetic resources. The other States have lagged behind failing to regulate against the ABS provisions of the CBD. Despite the recent introduction of State-based biodiversity conservation legislation in New South Wales (NSW)[5] and the Victorian biodiversity plan,[6] both again fail to properly address misappropriation issues and ABS rules. Western Australia (WA) has a new Biodiversity Conservation Act[7] that seeks to regulate ABS under certain conditions and there are also plans for an additional Biodiscovery Bill in WA. This suggests that the Northern Australian States and Territories with tropical biodiversity have taken their ABS obligations under the CBD more seriously than the Southern States.

To ensure consistency of ABS policy and law across the States and Territories, the *Nationally Consistent Approach for Access to and the Utilisation of Australia's Native Genetic and Biochemical Resources* (NCA) was developed in 2002.[8] This was developed at the same time as the CBD Working Groups on ABS had successfully developed the *Bonn Guidelines on Access to Genetic Resources and Fair and Equitable Sharing of the Benefits Arising out of their Utilization* (Bonn Guidelines).[9] Despite this, the international community

---

2 This is set out under the 1992 *Inter-Governmental Agreement on the Environment* with concepts in the agreement developed further and agreed as the *Heads of Agreement on Commonwealth and State Roles and Responsibilities for the Environment* (Department of Environment, 1997) available at <https://www.environm ent.gov.au/resource/heads-agreement-commonwealth-and-state-roles-and-resp onsibilities-environment> (accessed 18 May 2017).

3 *Biological Resources Act 2006* (NT).

4 *Biodiscovery Act 2004* (Qld).

5 *Biodiversity Conservation Act 2016* (NSW).

6 State of Victoria Department of Environment, Land, Water and Planning *Protecting Victoria's Environment – Biodiversity 2037* (2017), available at: <https:// www.environment.vic.gov.au/__data/assets/pdf_file/0022/51259/Pro tecting-Victorias-Environment-Biodiversity-2037.pdf> (accessed 12 August 2017).

7 *Biodiversity Conservation Act 2016* (WA).

8 Department of Environment and Energy, *Nationally Consistent Approach for Access to and the Utilisation of Australia's Native Genetic and Biochemical Resources* (2002), available at <http://www.environment.gov.au/system/files/ resources/bbfbde06-d13a-4061-b2f9-c115d994de2d/files/nca.pdf> (accessed 15 June 2017).

9 See Conference of the Parties to the Convention on Biological Diversity, *Report of the Sixth Meeting of the Conference of the Parties to the Convention on Biological Diversity* (2002) UNEP/CBD/COP/6/20, [342] and Annex I (Decision VI/ 24A, pp 253–269) (Bonn Guidelines).

continues to push for greater clarity on the expectations for both users and providers of genetic resources and of any associated IK.[10] This eventually led to the *Nagoya Protocol on Access to Genetic Resources and the Fair and Equitable Sharing of Benefits Arising from their Utilization* (Nagoya Protocol) to the CBD, which was adopted on 29 October 2010 in Nagoya, Japan and entered into force on 12 October 2014.[11]

There are presently 96 Parties and 92 Signatories to the Nagoya Protocol.[12] Australia signed the Nagoya Protocol on 20 January 2012 but is yet to ratify it. Australia has undertaken consultations with a view to ratifying the protocol since signing, however there have been long delays and ratification seems to have slipped off the political radar for the time being.[13] This is rather strange, given that during the negotiations leading to the Nagoya Protocol, the NCA framework and the Australian laws that did exist at the time were regularly cited as examples of how an ABS system might work.[14] In addition, Australia was a strong proponent for the Nagoya Protocol at the time because of its high levels of endemic biodiversity, and extensive IK about the use of bush foods and medicines.[15]

As a consequence of this promising and yet piecemeal approach to ABS in Australia, we have been investigating the existence of commercial R&D and patent activity using a 'patent landscape' approach. Our work has highlighted that more than 1300 patents and patent applications exist citing plant species with associated published IK.[16] Of these, there are more than 150 patents relating to endemic Australian species. Of all of the patents identified, there were only three that acknowledged an ABS agreement/partnership existed, or would be set up if a derived product becomes commercially successful. This

---

10 See Conference of the Parties to the Convention on Biological Diversity, *Access and Benefit-Sharing: Report of the Ad Hoc Open-ended Working Group on Access and Benefit-sharing* (2010) UNEP/CBD/COP/10/5 and the five addenda.

11 UNEP/CBD/COP/10/27, [103] and Annex (Decision X/1, Annex 1, pp 89–109) (Nagoya Protocol).

12 See Secretariat to the Convention on Biological Diversity, *Parties to the Nagoya Protocol* available at <https://www.cbd.int/abs/nagoya-protocol/signatories/default.shtml> (accessed 18 May 2017).

13 Department of Environment and Energy, *How Will Australia Implement the Nagoya Protocol?* available at <http://www.environment.gov.au/topics/science-and-research/australias-biological-resources/nagoya-protocol-convention-biological> (accessed 18 May 2017).

14 See, for example, Sarah Laird, Catherine Monagle and Sam Johnston, *Queensland Biodiscovery Collaboration: The Griffith University AstraZeneca Partnership for Natural Product Discovery – An Access and Benefit Sharing Case Study* (UNU, 2008).

15 Daniel Robinson *Biodiversity, Access and Benefit-Sharing: Global Case Studies,* (Routledge, 2015), pp 128–141.

16 Daniel Robinson and Margaret Raven, 'Identifying and Preventing Biopiracy in Australia: Patent Landscapes and Legal Geographies for Plants with Indigenous Australian Uses' (2017) 48 *Australian Geographer* 311.

study and earlier studies[17] have highlighted through examples, particularly the Mary Kay patents and applications relating to Kakadu Plum, that companies appear to be side-stepping the ABS laws in Australia.

Improved outcomes for Aboriginal and Torres Strait Islander Peoples requires the recognition that the use of IK for cultural and economic purposes is fundamental to Indigenous Peoples' self-determination enshrined within the United Nations *Declaration on the Rights of Indigenous Peoples* (UNDRIP)[18] that Australia adopted in 2009.[19] From this position, Indigenous Peoples and activists in Australia are starting to challenge current patents that might affect Indigenous rights to the use of IK, inhibit economic opportunities, or cause significant cultural offence. There are a growing number of scholars who acknowledge the centrality of self-determination in such a discussion and are actively collaborating with Indigenous Peoples to create positive change.

This chapter furthers this evidence by examining several other species of plants that have been patented, the issues associated with the patents, and concerns that are raised by Indigenous Peoples due to their 'prior art' and the spiritual and cultural significance of the plants. Below we first present our methods for patent landscaping, and then highlight the possibility of challenging patents and applications of concern.

8.2 Methods, patents and 'prior art': using public domain information and administrative processes to prevent biopiracy

Since the early 1990s there have been a small, but vocal, number of activists and researchers who have highlighted biopiracy cases.[20] Here, we also want to note that there are possibilities for members of the interested public, Indigenous Peoples, or concerned stakeholders to do their own searches and even to challenge patents.

First, it is simple to search patents for specific keywords (for example, the species name, the Indigenous use or application, the geographical location where the species is found, and so on) through both national and international patent databases. The best starting point is the WIPO PATENTSCOPE Portal[21] since:

17 See Daniel Robinson, *Confronting Biopiracy: Cases, Challenges and International Debates* (Earthscan, 2010) pp 75–76.
18 GA Res 61/295, UN GAOR, 61st sess, 107th plen mtg, UN Doc A/RES/61/295 (13 September 2007).
19 Australian Human Rights Commission, *UN Declaration on the Rights of Indigenous Peoples* http://www.humanrights.gov.au/our-work/aboriginal-and-torres-strait-islander-social-justice/projects/un-declaration-rights (accessed 16 August 2017).
20 See, for example, the ETC Group at: <http://www.etcgroup.org>, Public Eye (formerly Berne Foundation) at: <https://www.publiceye.ch/en>, and Natural Justice at: <http://naturaljustice.org> (accessed 16 August 2017).
21 World Intellectual Property Organization, *PATENTSCOPE* available at <http://www.wipo.int/patentscope/en> (accessed 18 May 2017).

The PATENTSCOPE database provides access to international *Patent Cooperation Treaty* (PCT) applications in full text format on the day of publication, as well as to patent documents of participating national and regional patent offices. The information may be searched by entering keywords, names of applicants, international patent classification and many other search criteria in multiple languages.[22]

The PATENTSCOPE portal also provides basic machine translations of non-English patents. This means it is possible and relatively simple for lay people and IK holders to check if specific biological resources are being patented, and then to ascertain if it appears that IK has also been used as a lead towards the claimed invention. Once a dubious patent or a patent of concern is identified, however, court proceedings to challenge the patent can be prohibitively costly and the process too technical. For the patent landscape that informed Robinson and Raven's study and identified the cases in this paper, a simple species name search was conducted in PATENTSCOPE for 321 Australian plants.[23] These 321 plants were all chosen from an ethnobotanical/economic botany text: the *CSIRO Handbook of Economic Plants of Australia*[24] and they are all listed as having known Indigenous uses (such as a bush food, medicine), or other uses (such as fibres, poisons).

In Australia, we are relatively lucky to have pre- and post-grant challenges built into the patent system, via an administrative mechanism. This has particular benefits with regards to 'biopiracy' cases because we are often talking about patents that relate to IK. Internationally, in many, if not all cases, it has been difficult for Indigenous Peoples to challenge dubious patents and biopiracy because of the costs and burdensome technical procedures involved. However, in Australia there are some options in the *Patents Act 1990* (Cth):

- Section 27(1) submissions (standard patents) (and Section 28 submissions apply also for an Innovation Patent) are allowed pre-grant: 'A person may, within the prescribed period after a complete specification filed in relation to an application for a standard patent becomes open to public inspection, notify the Commissioner, in accordance with the regulations, that the person asserts, for reasons stated in the notice, that the invention concerned is not a patentable invention'.
- Section 97(2) (standard patents) (and Section 101G submissions also apply for innovation patents) post-grant re-examination request: 'Subject to this section and the regulations, where a patent has been granted, the Commissioner may, and must if asked to do so by the patentee or any other person, re-examine the complete specification'.

22 Ibid.
23 See Robinson and Raven, above n 16, pp 316–317.
24 Michael Lazarides and Bernadette Hince, *CSIRO Handbook of Economic Plants in Australia* (CSIRO Publications, 1993).

Following patent searching in 2010, the identification of a patent application by Mary Kay company and consultations with relevant Indigenous organisations, Robinson filed a notice with IP Australia (at no cost) according to the *Patents Act 1990* (Cth) pre-grant challenge process.[25] This submission was used as evidence by the patent examiner to reject the claims made by the applicant who subsequently withdrew the application.[26] Further challenges are likely to be made against patents identified by Robinson and Raven, although if the challenge is made post-grant, there is an AUD800 fee for each request to re-examine the patent[27] (and this could be crowd-sourced).

These pre- and post-grant administrative procedures provide an important avenue for challenging patents that appear to be dubious. In the next sections, we examine some patents of concern relating to Australian plant species which are known to have Indigenous uses. While one of these is an Australian patent, which means it might be possibly to request re-examination, the others are patents granted in foreign jurisdictions (the United States and Japan) where these procedures are not available or are not presently clear.

8.3 Gumbi Gumbi (*Pittosporum angustifolium*)

Gumbi Gumbi (sometimes Gumby Gumby, Cumby Cumby, or Gumpii Gumpii which reputedly means 'medicine tree' in some local languages) is known by many names: native willow, native apricot, butter bush, poison berry tree, weeping pittosporum, meemeei and Berrigan amongst others (see Table 8.1).[28] The plant is known to be endemic to Australia, with its distribution in primarily arid, semi-arid and temperate zones.[29] According to the *Atlas of Living Australia*, the plant has numerous synonyms such as *Pittosporum phillyreoides DC* that were misapplied to another taxon during assessments in the past, and also to heterotypic 'subjective synonyms based on different types' or perceived variations including *Pittosporum phillyraeoides* var. microcarpa S Moore.[30] In a taxonomic revision by Australian botanists in

---

25 Robinson, above n 17, pp 75–76.
26 See Robinson and Raven, above n 16, pp 323–324; Robinson, above n 17, pp 75–76.
27 *Patents Act 1990* (Cth) s 97(2); *Patents Regulations 1991* (Cth) r 9.2.
28 Enrich Lassak and Tara McCarthy, *Australian Medicinal Plants: A Complete Guide to Identification and Usage* (2nd ed., Reed New Holland, 2011); Peter Latz, *Pocket Bushtucker: A Field Guide to the Plants of Central Australia and their Traditional Uses* (IAD Press, 1999).
29 See *Atlas of Living Australia*, '*Pittosporum angustifolium* Lodd.' available at <http://bie.ala.org.au/species/http://id.biodiversity.org.au/node/apni/7744138> (accessed 18 May 2017); Lindy Cayzer, Michael Crisp and Ian Telford, 'Revision of *Pittosporum* (Pittosporaceae) in Australia' (2000) 13 *Australian Systematic Botany* 845.
30 *Atlas of Living Australia*, '*Pittosporum angustifolium* Lodd.: Names and sources' available at <http://bie.ala.org.au/species/http://id.biodiversity.org.au/node/apni/7744138#names> (accessed 18 May 2017).

Table 8.1 A non-exhaustive list of the peoples, plant names, and regions where Gumbi
Gumbi (*Pittosporum angustifolium*) is found

Indigenous People	Name	Region
Yirendali and Bidjara	Cumbi Cumbi or Gumbi Gumbi	Central Queensland
Alyawarr	Ampwerrety, Welterr	Central Australia
E. Anmatyerr	Welter, Anawert, Atnawert	Central Australia
W. Anmatyerr	Anawert	Central Australia
E. Arrernte	Atnawerte	Central Australia
W. Arrernte	Tnawerte	Central Australia
Kaytetye	Eltwerreye	Northern Territory/Central Australia
Pitjantjatjara	Alita, Kumpalypa	Central/Southern Australia
Warlpiri	Ngamari, Pawurlirri, Wirnpir-arri, Yarnawurdu	Central Australia
Yankunytjatjara	Kumpaly(pa)	Central Australia

Sources: Peter Latz, *Pocket Bushtucker: A Field Guide to the Plants of Central Australia and their
Traditional Uses* (IAD Press, 1999); Everard et al., *Punu. Yankunytjatjara Plant Use* (Jukurrpa
Books, 2002); Janis Constable and Karen Love, *Aboriginal Water Values Galilee Subregion (Qld)*
(2015).

2000, numerous synonyms were re-classed into *Pittosporum angustifolium*.[31]
For example:

> Another species, widespread throughout Australia and included in *P. phil-
> lyraeoides* until now (as var. *microcarpa*), is reinstated here as *P. angusti-
> folium. Pittosporum angustifolium* has pendulous branches, falcate,
> glabrous leaves, and is not found on coastal limestone plains [like the *P.
> ligustrifolium* species].[32]

This taxonomic reclassification is important because it broadens the scope of
the recognised historical and Indigenous species uses as we explain below. Not
only has the plant had many changing names, it has many Indigenous uses,
applications and associated knowledges.

A Indigenous uses, understandings and cultural significance of gumbi gumbi

IK of Gumbi Gumbi and other biological resources is embedded within a
complex framework of cultural identity which is connected to ancient and
ongoing belief systems and community wellbeing. Indigenous practices are

31 Cayzer *et al.*, above n 29, p 847.
32 Ibid, p 847.

intrinsically associated with knowledge of Country, and are embedded in Dreaming beliefs and 'law-stories' wherein the plants and animals being used as genetic/biological resources are actually considered ancestors and kin.[33] Spiritual associations with knowledge held by Indigenous Peoples establish cultural protocols and processes for their use, management and conservation. In our experience, to take and use IK – without firstly negotiating with appropriate elders and knowledge-holders, and following correct 'cultural' process – causes detrimental impacts upon Aboriginal communities. These impacts are not solely economic, they may also impinge on self-determination, and there may be cultural and spiritual ramifications that are embodied by a community or specific individuals, particularly if a species is considered sacred or 'totemic'.[34]

There is evidence that Gumbi Gumbi is used in ceremonies and they are critical to creation stories by the Yirendali and Bidjara people, implying a regional cultural and spiritual significance of the plant in the Galilee Basin region of Central Queensland.[35] For example, Mr James Hall, a Yirendali man is recorded as explaining the centrality of Gumbi Gumbi to Yirendali Dreaming:

> Prairie Creek – The Plains Homestead water hole on the Prairie river, is the creation place for the Yirendali people, it is associated with the ceremonial bush medicine, common name gumbi gumbi. It is the story about the gumbi gumbi bush spirit, a women who lived alone by the water hole, and one day while out gathering food, she came across a male bush spirit. They courted and fell in love, and when the gumbi gumbi spirit lady fell pregnant, she gave birth, and the baby came out of the seed pod. This was the birth of the Moongaburra people, of the Yirendali people.[36]

Therefore the plant has a sacred significance to these people, with the plant representing their spirit ancestor in their Dreaming. This indicates that attempts to patent and monopolise embodiments of the plant may cause significant cultural offence.

There is also active medicinal use of Gumbi Gumbi within contemporary Aboriginal communities, especially in Queensland, and it has been reported that the plant forms an important part of connection to Country in the

---

33 Deborah Rose, *Reports from a Wild Country: Ethics for Decolonisation* (UNSW Press, 2004); Irene Watson, 'Kaldowinyeri-Munaintya-In the Beginning' (2000) 4 *Flinders Journal of Law Reform* 3.

34 Deborah Rose, *Nourishing Terrains: Australian Aboriginal Views of Landscape and Wilderness* (Australian Heritage Commission, 1996) p 28.

35 Janis Constable and Karen Love, *Aboriginal Water Values – Galilee Subregion: A Report for the Bioregional Assessment Programme* (Department of the Environment, 2015) available at <http://www.bioregionalassessments.gov.au/sites/defa ult/files/gal_indigenous_report.pdf> (accessed 18 May 2017).

36 Ibid, p 34.

Bundaberg Area.[37] General ethnobotanical texts note that Aboriginal Peoples used Gumbi Gumbi as a food, timber and a medicinal plant.[38] Aboriginal medicinal uses include the use of an infusion of seeds, fruit pulp, leaves or wood internally for the relief of pain and cramps, as well as a decoction of the fruits to be drunk or applied to the skin for eczema and pruritus.[39] For example, the Yankunytjatjara people of central Australia, who call it Kumpaly(pa), know that the fruits are poisonous.[40] In central NSW and other regions, heated native willow leaves were used as a compress to induce breast milk.[41] The Pitjantjatjara are reputed to grind the seeds for use as a poultice. In other areas of Australia, a decoction of the leaves is drunk for colds or used as a medicinal wash by Indigenous Australians.[42] The widespread and varying uses as well as the recognition by multiple names from various language groups highlight the importance of this plant to Indigenous Australians.

B. Scientific studies of Pittosporum angustifolium

Some texts note that the plant should not be used too frequently, since the phytochemical saponins that are present in the plant may have a haemolytic effect (damage red blood cells) and prove injurious.[43] Studies on the biochemical compounds from the plant have been noted as early as 1969 by German scientists,[44] with Enrich Lassak and Tara McCarthy indicating the '[f]ruits and leaves contain a haemolytic saponin hydrolyzing to the triterpenoid compounds pittosapogenin (R1-barrigenol) and phillyrigenin'.[45] More recent examination of extracts from the plant found that '[t]he low toxicity of the *P. phylliraeoides* extracts and their inhibitory bioactivity against bacteria and fungi validate Australian Aboriginal usage of *P. phylliraeoides* and indicates its medicinal

---

37 Barbara Blair, James Chapman, Bruce Little, Lavina Little, Kathy Prentice, Georgina Tanner and Coral Walker, *The Yarning Up! Project Report 2013–2014* (Phoenix House, 2014) pp 11 and 18, available at <http://www.aph.gov.au/DocumentStore.ashx?id=71c5b03b-3f3c-4224-b405-db4840308144&subId=253741> (accessed 16 June 2017).
38 Lazarides and Hince, above n 24, p 191.
39 Enrich Lassak and Tara McCarthy, *Australian Medicinal Plants* (Methuen Australia, 1983); Enrich Lassak and Tara McCarthy, *Australian Medicinal Plants: A Complete Guide to Identification and Usage* (1st edition Reed New Holland, 2001); Lassak and McCarthy 2011, above n 28, pp 135–136.
40 Pompey Everard *et al.*, *Punu: Yankunytjatjara Plant Use* (Jukurrpa Books, 2002) p 99.
41 Philip Clarke, *Aboriginal People and their Plants* (Rosenberg Publishing Pty Ltd, 2007) pp 105–106.
42 Latz, above n 28, p 182.
43 Lassak and McCarthy 2001, above n 39; Lassak and McCarthy 1983, above n 39.
44 See Leonard Webb, 'The Use of Plant Medicines and Poisons by Australian Aborigines' (1969) 7 *Australian Journal of Anthropology* 137; Robert Hegnauer, *Chemotaxonomie der Pflanzen*, Volume 2 (Birkhauser Verlag, 1969) pp 222–226 ('Oenotheraceae').
45 Lassak and McCarthy 2001, above n 39, p 136.

potential'.[46] These authors cite Semple *et al.*[47] 'that *P. phylliraeoides* leaf extracts were capable of inhibiting greater than 25% of Ross River virus (RRV) induced cytopathicity. This demonstrated the antiviral potential of *P. phylliraeoides* and provided support for the traditional Aboriginal use of *P. phylliraeoides* infusions to treat viral diseases including colds and coughs'.[48] In summary, a limited number of scientific studies have been conducted on the potential effects and toxicity of extracts from the plant, which have biochemically validated Indigenous Peoples' uses of the plant as early as the 1990s.

C *Patent application and trade marking of Gumby Gumby*

On the basis of the scientific studies, it is then surprising that a standard patent has been issued in Australia to an 'inventor' for a basic extract and extraction process relating to this plant. Through an international patent filing[49] a patent has been examined and granted in several countries including Australia.[50] The applicant/inventor is Klaus-Otto Von Gliszcynski from Yeppoon in Queensland. The patent as filed is for leaf extracts of *Pittosporum phillyraeoides* and the use thereof in medicine, and claims an extract from the leaves through an ethanol extraction process, the extract and its use for treating an array of malignant diseases or applications. This patent recently gained media attention on *The Wire* after lawyers representing the patent holders and their company Gumby Gumby sent a letter threatening another company run by Indigenous Australians, the Golden Gumby Gumby Company.[51]

Our analysis of the claims of the patent suggests that there are issues relating to novelty, obviousness and incorrect description. Regarding novelty, as listed under 1, 9 and 10 of the patent claims, we believe that the vague claims to extracts from leaves and uses for 'treatment of malignant diseases' are not novel. Enrich Lassak and Tara McCarthy in 1983, and several other authors of botanical and/or ethnobotanical texts have previously noted the Indigenous

46 J Vesoul and I Cock, 'An Examination of the Medicinal Potential of *Pittosporum phylliraeoides*: Toxicity, Antibacterial and Antifungal Activities' (2011) 1 *Pharmacognosy Communications* 8, 8.
47 See S Semple, G Reynolds, M O'Leary and R Flower, 'Screening of Australian Medicinal Plants for Antiviral Activity' (1998) 60 *Journal of Ethnopharmacology* 16.
48 Vesoul and Cock, above n 46, p 8.
49 Klaus-Otto Von Gliszczynski, Cornelia Krasser and Rudolf Kunze, *Production of Leaf Extracts of Pittosporum Phillyraeoides and the Use Thereof in Medicine* (2009) WO/2009/037225, available at <https://patentscope.wipo.int/search/en/detail.jsf?docId=WO2009037225> (accessed 16 June 2017).
50 Katja Amato and Klaus-Otto Von Gliszczynski, *Production of Leaf Extracts of Pittosporum Phillyraeoides and the Use Thereof in Medicine* (2008) AU2008300612, available at <http://pericles.ipaustralia.gov.au/ols/auspat/applicationDetails.do?applicationNo=2008300612> (accessed 16 June 2017).
51 Stephanie Richards, 'A War of Words over the Trademarking of Traditional Bush Medicine', *The Wire*, 16 June 2016, available at <http://thewire.org.au/story/a-war-of-words> (accessed 16 June 2017).

uses of the leaves and other parts of the plant for the treatment of various ill-nesses, skin conditions, coughs and colds.[52] There is a direct link between the IK and the claim in the patent for monopoly. There is also an existing published biochemical validation of these same Indigenous uses by other authors.[53] We argue that this existing biochemical validation presents strong prior art and should nullify any claimed novelty of the above patent claims. By granting this patent, there is a possibility and likelihood given *The Wire* story, that an unfair and unwarranted monopoly position will be granted that disregards prior art and will be detrimental to existing Indigenous uses and existing commercial uses.

Second, we argue that the patent is not inventive – the second critical bench-mark for achieving a patent. We would argue that in claims 2 through 7 (see Table 8.2) the 'inventors' extraction processes and methods do not appear to be inventive. Using an extraction process with water, methanol or ethanol is obvious to someone skilled in relevant fields like ethnopharmacognosy. For example, it is a very similar process to that used in Susan Semple *et al.* for making extractions for the same plant species.[54] Citing a range of temperatures (including room tem-perature) of 10–80°C and lyophilising (freeze drying) the extract also do not suggest any inventive activity. In claims 5–7 (Table 8.2) the range of administra-tions orally or to the skin for, vaguely, the 'treatment of malignant diseases' is worryingly broad and does not signify any inventiveness beyond that already undertaken by Indigenous Australians. There is also no chemical valida-tion of the extracts from the plant: the inventors do not claim to know *how* the plant extracts provide medical relief in any scientific way. We argue that this means they have not added an inventive step onto the existing IK of the plant.

Third, the patent relates in all its claims to an 'extract from leaves of *Pittos-porum phillyraeoides* DC, especially var. *microcarpa* S. Moore'. As we have explained, prior to the grant of the patent, Lindy Cayzer *et al.* issued a taxo-nomic revision of the various synonyms of *Pittosporum phillyraeoides* species to be replaced by *Pittosporum angustifolium*.[55] We argue that this revision also provides an evidence towards the invalidation of the patent claims, which incorrectly cited an outdated species description at the time of patent filing. Furthermore, the revision by Cayzer *et al.* dilutes any claims to distinct vari-eties existing. Indeed, the issue of claiming specific varieties of plants within intellectual property has been a subject of decades of debate with multiple revisions of plant variety conventions and laws such that plant varieties gen-erally need to be new, distinct, uniform and stable, to be eligible for protection under most modern plant variety protection laws.[56] To claim extracts from a

52 See Lassak and McCarthy 1983, above n 39, pp 135–136.
53 See Semple *et al.*, above n 47, pp 8–9.
54 Ibid, pp 9–10.
55 Cayzer *et al.*, above n 29.
56 See Jay Sanderson, *Plants, People and Practices: The Nature and History of the UPOV Convention* (Cambridge University Press, 2017); Brad Sherman, 'Taxo-nomic Property' (2008) 67 *Cambridge Law Journal* 560; Jay Sanderson, 'Intel-lectual Property and Plants: Constitutive, Contingent and Complex' in Kathy

Table 8.2 Australian Patent 2008300612 list of claims

Number	Substantive claim
1	An extract from leaves of *Pittosporum phillyraeoides* DC, prepared by a process comprising extracting the leaves with a solvent selected from the group consisting of water, methanol, ethanol and combinations thereof, at a temperature in the range of from 10 to 80 °C and fermenting the leaves and solvent to provide an extract.
2	The extract of claim 1 further comprising adding amylase to the leaves and solvent prior to fermentation.
3	The extract of claims 1 or 2 wherein the process further comprises lyophilising the extract.
4	The extract of any one of claims 1 to 3 wherein the leaves are *Pittosporum phillyraeoides var. microcarpa* leaves.
5	The extract according to any one of claims 1 to 4 further comprising stabilising pharmaceutical, chemical or biological auxiliaries.
6	The extract according to any one of claims 1 to 5 further comprising at least one other pharmacologically or medicinally active substance or mixtures of substances.
7	Use of an extract according to any one of claims 1 to 6 in the preparation of a medicament for oral administration; extracorporeal topical administration; intravenous, intramuscular or intracutaneous application; or for application as a clysma.
8	Use of an extract according to any one of claims 1 to 6 for the prophylaxis or treatment of malignant diseases.
9	"A medicament containing an extract from leaves of *Pittosporum phillyraeoides* DC, especially *var. microcarpa* S. Moore, according to claim 1."
10	"Use of the extract according to any of claims 1 to 8 for the treatment of malignant diseases."

Source: Katja Amato and Klaus-Otto Von Gliszczynski, *Production of Leaf Extracts of Pittosporum Phillyraeoides and the Use Thereof in Medicine* (2008) AU2008300612, available at <http://peri cles.ipaustralia.gov.au/ols/auspat/applicationDetails.do?applicationNo=2008300612> (accessed 16 June 2017).

wild plant variety (incorrectly taxonomically identified) appears somewhat questionable in this case because wild *Pittosporum angustifolium* plants have not been bred to be distinct, uniform and stable like modern plant varieties, and thus will have phenotypic (physical and biochemical) variations. These biochemical variations which are more likely to be found in the distributions of a wild plant variety than a modern variety somewhat dilute their patent claims, because the patent holder is only claiming a mixture-type product and is not isolating any biochemical active ingredients. The patent owners are themselves

Bowrey, Michael Handler and Dianne Nicol (eds.), *Emerging Challenges in Intellectual Property* (Oxford University Press, 2011) pp 164–182.

contradictory and undermine their own patent and trademark (discussed below) claims on this, noting on their website: 'There are many variations and to avoid confusion the following names also refer to EXACTLY the same Australian Native Plant', then listing a number of the plant's synonyms: *Pittosporum angustifolium, Pittosporum phylliraeoides,* Gumby Gumby, Gumbi Gumbi, Cumbi Cumbi, and others. The website indicates that different varieties exist and can be used with slightly different qualities.[57] On the one hand, they make specific claims in the patent to the uniqueness of an extract from a specific plant variety; whilst on their website making claims that it is exactly the same species and there are many variations and names for essentially the same thing. So what are they really claiming here with this patent? An incorrectly named variant or a variety of a wild species that they admit has different extract qualities? These sorts of questions are at the core of concerns about plant intellectual property, and have been for decades. As Brad Sherman notes of early plant intellectual property law development in the United States in the 1930s:

> The concerns about whether plant inventions could be described with the specificity required by patent law were exacerbated by the tendency for plants to change depending on where they are grown.[58]

Patent claims to plant extracts of a generic nature, like in this case, are problematic specifically because this wild native plant will vary depending upon conditions. The lack of any biochemical validation or the identification of the chemical actives in the plant suggests that there is no inventive step and the 'inventor' is free riding on IK.

We argue that these three factors indicate that the patent has been granted in error and that IP Australia should re-examine and reject these patent claims in light of prior art, obviousness and taxonomic revision. This is important to allow free market operation, including Indigenous businesses that trade in products that utilise 'Gumbi Gumbi' as well as to ensure that traditional uses and their adaptations (e.g. home-made remedies, soaps and creams) are also not threatened. On the other hand, *if* the patent continues to stand, this case will highlight that patent standards set too low a threshold for the grant of this kind of patent. This would further the justification for specific *sui generis* protections for IK associated with biological resources, given the current failures to protect and promote it for the benefit of Indigenous Peoples.

The Gumby Gumby.com company also holds a trademark in Australia covering: soaps, ointments, lotions and hair/body care products; teas, tonics and bath products; and herbal and flavoured teas.[59] The trademark is for a word 'Gumby

57 Gumby Gumby, *What is Gumby Gumby?*, available at <http://www.gumbygumby.com/whatisit.html> (accessed 16 June 2017).
58 Sherman, above n 56, 562.
59 Katja Ada Amato and Klaus Von Gliszczynski, *Gumby Gumby* (2016), 1760850 available at <https://search.ipaustralia.gov.au/trademarks/search/view/1760850?q=gumby+gumby> (accessed 16 June 2017).

Gumby' with an associated device/image of 'cupped hands holding a pile of leaves'. The company notes on their website: 'We have chosen to refer to our products by the most commonly known name Gumby Gumby. Gumby Gumby is the name invented by us for one particular variety named "cumpi cumpi" by an Aborigine elder's medicin[e] woman in the Emerald Queensland area'.[60] This raises two immediate issues: genericness and misappropriation. If the trademark owners themselves admit that they have chosen the most commonly known name, it is clear that it has an existing generic descriptive public use. That they also admit that they 'invented' a name near identical to a name for a variety (which contradicts their claim that Gumby Gumby is the most commonly known name) from an Indigenous elder directly points to an issue of name appropriation. Furthermore, the trademark could impact upon existing enterprises that recognise the traditional and ongoing uses of Gumbi Gumbi. For example, this trademark could be problematic for the Charleville and Western Areas Aboriginal and Torres Strait Islander Community Health Limited (CWAATSICH) where Gumbi Gumbi is the emblem of the health centre and is used as their logo including depictions in a mural that are quite similar to the trademark device/ image.[61]

We argue that this trademark to a generic Indigenous plant name, alongside the questionable patent claims, their obvious use of existing IK, and their attempts to monopolise this commercial space through both the patent extracts/process and name, mark this as a possible case of 'biopiracy'.[62]

8.4 Soap Tree (*Alphitonia excelsa*) and Giant Water Lily (*Nymphaea gigantea*)

Alphitonia excelsa is known by the common name 'Red Ash' and 'Soap Tree', Minjirrajirda in Burarra, Bani or Buwalawal in Djambarrpuyngu, and Mitjirribiya in Emi.[63] *Alphitonia excelsa* has a distribution across sub-tropical and semi-arid Australia in eastern and northern Australia.[64] *A. excelsa* is a tall tree with grey or pale bark, hairy leaves that are dark green on top and white underneath, small 5-petalled flowers and small blackish berries.[65]

Nymphaea gigantea is known commonly as Giant Waterlily and Blue Waterlily[66] and sometimes described as 'arnurna' by Aboriginal Australians.[67]

60 'What is Gumby Gumby?', above n 57.
61 Constable and Love, above n 35, p 15.
62 See Robinson, above n 17, p 21.
63 Aboriginal Communities of the Northern Territory, *Traditional Aboriginal Medicines in the Northern Territory of Australia* (Conservation Commission of the Northern Territory of Australia, 1993) pp 50–51; A Cribb and J Cribb, *Wild Medicine in Australia* (William Collins Pty Ltd, 1981) pp 18–19.
64 Cribb and Cribb, ibid.
65 Lassak and McCarthy 1983, above n 39, pp 27–28; Cribb and Cribb, ibid, pp 18–19.
66 Cribb and Cribb, ibid, pp 39–40.
67 Clarke, above n 41, p 101.

It is found in northern Australia in the tropics, and also New Guinea.[68] *Nymphaea gigantea* is an aquatic plant with floating leaves that can reach up to 30cm across. Its flowers are typically blue or blue-purple, but there is considerable variation, with some appearing white or pink.[69] *N. gigantea* has a distribution across tropical northern Australia in wetlands and still waters.[70]

A Indigenous use of Soap Tree and Giant Water Lily

Interest in Soap Tree (*Alphitonia excelsa*), as an Indigenous plant, perhaps began in earnest with Leonard Webb's (1969) publication 'The Use of Plant Medicines and Poisons by Australian Aborigines'.[71] Webb indicated that a concoction of *A. excelsa* bark and wood was drunk as a tonic, used as a liniment for muscle pain, or gargled for toothache; the young leaf tips were chewed for an upset stomach; and leaf tips were added to a warm bath for people with headaches or skin troubles. This information was gained through a research scholar at the University Queensland, one person from Bamaga, Queensland (who is identified in the text), and a non-identified source from Aurukun, Queensland. Referencing individuals and a community as a 'source' of the knowledge is significant, and could be used to support the recognition of geographically and culturally specific Indigenous governance as discussed in the discussions and conclusions of the chapter.

Some years later in relation to *A. excelsa*, Lassak and McCarthy indicated that:

> Aborigines used to apply leaves to sore eyes. An infusion of the leaves in warm water was used for bathing in cases of headache, and an infusion of the bark, root and wood was rubbed on the body as a liniment for body pains. A bark and wood decoction was used as a gargle for toothache; it was drunk as a tonic. Young leaf tips were chewed for an upset stomach.[72]

Lassak and McCarthy's entry for *A. excelsa* appears in the 'narcotics and pain-killer' section of their book. Most of the knowledge/information in Lassak and McCarthy's book on the Indigenous use of *A. excelsa* is referenced to earlier work of Webb. Even back in the 1980s, as indicated by Lassak and McCarthy's language, the accepted mistruth was that Aboriginal Peoples had ceased to use the plants, and associated knowledge, of many native plants including the Soap Tree. Contemporary ethnobotanical studies indicate that Yaegl people situated at two locations along the Clarence River in the Northern Rivers region of the

68 *Atlas of Living Australia* '*Nymphaea gigantean* Hook' <http://bie.ala.org.au/sp ecies/http://id.biodiversity.org.au/instance/apni/850745> (accessed 25 January 2017).
69 Cribb and Cribb, above n 63, pp 39–40.
70 No map available: see above note 68 (accessed 25 January 2017).
71 Webb, above n 44.
72 Lassak and McCarthy 1983, above n 39, pp 27–28.

NSW still have knowledge, and/or use of *Alphitonia excelsa*.[73] In the book *Traditional Aboriginal Medicines of the Northern Territory of Australia*, it is noted that the leaves of *A. excelsa* can be used as a mild topical antisepsis. The preparations and use describe:

> Two or three leaves are crushed and rubbed between the hands with a little water, producing a copious green lather. Both leaves and lather are rubbed over the skin as a cleanser, and as a mild antiseptic in the treatment or prevention of topical infection eg sores, pustular rashes, ringworm.[74]

The tree seems to have received its common name 'soap tree' because an instant soap can be made by crushing the leaves or pods of it and other saponin rich plants – with Aboriginal Peoples from the Kakadu area calling the cleansing lather 'andjana'.[75] Phillip Clarke notes uses of wood and bark of the Soap Tree for making a solution to deal with tooth-ache in the Cooktown area, and also for extracts to be used as a poison in small pools to catch fish.[76]

The Giant Water Lily (*Nymphaea gigantea*, sometimes *gigantean*) has been used to treat skin infections by Indigenous Australians and the use of the crushed leaves has been described by Clarke to be 'rubbed over the body to discourage leeches'.[77] The plant was also used as a food, with the roots and bulbs often collected and ground up with pestle and mortars to be used as staple food.[78] *N. gigantea* is, as Cribb and Cribb suggest:

> A well-known Aboriginal food plant, it was put to another use by Aborigines of Western Australia who rubbed the leaves over the body to prevent leech attack.[79]

Nymphaea species received numerous references in Les Higgins' (the self-proclaimed 'Bushtucker Man') book, where he suggested that:

---

73 Joanne Packer, Nynke Brouwer, David Harrington, Jitendra Gaikwad, Ronald Heron, Yaegl Community Elders, Shoba Ranganathan, Subramanyam Vemulpad and Joanne Jamie, 'An Ethnobotanical Study of Medicinal Plants Used by the Yaegl Aboriginal Community in Northern New South Wales, Australia' (2012) 139 *Journal of Ethnopharmacology* 244, 247.

74 Aboriginal Communities of the NT, above n 63, p 50.

75 Tim Low, *Bush Medicine. A Pharmacopeia of Natural Remedies* (Harper Collins, 1990) pp 185 and 226.

76 Clarke, above n 41, p 124.

77 Ibid, p 101.

78 C Rae, V Lamprell, R Lion and A Rae, 'The Role of Bush Foods in Contemporary Aboriginal Diets' (1982) 7 *Proceedings of the Nutrition Society of Australia* 45, 46; Nicolas Peterson, 'The Pestle and Mortar: An Ethnographic Analogy for Archaeology in Arnhem Land' (1968) 6 *Australian Journal of Anthropology* 567, 567–568.

79 Cribb and Cribb, above n 63, p 40.

The waterlily was an important part of the diet of Aboriginal people … The bulbs and roots can be eaten after roasting on hot coals. The seed pods, which are slightly larger than a golf ball, can be eaten raw, or were sometimes roasted before removing the seeds. The stems of the lily were also roasted and chewed or sometimes eaten raw. The leaves of the plant were crushed and rubbed over exposed areas of the body to prevent attacks by leeches.[80]

As with Lassack and McCarthy's reference to *A. excels*, Higgins uses past tense in his descriptions following the same mistruth that Aboriginal Peoples have ceased to use *Nymphaea gigantea* and the associated knowledge. Aside from these references, there are relatively few mentions of *N. gigantea* in Australian ethnobotanical texts.

B Scientific studies of Alphitonia excelsa and Nymphaea gigantea

George Branch *et al.* studied *Alphitonia* species for the compound triterpene and other useful extractives.[81] From the bark of *Alphitonia excelsa* a new tri-terpene, alphitexolide, was isolated in very small amount. Triterpenoid saponins have been found to have a range of immunostimulatory, hypocholesterolemic, anti-carcinogenic, anti-inflammatory, anti-microbial, anti-protozoan, molluscici-dal and anti-oxidant properties[82] making them a common focus of analysis when validating traditional medicines and botanicals, as also described in the case of Gumby Gumby in J Vesoul and Ian Cock.[83] The saponins are likely responsible for the soap-like quality of the soap tree extract.

Smyth *et al.*'s study of antibacterial activities of selected Australian medicinal plants, of which *Alphitonia excelsa* was one of the samples, states that 'the fact that the majority of these plants exhibit antibacterial activity demonstrates that their aboriginal uses, particularly for wound healing and infections, are well founded'.[84]

Only limited studies mentioning *Nymphaea gigantea* could be identified, and these were predominantly ethnobotanical, as described above.

80 Les Higgins, *Explore Wild Australia with Bush Tucker Man* (Penguin Books Australia, 1999) p 166.
81 G Branch, D Burgess, P Dunstan, L Foo, G Green, J Mack, G Ritchie and W Taylor, 'Constituents of *Alphitonia* species. III. Alphitexolide, a New Triterpene, and other Extractives' (1972) 25 *Australian Journal of Chemistry* 2209, 2209–2210.
82 Tessa Moses, Kalliope Papadopoulou and Anne Osbourn, 'Metabolic and Functional Diversity of Saponins, Biosynthetic Intermediates and Semi-synthetic Derivatives' (2014) 49 *Critical Reviews in Biochemistry and Molecular Biology* 439, 439–440.
83 Vesoul and Cock, above n 46, p 15.
84 T Smyth, V Ramachandran, P Brooks and W Smyth, 'A Study of Antibacterial Activities of Selected Australian Medicinal Plants' (2009) 1 *Journal of Pharmacognosy and Phytotherapy* 82, 83.

C *Patent application*

There are two patents published which acknowledge the utilisation of *Alphitonia excelsa* in their patent abstract, both for skin care applications. The first is United States Patent Number 8,173,184 titled *Topical Skin Care Formulations Comprising Botanical Extracts* which is assigned to Mary Kay Inc.[85] The second is Japanese Patent Number 4224387 titled *Skin Care Preparations for External Use* which is assigned to Nippon Menaade Keshohin.[86]

The patent granted to the Mary Kay company does not explicitly mention *Alphitonia excelsa* in the patent claims, which focus on the use of extracts of *Nymphaea gigantea* flower and *Plumeria alba* flower, for a dermatological application, but the abstract indicates:

Disclosed are compositions and corresponding methods of their use that include *Nymphaea gigantea, Syzygium moorei, Cupaniopsis anacardioides, Archidendron hendersonii, Tristaniopsis laurina, Brachychiton acerifolius, Stenocarpus sinuatus, Alphitonia excelsa, Eucalyptus coolabah, Plumeria alba, Cocos nucifera,* or *Tamarindus indica* extract.[87]

However, in the field of the invention, the patent indicates that the 'invention' relates to compositions that include 'any one or any combination of botanical extracts from the group consisting of' those listed in the above abstract, and any combination of such extracts. A number of these plants are found in Australia, and *Nymphaea gigantea* is native to Australia and Papua New Guinea.[88] The other main species used in the patent – *Plumeria alba* – is native to Central America,[89] but the patent document indicates that it is found 'throughout Australia'[90] and is indeed a commonly found/introduced garden plant. The patent itself notes that these plant species can be found in various parts of Australia, but it does not note IK relating to any plants.

As with our previous analysis of the Mary Kay company patent attempts and United States patents relating to Kakadu Plum,[91] key questions surround the sourcing of the genetic resources for utilisation towards this claimed R&D. As

---

85 Tiffany Florence, David Gan and Michelle Hines, *Topical Skin Care Formulations Comprising Botanical Extracts* (2009) United States Patent Number 8,173,184, available at <https://www.google.com/patents/US8173184> (accessed 16 June 2017).
86 Mizutani Eiji, Matsushita Hibiki and Osumi Kazuhisa, *Skin Care Preparations for External Use* (2009) Japanese Patent Number 4224387 available at <https://patentscope.wipo.int/search/en> (accessed 17 August 2017), p 1.
87 United States Patent Number 8,173,184, above n 85.
88 See *Atlas of Living Australia*, '*Nymphaea gigantean* Hook' <http://bie.ala.org.au/species/http://id.biodiversity.org.au/instance/apni/850745> (accessed 25/1/2017)
89 *Atlas of Living Australia*, '*Plumeria Alba*' <http://bie.ala.org.au/species/NZOR-4-107461> (accessed 25 January 2017).
90 United States Patent Number 8,173,184, above n 85.
91 See Robinson and Raven, above n 16; Robinson, above n 17.

with the United States patent citing Kakadu Plum, they have indicated that examples and extracts or blends of the botanicals have been obtained from Southern Cross Botanicals in the NSW.[92] This again suggests that the United States company is seeking to avoid compliance with Australian ABS laws by geographically circumventing them – the state of NSW does not yet have a clear ABS policy or law. This is highly problematic for the functionality of ABS in Australia, since neither Kakadu Plum, nor *Nymphaea gigantean* would normally be found in NSW. Both plants are tropical and they are unlikely to do well in sub-tropical climates like the one of NSW, so their origin is northern Australia (which has ABS laws) but their sourcing is occurring via a commercial trader in NSW. Southern Cross Botanicals have been contacted in the past but have refused to comment on their supply of ingredients to companies. The company website has been recently updated and linked to their global parent company website with a generic statement:

> After signing the *Convention on Biological Diversity* (CBD) in 1993 and the Nagoya Protocol in 2010, Australia is clearly committed to the sustainable and responsible development of its natural heritage.[93]

Since its inception, Southern Cross Botanicals has been committed to sustainable and ethical practices, showing the greatest respect for Australia's nature and Indigenous populations.

> Working regularly with local communities, the company is deeply devoted to ensuring fair pricing and high quality relationships built on trust, which it has developed over the years through hands-on involvement.[94]

Notably, the company does not say that it is committed to the CBD or the Nagoya Protocol, or mention ABS, which is a different issue to 'fair pricing'.

This patent, although extensive in description, is full of vague assertions and claims regarding the actual 'invention' being claimed. The lack of corre-lation between the abstract and the claims is notable, as well as assertions like: 'In certain embodiments, the compositions are formulated into topical skin or hair care compositions' with extremely broad ranges.[95] Indeed, they assert 'the compositions of the present invention can include any desired amount of' the extracts of the above species.[96] To get a sense of the inventiveness/

92 United States Patent Number 8,173,184, above n 85.
93 Cosmetics Business, *Southern Cross Botanicals*, available at <https://www.cosm eticsbusiness.com/company/single_company/Southern_Cross_Botanicals> (accessed 16 June 2017).
94 Lucas Meyer Cosmetics, *A Unique Combination of Expertise*, available at <http:// lucasmeyercosmetics.com/en/about-us/australian-plant-expertise.php> (accessed 16 June 2017).
95 United States Patent Number 8,173,184, above n 85.
96 Ibid.

non-obviousness of the patent, the patent's 'description of illustrative embodiments' does not indicate that the researchers have chemically validated the actual biochemical compounds that would benefit the skin. Rather, the patent states that 'the inventors have discovered that each of the extracts identified above have several biological activities, which can be beneficial to skin'.[97] There is no proof in the patent of *biochemical* synergies or naming of the compounds that cause the biological activity though; instead the patent is essentially a mixture of botanical extracts. As for method, the patent itself states that: 'A person of ordinary skill in the art would be able to isolate extracts from each of the above mentioned plants from parts of these plants by using any suitable method known in the art'.[98] These all suggest that this is a highly dubious patent.

The Japanese Patent 4224387 assigned to Nippon Menaade Keshohin titled *Skin Care Preparations for External Use* also cites extracts from several Australian plant species:

> The extracts of *Melaleuca quinquenervia, Alphitonia excelsa, Melaleuca linariifolia, Atriplex nummularia, Leptospermum petersonii* and *Tristaniopsis laurina* of the present invention have each excellent active oxygen-eliminating action, hyaluronidase-inhibiting action and collagenase-inhibiting action and have stability. The skin care preparation for external use comprising extracts of *Melaleuca quinquenervia, Alphitonia excelsa, Melaleuca linariifolia, Atriplex nummularia, Leptospermum petersonii* and *Tristaniopsis laurina* has high safety and exhibits excellent aging-preventing action.[99]

All of these species are endemic or near endemic (one also found in Melanesia). Given the earlier application date (2003), the researchers may have accessed Australian genetic resources prior to the existence of Australian ABS laws. Most of this patent is available in Japanese only, and there is minimal machine translation, so it is difficult to do further analysis. Some of these plants have been used by Indigenous Australians to treat skin ailments, suggesting their knowledge may have been a lead towards the research underpinning this patent.[100]

8.5 Operationalisation of ABS laws: closing gaps and legal avoidance

Doreen McBarnet argued in the late 1980s that it is 'possible to use legal techniques to achieve non-compliance with the intent of the law without technically violating its content. The law is not broken but it is, nonetheless,

97 Ibid.
98 Ibid.
99 Japanese Patent Number 4224387, above n 86, p 1.
100 See Lassak and McCarthy 2001, above n 39, pp 98 and 115.

entirely ineffective in achieving its aims. Despite the legislature, despite the enforcers, law becomes merely symbolic'.[101]

There are two types of avoidance tactics associated with accessing Australian biological resources. The first is through the use of existing legislation that facilitates access without providing benefits to Indigenous Peoples (for example, under the limited scope of the Queensland *Biodiscovery Act 2004* (Qld)). The second type, perhaps more mundane, is due to the patchiness and inconsistency of ABS policy and legislation across Australia.

The argument often given, both nationally and internationally, is that 'inventors' or 'researchers' will go to those places where there are less barriers to access. The possibility to avoid ABS legislation is also enabled by 'drafting skills' and 'time lag', which are often blamed for legal avoidance.[102] Following the CBD, those working with botanicals, plant extracts and biological diversity were made aware of the new expectations from ABS. Informed of this pending regulatory change, and as the negotiations towards a binding regime on ABS dragged on for more than 20 years after the CBD, there has been ample time for companies and researchers to accumulate biological resources with minimal restrictions and little or no obligation of ABS. At the same time, the Australian *Patents Act 1990* (Cth) has not been amended to sufficiently prevent the grant of patents that have failed to follow ABS procedures, or even to help interested parties to check on the erroneousness of patent claims without having to do a detailed research (as with this paper). As Charles Lawson explains, ABS has largely failed to achieve some of its core purposes to date in Australia:

(1) there is little evidence that benefits flow to conservers and curators of *in situ* biodiversity (such as protected areas), and (2) there is an evolving policy dissonance between patents as a means of promoting biodiversity conservation and patenting as an imperative without reference to any conservation purposes.[103]

Despite considerable experience, having been created in the early 2000s, the ABS laws in Australia have remained patchy with regards to geographical scope and the protection of traditional knowledge, as explained by Daniel Robinson and Margaret Raven with the Kakadu Plum example.[104] Until recently, the existence of functioning ABS laws in only two States or Territories in Australia plus the Commonwealth has been insufficient to prevent companies from accessing biological resources endemic to those States and Territories that already have laws in place. The resources were simply traded across the border

101 Doreen McBarnet, 'Law, Policy, and Legal Avoidance: Can Law Effectively Implement Egalitarian Policies?'(1988) 15 *Journal of Law and Society* 113, 114.
102 Ibid.
103 Charles Lawson, 'Biodiversity Conservation Access and Benefit-sharing Contracts and the Role and Place of Patents' (2011) available at <https://papers.ssrn.com/sol3/papers.cfm?abstract_id=1612552> (accessed 16 June 2017).
104 See Robinson and Raven, above n 16.

to NSW or a southern State where they are not endemic. The researchers and companies have done this by obtaining the biological resources from a commercial supplier in NSW, as also noted in the discussion here of Soap Tree (*Alphitonia excelsa*) and Giant Water Lily (*Nymphaea gigantea*). As we continue to trawl through the other 1,300 patents that we have identified, how many more examples will we find?[105]

These examples make a mockery of the NCA framework and the 1992 *Inter-Governmental Agreement on the Environment* (IGAE).[106] As Australia continues to deliberate about adopting the Nagoya Protocol, any window it had of preventing further biopiracy is rapidly closing.

The other main issue with the ABS laws nationally and across the States and Territories currently in force is that they do not all implicitly protect IK beyond the provision of some requirements for prior informed consent and benefit sharing (in line with Nagoya Protocol protections of IK). This essentially reduces IK protection down to the regulation of an economic transaction, when the extensive corpus of IK should be afforded alternative protections. IK systems should be a driver for community capacity building, self-determination and sustainable economies that ultimately facilitate the preservation of orally transmitted world views. Due to the cultural significance of many species, the gradual loss of orally transmitted knowledge over time, and its ongoing usefulness for bush foods and medicines, additional ways of protecting IK should be developed. These could include community protocols and a system for recognition of customary laws, most likely through a *sui generis* law (or laws across States and Territories). *Sui generis* protections for IK are being negotiated in the WIPO Intergovernmental Committee on Intellectual Property and Genetic Resources, Traditional Knowledge and Folklore (IGC). However, there are still major divisions between the negotiating parties about the substantive provisions and the forum has made relatively slow progress since its establishment in the year 2000.[107]

Last, the examples here and others in Robinson and Raven[108] highlight the need to improve patent examination processes. As the Gumbi Gumbi and Soap Tree cases demonstrate, there are still patent examination problems and

---

105   This survey also excluded Acacia and Eucalyptus genera because of the tens of thousands of patent hits that were being obtained, and which could not be checked or data cleaned for accuracy because of the sheer volume.

106   Concepts in the IGAE were developed further and agreed as the 1997 *Heads of Agreement on Commonwealth and State Roles and Responsibilities for the Environment*, Department of Environment and Energy, available at <https://www.envir onment.gov.au/resource/heads-agreement-commonwealth-and-state-roles-a nd-responsibilities-environment> (accessed 16 June 2017).

107   See Daniel Robinson, Pedro Roffe and Ahmed Abdel-Latif, 'Introduction: Mapping the Evolution, State-of-Play and Future of the WIPO IGC' in Daniel Robinson, Ahmed Abdel-Latif and Pedro Roffe (eds), *Protecting Traditional Knowledge: The WIPO Intergovernmental Committee on Intellectual Property and Genetic Resources, Traditional Knowledge and Folklore* (Routledge, 2017), pp 3–9.

108   See Robinson and Raven, above n 16.

questionable patents are still being granted in Australia and Japan, and particularly in the United States where patent approval rates are notoriously high. While databases are likely to help improve the identification of IK as prior art in patent applications, they are likely to be incomplete, and the documentation of IK has been a cause for concern for many Indigenous Peoples. In addition, without a genetic resource patent disclosure requirement, examiners may still miss some patent free riding on IK. But, even with a patent disclosure requirement, inventors may still be able to avoid detection by patenting synthetic analogues and natural mimics of the original compounds. As Sherman has explained, as plant breeding and biotechnological innovation has advanced, intellectual property law has also had to adapt to those advances.[109] By and large the beneficiaries of the intellectual property system have been corporations and private enterprises,[110] but now it is time to focus on new beneficiaries – space and political will must be ceded to support IK protection and promotion. The intellectual property system and ABS regulations may play a role in this, but a more progressive move would be towards greater recognitions of Indigenous customary laws and community protocols.

109 Sherman, above n 56, p 562.
110 Lawson, above n 103.

9 Reshaping the international access to genetic resources and benefit sharing process?

Overcoming resistance to change and correction

Manuel Ruiz Muller

9.1 Introduction

More than two decades of global experiences in designing and implementing access and benefit sharing (ABS) regimes show that their impact in achieving a fair and equitable sharing of benefits that arise from the access and use of genetic resources has been limited, in the best of cases.[1] Why is this so? Reasons do not lie in institutional and regulatory frameworks on ABS, as many believe and often highlight.[2] They are more profound and involve definitional aspects in the United Nations' *Convention on Biological Diversity* (CBD),[3] a limited or partial understanding of the economics applicable to genetic resources, and an ongoing resistance among ABS advocates to consider alternative approaches to ensure that the conservation, sustainable use and benefit sharing objectives of the CBD are met.

The scientific community has long acknowledged that genetic resources are essentially information[4] that are key to biotechnology and its process and that

---

1 Various studies and reports have arrived to, more or less, the same conclusion. See, for example, Sebastian Oberthür and Kristin Rosendal (eds), *Global Governance of Genetic Resources. Access and Benefit Sharing after the Nagoya Protocol* (Routledge, 2014).

2 Multiple studies and reports have reached this conclusion over the years. See, eg., Sarah Winands and Karin Holm-Muller, 'Bilateral vs. Multilateral? On the Economics and Politics of a Global Mechanism for Genetic Resources' (2015) 7 *Journal of Natural Resources Policy Research* 305. Furthermore, it can safely be argued that the *Nagoya Protocol on Access to Genetic Resources and the Fair and Equitable Sharing of Benefits Arising from their Utilization to the Convention on Biological Diversity* exists, among other reasons, because of the difficulties providing countries where experiencing with the effectiveness of their national ABS regimes: see Conference of the Parties to the Convention on Biological Diversity, *Report of the Tenth Meeting of the Conference of the Parties to the Convention on Biological Diversity* (2010) UNEP/CBD/COP/10/27, [103] and Annex (Decision X/1, Annex 1 (Nagoya Protocol), pp 89–109).

3 [1993] ATS 32 (CBD).

4 From the more intuitive perceptions by Darwin (1859) and Mendel (1865), to the more contemporary research by Schrödinger (1944) and modern theories by

respond well to the economics of information principles especially as they apply to intellectual property.[5] However, the CBD defines 'genetic resources' as 'genetic material of actual or potential value' and thus moves away from a long established and researched economic field. Institutional and regulatory regimes, which have resulted from the CBD, have also obviated the fact that genetic resources are essentially information. This is despite the fact that there is a readily available literature emphasising and explaining this particular feature of genetic resources, specifically in the context of policy, law and institutions related to ABS.[6] Again, why is this so? There are a few plausible explanations which include elements of path dependency, the *stare decisis* phenomenon, the principal-agent phenomenon, and what some have called 'studied ignorance',[7] for the lack of a more precise term.

This chapter offers some insights into why international processes seem to find it so hard to consider more efficient institutional and regulatory approaches to ABS and what may result if changes come about, particularly in the light of the painfully negotiated texts of the CBD and the *Nagoya Protocol on Access to Genetic Resources and the Fair and Equitable Sharing of Benefits Deriving from their Utilization* (Nagoya Protocol).[8] The paper is divided into

Watson and Crick (1953), and Dawkins and Venter over the past decades (to name a few), there is an implicit and often explicit recognition in science that genes are, in essence and fundamentally, coded information. See Richard Dawkins, *A River Out of Eden. A Darwinian View of Life* (Basic Views, 1995).

5 See, for example, Richard Posner, 'Intellectual Property: The Law and Economics Approach' (2005) 19 *Journal of Economic Perspectives* 57 available at <http://p eople.ischool.berkeley.edu/~hal/Courses/StratTech09/Lectures/IP/Papers/p osner05.pdf> (accessed 8 May 2017). See also, World Intellectual Property Organization, *The Economics of Intellectual Property: Suggestions for Further Research in Developing Countries and Countries with Economies in Transition* (WIPO, 2009) available at <http://people.ischool.berkeley.edu/~hal/Courses/StratTech09/ Lectures/IP/Papers/posner05.pdf> (accessed 8 May 2017).

6 Scholars like Timothy Swanson, Christopher Stone, Roger Sedjo and Joseph Vogel in the early 1990s recognised some of the policy, legal and institutional implications of considering genetic resources as information. For over two decades, Vogel, in particular, has been consistently arguing about the need to revisit the CBD and ABS from the perspective of genetic resources as natural information and the need for the economics of information to be applied thereof: see, for example, Joseph Vogel, 'Nothing in Bioprospecting Makes Sense Except in the Light of Economics', in Naomi Sunderland, Philip Graham, Peter Isaacs and Bernard McKenna (eds), *Toward Humane Technologies: Biotechnology, New Media and Ethics* (Sense Publishers Series, 2008) pp 65–74. More recently, see Joseph Vogel, 'The Tragedy of Unpersuasive Power: The Convention on Biological Diversity as Exemplary' (2013) 5 *International Journal of Biology* 44.

7 Omar Oduardo-Sierra, Barbara Hocking and Joseph Vogel, 'Monitoring and Tracking the Economics of Information in the Convention on Biological Diversity: Studied Ignorance (2002–2011)' (2012) 5 *Journal of Politics and Law* 29.

8 Nagoya Protocol, above n 2. Both the CBD and the Nagoya Protocol were formally adopted in Nairobi and Nagoya respectively, after long and tedious negotiation processes, with minutes to spare in regards to the time frame assigned for their approval. For a historic overview of the CBD see, Désirée McGraw, 'The

four broad parts. Part 2 addresses the current implementation status of ABS regimes around the world. Part 3 reflects on whether in the light of the shortcomings and limitations in ABS frameworks worldwide, a new, fresh look and approach may be needed to better institutionalise a fair and equitable system of ABS. Part 4 analyses some of the reasons which may be behind the decade-long resistance to change by policy makers and practitioners in regards to ABS processes. Even suggestions for adjustments and new analyses seem to have been consistently sidelined. Part 5 provides some suggestions for the type of changes and reorientations ABS discussions may need to ensure that the conservation, sustainable use and benefit sharing objectives of the CBD and the Nagoya Protocol are efficiently met.

9.2 The status of ABS regimes around the world: a rapid assessment

The implementation of ABS regimes can be assessed from two perspectives. For those who see the success of ABS in what policy and legal frameworks have been designed and implemented, a good argument can be made that we are heading in the right direction. The *number* of policies, laws, regulations and measures in place throughout the world are on the increase, which may be interpreted as progress and advancement. There are at least 60 or more countries (sometimes grouped in regional blocs such as the European Union, the Andean Community and the African Union),[9] which have introduced ABS frameworks,[10] although with different degrees of implementation.[11] However,

CBD: Key Characteristics and Implications for Implementation' (2002) 11 *Review of European, Comparative and International Environmental Law* 17.

9 See, Santiago Carrizosa, Stephen Brush, Brian Wright and Patrick McGuire (eds), *Accessing Biodiversity and Sharing Benefits: Lessons from Implementing the Convention on Biological Diversity*, IUCN Environmental Policy and Law Paper No 54 (IUCN, 2004). See also Jorge Cabrera Medaglia, Frederic Perron-Welch and Freedom-Kai Phillips, *Overview of Regional and National Measures on Access and Benefit Sharing. Challenges and Opportunities in Implementing the Nagoya Protocol* (3rd edition, CISDL, 2014) available at <http://www.cisdl.org/aichilex/files/Global%20Overview%20of%20ABS%20Measures_FINAL_SBSTTA18.pdf> (accessed 8 May 2017).

10 The World Intellectual Property Organization (WIPO) has developed a good data base with the texts of the many of these ABS and related traditional knowledge protection frameworks: available at <http://www.wipo.int/tk/en/databases/tklaws/> (accessed 8 May 2017).

11 Most examples of monetary benefits are often linked to research and development and value chains which are closer to biotrade-type endeavours (and using derivatives such as oils, resins, raw natural products) rather than success stories regarding the actual use and development of genetic resources (natural information) *per se*. These include cases such as Argan oil, Hoodia and business models by companies such as Natura (Brasil), Weleda (Germany), and Phytotrade Africa (South Africa). For an analysis of the relation between ABS and BioTrade and examples of benefit sharing see, United Nations Conference on Trade and Development (UNCTAD), *Facilitating BioTrade in a Challenging Access and Benefit Sharing Environment*

even for these initiatives evidence is very clear that in terms of *monetary* benefit sharing, their effect has been modest, at best.

One of the better and most profoundly analysed examples of a bioprospecting effort between a national institution and a foreign company – the National Biodiversity Institute (INBIO) of Costa Rica – stops short of any substantial and sustainable monetary benefit derived from access to and research and development (R&D) over genetic resources extracted from Costa Rica's protected areas.[12] Costa Rica has had ABS legislation in place since 1998.

Often cited as successful examples of monetary benefit sharing are biotrade-related projects and enterprises which deal with biological resources (mostly used and commercialised as bulk products or commodities), and where R&D and value added are not necessarily achieved through the development of modern biotechnologies.[13] Sometimes, phases in these projects and businesses are included under the scope of national ABS laws and regulations, especially at present where the Nagoya Protocol has opened its scope to derivatives and biochemicals.[14]

(UNCTAD, 2016) available at <http://unctad.org/en/PublicationsLibrary/web ditcted2016d4_en.pdf> (accessed 8 May 2017). See also Christian Prip and Kristin Rosendal, *Access to Genetic Resources and Benefit-sharing from their Use (ABS) – State of Implementation and Research Gap*, Report 5/2015 (Fridtjof Nansen Institute, 2015) pp 16–19.

12 In two of the better known and studied examples, that of Taxol and *Thermus aquaticus*, a multibillion dollar industry has emerged with limited benefits shared with the providers of original genetic resources (natural information). The often cited case of INBIO in Costa Rica is also very limited in terms of the monetary benefits derived from more than two decades of bioprospecting. Many of INBIO contracts have set the stage and standard for negotiating royalties in the 0.5–2.5% range. Quite ironically, after more than two decades of operation, INBIO is closing its bioprospecting operation and seeking a governmental bailout. See, Pablo Fonseca, 'A Major Centre of Biodiversity Research Crumbles' (2015) *Scientific American* available at <https://www.scientificamerican.com/article/a-major-cen ter-of-biodiversity-research-crumbles> (accessed 8 May 2017). After a seminal study by Kerry ten Kate and Sarah Laird in 1999, on the global value of genetic resources, reports continue to place again, in the billions, the annual sales and value of genetic resources in global biotechnology, pharmaceutical, crop protection and other related markets: Kerry ten Kate and Sarah Laird, *The Commercial Use of Biodiversity: Access to Genetic Resources and Benefit Sharing* (Earthscan, 1999).

13 Markets for biotrade products are steadily growing worldwide. However, most monetary benefits generated respond to classic market demand principles (prices) which could be arguably considered as fair and equitable along the value chain. The paper will not address this particular dimension in the use of biodiversity.

14 Carlos Correa, *Implications for BioTrade of the Nagoya Protocol on Access to Genetic Resources and the Fair and Equitable Sharing of the Benefits Arising from their Utilization* (United Nations, 2011) available at <http://www.biotrade.org/ ResourcesPublications/UNCTAD_DITC_TED_2011_9.pdf> (accessed 8 May 2017).

However, for those looking more closely at some of the substantial elements in ABS, including fairness and equity in benefit sharing, a rather different picture emerges. Monetary benefits are very limited, equity and fairness have not been achieved,[15] and ABS regimes have not been designed with appropriate incentives aligned to ensure that they are supportive of the two interlinked objectives of the CBD, that is, conservation and sustainable use of biological diversity and its components.[16]

Why is this so? Mainly because bilateralism in ABS negotiations (contracts) over widely diffused resources (both *in situ* and *ex situ*) leads to a downward pressure on prices and the impossibility to negotiate fairly and equitably. Jurisdiction shopping entails on the part of users and a price war results between countries sharing similar resources (natural information).[17] The issue merits further discussion given that answers are and have been available for at least a couple of decades.

9.3 The problems and challenges: is another approach to ABS neededand what might it look like?

To understand why a non-contractual approach to ABS is needed if fairness and equity in benefit sharing are to be achieved, there are a couple of premises that we need to consider. Firstly, there is a need for a new international policy process which implies reinterpreting or modifying (renegotiating) certain terms and definitions in the CBD. Though politically very complicated, it may be the only way to change the current trend in ABS worldwide. The key terms to be revised are 'genetic resources' and 'sovereignty'.

Genetic resources are (natural) information and regulatory or *ex ante* access barriers are *de facto*, ineffective and inefficient as with any information. As mentioned earlier, economics literature has for decades addressed the issue of information and intangibles. Intellectual property, and patents in particular, appear as an effective and efficient instrument to reward the value added to artificially created information, expressed in inventions.[18] Intellectual property

15　It seems rather odd that royalty rates of 0.5–3.0% are accepted globally and with little discussion as an appropriate measure of fairness and equity, as if the market should be the decider of this particular rate. Benefit sharing (fair and equitable) seems to mean something more than what would be negotiated under normal circumstances in a commercial agreement or transaction. If not, the CBD would not have included these terms: see, UNCTAD (2016), above n 11, pp 18–21.

16　See Manuel Ruiz, *Genetic Resources as Natural Information. Implications for the Convention on Biological Diversity and the Nagoya Protocol* (Earthscan, 2015) pp 1–8.

17　Angerer offers a compelling example on 'jurisdiction shopping' in regards to the dart frog (*Epipedobates*): Klaus Angerer, 'Case Study 1: *Epipedobates anthonyi* Under "Bounded Openness"' in Ruiz, ibid, pp 98–109.

18　This chapter will not address some of the ongoing critique of the intellectual property system and its stifling effects on innovation and broader effects on national development, especially in developing and least-developed countries: see

which protects innovations derived from natural information – mainly bio-technologies – and is commercially successful could serve to trigger benefit sharing. Given natural information is widely diffused among jurisdictions,[19] negotiating bilaterally – between a user and a provider – as if genetic resources were *tangibles*, leads, quite simply, to a price war or jurisdiction shopping, a common practice seen over time among companies and institutions.[20]

The idea of State sovereignty should not be restricted to the ability countries have to negotiate bilateral ABS agreements, but rather, should be expanded to explore the possibility to develop and agree to a new multilateral ABS regime. Rather counterintuitively, countries of origin and providers have heralded sovereignty almost as a synonym to bilateralism and ABS contracts, where mutually agreed terms (MAT) and prior informed consent (PIC) are the cornerstone of any ABS scheme. However, sovereignty could also pave the way for a negotiation to establish a more effective and efficient ABS regime, obviating MAT and PIC altogether.

A new way of looking at sovereignty may simply mean participating in a new multilateral, non-contractual regime on ABS,[21] which focuses on facilitating access to natural information upon one single condition: that if patents are sought over biotechnologies, the use of natural information is disclosed.[22] If commercial success is achieved, determination of the distribution of natural information among countries (providers) will be made, and benefits shared according to the conservation status of the species. Under this approach, controls are *ex post*. A new multilateral regime for ABS would take the form of an oligopoly where countries sharing the sources of natural information (such as

Joseph Stiglitz, 'Economic Foundations of Intellectual Property Rights' (2008) 57 *Duke Law Journal* 1693.

19 Paul Oldham is unequivocal. In some cases, genetic resources [natural information] may be unique to one specific country or a provider. However, 'species [from which genetic resources are obtained] that are limited to one or a very small number of cases, are likely, on the basis of available distribution data, to be the exception rather than the rule': Paul Oldham, Stephen Hall and Oscar Forero, 'Biological Diversity in the Patent System' (2013) 8 *PLoS ONE* 6 available at <http://journals.plos.org/plosone/article?id=10.1371/journal.pone.0078737> (accessed 8 May 2017).

20 See, Klaus Angerer, 'Frog Tales – On Poison Dart Frogs, Epibatidine, and the Sharing of Biodiversity' (2011) 24 *Innovation: The European Journal of Social Science Research* 353.

21 The Nagoya Protocol offers a glimmer of hope when it – paradoxically – considers the possibility of a Global Multilateral Benefit Sharing Mechanism (GMBSM) for cases when genetic resources are in transboundary situations (Article 10), or when resources are shared among two or more countries (Article 11). In this latter case, Contracting Parties should 'cooperate' among themselves with a view of implementing the Nagoya Protocol. These situations are presented as exceptional when they are in fact the common rule!

22 This in no way means disrupting existing and classic national permitting regimes for collecting biological samples or agreeing to non-monetary benefits. These regimes may co-exist with the new multilateral system – of bounded openness.

species) would share set and predefined benefits in a manner proportional to geographic distribution and conservation of the species.

These approaches can be synthesised into the concept of 'bounded openness', which has been advocated by Joseph Vogel. There is a long trajectory and peer reviewed literature which develops and reflects on the operational and procedural details of bounded openness.[23]

9.4 Resistance to correction and change by decision makers and practitioners in ABS

Over time, various aspects of bounded openness have been presented and discussed in ABS meetings, workshops and forums around the world. Related literature is abundant and accessible. Other than the non-argument of *stare decisis* (stand by the decision) and pointing to political unviability ('it's too late in the process'), bounded openness as an option has never been forcefully refuted or challenged during the events of the Conference of the Parties (COP) to the CBD or ABS workshops.[24] This seems quite striking.

Stare decisis and political unviability for any other option rather than ABS contracts or bilateralism stand, to date, as the strongest arguments made by ABS policy makers and practitioners. Why has there not been further attention and more solidly founded arguments against bounded openness or any other proposal for that matter? There are a series of interesting answers to this, in some cases, quite straightforward whilst others may require a more careful attention.

One possible reason is that bounded openness is simply not understood fully in its economic and institutional rationale. However, this situation is rather ironic. Even though there have been continued calls by a wide range of actors to ground decisions on solid scientific and economic foundations through the ABS processes, the truth of the matter seems to be that there is certain hostility from policy makers and many ABS actors towards both basic economic thinking and science.[25] Current approaches to the fair and equitable sharing of benefits for tangible and widely distributed resources, through bilateral contracts, invariably lead to inequity and unfairness.

Resistance to technocracy is neither new nor a unique feature of the CBD process. Examples abound in many realms. Paul Krugman, the 2009 Nobel Memorial Laureate in Economics, exemplifies this with the shameful fiscal

---

23 See Ruiz, above n 16, pp 74–92.
24 A recent event, attended by over 75 people was organised during the CBD COP 13 held in Cancun, México: see <http://www.iisd.ca/biodiv/cop13/enbots/ 9dec.html#event-4> (accessed 8 May 2017).
25 These actors include funding agencies, CBD negotiators (country representatives), Indigenous Peoples' representatives, ABS consultants, researchers and non-governmental organisations. All play an important role in setting the course and bearings for the CBD and ABS, in terms of their influence on specific policy and regulatory developments.

stimulus during the Great Recession and the underwhelming initiatives on climate change. Krugman accepts as a given that 'policy makers just keep finding reasons not to do the right thing'. This insight applies well to ABS decision makers and actors who have made non-negotiable any correction in the CBD process, including the definition and understanding of genetic resources as material, sovereignty as synonymous of ownership, and PIC and MAT as two obligations for bilateral ABS agreements or contracts.[26]

Krugman identifies a process of 'intellectual devolution' where the acceptance of a logical alternative – particularly in policy making – is not as straightforward as it would seem. The 'unpersuasive power [of logic]' comes to mind.[27] The issue of ABS puts intellectual devolution in high relief as the discussion is not only detached from logic but also the reality of biotechnology and R&D. The failures of ABS projects to deliver equitable and fair returns from multibillion dollar industries in pharmaceutical research, health care, cosmetics, crop protection, plant breeding and seeds are embarrassingly obvious.[28] Policies in ABS enabled through contracts and confidentiality move in the opposite direction from the viable alternative.

There may be another reason for continued resistances to correction and change. In the 1980s, the notion of 'path dependency' had fully permeated and had been incorporated into the economic literature, illustrated with examples that were commonplace such as the QWERTY typewriter keyboard, the convention of driving on the left- or right-side of the road, VHS versus BETA models of video tape recorders, and others. All these choices made sense at the time, but became anachronistic over the years and costly to reverse. The simplicity of path dependency meant that from a given starting point, say the CBD, accidental or random events, being 'noise' (such as sovereignty, PIC, MAT), can have a significant effect on the outcome – for example, bilateral contracts as the basis for ABS, even if these are not technically the optimal solution. Reversal in the prevailing trend is difficult due to positive feedback mechanisms, increasing returns and self-reinforcement.[29] The importance of

---

26 Paul Krugman, 'Why Economics Failed', *New York Times*, 1 May 2014 available at <http://nyti.ms/1kz4iZ7> (accessed 8 May 2017); Paul Krugman, 'Point of No Return', *New York Times*, 15 May 2014 available at <https://www.nytimes.com/2014/05/16/opinion/krugman-points-of-no-return.html?_r=1> (accessed 8 May 2017).

27 The physicist Lawrence Krauss laments that technical and scientifically grounded advice is routinely ignored and that until such inputs are appropriately assessed and acted upon, humanity faces grave and even existential threats: Lawrence Krauss, 'Deafness at Doomsday', *New York Times*, 15 January 2013 available at <http://www.nytimes.com/2013/01/16/opinion/deafness-at-doomsday.html?_r=0> (accessed 8 May 2017).

28 Ten Kate and Laird, above n 12, p 123.

29 Paul David, an economist at Stanford University, is credited with starting the path dependency conceptual framework with his essay Paul David, 'Clio and the Economics of QWERTY' (1985) 75 *American Economic Review* 332.

setting the efficient standards early on became apparent as a way to eliminate the transaction cost of a future correction.

Perhaps had policymakers been more conversant with the trends in economic theory, and emerging research and advancements in science and technology applied to genetic resources (for example, the genomics revolution and bioinformatics), they would have given greater thought to what path they were embarking on before they embraced bilateralism as expressed in the CBD and later affirmed through the ABS framework under the Nagoya Protocol. The 'distance' between advances in science and technology and ABS frameworks continues to grow. Reversing the policy and regulatory architecture in ABS is like changing the design of the QWERTY keyboard or expecting drives on the right-hand side of the road to change to the other side of the road (for those accustomed to the left). These changes incur tremendous costs and resistance. The criterion for reversal should be: do the future benefits of the change outweigh the costs? Inasmuch as the bilateral ABS contracts seem to have failed so visibly over time, one would respond resoundingly, yes![30] Yet no such response emanates from either the CBD COP or the ABS process that countries have introduced and/or implemented for benefit sharing between resource providers and resource users.

A third line of argument rests in fairly standard economics: vested interests and the principal-agent problem. Significant royalties would result (the vested interests would oppose this) from new biotechnologies using natural information, while transaction costs would be substantially lowered, eliminating the rationale for agents. Less transaction costs mean, by definition, less legal, administrative and procedural complexities, and thus, less need for legal experts, consultants and formal bureaucracies to resolve ABS complexities. A recent example from a law firm Wilmer-Hale is very illustrative of what is at stake. The firm expressly states:

> with the entry into force of the Nagoya Protocol, companies and researchers utilizing genetic resources occurring in foreign countries are subject to *new requirements* governing [ABS]. These *restrictions* raise an *array of legal questions* cutting across distinct areas including compliance, international trade, international litigation, *transactional and licensing arrangements*, and protection of intellectual property rights. Wilmer-Hale Attorneys have access to many of the foreign laws adopted by countries to implement the Protocol and the firm has assisted clients on matters arising under this new framework, both at the international and domestic levels (emphasis added).[31]

---

30 The intellectual property regime took centuries to evolve and consolidate, and ABS is a new ground. Should we give it time to settle and consolidate? I would answer in the negative: at a species loss of one every 20 minutes the planet pays a hefty price. Biodiversity loss is an issue of (literally) survival and we cannot wait for another 20 years to ensure that ABS regimes respond to human needs and effectively contribute to conservation and sustainability.

31 See Bruce Manheim, *Nagoya Protocol Spurs New and More Stringent Requirements for Prior Informed Consent and Benefit Sharing for research and Commercial*

Law firms are already craving the opportunities of providing legal counselling about the 'complexities' (transaction costs) of ABS. Furthermore, without exception, the ABS projects funded by the Global Environment Facility (GEF) worldwide include a component of technical assistance in ABS, invariably linked to legal advice and counsel. Likewise, dozens of courses and capacity building modules in ABS include a section on support to 'negotiating ABS agreements' which is, in practice, impossible – if fairness and equity are expressly included into the equation.

Finally, there seems to be sufficient evidence to argue that many of the economic arguments surrounding bounded openness have been 'studiously ignored'. This concept is both descriptive and emotive. It captures well the resistance of ABS stakeholders to the academic literature as well as a certain exasperation.[32] As a phenomenon it cuts across disciplines. Omar Oduardo-Sierra *et al.* cite prominent scholars in different fields of work (for example, George Stigler, Herman Daly and Edward Wilson) who lament that their contributions to their respective fields were ignored by their peers for needlessly long periods of time, until they were vindicated.[33]

The same seems to be true for ABS. For almost a half century, a distinguished and peer reviewed literature exists on the policy implications of the economics of information. Similarly, the explicit recognition of genetic resources as information is just as old. A detailed application of the economics of information to genetic resources as natural information has been developed over the last generation, whose original founding blocs can be traced to the works of Timothy Swanson and Joseph Vogel in the early 1990s.[34]

Activities Involving Genetic Resources from Plants, Animals and Microorganisms, 17 October 2014 available at <http://www.mondaq.com/unitedstates/x/347698/Life+Sciences+Biotechnology/Restrictions+Governing+International+Trade+in+Genetic+Resources+Enter+Into+Force> (accessed 8 May 2017).

32 Joseph Vogel, Nora Álvarez-Berríos, Norberto Quiñones-Vilches, Jeiger Medina-Muñiz, Dionisio Pérez-Montes, Arelis Arocho-Montes, Nicole Val-Merniz, Ricardo Fuentes-Ramírez, Gabriel Marrero-Girona, Emmanuel Valcárcel Mercado and Julio Santiago-Ríos, 'The Economics of Information, Studiously Ignored in the Nagoya Protocol on Access to Genetic Resources and Benefit Sharing' (2011) 7 *Law, Environment and Development Journal* 52.

33 Oduardo-Sierra *et al.*, above n 7, 30.

34 Two short articles appeared in the newsletter of CIRCIT, an Australian think tank: Joseph Vogel, 'Intellectual Property and Information Markets: Preliminaries to a New Conservation Policy' (1990) *CIRCIT Newsletter*, May 1990, p 6; Joseph Vogel, 'The Intellectual Property of Natural and Artificial Information' (1991) *CIRCIT Newsletter*, June 1991, p 7. This set the basis to the conceptual development of applying the economics of information to genetic resources (as natural information). Timothy Swanson on the other hand wrote a discussion paper entitled *The Economics of the Biodiversity Convention*, CSERGE Discussion Paper GEC 92–08 (Centre for Social and Economic Research on the Global Environment, 1992) available at <http://www.cserge.ac.uk/sites/default/files/gec_1992_08.pdf> (accessed 9 May 2017). In this paper, Swanson discusses the informational dimension of biodiversity and its implications for conservation.

Just like some legal frameworks do indeed recognise the informational nature of genetic resources (for example, Brazil and Costa Rica), they fail to develop the subsequent logical regulatory framework of that recognition. Some authors and scholars make reference to genetic resources as information but stop short of fleshing out the political consequences for the CBD COP process and the ABS trajectory in general.[35]

Oduardo-Sierra *et al.* track the presence of the theoretical framework for the economics of information in ABS literature and CBD-related forums. The results were startling: when searching in Google and Google Scholar for hits on 'Convention on Biological Diversity' and 'access', 'benefit sharing', 'openness' and 'information', hits are substantial and go into the millions. When 'economics of information' is added to the search, results drop to almost nil, other than those related to Vogel, Vogel *et al.* and a few others. The dearth is surprising. Land use and habitat conservation belong to the discipline of economics, and as stressed repeatedly, genetic resources are essentially natural information for the purposes of R&D. How and why did almost everyone fail to connect the two?[36]

Oduardo-Sierra *et al.* concede the possibility that during the first ten years (1993–2001), the lack of due diligence was an explanation. In other words, researchers and scholars missed both the literature and the connection though one would think that many would have converged on it. The Nobel Memorial Prize in Economics in 2001 was on the economics of information and the 'omics' revolution well under way. For the period (2002–2011), Oduardo-Sierra *et al.* suggest the 'economics of information' was 'studiously ignored', recognising a high bar in attributing intent. To paraphrase, the failure to mention the implications of the economics of information was, likely, intentional. After a rather creative survey and data analysis on which to base their affirmations regarding 'studied ignorance', Oduardo-Sierra *et al.* also conclude that 'the lack of due diligence is not a credible explanation for failure to apply the economics of information in the CBD once one recognizes genes as information'.[37]

9.5 Conclusions

The resistance to any re-definition of genetic resources as natural information and to change in direction away from bilateralism is notably steadfast. Any

---

35 See Peter Drahos, *Intellectual Property, Indigenous People and their Knowledge* (Cambridge University Press, 2014); Gerd Winter, 'Knowledge Commons, Intellectual Property and the ABS Regime' in, Evanson Chege-Kamau and Gerd Winter (eds.), *Common Pools of Genetic Resources, Equity and Innovation in International Biodiversity Law* (Routledge, 2013); Timothy Swanson, *Global Action for Biodiversity* (Earthscan, 1997); Christopher Stone, 'What to Do About Biodiversity, Property Rights, Public Goods and the Earth's Biological Riches' (1995) 68 *Southern California Law Review* 577.

36 For a detailed overview of this survey and its results, see Oduardo-Sierra *et al.*, above n 7.

37 Ibid 2.

move away from bilateralism – MAT, PIC and ABS contracts – is usually dismissed and when pressed, strongly contested. Resistance to technocracy, path dependency, principal-agent problems and studied ignorance may explain this resistance. One additional possible explanation may lie in the proclivity of lawyers and really all actors involved in ABS to adhere to *stare decisis*, and the subtle dominance of lawyers in many CBD COP and ABS processes. Indication that the flaw of the CBD is foundational is the very number of COPs – thirteen – since 1994. Many conversions of land use also transpired largely because incentives for conservation were and are illusory. Bilateral ABS policy has failed and as the old adage goes, when all else fails, try the truth. The truth begins with a correct classification of the object of access for the purposes of R&D, that is, natural information. It continues with the recognition that in most cases natural information is dispersed across jurisdictions and culminates with a justification for a new multilateral regime on ABS as an expression of sovereignty, based on the bounded openness conceptual framework. Neither the CBD nor the Nagoya Protocol are carved in stone. We need creative, innovative and sound policy and legal approaches to realise the fairness and equity dimensions in ABS. Reversing a trend as difficult as it is, becomes a must when looking at the current situation in bilateralism in ABS and its dismaying record in ensuring fair and equitable sharing of benefits for both resource providers and resource users.

10 Certified ABS: the Union for Ethical Biotrade and the use of trade and certification marks to encourage and facilitate behaviour change

Jay Sanderson, Leanne Wiseman and Drossos Stamboulakis[1]

10.1 Introduction

Certification is used to indicate that goods, services or business practices meet certain standards.[2] It is used in a wide range of fields (e.g. forestry, livestock, banking, agriculture and electrical goods), on a variety of products and services (e.g. food, finance and fridges), and to advance various goals and objectives (e.g. organic practices, labour conditions and sustainability). In addition to recognising the attainment of certain standards and advancing particular ends,[3] certification is often justified because it enables certified goods or services to be differentiated from those that are not. In so doing, certification may help consumers decide which products and services to purchase, and which ones to pay a premium for. Certification, therefore, can play an important role in increasing the market value of goods or services being certified. For instance, according to an empirical study conducted by the International Accreditation Forum, 83 per cent of businesses felt that certification added value to their organisation, 17 per cent found a significant increase in sales as a direct result of certification, 32 per cent indicated a minor rise in sales due to certification, and 16 per cent considered certification being important to direct customers.[4]

1 The authors thank Maria Julia Oliva, Senior Coordinator for Policy and Technical Support at the Union for Ethical BioTrade (UEBT) and David Vivas Eugui, Legal Officer at the Trade, Environment, Climate Change and Sustainable Development Branch (DITC at UNCTAD, for their comments and suggestions on an early draft of the chapter.
2 While there are theoretical and practical differences between certification, verification and accreditation we use the term certification broadly throughout this chapter to indicate a formal process by which an authorised person or agency assesses and certifies attributes, characteristics or quality of goods or services.
3 For a summary of some of the justifications of certification in business see: Michael Conroy, *Branded!: How the Certification Revolution is Transforming Global Corporations* (New Society Publishers, 2007).
4 International Accreditation Forum, *The Value of Accredited Certification: Survey Report* (May 2012) available at <http://www.iaf.nu/upFiles/The_value_of_accredited_certification_survey_report.pdf> (accessed 15 June 2017).

A crucial part of certification, therefore, is letting others know that you are certified. One of the ways to make others – usually, the ultimate consumers of products – aware of your certified status is via the use of trade and certification marks.[5] As we will see in Part 5 of this chapter, the difference between trade and certification marks is significant when thinking about developing and administering access and benefit sharing (ABS) marks. For now, it is worth noting that, on the one hand, a trade mark indicates the trade origin of a product or a service sold under that trade mark. A trade mark can also indicate that the trade mark owner is happy for the good or service to be marketed using the 'banner' of his/her trade mark.[6] A trade mark, however, does not necessarily say anything about the quality of the good or service: just that the trade mark owner is happy for the mark to be used. On the other hand, a certification mark indicates that a good or a service has been certified as having particular qualities or characteristics.[7] In this way, a certification mark will indicate that the certified product or service has met certain approved standards.

Importantly, because trade and certification marks can help consumers decide which products and services to purchase, and which ones to pay a premium for, they can also be used to encourage producers and marketers to transform behaviour so that they are able to acquire and use the relevant marks on their products.[8] One of the best known marks of this kind is Fairtrade (see Figure 10.1). The Fairtrade trade mark is a globally recognised independent

Figure 10.1 Australian Trade Mark 1612515[9]

5 We will use the term 'mark' throughout the chapter to refer to both trade and certification marks, and will distinguish between them where relevant and necessary.
6 *Glaxo Group Ltd v Dowelhurst Ltd (No 2)* [2000] All ER (D) 256, [540]–[541] (Laddie J).
7 For a history and discussion of certification marks in the United States see Jeffrey Belson, *Certification Marks* (Sweet & Maxwell, 2002).
8 See Margaret Chon, 'Slow Logo: Brand Citizenship in Global Value Networks' (2014) 47 *University of California* 935; Deven Desai, 'From Trademarks to Brands' (2012) 64 *Florida Law Review* 981.
9 Black and white version of Australian Trade Mark 1612515, registered on 12 September 2013 (owned by Fairtrade Labelling Organization International).Our thanks go to Kelly Armiger, Fairtrade Australia and New Zealand, for permitting reproduction of this mark. Globally, Fairtrade has numerous registered marks including in the United States (e.g. trade mark registered number 3811009); Brazil (e.g. trade mark number 831077522); and Europe (e.g. EU007408917).

trade mark that is used in over 50 countries to guarantee that products have been sourced according to Fairtrade's social, environmental and economic standards.[10] The Fairtrade trade mark has been used on a wide range of products, from coffee and tea to footballs and cotton products. While often criticised and derided,[11] the Fairtrade mark is premised on the idea that it helps transform both the behaviour of consumers (who can use certification marks to easily identify and purchase Fairtrade goods) and producers (who change their practices to comply with Fairtrade's social, environmental and economic standards).[12] In addition, and perhaps most importantly, it is argued that local communities benefit from Fairtrade certification.[13] This is because the standards of Fairtrade are targeted towards facilitating safe and healthy working conditions, protecting the environment, and empowering communities to build strong, thriving businesses.

One of the most important aspects of the Fairtrade strategy is communicating to consumers that products are certified Fairtrade. While individuals have different reasons for choosing Fairtrade products, the Fairtrade mark is crucial for many consumers.[14] After conducting over 100 interviews with consumers, entrepreneurs, workers and activists, Keith Brown argued that there were three (composite) ethical shoppers – conscientious consumers, purchasers and promoters – who have various reasons for choosing Fairtrade such as utility, aesthetics and social responsibility.[15] Where consumers organise all of their purchases around ethical choices, or prefer to make ethical decisions (but do not always do so), Fairtrade branding, including the use of the Fairtrade trade mark, allows them to do this. Referring to the potential effect of marks on influencing markets and as a form of 'rectitude', Margaret Chon claims that '[s]ustainability standards in particular potentially restructure markets for farmers or other producers of commodities and goods, as well as third parties

---

10 For a discussion of Fairtrade: see, for example, Keith Brown, *Buying into Fair Trade: Culture, Morality, and Consumption* (New York Press, 2013); Mark Moberg, *Fair Trade and Social Justice: Global Ethnographies* (New York Press, 2010).

11 Laura Raynolds, 'Fairtrade, Certification, and Labor: Global and Local Tensions in Improving Conditions for Agricultural Workers' (2014) 31 *Agriculture and Human Values* 499; Elizabeth Anne Bennett, 'A Short History of Fairtrade Certification Governance' [2013] *The Processes and Practices of Fair Trade: Trust, Ethics, and Governance* 53.

12 See Valerie Nelson and Barry Pound, *The Last Ten Years: A Comprehensive Review of the Literature on the Impact of Fairtrade* (Natural Resources Institute, 2009) pp 1–48.

13 Sanjay Bavikatte, Daniel Robinson and Maria Julia Oliva, 'Biocultural Community Protocols: Dialogues on the Space Within' (2015) 1 *IK: Other Ways of Knowing* 1.

14 See also Virginie Diaz Pedregal and Nil Ozcaglar-Toulouse, 'Why Does Not Everybody Purchase Fair Trade Products? The Question of the Fairness of Fair Trade Products' Consumption for Consumers' (2011) 35 *International Journal of Consumer Studies* 655.

15 Brown, above n 8.

in the global supply or value chains, through the value added to products from social premiums'.[16]

In keeping with the theme of this collection – developments in ABS and associated traditional knowledge – this chapter takes a 'big picture' view of ABS and considers how ABS marks (both trade and certification) can be used to encourage and facilitate a fair and equitable sharing of benefits that arise from the use of genetic resources and associated traditional knowledge. While the potential for marks to assist with trade and sustainable development has been largely overlooked there are some notable exceptions. For example, the key transnational intergovernmental organisation concerned with trade and development, the United Nations Conference on Trade and Development (UNCTAD), contemplates the use of trade marks and other labelling in developing the market around BioTrade, particularly in '[p]romoting the development of conceptual and methodological instruments that contribute to developing value in markets for sustainably produced products'.[17] In this way, marks can be used, in a manner consistent with approaches contemplated by market participants, and private transnational authorities to lead to biodiversity and sustainability premised upon value-creation around ABS.

In order to examine how marks might be used to facilitate ABS, this chapter is divided into four key parts. The chapter begins (in 10.2) by situating the use of ABS marks in context: both in terms of their consistency with transnational approaches, and their potential use as one aspect of a multi-faceted approach to 'smart regulation'.[18] In brief, while there are existing principles and legal frameworks on ABS, marks represent a complementary, flexible and responsive option to also encourage and facilitate ABS.

Part 10.3 of the chapter examines the primary reason for the use of marks: as a driver of positive behavioural change in favour of a fair and equitable system of ABS. We do so by considering the key impacts on all interested stakeholders: local producers, suppliers and communities overall, and the 'market impact' between consumers and suppliers. First, because the certification of ABS can be viewed as a *process* in which certain standards such as prior informed consent and mutually agreed terms are met – or at least a commitment is made to meet those standards in the future – it can provide a locally oriented solution to ABS. This creates awareness about, and supports local participation in, ABS. It also has a market impact, as it appears that consumers have a desire for goods and services that are ethical, sustainable and biodiverse. Indeed, a study conducted and published by the Union of Ethical BioTrade

16 Margaret Chon, 'Marks of Rectitude' (2008) 77 *Fordham Law Review* 2311, 2313.

17 UNCTAD, *UNCTAD Biotrade Framework 2020*, p 26 available at </?sourceid=-chrome-instant&ion=1&espv=2&ie=UTF-8> (accessed 7 March 2017).

18 For a discussion of 'smart regulation' and its key requirements and concepts see Robert Baldwin *et al.*, *Understanding Regulation: Theory, Strategy, and Practice* (Oxford University Press, 2012) pp 329–334.

(UEBT) indicates that awareness of biodiversity has grown:[19] with over two-thirds of the 54,000 respondents (from 16 countries) concerned about biodiversity,[20] and 60 per cent of consumers positively perceiving companies that respect biodiversity.[21] Significantly, then, consumer interest in biodiversity provides an opportunity for the marketing of products based on ABS certification (i.e. compliance with standards consistent with ABS). In so doing, ABS marks can bring together farmers, producers and consumers in a way that benefits the whole community, and in a way that is more likely to lead to long-term benefits around ABS.

After contextualising ABS marks and making the argument for their use as potential drivers of positive behavioural change, Part 10.4 of the chapter then examines one transnational source of standards and certification internationally: the UEBT. The UEBT is a non-profit organisation that was established in 2007 to promote and facilitate the 'Sourcing with Respect' of ingredients that come from biodiversity in a way that is consistent with the United Nations' *Convention on Biological Diversity* (CBD)[22] and the *Nagoya Protocol on Access to Genetic Resources and the Fair and Equitable Sharing of Benefits Arising from their Utilization to the Convention on Biological Diversity* (Nagoya Protocol).[23] After examining the UEBT's approach to marks, in Part 10.5 of this chapter presents and elaborates four general observations around the potential use of ABS marks: (A) it is necessary to understand the subject matter of protection as well as the intent and objectives of certification; (B) ABS trade marks are more flexible and less onerous than ABS certification marks; (C) it is important to ensure that appropriate and dynamic ABS standards and licensing arrangements are established; and (D) an important part of ABS marks is providing support for behaviour change, and ensuring that there are effective compliance tools to detect and punish undesirable and non-compliant behaviour.

Our hope is that by arguing for the development and use of ABS marks we contribute to a vigorous discussion on the scope and design limitations of transnational legal instruments (such as the CBD and the Nagoya Protocol) that promote State-driven regulation in encouraging and facilitating ABS. At the same time, while acknowledging that ABS marks are not the panacea of ABS, we argue that they are one mechanism that can be used as part of a sophisticated 'regulatory mix'. This is because they can be used in a manner

---

19 UEBT, 'UEBT Biodiversity Barometer, 2009–2016' (2016) p 3 available at <http://ethicalbiotrade.org/dl/Baro-2016-web.pdf> (accessed 3 April 2017).
20 Ibid.
21 Ibid, p 4.
22 [1993] ATS 32 (CBD).
23 Conference of the Parties to the Convention on Biological Diversity, *Report of the Tenth Meeting of the Conference of the Parties to the Convention on Biological Diversity* (2010) UNEP/CBD/COP/10/27, [103] and Annex (Decision X/1, Annex 1, pp 89–109) (Nagoya Protocol).

consistent with the goals of transnational instruments to achieve ABS by bringing together producers, consumers and local communities. Specifically, ABS marks can do so by facilitating a market-driven low-intervention *nudging* of consumers and producers towards ABS practices such as equitable pricing, prior informed consent and mutually agreed terms.

10.2 ABS marks in context: using marks to facilitate fair and equitable ABS

ABS marks – whether in the form of trade marks or certification marks – can be used as part of the 'smart regulation' toolkit, for the ultimate purpose of facilitating sustainability and biodiversity predicated on ABS. Doing so is likely to assist with reaching the overarching transnational goal of facilitating a 'fair and equitable' system of ABS, in a manner consistent with the policy goals and legal approaches of the present transnational legal order.[24] While the existing transnational practice focuses on a State-centric model of regulation to achieve this goal, in this Part we argue that ABS marks can be conceived of more broadly as a tool – designed and employed by a range of interested stakeholders, including a diverse mix of State and non-State actors – to encourage behavioural change in favour of ABS. Before considering the use of ABS marks as a form of 'smart regulation', we first set out the transnational context surrounding ABS, and how ABS marks can be used to supplement and complement the prevailing transnational legal order.

A. ABS marks supplement and complement the prevailing transnational legal order

The use of ABS marks represents a mechanism that can be used to encourage ABS, and may assist with addressing public and scholarly concern over the way in which ABS is pursued on a transnational level. In brief, the overarching goal shared by transnational instruments and approaches is the facilitation of a 'fair and equitable' system of ABS. This goal is central to the prevailing transnational legal order surrounding ABS: it is one of the three central objectives of the CBD[25] and forms part of the core approach – and title – of the 2002 *Bonn Guidelines on Access to Genetic Resources and Fair and Equitable Sharing of the*

---

24 The term 'transnational legal order' is used in this chapter to refer to the 'collection of formalized legal norms and associated organizations and actors that authoritatively order the understanding and practice of law across national jurisdictions' with respect to ABS: Terence Halliday and Gregory Shaffer, 'Transnational Legal Orders' in Gregory Shaffer and Terence Halliday (eds), *Transnational Legal Orders* (Cambridge Studies in Law and Society, Cambridge University Press 2015) p 5. This legal order is constituted by three key transnational instruments, as set out in this chapter.
25 See CBD, Art. 1 ('Objectives').

Benefits Arising out of their Utilization (Bonn Guidelines).[26] The Nagoya Protocol, a protocol arising out of the CBD, is also expressly designed to provide a transparent legal framework to facilitate a 'fair and equitable' system of ABS internationally.[27] While guidance as to the ways in which the goal of ABS is pursued transnationally has developed significantly from the CBD through until the most recent Nagoya Protocol, the precise details of the implementation of ABS procedures largely remain a matter for implementing States to regulate. Due in no small part to the incremental transnational law and norm development process,[28] the transnational ABS approach – focusing predominantly on policy rather than implementation – has been criticised by legal and socio-legal scholars concerned with assessing the law 'in action' rather than as expressed 'on paper'.[29]

A longstanding criticism levelled against the prevailing transnational legal order – focusing on the CBD and the Bonn Guidelines – is that the transnational work on ABS has been dominated by words, rather than action, policy and implementation.[30] In considering the challenges of implementing the CBD and other conservation initiatives, Alvin Chandra and Anastasiya Idrisova identify numerous problems including limited capacity, knowledge and accessible information; inadequate economic policy and financial resources; and lack of cooperation and stakeholder involvement.[31] According to Chandra and Idrisova, underlying the problem of implementation is 'that limited capacity in developing countries and transition economies undermines conservation initiatives'.[32] These issues are not easily solvable, but serve to highlight the practical need for the implementation of ABS in a flexible and diverse manner that can be structured to solve local needs.

---

26 Conference of the Parties to the Convention on Biological Diversity, *Report of the Sixth Meeting of the Conference of the Parties to the Convention on Biological Diversity* (2002) UNEP/CBD/COP/6/20, pp 60–62 and 253–269 (Bonn Guidelines).

27 Secretariat of the Convention on Biological Diversity, *Nagoya Protocol on Access to Genetic Resources and the Fair and Equitable Sharing of Benefits Arising From Their Utilization to the Convention on Biological Diversity: Text and Annex* (CBD, 2011) p 1.

28 As Gregory Shaffer notes, because 'transnational legal norms interact with domestic institutional, political, and cultural contexts, changes are often evolutionary and incremental over time': Gregory Shaffer, 'Transnational Legal Ordering and State Change' in Gregory Shaffer (ed), *Transnational Legal Ordering and State Change* (Cambridge University Press 2012) p 12.

29 See, for example, Alvin Chandra and Anastasiya Idrisova, 'Convention on Biological Diversity: A Review of National Challenges and Opportunities for Implementation' (2011) 20 *Biodiversity and Conservation* 3295.

30 See Muriel Lightbourne, *Food Security, Biological Diversity and Intellectual Property Rights* (Ashgate, 2009) pp 80–83.

31 Chandra and Idrisova, above n 27.

32 Ibid, p 3312.

At a transnational level, the Nagoya Protocol attempts to meet this call for 'action' by advancing the implementation of ABS under the CBD via a State-driven ABS 'permit' system facilitated by a transnational ABS 'Clearing-House'.[33] The Nagoya Protocol builds on the Bonn Guidelines, which were adopted as an integral part of the CBD in 2002 to provide guidance for developing both policy measures and contracts and other agreements for ABS.[34] Unlike the Bonn Guidelines, however, the Nagoya Protocol – upon ratification, accession, acceptance or approval by States[35] – provides a legally binding framework which elaborates on the CBD's terseness in terms of when ABS applies and, perhaps most importantly, how ABS should take place.[36] At the same time, however – and despite concerted transnational attempts to move from policy to action – criticisms continue to be levelled about the implementation of ABS, including about the Nagoya Protocol's alleged excessive bureaucracy,[37] utilisation of vague and obfuscate language,[38] and its failure to fully meet the needs of developing countries. For example, it has been suggested that the *obligation* to negotiate an ABS agreement and obtain a permit under a national regulatory scheme is likely to increase the complexity, time and costs associated with accessing, and providing access to, genetic resources.[39] Further, many developing countries were disappointed with the final text of the Protocol, as they were hoping to receive greater assistance to achieve Nagoya targets, and support for a separate and independent international clearing house with

---

33 See Kabir Bavikatte and Daniel Robinson, 'Towards a People's History of the Law: Biocultural Jurisprudence and the Nagoya Protocol on Access and Benefit Sharing' (2011) 7 *Law Environment & Development Journal* 35.

34 See, for examples, Thomas Greiber *et al.*, *An Explanatory Guide to the Nagoya Protocol on Access and Benefit-sharing* (IUCN, 2012) p 19; Matthias Buck and Clare Hamilton, 'The Nagoya Protocol on Access to Genetic Resources and the Fair and Equitable Sharing of Benefits Arising from Their Utilization to the Convention on Biological Diversity' (2011) 20 *Review of European Community & International Environmental Law* 47.

35 For a list of the status of ratification, acceptance, approval or accession see: Secretariat of the Convention on Biological Diversity, *Parties to the Nagoya Protocol*, available at <https://www.cbd.int/abs/nagoya-protocol/signatories> (accessed 3 April 2017).

36 The Nagoya Protocol, similar to the Bonn Guidelines, operates within the legal remit of CBD, Art 15, and further expands upon the benefits of ABS, as well as clarifying the concept of ABS under international and domestic law.

37 See, for example, Daniel Cressey, 'Biopiracy Ban Stirs Red-Tape Fears' (2014) 514 *Nature* 14.

38 See, for example, Saskia Vermeylen, 'The Nagoya Protocol and Customary Law: The Paradox of Narratives in the Law' (2013) 9 *Law Environment & Development Journal* 185.

39 See, for example, Evanson Kamau *et al.*, 'The Nagoya Protocol on Access to Genetic Resources and Benefit Sharing: What is New and What Are the Implications for Provider and User Countries and the Scientific Community' (2010) 6 *Law Environment & Development Journal* 246; Bart Van Vooren, 'Impact on the Food Industry of New EU Rules Implementing the Nagoya Protocol' (2016) 11 *European Food & Feed Law Review*.

embedded compliance mechanisms.[40] While it is too early for a comprehensive assessment of the Nagoya Protocol's benefits and limitations, its coming into force in 2014 nonetheless represents a significant development in ABS. More specifically, the Nagoya Protocol is likely to continue to play a key role in guiding the implementation of ABS principles, with its impact increasingly felt when the legal rules and norms it establishes 'settling' upon implementation, interpretation and enforcement at a national level.

Yet, assuming, for the moment, that any transnational implementation issues (such as interpretative ambiguities, or lack of developmental capacity) are readily and uniformly overcome, there are still limits to what the CBD and the Nagoya Protocol – as binding instruments of State-driven regulation – can do to promote ABS. Recognising these inherent limits, and conscious of an overarching goal of facilitating a 'fair and equitable' system of ABS, the transnational legal order with respect to ABS is designed in a non-exhaustive way. That is, while the Nagoya Protocol provides for a range of legal mechanisms aimed at achieving a fair and equitable outcome of ABS, it does not preclude other mechanisms that may also assist in reaching this goal. For example, an explicit provision is made for States to draw upon private voluntary standards or norms to develop their approaches to ABS, in Article 20(1) of the Nagoya Protocol, which provides that: '[e]ach Party shall encourage, as appropriate, the development, update and use of voluntary codes of conduct, guidelines and best practices and/or standards in relation to [ABS]'.[41] It is in this context, entirely consistent with prevailing transnational legal instruments, that the use of ABS marks as a form of 'smart regulation' arises.

B. Using ABS marks to facilitate 'smart regulation'

ABS will be more effectively achieved if there is a mixture of both compulsory and voluntary regulation, employed at different levels by interested stakeholders. An umbrella term for this diverse regulation is 'smart regulation'.[42] In the context of ABS, smart regulation is likely to require a mix of social, legal and economic influences, actors and institutions: ranging from State-driven regulation to 'market-driven' self-regulation by corporations and professional bodies to regulation via third parties such as public interest groups and

---

40   See, for example, Gurdial Singh Nijar *et al.*, *The Nagoya Protocol on Access and Benefit Sharing of Genetic Resources: Analysis and Implementation Options for Developing Countries* (South Centre 2011); Buck and Hamilton, above n 32; Elisa Morgera *et al.*, *Unraveling the Nagoya Protocol* (Brill, 2016).

41   For a discussion of the use of 'private standards' in implementing the Nagoya Protocol in Europe: see Maria Julia Oliva, 'Private Standards and the Implementation of the Nagoya Protocol: Defining and Putting in Practice Due Diligence in the Proposed EU Regulation' in Brendan Coolsaet, Fulya Batur, Arianna Broggiato, John Pitseys and Tom Dedeurwaerdere (eds), *Implementing the Nagoya Protocol: Comparing Access and Benefit-sharing Regimes in Europe* (Hotei Publishing, 2015).

42   See Baldwin *et al.*, above n 16, pp 265–266, 329–334.

non-governmental organisations (NGOs).[43] This multi-faceted approach of smart regulation is consistent with the use of alternative, decentralised instruments and standards, each driven by a range of interested stakeholders, as seen in the pursuit of the regulation of challenging environmental goals.[44] In this way, ABS marks offer an additional avenue to assist in achieving a fair and equitable outcome of ABS, as they can be used to harness both State and non-State regulatory capacity to provide 'flexibility of response'. In particular they can assist with allowing 'sanctioning gaps to be filled so that if escalation up the [S]tate system is not possible (e.g. because a legal penalty is not provided or inadequate) resort can be made to another form of influence'.[45] This fits squarely within the other arguments made in this chapter on why ABS marks should be contemplated as a driver of behavioural change. For instance: to develop, and benefit from, the market value of differentiated ABS goods and services, and to bring together producers, consumers and local communities to work towards ABS principles such as equitable pricing, prior informed consent and mutually agreed terms.

What, then, does 'smart' (or 'mixed') regulation mean for ABS? First, it suggests the need for creative and multi-faceted approaches to the regulation and promotion of ABS. As we have already noted, while the CBD and the Nagoya Protocol play significant roles in promoting ABS, they are not, in and of themselves, exhaustive, and nor are they designed to be. This is not necessarily due to any significant deficiencies in the approach of these transnational instruments, but simply represents the bounds of transnational legal ordering given practical effect via State-driven regulation. For example, across a diverse range of environmental issues, national governments are 'now widely seen as lacking capacity to implement and enforce detailed environmental regulations, or as too often acting for a narrow national interest against global environmental problems'.[46] Second, there are benefits to a low-intervention alternative to facilitating ABS (such as trade and certification marks) that is market-driven. This is because effective ABS marks can be perceived as 'quality signalling' devices for consumers, allowing them to select products or services that have been sourced or developed based on ABS principles. If there is sufficient

---

43 See Neil Gunningham *et al.*, *Smart Regulation: Designing Environmental Policy* (Oxford University Press, 1998). Although the State remains central to governance and the legitimacy of non-government regulation is predicated on compliance, or at least consistency, with legislative frameworks: see, for example, Stephen Bell and Andrew Hindmoor, *Rethinking Governance: The Centrality of the State in Modern Society* (Cambridge University Press, 2009).
44 See, for example, Jason Morrison and Naomi Roht-Arriaza, 'Private and Quasi-Private Standard Setting' in *The Oxford Handbook of International Environmental Law* (Oxford University Press, 2008) pp 498–528.
45 Baldwin *et al.*, above n 16, p 264.
46 Peter Vandergeest, 'Certification and Communities: Alternatives for Regulating the Environmental and Social Impacts of Shrimp Farming' (2007) 35 *World Development* 1152, 1152.

consumer demand for ABS mark certified goods and services, this will encourage producers to insist in their dealings with suppliers on 'chains of certification' based upon approved or licensed standards that may assist in ensuring fair and equitable ABS outcomes.

In terms of regulatory theory, then, ABS marks are not only a low-cost and low-intervention way to assist with 'smart regulation' of ABS. They also provide a mechanism to facilitate informed consumer and producer choices about the use and supply of products that are sourced consistent with the goal of ABS espoused in the CBD and the Nagoya Protocol. ABS marks are likely to also benefit from 'network effects': that is, the more the marks are used effectively, the stronger the signalling value of the marks, and hence, the case for their use. In this way, States that make provision or allowance for the operation of an effective and accessible ABS mark scheme (that need not be State-driven) – coupled with private regulatory bodies who can design, implement and monitor certain ABS standards – can be influential in designing 'choice architecture': that is, structuring decision-making in a way that it is easier for consumers, producers or suppliers to act in ways that are beneficial or desired for facilitating ABS.[47] This includes, relevantly for present purposes, a regulatory architecture that employs as part of its regulatory mix ABS marks, making it easier for all interested stakeholders to make decisions consistent with the overall goal of establishing a fair and equitable system of ABS.

10.3 ABS marks as drivers of behavioural change

Given the potential of ABS marks to assist with the CBD's goal of ABS, in this part we present two related arguments for their use based on their potential to drive positive behavioural change towards ABS. We focus on the impact on local producers, suppliers and communities, and the 'market impact' of consumer-facing marks.

A. The impact on local producers, suppliers and communities

One of the key arguments for the use of ABS marks is their potential impact on local and Indigenous communities. As we discuss in Parts 4 and 5 of this chapter, the use of ABS marks can help set and normalise standards around environmental, social and economic conditions. The use of an ABS mark is only permitted and effective if the entire supply chain works together to achieve these standards. It is likely, therefore, that the use of ABS marks will encourage and support local participation in the sourcing, manufacture and distribution of genetic resources in a way that encourages and supports ABS practices. This is likely to include, for example, attempts to ensure that prior

---

47 Richard Thaler and Class Sunstein, *Nudge: Improving Decisions about Health, Wealth, and Happiness* (Penguin Books, 2009).

informed consent is given, and that any terms that are reached are mutually acceptable, including the provision of equitable pricing. An example of marks and community-based strategies can be found in relation to the manufacture of Plumpy'nut, a ready-to-use therapeutic food for acutely malnourished children.[48] In terms of Plumpy'nut, and the use of intellectual property protection including trade marks, it has been argued that intellectual property helps to 'encourage and support local partners in the [developing] countries to produce their own food and nutritional products', and in so doing increases 'the economic and social effect' of products in developing countries.[49] The significance of locally oriented solutions to long-term ABS cannot be underestimated. Referring to the synergies between trade, local communities and biodiversity, Sanjay Bavikatte, Daniel Robinson and Maria Julia Oliva suggest that ethical biotrade provides an:

interesting context for analysing how commercial ventures are able to go beyond use value and incentives and focus on relationships. Ethical Bio-Trade has also provided a useful testing ground for some of the tools seeking to address some of the tensions and synergies between approaching biodiversity as a resource and approaching biodiversity as part of a community's culture and heritage.[50]

In this way, ABS marks – and the standards or the certification process coinciding with these marks – can be used as a short-hand mechanism for assisting local producers, suppliers and communities with fair and equitable ABS practices. Importantly, if ethical biotrade receives significant focus at all stages of the supply chain, it sends signals to all involved stakeholders that there are certain standards of fair and equitable dealing that they should meet or can insist upon. ABS marks can be used to support this goal in a self-reinforcing manner. That is, if ABS marks and certifications are broadly accepted and insisted upon by the wider community, this will influence the norms relating to ABS. When this occurs, supply that occurs taking into consideration ABS becomes the 'new normal'. Taken to its extreme then, the greatest success of ABS marks would make the need for these marks obsolete: if sourcing according to ABS standards becomes part of the internalised norms of the sourcing process internationally, there is little need to 'signal' compliance with minimum ABS standards. Yet, in an environment where a fair and equitable

---

48 Nuriset, *Nutriset: Plumpy'Nut® Ready-to-Use Therapeutic Food (RUTF)*, available at <http://www.nutriset.fr/en/product-range/severe-acute-malnutrition/plump y-nut-ready-to-use-therapeutic-food-rutf.html> (accessed 20 March 2017).

49 Jay Sanderson, 'Can Intellectual Property Help Feed the World? Intellectual Property, the PLUMPYFIELD® Network and a Sociological Imagination' in Charles Lawson and Jay Sanderson (eds), *The Intellectual Property and Food Project: From Rewarding Innovation and Creation to Feeding the World* (Ashgate, 2013) pp 152–153.

50 Bavikatte *et al.*, above n 11, 10.

system of ABS is still largely an aspirational goal, ABS marks continue to represent important signals about the production process. While the signalling impact of ABS marks can be directly seen at the level of local community, it is perhaps most clearly demonstrated in the market impact of marks that are consumer-facing.

B. The market impact of consumer-facing marks

The interface between consumers, producers and ABS brings us to our second argument for the use of ABS marks as drivers of behavioural change: that consumers increasingly make value-driven choices that can be supported by effective ABS marks. A regulatory regime that encompasses ABS marks provides an opportunity for differentiation of products and services based on ABS. Such differentiation may be communicated and translated through certifying companies that demonstrate a respect for biodiversity through ABS and compliance with agreed ABS standards.

Much recent evidence suggests that consumers have an increasing desire for goods and services that are ethical, sustainable and biodiverse.[51] For example, a 2015 global survey of over 30,000 individuals found that the characteristics of foods were crucial to consumer choices. Over 80 per cent of respondents were willing to pay more for products that claimed health benefits;[52] approximately 30 per cent of the respondents stated that whether foods were sustainably sourced or organic was important in their purchasing decisions; and more than 25 per cent of the respondents claimed that local ingredients were desirable.[53]

An international study conducted by UEBT from 2009 to 2015 – covering 54,000 people in 16 different countries – saw 87 per cent of respondents say it was important to 'contribute to the biodiversity conversation'.[54] Further, during the time span of the survey, awareness of biodiversity grew by up to 20

---

51 See Ekaterina Volkova and Cliona Ni Mhurchu, 'The Influence of Nutrition Labeling and Point-of-Purchase Information on Food Behaviours' (2015) 4 *Current Obesity Reports* 19; Alessandro Banterle and others, 'Food Labelled Information: An Empirical Analysis of Consumer Preferences' (2013) 3 *International Journal on Food System Dynamics* 156; Nadia Prinsloo *et al.*, 'A Critical Review of the Significance of Food Labelling during Consumer Decision Making' (2012) 40 *Journal of Family Ecology and Consumer Sciences* 83.

52 The Nielsen Company, *We Are What We Eat: Healthy Eating Trends Around the World* (2015), available at <http://www.nielsen.com/content/dam/nielsenglobal/eu/nielseninsights/pdfs/Nielsen%20Global%20Health%20and%20Wellness%20Report%20-%20January%202015.pdf> (accessed 15 June 2017).

53 Ibid.

54 'UEBT Biodiversity Barometer, 2009–2016', above n 17, 2.2. Since its first edition in 2009, 54,000 consumers in 16 countries have been interviewed (i.e. Brazil, Colombia, China, France, Germany, India, Japan, Peru, South Korea, Switzerland, the United Kingdom, the United States of America, Vietnam, Mexico, Ecuador and the Netherlands).

per cent,[55] with the survey suggesting that 69 per cent of the population is concerned with biodiversity.[56] Specifically, the survey revealed that 60 per cent of consumers positively perceive companies that respect biodiversity.[57] In the UEBT survey, respondents listed brands they believe respect biodiversity including Natura Cosmetics and The Body Shop. The brands listed were brands that explicitly market their positon on biodiversity via branding, television commercials and other advertisements.[58] Thus companies employing ABS marks would clearly demonstrate a commitment to biodiversity, which would likely, in turn, translate into commercial and non-commercial benefits.

It is worth noting here something of the psychology of branding. In short, an ABS mark – along with brand reputation and other marketing strategies – would provide consumers looking for biodiverse products with a short-cut: that is, a heuristic upon which to base their decision. In 2013, the then Executive Secretary for the CBD, Braulio Ferreira de Souza Dias, noted the increasing awareness of biodiversity and stated that there was 'a growing consciousness' and that 'respecting biodiversity provides tremendous opportunities for business around the world'.[59] And, as already noted in the introduction to this chapter, the use of trade marks to develop markets around BioTrade is explicitly contemplated by UNCTAD, particularly in '[p]romoting the development of conceptual and methodological instruments that contribute to developing value in markets for sustainably produced products'.[60] More precisely cognitive and behavioural psychologists have long known that humans employ two fundamentally different modes of thought, and more often than not, humans are not rational decision-makers.

In *Thinking Fast and Slow*, Daniel Kahneman identifies two systems of thought that, for simplicity and ease of reference, he calls System 1 and System 2.[61] System 1 is fast, intuitive and associative. It is unconscious and cannot be turned off. According to Kahneman, System 1 is the 'secret author of many of the choices and judgments [we] make'.[62] By contrast, System 2 is logical, deliberate and slow. System 2 tires easily and, perhaps most importantly, it tends to accept what System 1 tells it. Explaining the differences between System 1 and System 2, Kahneman argues that System 1 jumps to intuitive conclusions based on heuristics and shortcuts, while System 2 tends to endorse or rationalise ideas and decisions. For the most part, it is sufficient to rely on System 1 because it is sensitive to subtle environmental cues, signs of danger and other similar factors.

---

55 Ibid, 3.
56 Ibid.
57 Ibid, 4.
58 Ibid, 7.
59 Ibid. See also Maria Julia Oliva, 'Sharing the Benefits of Biodiversity: A New International Protocol and Its Implications for Research and Development' (2011) 77 *Planta Medica* 1221.
60 *UNCTAD Biotrade Framework 2020*, above n 15, p 26.
61 Daniel Kahneman, *Thinking, Fast and Slow* (Macmillan, 2011) pp 20–30.
62 Ibid, p 13.

Kahneman observes that relying on System 1 is 'efficient if the conclusions are likely to be correct and the costs of an occasional mistake acceptable, and if the jump saves much time and effort'.[63] It is System 1, therefore, that tends to enable consumers to make the myriad of decisions necessary in determining which products they purchase.[64]

Thus, while individuals can take time to evaluate the attributes of products they buy, people tend to make decisions quickly, sometimes with little more than a glance. This is an efficient way to make decisions and has not been lost on judges and lawyers. In the Federal Court of Australia, Chief Justice Allsop, for example, observed:

> the ordinary or reasonable person may be intelligent or not, may be well educated or not, will not likely spend any time undertaking an intellec-tualised process of analysis, will often be shopping for many other items, and will be likely affected by an intuitive sense of attraction rather than by any process of analytical or logical choice.[65]

This intuitive sense of attraction – a System 1 conclusion – can readily be harnessed by the use of ABS marks on consumer-facing goods or services. If the mark is effective at communicating that a particular product is biodiverse or ethically sourced, it can serve as a shortcut in consumers' minds when making purchasing decisions.

C. A brief recapitulation

So far in this chapter, we have considered the use of ABS marks in their transnational and regulatory context (in 10.2) and the use of ABS marks as drivers of behavioral change across two key levels (in this part, 10.3). On one level, the certification of ABS can be viewed as a *process* in which certain standards (e.g. ensuring prior informed consent and mutually agreed terms) are met, and thus can provide a locally oriented solution to ABS. On another level, ABS marks allow consumers to make informed value-driven choices. ABS marks do so by providing a simple heuristic for consumers to identify and choose ABS products and services, targeting the 'secret author of many of the choices and judgments [consumers] make' and *nudging* producers and consumers towards goods and services that are sourced based upon fair and equitable principles of ABS.[66] For these reasons, ABS marks can bring together farmers, producers

---

63 Ibid, p 79.
64 Klaus Grunert and Josephine Wills, 'A Review of European Research on Con-sumer Response to Nutrition Information on Food Labels' (2007) 15 *Journal of Public Health* 385.
65 *Australian Competition and Consumer Commission v Coles Supermarkets Australia Pty Ltd* (ACN 004 189 708) (2014) 317 ALR 73, 81–82 ([43]).
66 Kahneman, above n 59, p 13.

and consumers in a way that benefits the whole community, and in a way that is more likely to lead to long-term benefits around ABS.

Having set out the regulatory context and use of ABS and the ways they may be used to drive behavioural change, we now turn our attention to UEBT, and the verification it undertakes around the ethical sourcing of natural ingredients and the use of the UEBT Member trade mark (see Figure 10.2). In so doing, we hope to draw out some important features of ABS marks that can then be used to guide future developments and uses of ABS marks. More specifically, the intention of the next Part of the chapter is to highlight some key features of the UEBT's verification process and the role that the UEBT Member trade mark plays in achieving the goal of ABS. Importantly, the use of ABS marks is not a one-size fits all approach, with UEBT viewing ABS verification as a 'path' or 'journey' towards ABS, a *process* in which Members work innovatively, collaboratively and gradually towards addressing the issues around ABS.[67]

10.4 The Union for Ethical Biotrade

Established in 2007, UEBT is a non-profit organisation that aims to make real and tangible practical contributions to biodiversity and sustainability. In order to achieve this, UEBT promotes the sourcing of natural ingredients in a way that is consistent with the goals of the CBD and the Nagoya Protocol.[68] In joining UEBT, companies in the cosmetics, food and pharmaceutical sectors commit to respecting the *Ethical BioTrade Standard* in their operations and supply chains.[69] UEBT Members adopt a gradual approach towards compliance, giving priority to those ingredients that are most relevant for ethical sourcing of biodiversity.

Figure 10.2 The Union for Ethical BioTrade Member logo used by UEBT Members such as Beraca and Weleda[70]

67 Maria Julia Oliva interview with Jay Sanderson on 3 March 2017.
68 See, for example, UEBT, *Ethical BioTrade Standard*, STD01 (11 April 2012), 5.1 (Compliance with national and international legislation), available at <http:// ethicalbiotrade.org/dl/STD01_Ethical%20BioTrade%20Standard_2012.04.11_ Eng.pdf> (accessed 17 June 2017).
69 Ibid, p 4.
70 Source: Australian trade mark number 1357308 (registered on 10 December 2009). Our thanks go to Maria Julia Olivia, UEBT, for permitting reproduction of this mark. UEBT's mark is also registered in other countries including: United States trademark 3919051; European trade mark WE00001034692; and Brazil trade mark 830362720.

A key part of the UEBT's strategy is an independent verification system.[71] On joining UEBT, Members undergo an initial audit against the *Ethical Bio-Trade Standard*. The audit assesses conformity with a number of entry-level requirements such as not using pesticides that are banned under the *Stockholm Convention on Persistent Organic Pollutants* (POPs), that fall under Categories I and II of the World Health Organization (WHO), and that are listed in the *Rotterdam Convention on the Prior Informed Consent Procedure for Certain Hazardous Chemicals and Pesticides in International Trade* (Rotterdam Convention).[72] The audit also identifies areas for improvement to bring operations in line with the *Ethical BioTrade Standard*. Further audits occur every three years and focus on the company's policies and procedures linked to biodiversity, and the prioritisation of ingredients and progress made in the implementation of the *Ethical BioTrade Standard* along supply chains.[73] In this way the UEBT system is a *process* in which companies in the cosmetics, food and pharmaceutical sectors commit to gradually improving their practices around BioTrade. Indeed, UEBT's Maria Julia Oliva views the UEBT verification scheme as a 'path' and 'journey' in which companies gradually work towards compliance with the *Ethical BioTrade Standard*.[74]

The commitments made by UEBT Members are set out by, and measured against, the implementation of the *Ethical BioTrade Standard* in their business practices.[75] The *Ethical BioTrade Standard* 'builds on the BioTrade Principles and Criteria that were developed by the UNCTAD BioTrade Initiative'.[76] It elaborates on the seven BioTrade Principles, developed by the UNCTAD BioTrade Initiative: (1) biodiversity conservation; (2) sustainable use; (3) fair and equitable benefit sharing; (4) socio-economic sustainability; (5) legal compliance; (6) respect for the rights of actors; and (7) clarity about land tenure.[77] The *Ethical BioTrade Standard* is more detailed than the BioTrade Principles and sets out specific criteria and indicators for each of the seven Principles. In total, there are nearly 60 individual criteria.[78] For example, the

71 The difference between verification and certification is important, with UEBT viewing verification as on on-going *process* in which there is a commitment to meet the *Ethical BioTrade Standard* in the future: Maria Julia Oliva interview with Jay Sanderson on 3 March 2017.

72 UEBT, *Ethical BioTrade Standard*, above n 66, p 15.

73 Ibid, pp 5–6.

74 Maria Julia Oliva interview with Jay Sanderson on 3 March 2017.

75 Ibid. Significantly, UEBT is a full ISEAL member, which means that the Ethical BioTrade Standard complies with ISEAL's codes on standard-setting, assurance and impact. See <https://www.isealalliance.org/about-us> (accessed 20 March 2017).

76 UEBT, *Ethical BioTrade Standard*, above n 66, p 4.

77 See UEBT, *Ethical BioTrade Standard*, available at <http://ethicalbiotrade.org/verification/ethical-biotrade-standard> (accessed 3 April 2017); UEBT, *Draft Proposal* (April 2007) p 2 available at <http://earthmind.org/files/eibb/workshop-a-uebt-2007-draft-proposal.pdf> (accessed 3 April 2017).

78 Originally introduced in 2007, the *Ethical BioTrade Standard* was reviewed and amended in 2012.

criteria for 'fair and equitable sharing of benefits derived from the use of bio-diversity' are set out in Part 5C of this chapter.

In addition to the verification and the associated use of the UEBT Member mark, UEBT more recently offered its Members certification possi-bilities for ingredients used for herbal teas. Specifically, UEBT certification allows claims over ingredients originating from fully monitored supply chains that comply with the requirements of relevant certification protocols, based on the Ethical BioTrade system. There are currently two options for UEBT certification:

1   UEBT Ethical BioTrade Certification for natural ingredients: however, the UEBT trade mark is not available for use on products; and
2   Combined UEBT/UTZ certification for ingredients used for herbal teas, which allows for the use of the UTZ trade mark on herbal tea packaging.[79]

Each of the UEBT certification options and their use of trade marks will be considered in the remainder of this Part.

A. UEBT Ethical BioTrade Certification for natural ingredients

UEBT membership and the use of the UEBT Member trade mark (see Figure 10.2) attest to companies having adopted policies and procedures to implement the *Ethical BioTrade Standard* in operations and supply chains. Part of the reason for having a UEBT Member trade mark is to allow companies to explicitly communicate their commitment to ethical biotrade on corporate communication such as their websites, catalogues and business cards. Both the verification process and the use of the trade mark are used to differentiate companies based on their biodiversity credentials including awareness and measures on ABS.[80] UEBT membership and the use of the UEBT Member trade mark do not certify or attest compliance with the provisions of the stan-dard. Importantly, while there are minimum standards,[81] total compliance with the *Ethical BioTrade Standard* is not expected from day one, nor is compliance required for UEBT membership and the use of the UEBT Member trade mark. Instead, UEBT membership and the use of the Member trade mark are granted when UEBT has approved the Member's work-plan outlining the measures and timeframe by which the Member organisation will complete its

---

79 The UTZ certification is an independently monitored 'program and label for sus-tainable farming' of tea, coffee, cocoa and hazelnuts: see <https://utz.org> (accessed 3 May 2017).
80 As we will see in Part 5A of this chapter, certification marks are registered domestically so that the requirements for registration and conditions for use of the certification mark may vary.
81 While referred to as 'minimum' standards, the standards are not negligible.

'Critical Path' to achieve compliance with UEBT's Standard.[82] Further, in order to comply with membership obligations and thus be able to use the UEBT mark, UEBT Members must report annually on progress with their work plans. This progress is also independently verified every three years.

Despite this pathway to compliance, the UEBT Member trade mark cannot be used in relation to specific products or in product packaging. The mark is instead intended to represent an ongoing and externally verified 'commitment' by companies to biodiversity and acting in a fair and equitable way with respect to sourcing. It is intended to communicate an ongoing commitment to ethical practices along the supply chain, not at one particular point along the supply chain. Take, for example, Weleda, a Swiss-based company that was established in the 1920s by humanitarian and philosopher Rudolf Steiner to manufacture antroposophic pharmaceutical/homeopathic products as well as natural and organic cosmetic products. In communicating its commitment to biodiversity, Weleda's website displays the UEBT Member trade mark and claims:

> Our focus is not only on creating exquisite natural and organic products, but to do so in a way that is ethically, socially and environmentally responsible. For these reasons, the [UEBT] accredited Weleda as a member. Not only do they demand fair trade, but they work to ensure everyone and everything along the entire growing, harvesting and manufacturing process is treated fairly, with care and respect.[83]

The main reason why the UEBT trade mark is not designed to be used on products is a technical one. UEBT Members and their products tend not to be 'consumer facing'. Instead they are focused on the natural ingredients (e.g. cold pressed oils, butters and essential oils) sourced by the producers of consumer products such as cosmetics and pharmaceuticals.[84] Rather than communicate directly to consumers, the UEBT trade mark is meant for business to business (B2B) communication among companies in the cosmetic, pharmaceutical and nutraceutical sectors. UEBT Members include Naturik (a company that produces cold pressed oils and butters from seeds and fruits from Peru for the cosmetic and nutraceutical industries), Aldivia (a company that specialises in sourcing, designing, manufacturing and marketing of vegetable lipids for the cosmetic industry) and Villa Andina (a company that sources grains and cocoa derivatives).[85] UEBT Membership and the UEBT Member trade mark, therefore, provide a way for these companies to distinguish themselves from

82 UEBT, *Who May Join UEBT?* (*UEBT*, September 2013), available at <http://ethicalbiotrade.org/membership/> (accessed 20 March 2017).

83 Weleda, *About Us: Beautiful Products, Ethically Sourced Natural, Organic and Sustainable*, available at <http://www.weleda.com.au/about-us/w1/i1133306> (accessed on 3 April 2017).

84 Maria Julia Oliva interview with Jay Sanderson on 3 March 2017.

85 UEBT, *Trading Members*, available at <http://ethicalbiotrade.org/our-members/trading-members> (accessed 3 April 2017).

companies not bearing the UEBT Member mark. It also communicates that they have met minimum standards and have committed to achieving compliance with the UEBT *Ethical BioTrade Standard* by developing a supply chain management system for continuous improvement. Importantly, though, the communication is between the UEBT Member and cosmetic, food or pharmaceutical companies. For example: a 'consumer-facing' company such as cosmetics company L'Oreal – who wants to know that the companies they are sourcing ingredients from are concerned with, and working towards, biodiversity conservation – can check that the supplier is verified and certified by UEBT. If so, it can be confident that the supplier has made a commitment to, and taken steps towards, ethical biotrade. Consumers, however, generally do not purchase products from companies based on their UEBT Membership.

B. *UEBT/UTZ certification for ingredients used for herbal teas*

In addition to use of the UEBT Member trade mark, UEBT offers certification for ingredients used for herbal teas. This allows for the use of a UTZ trade mark on herbal tea packaging.[86] Unlike UEBT Ethical BioTrade Certification for natural ingredients – which is not used on products – because the natural ingredient (tea) is also the product (tea), this is a 'consumer-facing' product and the UTZ trade mark can be used on the product. The UEBT/UTZ Herbal Tea Certification Program allows UEBT Members to use the UTZ logo on herbal tea blends composed of herbs originating from fully monitored supply chains that are in compliance with the requirements of the UEBT/ UTZ Herbal Tea Certification Protocol. Companies that buy UEBT/UTZ certified herbs can use the UTZ label. They need to apply the UTZ Chain of Custody requirements, follow the UTZ Labelling Policy for herbal teas, and pay a premium.[87]

To become UEBT/UTZ certified, suppliers have to comply with a joint UEBT/UTZ protocol and checklist,[88] that applies:

a comprehensive field checklist, which consists of UEBT Standard requirements applicable to the field as well as UTZ supplementary requirements from the UTZ Core Code. Incorporated in the Field

86 Australian Trade Mark 1543657 (registered on 24 August 2012); United States trademark 1149680 (registered on 5 November 2013); European trade mark WE000001149680 (registered on 24 August 2012); and Brazil trade mark 8310777522 (registered on 21 October 2014).
87 UEBT, *Certification conditions*, UEBT/UTZ Herbal Tea Certification Program, available at <http://ethicalbiotrade.org/certification-conditions> (accessed 20 March 2017).
88 See *Certification Protocol for UEBT/UTZ Herbal Tea: Internal Monitoring System Certification Approach*, Version 1.2, July 2016 available at <http://ethicalbiotra de.org/dl/Certification-Protocol-for-UEBT_UTZ-Herbal-Tea-version-1. 2-July-2016.pdf> (accessed 20 March 2017).

Checklist is also a Scoring System to provide critical guidance for the compliance assessment.[89]

Having considered the standards for, and the use of, the UEBT and UEBT/UTZ Member trade marks in the preceding paragraphs we would like to set out some broader observations around which ABS marks can be developed. Thinking about how ABS marks may be developed and administered will not only help assess the relevance and effectiveness of ABS marks but will also provide insights for anybody considering using marks associated with ABS principles and practices. To this end, in the next part of the chapter we set out a number of important *indicia* around the use of ABS marks. We do not, however, provide an exhaustive list of issues, opportunities and challenges around ABS marks.

10.5 Observations and guidance on the use of ABS marks

In this part of the chapter we make four broad observations about the use of ABS marks. These are:

1   It is necessary to understand the subject matter of protection as well as the intent and objectives of the proposed ABS mark;
2   ABS standard trade marks are more flexible and less onerous than ABS certification marks. Notably, the UEBT Member mark is registered as a standard trade mark; so too Fairtrade and UTZ Organic;
3   It is important to ensure that appropriate and dynamic ABS standards and licensing arrangements are established; and
4   An important part of ABS marks is providing support for behaviour change, and ensuring that there are effective compliance tools to detect and punish undesirable and non-compliant behaviour.

Each of these observations will now be elaborated.

A. Understand the subject matter and intent of the proposed ABS mark

When determining whether to use an ABS mark it is necessary to understand the subject matter of protection (e.g. raw materials or products containing genetic resources) as well as the intent and objectives of certification (e.g. consumer or business recognition of ABS; quality assurance around ABS practices; or as a starting point in a long-term 'journey' towards ABS practices). Understanding something of the subject matter and objectives of certification is an important first step because verification or certification of ABS will not always lead to the use of marks. Or, if an ABS mark is appropriate, it may be

89 Ibid, p 6.

necessary to use it in a particular way depending on context. For example: if an ABS standard is not directed to an end-consumer in a retail context, but rather to a middle firm in a supply chain, then a mark may not be necessary or may need to be used in a particular way. As we saw in Part 10.4 of this chapter, the UEBT Member trade mark cannot be used in relation to specific products or in product packaging. Instead the UEBT Member trade mark allows companies to explicitly communicate their commitment to ethical biotrade on corporate communications such as their websites, catalogues and other trade material. In contrast to the UEBT Member mark, the Fairtrade and UTZ organic marks are used on product packaging. How the UEBT, Fairtrade and UTZ Certified marks are used is largely predicated on whether they are to be used on 'consumer-facing' products; if so, marks are used to promote identification and recognition in consumers' minds when making a purchasing decision.

In addition to considering the nature and intent of ABS certification, it is also necessary to give some thought to the broader context of the Nagoya Protocol and the State-driven 'permit' system it provides for. For example: how might ABS marks interact with the Nagoya Protocol? The Nagoya Protocol is essentially an international compliance system administered by national governments.[90] Perhaps ABS marks provide a way to link consumers with products that comply with national ABS laws. That is, ABS marks may be used in conjunction with national laws implementing the Nagoya Protocol: a consumer-facing sign indicating compliance with national ABS laws and the issuance of an international permit. Due to the transnational approach of the Nagoya Protocol, this in turn suggests that this compliance is not only with national laws, but also with an internationally accepted set of laws or norms relating to ABS. In this way it is possible that ABS marks can add to the current frameworks on ABS: for example, by linking consumers and producers, in a manner consistent with existing transnational regulatory approaches.

B. ABS trade marks are more flexible and less onerous than ABS certification marks

Another significant consideration when determining whether to use an ABS mark is the difference between trade and certification marks. On the one hand, an ABS trade mark indicates the trade origin of a product or a service sold under that trade mark. An ABS trade mark can also indicate that the trade mark owner is happy for that good or service to be marketed using the

90 Nagoya Protocol, Art 17(2). Also see Arts 6(3)(e) which provides 'for the issuance at the time of access of a permit or its equivalent as evidence of the decision to grant prior informed consent and of the establishment of mutually agreed terms, and notify the Access and Benefit sharing Clearing-House accordingly' and 14(2) (c) which establishes that '[p]ermits or their equivalent issued at the time of access as evidence of the decision to grant prior informed consent and of the establishment of mutually agreed terms'.

'banner' of his/her trade mark.[91] A trade mark, however, does not necessarily say anything about the quality of a good or a service: merely that the trade mark owner is happy for the mark to be used for that good or service. On the other hand, an ABS certification mark would indicate that a good or service has been certified as having particular qualities or characteristics. In this way, an ABS certification mark will indicate that a product or service has been certified as having met some form of approved standards.

As we have already seen, though, many of the marks used in certification schemes are registered as standard trade marks. UEBT, Fairtrade and UTZ Organic, for instance, are all registered as trade marks, not certification marks.[92] Generally speaking, companies need to obtain a licence from the mark holder to validly use a trade mark on their products or services. This is where the distinction between trade and certification marks is blurred, and, as far as consumers are concerned, it is perhaps a moot point whether producers or suppliers register an ABS trade mark or an ABS certification mark. Consumers are largely unaware of the differences, and used in the right way a standard trade mark can convey the same message as a certification mark. Often the licensing agreement sets out the standards upon which the trade mark owner is happy for the licensee to use his/her trade mark on the product. For example, in order to be eligible to obtain a licence to use the UEBT Member trade mark or the UTZ trade mark, companies must comply with the standards set out in UEBT's *Ethical BioTrade Standard* or UTZ's Standard respectively.[93] Strictly speaking, then, this is a trade mark licensing scheme rather than a certification mark scheme.

Importantly, though, registering ABS trade marks is more flexible and less onerous than registering ABS certification marks.[94] This is in large part because the procedures for registering an ABS certification mark are more demanding than those for a standard trade mark. While the grant of a standard trade mark is generally based on the examination of requirements centred on distinctiveness, and potential confusion and deceptiveness, the examination of certification marks consists of an additional distinct stage: the examination of the rules, standards or criteria that govern the use of the certification mark. In some countries, the examination of the rules, standards or criteria that govern the use of the certification mark requires the participation and approval of a regulator or consumer watchdog. In Australia, for example, approval from the Australian Competition and Consumer Commission (ACCC) is required before certification marks can be registered under the *Trade Marks Act 1995* (Cth).[95] In the

---

91 *Glaxo Group Ltd v Dowelhurst Ltd (No 2)*, above n 5, [540]–[541] (Laddie J).
92 Others examples including Pink Lady apples, USDA Organic and Natrue Certification.
93 UEBT, *UEBT/UTZ Herbal Tea Program*, available at <http://ethicalbiotrade.org/herbal-tea-program> (accessed 3 April 2017).
94 For an overview of the key difference between trade and certification marks in the Australian context see: Peter Hallett, 'Certification Marks – Are They Really Worth the Hassle?' [2012] *Australian Intellectual Property Bulletin* 223.
95 *Trade Marks Act 1995* (Cth) ss 173–175; *Trade Marks Regulations* 1995 (Cth) Pt 16.

United Kingdom, it is the Trade Mark Register which approves the standards and rules associated with certification marks under the *Trade Marks Act 1994* (UK).[96]

In assessing whether to approve the ABS standards – and therefore grant the certification mark – a range of factors may be considered, based on an assessment of the ABS standards. These include an assessment of the proposed process by which compliance with ABS certification will be judged, and an examination of the ABS standards to ensure that they are not to the detriment of the public, or likely to raise any concerns relating to competition, unconscionable conduct, unfair practices or product safety. Once approved by the consumer regulator or Trade Mark Register any changes or amendments to approved ABS certification standards need to be approved in much the same way. This adds time, cost and complexity to the registration of an ABS certification scheme: issues that are largely avoided if a standard trade mark is registered. Another related advantage of registering a standard ABS trade mark is that the trade mark owner can more freely alter the conditions upon which the ABS trade mark is licensed and used. Notably, in 2012, UEBT revised the *Ethical BioTrade Standard*,[97] prompted largely by lessons learnt through experiences and developments in the transnational legal order. More specifically:

> The purpose of the revision process was to capture the lessons learned with the implementation of the standard since UEBT's creation in 2007, to reflect modifications in the UEBT membership Conditions and Obligations … and to reflect developments in the international regulatory framework regarding biodiversity (e.g. Nagoya Protocol). The revised standard and verification system should allow UEBT to better adapt to the realities of those working on Ethical BioTrade, setting the stage for further growth of the UEBT membership base.[98]

In addition to the flexibility of an ABS trade mark, there is greater discretion about who can use the ABS mark if it is registered as a standard trade mark. Certification marks tend to be non-discriminatory. Consequently, it is possible

---

96 *Trade Marks Act 1994* (UK) Sch 2.
97 As the Union for Ethical BioTrade is a member of ISEAL Alliance, the *Ethical BioTrade Standard* was revised in accordance with the *The ISEAL Code of Good Practice for Setting Social and Environmental Standards*: see ISEAL Alliance, *Standard-Setting Code*, available at <http://www.isealalliance.org/our-work/defining-credibility/codes-of-good-practice/standard-setting-code> (accessed 3 April 2017).
98 UEBT, *Final Report on Public Consultation Phases of UEBT Standard_2012-04-11* (2012) p 1, available at <http://ethicalbiotrade.org/dl/Final%20Report%20on%20public%20consultation%20phases%20of%20UEBT%20Standard_2012-04-11.pdf> (accessed 20 March 2017).

244 Jay Sanderson, Leanne Wiseman and Drossos Stamboulakis

that a licensee might satisfy the standards related to the ABS certification mark but, by doing so, may more broadly damage the credibility of the mark. In Australia, for example, there was a peculiar and unwanted situation where the National Heart Foundation Tick, which is registered as a certification mark,[99] was awarded to certain approved McDonalds meals. Not surprisingly there was considerable negative publicity about the Heart Foundation certification mark being awarded to the fast food giant.[100] At the time, the Heart Foundation argued that McDonalds was a popular food choice and that the items with the tick were healthier choices when compared to others in the same category. Yet there is another reason for the award of the Heart Foundation certification mark to McDonalds: it is difficult if not impossible to refuse to licence a certification mark to a company who has complied with the approved standards of the certification. This is not the case with a standard trade mark, which is licensed at the discretion of the trade mark owner or their licensee.

C. Establish appropriate and dynamic ABS standards and licensing arrangements

One of the most important aspects of an effective ABS mark is establishing appropriate standards and licensing arrangements. This means that organisations and groups concerned with encouraging ABS via marks need to identify and target the most important ABS concerns such as equitable pricing, transparency, prior informed consent and mutually agreed terms. Identifying the most important ABS problems allows the ABS mark holder to decide what standards he/she will focus on and what can be done to ensure the greatest outcomes for the environment while making the best use of the resources available. Margaret Chon argues that, to do so, these kinds of '[m]arks of rectitude should represent accurately the standards purported to be embodied within the products (and services) being purchased by consumers in this disaggregated global marketplace'.[101]

At the least, and perhaps as a starting point, any ABS standards should be compliant with the prevailing transnational legal order, as represented by the CBD and the Nagoya Protocol. However, an ABS marks scheme could use alternative, additional or more specific ABS standards. A specific example of ABS standards can be found in the *Ethical BioTrade Standard* of UEBT. Importantly, the *Ethical BioTrade Standard* is both detailed and flexible. For example, the criteria for a 'fair and equitable sharing of benefits derived from the use of biodiversity' are set out in Table 10.1 below.

---

99 In Australia, the Australian Heart Foundation own a range of marks including Australian Trade Marks 498189 and 498189.
100 Simone Pettigrew *et al.*, 'Tick Tock: Time for a Change?' (2016) 27 *Health Promotion Journal of Australia* 102.
101 Chon, above n 14, 2312.

Table 10.1 The specific criteria for fair and equitable sharing of benefits derived from the use of biodiversity, Ethical BioTrade Standard, 2012

3.1	Negotiations related to the sourcing of biodiversity shall be transparent and based on dialogue and trust.
3.2	The organisation shall pay equitable prices for the natural ingredients that it sources.
3.3	The organisation shall contribute to local sustainable development goals in sourcing areas, as defined by producers and their local communities.
3.4	Traditional practices linked to the sourcing of species and ingredients shall be recognised.
3.5	The organisation shall comply with legislative or regulatory requirements on access to biodiversity and associated traditional knowledge for research and development and the sharing of resulting benefits.
3.6	For research and development activities, even if there are no legislative or regulatory requirements on access to biodiversity and associated traditional knowledge, such access shall be subject to prior informed consent and based on mutually agreed terms.
3.7	For research and development activities, even if there are no legislative or regulatory requirements on the sharing of benefits arising from the use of biodiversity and associated traditional knowledge, as well as subsequent application and commercialisation, benefits shall be shared in a fair and equitable way and based on mutually agreed terms.
3.8	Patents and other intellectual property rights shall be exploited and enforced in a manner that is supportive to the objectives of the CBD and the Ethical BioTrade standard.

Each of the broad criteria are further broken down into a set of specific requirements. So that, for example, the requirement on prior informed consent and mutually agreed terms (Criterion 3.6) requires that:

- Negotiations related to benefit sharing are transparent and based on dialogue and trust, as defined by Criterion 3.1 of this standard;
- The organisation has identified government agencies, groups, indigenous and local communities or individuals having contributed to the research, development or commercialisation processes;
- The organisation takes measures to share benefits in a fair and equitable way with these agencies, groups, communities or individuals having contributed to research, development or commercialisation processes, on the basis of the mutually agreed terms;
- In determining benefits to be shared, the organisation considers their contribution to local sustainable development goals, as defined by Criterion 3.3 of this standard;
- Other benefits may include access fees; milestone payments; special fees to be paid to trust funds supporting conservation and sustainable use of biodiversity; sharing of research and development results; collaboration,

cooperation and contribution in scientific research; and institutional and professional relationships; and

• The organisation identifies and addresses concerns on the sharing of benefits on the basis of mutually agreed terms.

While there is one UEBT standard, it is assessed on specific compliance expectations that are established at an initial 12 month audit in which the company is verified against the *Ethical BioTrade Standard*. Then a specific and targeted 'work plan' is developed aimed at reaching compliance with the *Ethical BioTrade Standard* within five years.[102] It is the specific 'work plan' that UEBT Members work towards and are held accountable to, not the *Ethical BioTrade Standard* as such. What this means is that each UEBT Member has different obligations and is held accountable to their own standards and criteria. As we saw in Part 5A above, flexibility in ABS standards and licensing is less possible with an ABS certification mark than it is with a standard trade mark.

Related to appropriate and dynamic ABS standards are the associated licensing arrangements. Put simply, a licence grants a party the legal right to use a product or service that has a trade or a certification mark that is owned by someone else. Successful licensing of ABS marks is critical to their economic and social success and therefore it is important that the scope of ABS mark licences is clear. Clarity is required in key terms such as the duration of the licence (e.g. a limiting period so you have the flexibility to re-negotiate its conditions); limitations on use of the ABS mark (e.g. on what products or in which countries); fees (e.g. how much, and when is the licence fee payable?); and suspension or termination of the licence and the cessation of use of the ABS mark. Importantly too, ABS standards and licensing arrangements should contemplate and promote continuous improvement around ABS. For example, ABS standards and licensing could reflect a set of development standards, that encourage continuous improvement and investment in the advancement of best practices around ABS.

D. Provide support for behaviour change, and ensure that there are effective compliance tools to detect and punish undesirable and non-compliant behaviour

The key justification for developing and administering ABS marks is behaviour change. That is, an ABS mark should help transform both the behaviour of consumers (who can use the ABS mark to easily identify and purchase ABS goods) and producers (who change their practices to comply with the ABS standards). An ABS mark on its own is not enough. This means that in addition to establishing ABS standards and certifying compliance, a range of strategies and resources need to be provided to build and strengthen competencies and

---

102 Maria Julia Oliva interview with Jay Sanderson on 3 March 2017; UEBT, *Membership Conditions*, available at <http://ethicalbiotrade.org/membership/condi tions> (accessed 3 April 2017).

knowledge around ABS. Positive ABS behaviour strategies should focus on the capacity and capability of farmers, producers and suppliers that lead to ABS; by providing safe, interesting and appropriate experiences and environments, fair and consistent rules, clear instructions, and logical strategies. For example, it is necessary to stimulate industry interest in actively working towards best ABS practices. This can be achieved by facilitating pro-active discussion with actors in the supply chain about the market and commercial value of ABS practices, independent certification, the use of ABS marks, and broader branding and marketing strategies.

Another crucial aspect of supporting behaviour change around ABS is the provision of appropriate technical advice and support. Again, this can be achieved by numerous methods including the provision of technical resources, and education and training of actors along the supply chain. At a transnational level, UNCTAD runs capacity building exercises, such as educational initiatives aimed at assisting developing countries to develop their approaches to ABS. For example, it regularly conducts workshops tailored towards particular countries on ABS and the intersection or implementation of the Nagoya Protocol, ABS rules, and biotrade.[103] Private certification providers also can provide technical advice and support. For example, UTZ Certified provide numerous supports for farmers, traders, producers and retailers, aimed at improving working conditions of farmers and taking care of the environment. These supports compliment certification and the use of the UTZ trade mark, with UTZ Certified stressing that '[t]raining is key to the success of the UTZ programs'.[104] One of the ways in which UTZ Certified assists companies and individuals to comply with their standards is through its UTZ Academy, a network of professional trainers who offer a wide range of courses in 37 countries, in 10 languages. In addition, UTZ Certified offers:

- Training courses for farmers on the implementation of sustainable agricultural practices;
- Training courses for certification bodies on how to thoroughly audit to the UTZ standards and rules; and
- Training trainers to increase the impact of their courses by using a proven didactic model.[105]

---

103 For a list of BioTrade 'Meeting and Events', many of which focus on ABS, see UNCTAD, *About BioTrade*, available at <http://unctad.org/en/Pages/DITC/Trade-and-Environment/BioTrade.aspx> (accessed 15 June 2017). Two recent workshops focusing on ABS include: UNCTAD, 'Exploring the relationship between the implementation of the Nagoya Protocol, Access and Benefit Sharing and BioTrade' (21–22 September 2016, Lima, Peru); and, UNCTAD, 'Addressing the intersection between the Nagoya Protocol, access and benefit sharing rules and BioTrade' (27–28 June 2016, Hanoi, Viet Nam).

104 UTZ, *Training* available at <https://utz.org/what-we-offer/training> (accessed 3 April 2017).

105 Ibid.

Another crucial aspect of certification is compliance. Any organisation administering an ABS mark needs to be able and prepared to identify and act upon non-compliance against the ABS standards where Members or potential Members' behaviour is not satisfactory or compliant. This is important for the credibility and reputation of the ABS certification scheme and mark. To ensure compliance with the *Ethical BioTrade Standard* UEBT Members undergo an independent verification process.[106] This process includes regular audits by certification bodies and internal management systems for certified natural ingredients, and regular audits of local supplier communities. In summary, the verification and compliance processes require Members to prepare work plans and report annually on their implementation, and commitment of ethical biotrade.[107] Importantly, UEBT has the capacity to suspend Members.[108] Specifically, UEBT membership can be suspended in cases of lack of compliance with the UEBT membership conditions and obligations. Suspended Members lose their statutory voting rights, can no longer use the UEBT Member trade mark, and risk losing their membership upon decision of the Membership Committee. Membership is reinstated when Members regain compliance with the UEBT membership conditions and obligations, in which case they recover all their rights.

Finally, organisations administering an ABS mark must be prepared to act against non-Members. In examining various trade marks – such as 'Jasmati' and Roobios Tea – Daniel Robinson laments the ability of companies to trade mark indigenous names.[109] Robinson views this kind of behaviour as 'trade mark biopiracy' because it often leads to concern from countries of origin about deception surrounding the origins and qualities of products.[110] In terms of ABS marks, biopiracy may exist in two forms. On one hand, it is possible that companies will try to register an ABS trade mark to exploit consumer demand for biodiverse products without truly seeking to pursue fair and equitable ABS practices. On the other hand, ABS mark owners need to be aware that some companies or individuals will use their ABS marks without permission. In addition to being a form of trade mark biopiracy, using an ABS trade mark without permission from the trade mark owner is also trade mark infringement. The unlawful use of an ABS mark has already occurred with the UEBT Member trade mark, which has previously been unlawfully displayed by companies that are not UEBT Members and have not committed to the

106 UEBT, *Ethical BioTrade Standard*, above n 66.
107 Ibid.
108 Current members with suspended membership include Espave, Inversiones2a, and Productos Alimentarios Misky SAC (Peru): UEBT, *Suspended Membership*, available at <http://ethicalbiotrade.org/our-members/members-suspended-from-the-union-for-ethical-biotrade> (accessed 3 April 2017).
109 Daniel F Robinson, *Confronting Biopiracy: Challenges, Cases and International Debates* (Earthscan 2010) pp 85–90.
110 Ibid, p 85.

Ethical BioTrade Standard.[111] Importantly, upon becoming aware of the misuse of the UEBT Member trade mark, UEBT was prepared to act and sent a carefully drafted letter to the offending company requesting that the unauthorised company stop using the UEBT mark.[112]

10.6 Concluding remarks

Implementing effective ABS has proven difficult. While the Nagoya Protocol is helping to develop and clarify the concept of ABS at a transnational level – and focusing on State-driven regulation of compliance with international norms – there is still space, and arguably, need, for alternative approaches to ABS. In this sense we are optimistic. And in this chapter we have argued that while ABS is a difficult and complex problem it is not an intractable one. More specifically ABS marks can be used to complement the existing transnational legal order aimed at facilitating ABS, and are consistent with a 'smart' approach to regulation abstracting away solely from State-driven regulation.

The use of ABS marks facilitate a consumer's ability to make value-driven product and service choices, by serving as a simple identification heuristic. In so doing, ABS marks help *nudge* producers and consumers towards ABS. At the same time, because the certification of ABS marks can involve a *process* by which certain local ABS standards are identified and adhered to, it can provide a locally oriented solution to ABS. This, in combination with the market-impacts of ABS marks' signals, can bring together farmers, producers and consumers and lead to long-term benefits around ABS.

Despite our optimism on the use of ABS marks, we realise that they are not the panacea for ABS. In Part 10.5 of the chapter we presented and elaborated four general observations around the potential use of ABS marks including understanding the subject matter of protection as well as the intent and objectives of certification and providing support for behaviour change, and ensuring that there are effective compliance tools to detect and punish undesirable and non-compliant behaviour. Most importantly, perhaps, organisations looking to establish an ABS mark should first consider registering and licensing a standard trade mark instead of a certification mark. In many cases, licensing a standard ABS trade mark will be more flexible and less onerous than the registration of an ABS certification mark. Indeed, the benefits of an ABS certification mark can be achieved by registering a standard trade mark and adopting appropriate business practices and licensing arrangements. In this way, a standard ABS trade mark can achieve the same recognition by consumers as an ABS certification mark. There may, however, be advantages to registering and administering an ABS certification mark. In some circumstances, an ABS certification mark may help ensure independence, transparency and credibility. Indeed, the legitimacy and effectiveness of an ABS mark system may be

111 Maria Julia Oliva interview with Jay Sanderson on 3 March 2017.
112 Ibid.

enhanced through the involvement of others outside of an organisation. As a certification mark relies on objective standards determined and approved in advance, it is possible that an ABS certification mark, as distinct from a standard trade mark licensing regime, promotes the perception of impartiality and objectivity around the nature and application of the ABS standards.

Finally, our hope is that by arguing for the development and use of ABS marks we contribute to the discussion around the options for encouraging and facilitating ABS. Marks represent an important instrument in the fight for ABS, and provide a way of bringing together farmers, communities, producers and consumers.

Index

Printed in the United States
by Baker & Taylor Publisher Services